P9-EA1-675

Inveighing We Will Go

William F. Buckley, Jr.

INVEIGHING
WE WILL GO

G. P. Putnam's Sons
New York

IN MEMORIAM

Julie Galbraith
1965-1972

'Elle est venue
Elle a souri
Elle est partie'

Acknowledgments

My thanks to the proprietors of *Life, National Review, Newsday,* the New York *Times, Playboy* magazine, Walker and Company, the Washington Star Syndicate, for whom I originally wrote most of the material in this book. My special thanks to Mrs. Agatha Schmidt Dowd, without whose help this book would be an unintelligible mess, for making it sublime. And to Joseph Isola for his great kindness and skill in copyreading the galleys.

Contents

Inveighing We Will Go

Introduction

Herewith another collection, taken from writing I have done over the past three years, and served up here without the customary apologies inasmuch as, after all, unlike the thoughts of Chairman Mao, mine are rejected or ignored without direct political consequence, whatever the strategic damage to the republic or to one's soul.

I have found that there is no significant difference in the reception given to my collections as distinguished from those of my books that are conceived as whole. As a matter of fact, my last two collections did a little better than my most recent book, the autobiography of a week of my life, done in overdrive, and not at all easy to publicize. One lady, on one of the morning television programs, asked me whether I didn't think it a bit much to devote an entire book to a single week in my life, and I found myself saying, "I don't know. After all, Keats devoted an entire ode to a single Grecian urn." I might have won the exchange, but no doubt she won the war. There is a sense in which all books written primarily to project one's own opinions can be viewed as exercises in vanity. But I have elsewhere touched on the difficulty by explaining that after all, one forms one's opinions because they are the very best one can come up with, and then one does or doesn't ventilate them publicly. All else follows.

I thought, on one occasion, to dedicate a book to the Invincibly Ignorant of this world, except that by definition I would then be addressing it to the body of men and women who cannot appreciate the wisdom of Conservative Doctrine, let alone conservative doctrine as imperfectly stated and adumbrated as it is between the pages of my books. That would be pointless, which I have no desire to be. I like to think that I would reason as I do, and express myself as I do, if I were all that was left of the biblical

Remnant. But I know that I probably would not, could not, so much sustenance do I get from the knowledge that I along with others serve a communion which if it is neither in control of the world, nor in prospect of achieving control of it, is nevertheless there, pensive, literate, grateful, as I am grateful, indescribably so, to all the better minds and spirits whose intellectual and moral example maintains me erect, and working.

I find, on completing the selections for this book, that I am a *little* less circumlocutory than I used to be, for instance in making up the general chapter headings. I am not exactly sure why, less sure whether the reasons for it, such as they are, are worth publicly exploring. In the other collections I think there was a little more anfractuosity than in this one, in which here and there I blurt forth more plainspokenly on some of the concrete problems of the day, and indeed in the chapter on The Issues I write, tout court, about things like pollution, conscription, ecology, social welfare, and even Women's Lib. Oh, I suppose the style does not change all that much, but the focus is probably more straightforward. That may be good news for some readers, though there is the obvious danger that the more directly one expresses oneself, the more alarming are the implications of that thought to those whose vested interest, material or emotional, is in the status quo, or in a direction other than that which I advocate. I greatly fear that this might mean that I shall more deeply antagonize here than I have in some of my other books, and that is too bad, because antagonizing people is something I care less and less to do. I forget who told me that Edward Heath, the Prime Minister of England, has somebody around who at his insistence plucks every lint of grace and humor and embellishment from his speeches, so as to leave him exclusively with the tonalities, for direct and unencumbered communication with his listeners. I couldn't do it that way, and I can make a very robust case against doing it that way, but increasingly I can see that there are advantages in the mode.

Which leads me to explain briefly my decision to begin this collection by reprinting my interview with *Playboy* magazine. The techniques used by the *Playboy* interviewers are instructive. Mr. David Butler, a young, affable, intense, and talented editor and writer, followed me about for several days with a briefcase full of questions written out on cards, and we did a dozen hours of work. He returned to Chicago where he and his superiors pored over the transcript and came up with more questions, based on the answers already given. Then a third round, after which I was given the transcript and permitted to make any adjustments I chose to make at my end. Except that the interview had then to be trimmed for length, the result was, as these things go, gratifyingly systematic, and more generally than not B was made to follow A, with a minimum of windbaggery, tu quoquéism, and our old friend, *ignoratio elenchi.* To be sure, I can think of some questions even the resourceful Mr. Butler and his colleagues didn't think to ask, and no doubt the reader will think of some on which I might have been even more effectively impaled. In any event I find, on rereading the interview after two years, a refreshing directness and tough-mindedness in the exchange, and no doubt it will bring relief to the antagonistic reader who will be gritting his teeth through much of the rest of the book in mad frustration at the licentious flow of one man's opinions.

I note also that in the interview I ventured certain conclusions about the lay of Richard Nixon's foreign policy concerning which, two years later, I was expressing reservations, most markedly in the pieces I did on Mr. Nixon's visit to China. I thought it most candid to put the two pieces back to back, rather than attempt to bury one or the other in the interstices of this volume. Mr. Nixon has after all proved to be a quite flexible Chief Executive on most matters, and it is perhaps not uninteresting to the reader who is gratified by the President's zags, to know that they have indeed mystified some of his supporters. When you come to think of it, Mr. Nixon's unpredictability may very well give him, before he is quite through with us, or us with him, that glamor which it is so widely complained he was never able to generate by his rhetoric, or by the cut of his manner. A very interesting point.

At this writing we are midway through the political primaries, and several of the politicians who figure prominently in the section on Politics will be out of the public eye when this book is published. But each in his way, they have contributed to the climate of political opinion and it is worthwhile to do their portraits, even if they finally bored the voters in New Hampshire. They are a part of the color of public life, and certainly they are grist for commentary. Sometimes I feel that John Lindsay is much more useful as a failure, than ever he would have been as a success. In that not insignificant sense, we are indebted to him. In any event, it is the tentative burden of several of the chapters of this book that nobody knows quite what is happening to America, and it is my own position that whatever it is, it couldn't have happened to a nicer country.

W. F. B.

Rougemont, Switzerland
March, 1972

I. A Playboy Interview

May, 1970

PLAYBOY: It's already a cliché to say that the sixties were a remarkable decade. Looking back, what event or development stands out in your mind as most important?

BUCKLEY: The philosophical acceptance of coexistence by the West.

PLAYBOY: Why "philosophical"?

BUCKLEY: Because a military acceptance of coexistence is one thing; that I understand. But since America is, for good reasons and bad, a moralistic power, the philosophical acceptance of coexistence ends us up in hot pursuit of *reasons* for that acceptance. We continue to find excuses for being cordial to the Soviet Union; our denunciations of that country's periodic barbarisms— as in Czechoslovakia— become purely perfunctory. This is a callousing experience; it is a lesion of our moral conscience, the historical effects of which cannot be calculated, but they will be bad.

PLAYBOY: Among the reasons cited for a *détente* with the Soviet Union is the fact that the money spent on continuing hot and cold wars with the Communist bloc would be better spent for domestic programs. With the $150 billion we've spent in Vietnam since 1965, according to some estimates, we could have eliminated pollution throughout the country and rebuilt twenty-four major cities into what New York's Mayor Lindsay has said would be "paradises." Do you think our priorities are out of order?

BUCKLEY: When I find myself entertaining that possibility, I dismiss my thinking as puerile. But first let me register my objection to your figures: It's superficial to say that the Vietnam war has cost us $150 billion. It has cost us X dollars in excess of what we would have spent on military or paramilitary enterprises even if there had been no war. That sum I have seen estimated at between $18 and $22 billion a year. Now, suppose I were to tell you that if Kerenski had prevailed in Russia in 1917, we would at this point have a budget excess sufficient to create the city of Oz in Harlem and everywhere else. The correct response to such a statement, for grown-ups, is twofold. First, we are not— unfortunately— in a position to dictate the activity of the enemy; we cannot ask him please to let down because we need money for Harlem. Second, there are no grounds for assuming that the American people would have consented to spending the kind of money we're spending on the Vietnam war for general welfare projects. They might have said, "No, we'd rather keep the money and do what we want with it." I suspect they *would* have said just that, and with justification: The bulk of the progress that has been made in America has been made by the private sector.

PLAYBOY: With reference to the first part of your answer: At the strategic-arms-limitations talks, aren't we actually asking the Russians to let down their guard if we let ours down?

BUCKLEY: Yes, we are. And, ideally, there would be massive, universal disarmament. But we don't live in an ideal world. The fact is that the Soviet Union is prepared to make remarkable sacrifices at home in order to maintain its military muscle abroad. It is prepared to do so in a world that has seen the United States pull out from dozens of opportunities to imperialize. We have walked out of twenty-one countries— I think that's the accepted figure— that we've occupied in the past thirty years. The Soviet Union has walked only out of Austria, for very complicated reasons. Under the circumstances, one must assume that the arrant armament expenditures by the Soviet Union— for instance, $20 billion to develop its ABM system and its MIRV's— have to do with the attraction of a first-strike capability. There is only one known explanation, for instance, for the known "footprint"— the configuration— of the MIRV's the Soviet Union has been practicing with. Those missiles are exactly patterned after our Minuteman installations. If the Soviets intended their MIRV's only as a deterrent to an American first strike, they would aim those missiles at American cities. But they aren't being fashioned that way. Now, I don't think the collective leadership of Russia would dream of making a first strike for so long as we are in a position to inflict insupportable damage in a second strike, whatever the urgings of their Dr. Strangeloves, who are not without influence. But, manifestly, America is not preparing for a first strike. If we were, we would be aiming our weapons not at Russia's population centers but at her military installations— and we're not.

PLAYBOY: The best information available— from hearings of the Senate Foreign Relations Committee at which Deputy Secretary of Defense David Packard appeared— is that we are well ahead of the Soviet Union in the development of MIRV's, and it's generally conceded that we conceived the system. Doesn't this suggest both that the threat posed by the Russian MIRV's is less than you imply and that their MIRV's may have been developed as a defense against ours?

BUCKLEY: The question of who conceived the system is immaterial. Who makes it operational is what matters. It is only a happy coincidence that Jules Verne was a non-Communist. On the question of whose MIRV's are more advanced, a) your information is, unhappily, incorrect and b) it is irrelevant to the question of whether MIRV's are designed for offensive or defensive purposes.

PLAYBOY: MIT professor Leo Sartori, writing in the *Saturday Review,* implies that some of our ICBM's are aimed at Russia's missiles rather than at her cities. Doesn't this indicate that the U.S. is prepared— to the point of overkill— for a massive first strike against the Soviet Union?

BUCKLEY: Look. The intellectual, attempting to evaluate the military situation, tends to fasten on a frozen position. He says, "Assuming apocalypse were tomorrow, how would the two sides stand?" But it is the responsibility of the military to understand how military confrontations actually work— which means that you cannot prepare for Tuesday by being absolutely prepared for Monday. In a world in which it takes between four and eight years to develop what is actually intended as a first-strike *defensive* system, you may, in the course of preparing for that system, find yourself temporarily with a first-strike superiority. A caricature of what I'm talking about is the sudden apprehension by Darryl Zanuck when he was filming *The Longest Day*— on the Normandy invasion— that he actually found himself in command of the third largest military force in the world. Presumably, he would not have used it even to attack Otto Preminger. You need to ask yourself the subjective question: Do I know people in the United States whose hands are on the trigger, who are actually conspiring to opportunize on the temporary military advantage? It seems plain to me that the recent history of the United States ought to be sufficient to appease the doubts of the doubters. In fact, we have had such superiority even at moments when the enemy was at its most provocative— and yet we haven't used it.

PLAYBOY: Hasn't it been authoritatively asserted that U.S. superiority is overwhelmingly beyond the defensive or offensive necessity of any conceivable threat from another nuclear power?

BUCKLEY: That's a military judgment and I don't feel qualified to pronounce about it. I feel confident only to make an elementary philosophical point. I tend to believe that what the lawyers call "an excess of caution" is not something we should penalize the military for. I *want* an excess of caution, because I understand a mistake in that direction to be apocalyptic in its consequences. Now, if you say, "I can establish that we are spending money to develop a redundant weapon," my answer is: Go ahead and establish it. Meanwhile, I would rather side with the cautious, the prudent people. And here I find myself wondering how it is that Robert McNamara— who, for some reason, tends to be rather beloved by the liberals— how come *he* didn't object to the technological-military evolution that nowadays strikes so many people as untoward. And, again, why have we so drastically reversed our attitudes concerning what was for so long considered the liberal thing to do? During the fifties, the great accent was on defense. The military-industrial complex— as you know— used to be called the "Arsenal of Democracy." Now, all of a sudden, when you talk about ABM's, the same people who encouraged us to spend $50 billion— yes, $50 billion— on defense during the fifties object to spending an extra $5 billion on defense in the sixties.

PLAYBOY: You seem to delight in reminding people that liberals are capable of changing their minds in the light of changing circumstances. Why?

BUCKLEY: Quite apart from the fact that delightful pursuits are delightful, it is important for any ideological grouping to confront historical experience. For one thing, it makes the ideologists less arrogant; or it should. That ought to be a national objective, after we eliminate poverty.

PLAYBOY: Ten years ago, wasn't there more reason than there is now to believe that the Russians wanted to bury us, militarily as well as ideologically?

BUCKLEY: That is an exercise in ideological self-indulgence. How do you account for the anomalies? Such as the crash program the Soviet Union has developed in ABM's and MIRV's.

PLAYBOY: One can only repeat that the U. S. is developing these systems as furiously as Russia is; and many observers feel that the Soviets have, therefore, just as much reason to suspect our intentions as we do theirs. But we'd like to return to your observation that the United States has walked out of twenty-one countries in the past thirty years and ask this: Doesn't the fact that we've also walked *into* Vietnam and Santo Domingo, tried to walk into Cuba at the Bay of Pigs and attempted to control many other countries through quasi-military, CIA-type operations leave us open to the charge of imperialism you impute to the U.S.S.R.?

BUCKLEY: Of course. But we are always at the mercy of the naïve. Imperialism suggests the domination of a country for the commercial or glorious benefit of oneself. The Soviet Union began its experience in imperialism not merely by jailing and executing people who disagreed with it but by systematic despoliation. In Czechoslovakia, for instance, they took one, two, three billion dollars' worth of capital goods and removed them physically to the Soviet Union. Far from doing anything of the sort, we did exactly the contrary: we sent our own capital goods to places like France and England and Spain and Latin America. I can't think of any country that we've "dominated" or "imperialized"—in the sense in which you use those words—that is worse off as a result of its experience with America than it would have been had we not entered into a temporary relationship with it.

PLAYBOY: One could argue that South Vietnam is such a country.

BUCKLEY: South Vietnam? My God! Above *all*, not South Vietnam. Not unless one is willing to say that South Vietnam would be better off satellized by North Vietnam—and derivatively by Asian communism—and consigned to perpetual tyranny. Put it this way: I will assent to the proposition that South Vietnam has been harmed by America's efforts during the past five years only to somebody who would say that France was harmed by the efforts of the Allied armies to liberate it during the Second World War.

PLAYBOY: We won't say that, but we will agree with the increasingly popular opinion that our adventure there has been a disaster— to us, as well as to South and North Vietnam— from the beginning. Yet you said recently that "the indices in Vietnam are good," which is something even McNamara and Westmoreland stopped saying three years ago. Why?

BUCKLEY: Because the indices *are* good, right down the line: First, there is the prestige of Thieu and our increased identification with him. A week or so after the 1968 Tet offensive, Professor J. Kenneth Galbraith gave it as the conventional wisdom that Thieu's government would fall within a matter of weeks. I predict that in the next election, he will get a significantly greater vote than he got the last time. Second, there is a lower rate of infiltration from the North. Third, the area controlled by the good guys is now much greater than it has ever been. The fourth positive index is the introduction in South Vietnam of a nonregular army, the equivalent of a militia, which makes it possible for people simultaneously to till their land during the day and yet be part of a large constabulary. Still another indication is the relative rise in South Vietnamese casualties and decrease in American casualties, which shows that they are beginning to shoulder even more of the human burden of the war.

PLAYBOY: How do you feel about Thieu's suppression of dissent among his political opposition— even moderate Buddhists and Catholics who have done nothing more subversive than suggest consideration of a postwar coalition government?

BUCKLEY: I am not in a position to judge whether Thieu suppresses more or fewer people than he should suppress in order to achieve his goals. I know that my own countrymen were prepared to take tens of thousands of innocent Japanese and throw them in jail during World War II. And I know that moral-political revulsion over that act didn't come until years later— when we recognized that what we had done to the nisei was, in fact, historically unnecessary. But it remains that a man who was tempered by four centuries of parliamentary experience— Franklin D. Roosevelt— thought it an altogether appropriate thing to do. I am not, under the circumstances, confident that I can authoritatively advise Thieu what is the right kind of suppression to engage in during a civil war.

PLAYBOY: Then it *is* a civil war and not a case of Communist expansionism exported from Russia and China?

BUCKLEY: Yes, it is a civil war, provided one is prepared to define any war as a civil war if one finds a significant number of collaborationists within the indigenous population. There are South Vietnamese Communists, even as there were Norwegian quislings, Northern Copperheads and French appeasers. General Pétain was sentenced to death for obliging the Nazis less effusively than the Viet Cong have done the northern imperialists. If the "civil" insurrection in Vietnam had depended on its own resources, it would have lasted about as long as the insurrection of the Huks in the Philippines.

PLAYBOY: You frequently use the fact that Thieu has fired twelve hundred civil servants to demonstrate what you consider his opposition to corruption. But weren't many of those firings really intended to get rid of his political opponents?

BUCKLEY: I didn't think to ask Thieu when I was over there. I assume it is because they were corrupt— at least the ones I'm talking about. I don't know how many he has fired for opposing his policies. I don't know how many officials Lyndon Johnson fired because they opposed *his* policies, or exactly how many F. D. R. did— plenty, I assume. Incidentally, I thought John Roche made a rather good point when he said that the critics of Thieu fail to account for the fact that he moves about without any difficulty at all— without bodyguards or any other protection— throughout South Vietnam. And they fail to point out that he has done something no tyrant *ever* does, which is to arm the citizenry. The very first thing he did, when he became president, was to ask Westmoreland to increase the arming of the people. In Cuba, if you're caught with an unlicensed rifle, you're liable to be executed.

PLAYBOY: Your satisfaction with the relative rise in South Vietnamese casualties indicates that you believe in Vietnamization. If, as Presidents Johnson and Nixon have claimed, we have a moral and legal commitment to defend the South Vietnamese, why are we now disengaging?

BUCKLEY: We're not disengaging. We have a moral and legal commitment to give aid to the South Vietnamese in resisting aggression, pursuant to the protocol that extended the SEATO treaty to that area. We did not specify in SEATO the nature of the aid we would give. It is Nixon's strategy to arrive at a realistic formula: indigenous manpower and external material aid, precisely the way the Soviet Union and China have been handling the situation in behalf of North Vietnam. I advocated such a formula five years ago. Allowing for the culture lag, it is time for its adoption.

PLAYBOY: Do you feel it was wrong, then, to send our troops in the first place?

BUCKLEY: No, we had to. The South Vietnamese were not prepared to defend themselves.

PLAYBOY: In other words, though it was right to send them in when we did, it's right to withdraw them now. Are you saying that everything we've done there has been correct?

BUCKLEY: Not at all—there are plenty of things we've done wrong. We shouldn't have stopped the bombing of the North and put the restrictions on it that we did. And, above all, I continue to believe that Japan is the key to that part of the world and that we may very well wish, before this decade is up, that she had the defensive nuclear weapons the nonproliferation treaty denies her.

PLAYBOY: Do you think that if America remains steadfast in Vietnam—with or without the support of our allies in Asia or Western Europe—the Communists will be less likely to test our commitments elsewhere in the world?

BUCKLEY: It's hard to say. In order to answer that question, you have to ask yourself: What is the point of view of the enemy? I have always maintained that the Soviet Union has been delighted over our experience in South Vietnam. It has cost them very little. But, at the same time, the Soviet Union has to reckon with the psychological realities. The psychological realities in the case of Vietnam are that America isn't prepared to do this sort of thing two or three times a decade. We did it in Korea and we're doing it in South Vietnam. If the Soviet Union decides to mount a challenge—let's say in the Mideast—it will probably have to reckon with the fact of a shortened American temper. The shortened American temper could result in one of two things. It could result in isolationism, which would please the Soviet Union dearly and encourage it; or that shortened American temper could result in our saying, "Since we cannot afford protracted, graduated South Vietnam-type resistances, we're going to go back to another kind of resistance. We're going to knock the hell out of you."

PLAYBOY: Do you think that bellicose attitude *will* develop—and can you imagine it resulting in a nuclear strike by the U.S., say, over Berlin or in the Mideast?

BUCKLEY: Only if the Soviet Union is capable of a miscalculation on an order that is unimaginable, on the basis of our historical experience with a society that on the one hand is ideologically rabid but on the other appears to have a positively Rotarian instinct for survival.

PLAYBOY: Critics of the war point to the alleged massacre at My Lai to prove our indifference to the lives of Vietnamese civilians. How do you react to that incident, as it has emerged in the press?

BUCKLEY: If, indeed, there were no extenuating circumstances in the case— if everything that Captain Medina has said is proved wrong, for instance— then either we have a case of collective hysteria or we face the appalling alternative that what happened there expresses a trend within America. I find it extremely difficult to indulge that conclusion, for the reason that if it were so, we would have had many more such incidents.

PLAYBOY: In January, 1967, ten Marines were court-martialed on charges resulting from the murders of a farmer, his mother, his sister, his three-year-old son and five-year-old niece and the gang-rape of his wife. From the beginning of 1966 through October, 1969, twenty-seven soldiers were convicted by U.S. courts-martial of murdering Vietnamese civilians; and since March, 1965, twenty-one sailors and Marines have been so convicted. The speculation is that most such crimes by U.S. military personnel against civilians in Vietnam go unreported. So it would seem that there *have* been many other such incidents, though perhaps on a smaller scale.

BUCKLEY: They are either so routine as to go unremarked— like, say, the incremental murder in Manhattan— or so spectacular as to be unbelievable. It took the most extraordinary coordination of ineptitudes to fail to bring the My Lai incident to light. Here we have a Pulitzer Prize-winning story— I predict that it will get the Pulitzer Prize— and yet the two newspaper people who had the story couldn't interest anybody in it for months. Editors wouldn't buy it precisely because they couldn't believe that kind of thing could have been committed on such a scale.

PLAYBOY: Do you think there should be or will be extensive war-crimes trials of American servicemen and policy makers, conducted either by the United Nations or by us?

BUCKLEY: No. There shouldn't be and there won't be. The whole Nuremberg Doctrine, I continue to believe, is an elaboration of the crime of losing wars. It was, for one thing, obviously and intrinsically contaminated by the presence on the tribunal, in the capacity of judges, of the principal massacre-makers of the twentieth century, namely, the representatives of Stalin. America is not about to invite the United Nations to preside over trials of American soldiers. Those people who have been guilty will be punished, most of them, by America. I grant that we have a technical problem of how to reach out and get some of those individuals who apparently ought to be defendants, but my guess is we're going to crack that problem.

PLAYBOY: Do you see a moral difference between what is alleged to have happened at My Lai and the aerial bombardment of free-fire zones where, it's generally granted, some civilians almost always get killed?

BUCKLEY: Of course. It's a difference explicitly recognized in Thomistic doctrine, where the whole definition of a just war was arrived at. If, in order to achieve a military objective, someone gets killed, that is on one scale of morality— on the permissible scale in warfare. If, however, someone is killed simply for the sake of killing him, unrelated to any military objective, that's different. Nobody would have thought twice about My Lai if there had been a machine-gun nest there and we had plastered the village from the air, resulting in an identical loss of life.

PLAYBOY: But, of course, there wasn't a machine-gun nest there. Most critics of the war put little trust in those who decide which villages and which other targets are legitimate military objectives. Do you?

BUCKLEY: I trust that somewhere along the line there is a constant monitoring of the criteria that are used by people who have that kind of authority. In the specific case of Lyndon Johnson, I am informed that only he *personally* could authorize the bombing of certain targets where considerable civilian carnage might have resulted. I believe that he took that kind of meticulous concern not merely out of political considerations but because he was always very sensitive to the notion that he was an indiscriminate killer.

Let me digress at this point: A few months ago, in Hawaii, a professor informed my audience that we had dropped one and a half times as many bombs on a very small area of Vietnam as were dropped on Germany throughout World War II. That statistic, he claimed, proves that we are committing genocide in Vietnam. I read the figures differently. It seems to me that if we have dropped that many bombs and killed as few people as we have— there are an awful lot of live Vietnamese left, no matter how you look at it— it must mean that an enormous effort is being made to drop bombs where people *aren't*.

PLAYBOY: According to official sources, several hundred thousand North and South Vietnamese civilians have been killed by American bombing raids. In view of those statistics, do you think the bombing has been justified?

BUCKLEY: It depends on whether there was an alternative, less bloody means of achieving the military objective. How many of those dead would be alive today if the North Vietnamese had desisted from infiltration as their principal technique? And if historical contexts interest you, bear in mind that we killed about as many German civilians in the course of a couple of raids over Dresden as we have killed Vietnamese in the five years in Vietnam.

PLAYBOY: For all our bombing— precise or indiscriminate— we have not yet won the war. Do you think North Vietnam could successfully have resisted the most powerful military nation on earth for this long if it didn't have the support of most Vietnamese, North and South?

BUCKLEY: There are both extensive and succinct ways to answer that. The succinct way is for me to ask you: Could Nazi Germany have triumphed over France without the overwhelming support of the French? My answer is— obviously— yes, Germany could, and did. The South Vietnamese situation is one in which the critical weapon was terror. I have great admiration for my countrymen, but I haven't the *least* idea whether or not we would have the stamina to resist an enemy that had strung up an equivalent number of our elite in the public squares. Roughly speaking, what the South Vietnamese suffered during the high period of terror from 1959 to 1963 would be the equivalent of, say, 3,000,000 of our politicians, teachers, doctors, engineers and civil servants being executed. How we would behave under the circumstances I don't know. I tend to reject the ethnocentrically arrogant assumption that we Americans are uniquely valiant. I think it's not at all impossible that years from now, people will think of the South Vietnamese resistance through this entire period as one of the truly heroic historical efforts.

PLAYBOY: Weren't many of the South Vietnamese elite, during this same period, jailed or killed by the Diem regime?

BUCKLEY: What you're saying is: Did Diem and the rest of them go to lengths they needn't have gone in order to effect what they wanted to effect, which was the independence of Vietnam? My answer is—I don't know. A very good argument may be made that they didn't go to great enough lengths. In fact, such an argument could appropriately be engraved on Diem's tombstone.

PLAYBOY: That sounds like an endorsement of political imprisonment and assassination.

BUCKLEY: In time of war? Of course. The detection and shooting down of Admiral Yamamoto was one of the triumphs of American intelligence during the Second World War, and it gets described at least once every ten years in the *Reader's Digest*. You do remember, don't you, how Walter Pidgeon almost assassinated Hitler at Berchtesgaden? Do you remember the political prosecutions during the Second World War, when the New Deal decided that [pro-Nazi authors] George Sylvester Viereck and Lawrence Dennis should be put behind bars, so that we could get on with the War? I think we overdid it. I hope the South Vietnamese aren't as jumpy as we were.

PLAYBOY: Is your claim that the leaders of South Vietnam have been motivated by a desire for independence consistent with their near-total reliance on the U.S.?

BUCKLEY: Of course they've depended on us. They are waging war not against an autarchic aggressor that is satisfied to use its own resources but against an aggressor that—from the very beginning—has been armed by great powers, namely, Red China and the Soviet Union. The South Vietnamese didn't have a *rifle factory* in 1954. As far as I know, neither do they now. And neither did the North Vietnamese.

PLAYBOY: Since you applaud the fact that we rushed to the assistance of the besieged South Vietnamese government, do you also think we should oppose any war of national liberation that happens to have Communist support?

BUCKLEY: No, I wouldn't be willing to make that generality. I'd want to know where it was, what the surrounding situation was, how important it was to either Russia or China at the moment—in short, what the consequences might be. I would like to note that neither of those countries has ever supported a *real* war of national liberation—in lower-case letters—that is, a war in which the objective really *was* national liberation. When the Communist powers get involved, the point is *never* national liberation, always satellization. Now, it seems to me that the United States position ought to be to support whatever elements in a particular country are heading in the better of the apparently available directions. John Stuart Mill says that despotism is excused as a temporary arrangement, provided the purpose of that despotism is to maximize rather than minimize freedom.

PLAYBOY: Isn't the idea of despotism maximizing freedom a contradiction in terms – at least in practice?

BUCKLEY: No. Lincoln put it well when he argued that it could not have been the intention of the framers of the Constitution to sacrifice all future prospects for freedom in order to celebrate constitutional punctilio.

PLAYBOY: Isn't it true that most indigenous Communist movements in Southeast Asia are motivated more by nationalism or by economic needs than by ideological communism?

BUCKLEY: No, it isn't. Most troops simply do what they are told. Intermediaries interpret the formulation that will most inspire a particular group of soldiers to act enthusiastically in obedience to orders— whether that's a matter of telling them that their kamikaze raids will instantly elevate them into the heavenly spheres, to live forever after in glory, or that they will become large landholders, or whatever. But the people who are directing the drives in that part of the world are, in my opinion, genuinely committed to a Communist vision. The general Western assumption has been that time erodes that vision; but it is, nevertheless, true that there is a fundamentalist Marxism-communism rampant in China today. It may be inevitable that time will overcome that ideological pretension, but that is not the kind of thing around which one writes a foreign policy for the here and now.

PLAYBOY: It is also part of liberal orthodoxy— based on his long-standing animosity toward China— that Ho Chi Minh would probably have reached a Titoist accommodation with Peking had he succeeded throughout Vietnam. Do you think that might have happened?

BUCKLEY: I have no doubt that Ho Chi Minh would have preferred to be the master of Vietnam rather than merely the surrogate in that area for Mao Tse-tung. But we have to recognize that Ho Chi Minh is dead and that it was foreseeable even six or seven years ago that he would be dead in due course, since he was an old man even then. The usefulness of Ho to Mao had to do with the veneration of Ho as an individual figure, which veneration would not and did not flow to his successor. In Chinese, Vietnam means "farther South," a fact that suggests the ancient Chinese attitude toward the area: that it was never really licensed as a separate territory— the same feeling they have toward Tibet.

PLAYBOY: Considering your hard-line view of China, how do you feel about Nixon's recent diplomatic overtures to Peking?

BUCKLEY: I don't really see why our attitude toward Red China ought to be different from our attitude toward the Soviet Union. The principal international leverage we have at this particular moment has to do with the Russian-Chinese feud. It strikes me as supremely intelligent to constantly advertise to the Soviet Union that, just as we were prepared to side with the Soviet Union in order to effect a victory over Hitler, so are we prepared to understand the potential desirability of a flirtation with Red China in order to contain the Soviet Union. Or the other way around. This strikes me as simply a return to traditional diplomacy.

PLAYBOY: Do you think that we should— and will— recognize Red China?

BUCKLEY: I think we should not recognize her— and that it is unlikely that we will. For one thing, it becomes increasingly apparent that all of the old arguments for recognition of Red China are meaningless. The old arguments were, first, "You can't ignore a nation of 800,000,000 people." But it has gradually become manifest that we are hardly ignoring a country by failing to recognize it. As a matter of fact, we are sort of *super*recognizing it. The easy thing to do is to recognize; if you *don't* recognize, you're giving it very special attention. Point two: The notion that if we recognize Red China, we would then be able to transact some differences with her— to talk about them— has been discredited by experience. We've had hundreds of meetings with Red China: we are probably having one tonight. So we go ahead and have the meetings anyway. Number three: We have discovered from the British experience that the mere fact of having an active consulate or an ambassador in Red China has no effect at all in terms of a thaw. The English have not been able to show that they've accomplished a single thing— even concerning the protection of their own citizens— that they might not have accomplished if they hadn't had their people there. Number four, and finally: It was Lyndon Johnson who said that he would agree to give passports to Americans who wanted to visit Red China—journalists and so on. What then happened, of course, was that Red China refused to grant visas. So that we are therefore left with no adverse practical consequences of a diplomatic nature having to do with the recognition of Red China, but purely with symbolic consequences. And those consequences, in my judgment, argue against recognition.

PLAYBOY: So far, you haven't disagreed with any aspect of President Nixon's foreign policy. One critic has suggested that you may feel a sense of obligation to him for appointing you to the advisory commission of the USIA.

BUCKLEY: Oh, for God's sake. The point is that when I look around the world today and ask myself what it is that I truly care about in international affairs that Nixon has let me down on, I don't come up with anything. On the other hand, I acknowledge that there may be a feeling of restraint deriving not from my appointment to the commission but from the fact that I have seen him once or twice privately. I have discovered a new sensual treat, which, appropriately, the readers of *Playboy* should be the first to know about. It is to have the President of the United States take notes while you are speaking to him, even though you run the risk that he is scribbling, "Get this bore out of here." It's always a little bit more difficult to be rhetorically ruthless with somebody with whom you spend time. For example, I find it more difficult to be verbally ruthless with Hugh Hefner after meeting him as my guest on *Firing Line* and seeing him on a couple of other occasions. Beyond that, if I'm kind to Nixon, it's also because I think he needs to be protected from that part of the right whose emphasis is unbalanced in the direction of the paradigm.

PLAYBOY: Is Nixon conservative enough for you?

BUCKLEY: My ideal conservative President would be one who would strike out for certain radical reforms that, in my judgment, would greatly benefit America and augment human freedom. But such a President cannot be elected—at this time—and couldn't get his programs through Congress. It is also true, I think, that the paramount need of this highly divided society at this particular moment is for conciliation; and Nixon—who is making gradual progress while attempting to fortify the bonds of common affection—is a good President from the conservative point of view.

PLAYBOY: Do you think that Vice President Agnew served the

purpose of conciliation when he referred to the leaders of last
October's Moratorium as "an effete corps of impudent snobs"?
BUCKLEY: No, he served other purposes. There *are* other
purposes to be served, such as isolating the sources of discontent
and the agitators and merchants of it. Some Presidents do that
kind of thing adroitly, some don't. At a moment when we needed
reconciliation after Pearl Harbor, I think it was wrong for F. D. R.
to call those who were against the War "the New Copperheads."
But history appears to have forgiven him.

PLAYBOY: To many liberals, Agnew's attacks on the media late
last fall brought to mind the Chinese emperors who executed
messengers bringing bad news. Do you think that the press is as
objective as it professes to be?

BUCKLEY: When Mr. Nixon in November said that North
Vietnam cannot defeat or humiliate the United States, only
Americans can do that, he meant that if the American people
refuse to back an enterprise that— in the judgment of the men
they elected to write their foreign policies— is essential to the
good health of this country and of this century, then one must
face two alternative explanations for their failure to do so. One is
that they have run out of stamina. The other is that they have
been constantly hectored into taking an erroneous position
because they are insufficiently aware of the dimensions of the
problem. He would obviously prefer the latter explanation to the
former, as would I. He tends to feel that the majority of morally
alert people in America have, for the most part, heard only a
single side on the Vietnam issue— in the universities as well as in
the press. He is absolutely correct. It is almost impossible, you
know, to work your way through Yale or Harvard or Princeton
and hear a pro-Vietnam speech. This is a pure caricature of
academic freedom.

PLAYBOY: Aren't campus conservatives free to speak— and
don't they, often and at length?

BUCKLEY: Well, you must mean students, because there are very
few conservative professors. At Princeton, for example, 65 percent
of the faculty voted for Humphrey in 1968, 7 percent for Dick
Gregory and 7 percent for Nixon. And it's the professors I'm
talking about; their capacity, at a college, is to instruct.

PLAYBOY: Then you're suggesting that the faculty allows its
political bias to creep into every course.

BUCKLEY: Constantly. In any course in the humanities or social sciences. And not only in their teaching but in the books they assign. It seems to me that the entire academic community collaborated in the demonstration of academic bias when Walt Rostow and Dean Rusk went around looking for an academic post after they left Lyndon Johnson. What kind of a demonstration do you need beyond that? Here are two people whose academic credentials are absolutely first-rate. But all of a sudden, you find MIT—that paragon of academic freedom and scientific devotion—saying that they assumed Walt Rostow had "forgotten" what he knew about economics as the result of his stay in Government. That was one reason given by a senior faculty member; even James Reston made fun of it. You will notice nobody at Harvard went around saying that Galbraith "forgot" what he knew about economics as the result of his service for John Kennedy. Though I don't know. Maybe they hoped he had.

I think the health of any university is damaged by this monopoly of opinion. I spoke at the University of Minnesota a few months ago. A professor—a very distinguished historian—stood up and said that there are fifty professors of history at the university and one Republican, himself; that is, the ratio is fifty to one. Now, how much real political dialogue is the typical student at the University of Minnesota going to be exposed to, under the circumstances? And if he is *not* subjected to a true dialogue, then he tends to think dialogue is unnecessary, that what you need is asseveration. Placard justice: "Hey, hey, L. B. J.—how many kids did you kill today?"

PLAYBOY: Don't you think most students get the pro-Vietnam argument from their fathers?

BUCKLEY: That's unrealistic. Students are terrific snobs. I was one myself, though I had no right to be with my own father. The fact is that unless your father is right up with the academic vernacular—unless he's read Douglas Pike as recently as last week—you tend to feel that he's not equipped to discuss serious intellectual matters with you. In any case, I think that this hegemony of thought within the colleges is something that— perhaps without even knowing it—Agnew is scratching up against.

PLAYBOY: In his speech on TV news, the Vice President's avowals of distaste for censorship, coupled with his allusions to the power of the FCC to withhold broadcasting licenses, struck many liberals as hypocrisy. How do you feel about it?

BUCKLEY: I think they were entitled to think of it as at least potentially hypocritical. I find absolutely mysterious the way in which the debate was ultimately joined. My devoted friend Frank Stanton, who emerged as the spokesman for the victims of this pogrom—or intended pogrom—didn't, for instance, pause to remark that Congress has *already* withheld total freedom from the industry. The whole equal-time provision is an effort by the Congress of the United States to say to the networks and television and radio stations, "Certain freedoms you don't have." The FCC finds as much in the fairness doctrines every year as the Supreme Court finds in the First Amendment.

PLAYBOY: So it was really unnecessary for Agnew to refer to licensing?

BUCKLEY: It may be that Agnew's speech will serve some sort of a maieutic function—that it will tease out of the system a public policy concerning the tendentious limits to which an individual station owner may go. Such a policy would be a refinement of the fairness doctrine, which was not only accepted but applauded by liberals as recently as four or five years ago. In any case, *I* would like to say: Let any radio or TV station owner do what he wants. If he wants to put only Benjamin Spock on from midnight to midnight, let him do it. But make it as hard as possible for him to achieve monopoly status—by licensing pay-TV, which is precisely the way to wed the individual eccentric with his individual network or station.

PLAYBOY: What was your reaction to the Vice President's blast at the liberal Washington *Post* and New York *Times*?

BUCKLEY: If the press is so easily intimidated as to feel threatened by three speeches by the Vice President of the United States—if all those effete snobs are moral pygmies after all—then I ought to be even more worried about the press than I am. Mr. Agnew is not Mussolini; for better or worse, he cannot close down the New York *Times*. To sum up: I think what Mr. Agnew was attempting to say to the American people was that, particularly in New York, the networks and the commentators tend to reflect a single point of view—they look and act like the Rockettes—and that it is necessary for people to escape from the assumption that that is the only point of view. I think he has done an extremely useful service. Of course, it isn't just Mr. Agnew who came to such a conclusion: The identical conclusion was arrived at a few weeks earlier by Theodore White, who is a renowned liberal, on my television program. Agnew was simply accenting the obvious; and the obvious, when it has been taboo to state it, tends to hurt. *Ce n'est que la vérité qui blesse,* as Mr. Agnew would put it.

PLAYBOY: How would you feel if Agnew were to become President?

BUCKLEY: I have been persuaded for several years that the office of the President is so staggeringly complicated that nobody can, by conventional measurement, be "a good President." That is to say that nobody can conceivably oversee the range of activities that, technically, the President is responsible for overseeing. Under the circumstances, whereas it is widely supposed that the President needs to be a man of more and more complicated attainments, I tend to feel that he needs to be less and less a man of complicated attainments. A hundred years ago, a President really had to run the Post Office, among other things. Today, what one needs most from a President is goodwill, a working intelligence and sound character. The people who praise Harry Truman were willing to point this out at the time, incidentally, but were not willing to remember the thought when it looked as though Goldwater might be nominated by the Republican Party. Second, I do think that when a man becomes President, a transmogrification takes place; that which was theretofore inconceivable becomes somehow conceivable. Nobody could really imagine Harry Truman— even himself, as he subsequently confessed— as President, until all of a sudden, he *was* President. Allen Drury dwells on this in one of his books. On Monday, the man is just that vicious, sniping, polemical, Nixonite Vice President; on Tuesday, he's inaugurated and suddenly things happen not only to his critics and to the people but also to him. In short, Agnew wouldn't sound like Agnew if he were President— and, in a sense, properly so.

PLAYBOY: When you list goodwill, a working intelligence and sound character as what we need most from a President, do you mean regardless of ideology?

BUCKLEY: A man can't have a working intelligence, as distinguished from an abstract intelligence, without a reasonably sound "ideology"— a word I don't use much.

PLAYBOY: By reasonably sound, you mean reasonably conservative.

BUCKLEY: Yes. Conservatism is the politics of reality.

PLAYBOY: Do you think the Administration is using Agnew in

an attempt to wrest away some of the support for George Wallace in the South?

BUCKLEY: I hope so. Anybody who can take the 9,000,000 votes that went to George Wallace, baptize them and rededicate them to a hygienic conservatism certainly has my best wishes. It would be as though Adlai Stevenson had addressed the Communist Party and urged them to desert and follow the Democratic Party.

PLAYBOY: Kevin Phillips, in *The Emerging Republican Majority*, argues that Republicans can strengthen their current national advantage by building an alliance of heretofore solid Democratic voters in the South, already conservative citizens in the traditionally Republican heartland states, and middle-class whites everywhere who are disenchanted with costly Democratic social engineering. Do you think this so-called Southern strategy is a correct one for the Republican Party?

BUCKLEY: Any strategy is correct that isn't practiced in such a way as to persecute the people who do not acquiesce in the goals of the winning party. Kevin Phillips is saying that a single politics, in fact, can, given the foreseeable future, appeal to the majority of the American people. If it follows that that particular appeal is at the expense— indeed has as its intention the persecution— of people who do not agree with it, then one would have to renounce it. But in all the criticism I have seen of Mr. Phillips' book, I have never seen that made plain. Of course, I start on the heretical assumption that Southerners are people and that, under the circumstances, it is not immoral to appeal to somebody merely because he is a Southerner. If you're going to appeal to Southerners by promising to re-enslave the black people, then I consider that to be immoral, but I don't see any suggestion of this in Mr. Phillips' book. I think, actually, that the horror Mr. Phillips has inspired in such people as George McGovern derives not from any moral abhorrence of the thesis but out of a recognition by a very shrewd professional— which Senator McGovern is— that Mr. Phillips has the clue to how to stitch together a winning majority. Franklin D. Roosevelt, McGovern's patron saint, found such a clue, which remained operative for an entire generation.

PLAYBOY: Whatever the intention of Phillips' Southern strategy— which you seem to be endorsing, with some qualifications— its effect is clearly to exclude blacks from the "emerging Republican majority." And we note that in citing the West's acceptance of coexistence as the most significant development of the sixties, you apparently downgrade the importance of the black revolution, which many consider the milestone of the decade. Why?

BUCKLEY: I think that the important philosophical fight in the area of American black-white relations was won by Abraham Lincoln, who insisted on the metaphysical fact of human equality. This was the great achievement of the American nineteenth century. The next milestone, as far as the Negroes are concerned, will come when whites turn to— and seek out— Negroes as a result of their individual achievements. This has come in some places and will come in others, but it is going to take time. It is certainly open to speculation whether all of the activities of the past fifteen years have significantly accelerated that emancipation.

PLAYBOY: Do you think the black struggle in the past fifteen years has *retarded* that emancipation?

BUCKLEY: America has, lately, given herself over to the promulgation of unrealizable goals, which doom her to frustration, if not to despair. Voegelin calls it the immanentization of the eschaton— broadly speaking, consigning that which properly belongs to the end of life to the temporal order. That can lead only to grave dissatisfactions. The very idea of "Freedom now" was an invitation to frustration. *Now* means something or it means nothing. When months and then years went by and the kind of dream that Martin Luther King spoke about in 1963 in Washington didn't come true, a totally predictable frustration set in. It is one thing to engage in great ventures in amelioration; it is another to engage in great ventures in utopianization.

PLAYBOY: Couldn't it be argued that the career of Martin Luther King— even if it didn't create freedom— inspired a sense of dignity in the masses of black people?

BUCKLEY: It could. It could also be argued that the dignity was already there. What Dr. King inspired was more nearly self-assertion, which sometimes is and sometimes isn't the same as dignity.

PLAYBOY: Your belief that black Americans had dignity before the appearance of King strikes us as less important than the fact that millions of blacks themselves didn't think so.

BUCKLEY: Look. There was anti-black discrimination pre-King, there is anti-black discrimination post-King. If dignity is something that comes to you only after you succeed in putting an end to discrimination, then the blacks didn't have dignity then and don't have it now. If dignity is something that comes to you by transcending discrimination, then I say they had it then even as they have it now. What some blacks— and a lot of whites— now have, which is distinctive, is a greater tendency to self-assertion. I am trying to insist that that isn't the same as dignity.

PLAYBOY: In an *Atlantic* magazine interview on the occasion of your unsuccessful candidacy for membership in the Yale Corporation two years ago, you made the unluckily timed crack: "It was only a very few years ago that official Yale conferred a doctor of laws on Martin Luther King, who more clearly qualifies as a doctor of lawbreaking." A few weeks later, Dr. King was assassinated. Did you regret the publication of your quote? And do you think of Martin Luther King as a pernicious force in American history?

BUCKLEY: I regret but am philosophical about the fact that there is a lead time in journalism, so that you sometimes find yourself reading something that is inappropriate the day you read it, which, however, was altogether appropriate the day you wrote it. *Look* magazine's cover, after J. F. K.'s assassination, had on it, "Kennedy Could Lose." As regards what I wrote, I think it was correct. I wrote it a couple of days after Dr. King threatened massive civil disobedience if the forthcoming demands of his poverty marchers were not met. I don't want to answer your question about whether he will be seen as a good or a bad force in history, because I don't know. He was clearly a bad force on the matter of obeying the law. His attempt to sanctify civil disobedience is at least one of his legacies; if it emerges as his principal legacy, then he should certainly be remembered as a bad force. If, on the other hand, his principal legacy emerges— the wrinkles having been ironed out by the passage of time— as a spiritual leader of an oppressed people whom he urged on to great endeavors, then he will be a great historical force.

PLAYBOY: Could you yourself ever justify breaking a law?

BUCKLEY: Yes. I would justify the breaking of a law that, by more or less settled agreement on the separation of powers since the time of Christ, is ontologically outside the state's jurisdiction. For instance, when the government of Mexico, beginning a government or two after the overthrow of Díaz, forbade Mexicans to attend church, hundreds of thousands of them did so anyway, in underground churches. It seems to me that this is an excellent example of justified breaking of the law, against which there could be no reasonable recrimination.

PLAYBOY: Then it depends on the individual's idea of the character of the government as well as of the laws.

BUCKLEY: No, it doesn't. I didn't say the individual's idea and I didn't say the character of the government. I said the settled idea of the separation of powers and I said the character of the law, not of the government. Scholars, secular and religious, have agreed for two thousand years that the state has no business interfering in the traffic between man and his God; any attempt to do so breaks the legal bond that the government has over the individual. I assume, of course, that we are talking about free or relatively free societies. If we're talking about totalitarian societies, the essential relationship of the subject to the slavemaster ought to be mutinous.

PLAYBOY: Since you have referred to the religious justification for lawbreaking: Do you think a young man has the right to use the Fifth Commandment— thou shalt not kill— as justification for refusing induction into the Armed Forces?

BUCKLEY: The Fifth Commandment obviously is not a proscription against taking another man's life under any circumstances. Moses led a pretty robust army even after he came down from Mount Sinai. The rendering should have been, "Thou shalt not murder." I am not correcting God— He had it right. The imprecision was King James'.

PLAYBOY: You said that the essential relationship of subject to slavemaster ought to be mutinous in totalitarian societies. Aren't there degrees of unfreedom— and isn't there a point at which the erosion of freedom must be resisted, perhaps by civil disobedience?

BUCKLEY: There is a point at which an individual citizen rejects his society. He has at that point several options. One is to leave. The society ought not to hinder his doing so. A second is to agitate for reform. The society ought to protect his right to do so. A third is to drop out. The society ought to let him alone, to the extent it is possible to disengage reciprocating gears. A fourth is to disobey the laws or to revolutionize. In that event, the society ought to imprison, exile or execute him.

PLAYBOY: You've identified what you consider the utopianism of Martin Luther King's call for "Freedom now" as a negative aspect of the civil rights revolution. Do you see any positive aspects to that revolution?

BUCKLEY: Yes, several. I supported Dr. King in Montgomery. I very much believe in voluntary boycotts. If Woolworth's isn't going to let you sit down and buy a Coca-Cola, then, goddamn it, don't patronize Woolworth's. I certainly believe in equal access to public accommodations and I have always opposed the denial to anyone of any constitutionally specified right, by reason of race, color or creed.

PLAYBOY: Including the right to vote?

BUCKLEY: Yes.

PLAYBOY: But you have argued, haven't you, for limiting the franchise?

BUCKLEY: Yes. I think too many people are voting.

PLAYBOY: Whom would you exclude?

BUCKLEY: A while ago, George Gallup discovered that 25 percent or so of the American people have never heard of the United Nations. I think if we could find that 25 percent, they'd be reasonable candidates for temporary disfranchisement.

PLAYBOY: How would you find them?

BUCKLEY: Ask the Ford Foundation where they are. Incidentally, there's an interesting paradox here. I think that as power is centralized, one can make less of a case for extending the vote. In the ideal world, where power is decentralized—in my kind of a world—one wouldn't have to know what the United Nations was in order to assess intelligently the local situation and express yourself on it.

PLAYBOY: You didn't include the school-desegregation decision of the Supreme Court in your list of the beneficent results of the civil rights movement. Why?

BUCKLEY: When *Brown vs. Board of Education* was passed, we at *National Review* called it "bad law and bad sociology." I continue to think it was lousy law, historically and analytically. There are, unfortunately, increased grounds for believing that it was also bad sociology. Coerced massive integration is simply not working at primary and secondary school levels, and I notice that, for instance in Harlem, the voters don't list integrated schooling as among their principal demands. What they want, and should have, is better education. The superstition that this automatically happens by checkerboarding the classroom is increasingly apparent to blacks as well as to whites. Meanwhile, in the total situation, you are taking very grave risks in jeopardizing the good nature of the white majority.

PLAYBOY: Could your concern for the good nature of the white majority be interpreted as acquiescence to their prejudice?

BUCKLEY: The word prejudice becomes a little strained, used in that way. Look, 95 percent of the white people who live in Washington are Democrats, political liberals who give speeches in favor of integration and vote for politicians who favor integration— and then take their children out of the public schools when Negroes enter those schools. If you call them prejudiced, they reply that that isn't it, but that they want for their children a better education than they will get at the public schools in Washington.

PLAYBOY: If every school in the country were integrated by law in the next two years, wouldn't you have a generation twenty years from now that was relatively free of race prejudice?

BUCKLEY: I fear not. There is still anti-Italian prejudice in Jewish sections of New York and anti-Jewish prejudice in Italian sections of New York, and they've been going to school together for more than twenty years. It may be, ages hence, when the final sociological report is stapled and submitted, that we will discover that it all had something to do with numbers. It may be that a school that has 10 percent Negroes will be successful and a school that has 30 or 40 percent Negroes won't make it; either the whites will pull out or racial antagonisms will disrupt the school. Meanwhile, the things to stress and restress are better education and better job opportunities for Negroes.

PLAYBOY: How should black demands for better education be met— or do you think they shouldn't be met?

BUCKLEY: The discussion so far has been within the context of the existing system. I have always been attracted to the twin notions that what we need are many more private schools and that public schools ought to approximate private schools as closely as possible, which means that public schools ought to have the same rights as private schools. These are among the reasons why I am so strongly attracted to the so-called voucher plan, which would work this way: A parent would be given a voucher for $500— or whatever it costs to educate a child— which the parent would then take to any school, public or private, close to home or distant, where he wanted to matriculate that child. The school would get its money by cashing in these vouchers. The

virtues of the plan are the virtues of the free-enterprise system—
concerning which, incidentally, you are strangely uncurious.
Specifically, it gives freedom of choice to the parent, whether he's
rich or poor. Under the voucher plan, schools would become
more competitive; they would strive to serve their customers—
namely, the students.

PLAYBOY: How much do you think remains to be done to
improve black job opportunities?

BUCKLEY: Plenty. I am convinced that the truly important way
for the Negro to advance is economically. We should, first,
deprive labor unions of their monopolistic privileges. In fact, I'd
do that anyway, even if no Negroes existed. But when we know
that those privileges are being exercised in part to prevent
Negroes from getting jobs in certain industries, the very least the
Government ought to do is act in *those* cases. Second, we should
encourage preferential hiring in situations where there isn't
unemployment. It's unrealistic to think that you can refuse to hire
a white in order to make room for a Negro if there is wide
unemployment. Point three: A revival of the whole ap-
prenticeship idea would be extremely useful at this point. It
would involve, among other things, modifying— and preferably
repealing— many of the minimum-wage laws. I digress to say that
the minimum-wage laws are, of course, the great enemy,
especially of teenage Negroes. Professor Milton Friedman has
shown that there was approximately a 100 percent relative rise in
Negro teenage unemployment after the last increase in the
minimum wage. Further, I would like to see somebody draw up a
sophisticated table of tax deductions given to individuals who
hire Negroes as apprentices, the idea being to teach them a
profitable trade— in construction, in electricity, in plumbing, in
newspaper offices, wherever.

PLAYBOY: Beyond increasing job opportunities, what else can
be done to eliminate poverty in America? Specifically, are you in
favor of President Nixon's welfare-reform proposals?

BUCKLEY: We are eliminating poverty in this country faster
than any society ever has. There is a downward-bound graph that
begins with about 50 percent of the population poor at the turn
of the century and dips to the present, where there are about 9
percent poor, using the same indices. So my first comment is that
I don't want anything to interfere with the direction of that
graph, which the overhead costs and economic strategy of many

social-welfare programs tend to do. Now, it may be that the curve
is asymptotic, that it will never quite close. The residual poor will,
of course, have to have some kind of a relief program, even as they
do now. I myself would buy the Moynihan plan, or the Nixon
plan, or the New Federalism— whatever you call it— as a substitute for all existing measures. It may well come down to a
matter of American know-how moving in on a congeries of
welfare systems to make welfarism both more mangeable and an
instrument that itself might break the so-called vicious cycle that
everybody agrees has discredited the existing system.
PLAYBOY: What sort of program— if any— do you favor for
eliminating hunger?
BUCKLEY: I'm attracted to the notion of giving out four basic
food materials, free, to anybody who wants them. The cost, according to one economist, would come to about a billion dollars a
year. The idea is that these ingredients would be available at food
stores to anybody— you, me, Nelson Rockefeller— because it
simply wouldn't be worthwhile trying to catch anyone who was
taking the free food and didn't need it. With such a plan, you
could officially and confidently say that the residual hunger in
America was simply the result of people not knowing how to
utilize these materials.
PLAYBOY: What are they?
BUCKLEY: Powdered skim milk, bulgur wheat, soybeans and a
kind of lard. You can make very good bread out of them, for
instance. This bulgur wheat, incidentally— which is a staple in
the Mideast— is not much liked by Americans and yet Alice
Roosevelt Longworth loves it, considers it a delicacy.
PLAYBOY: Do you agree with those analysts who feel that— in
part because of the black revolution and because of Federal
"handout" programs— the general electorate is moving to the
right?
BUCKLEY: There are all sorts of conflicting indices. The
Moynihan plan that we just talked about is left by orthodox
conservative standards; if it had been proposed by Franklin
Delano Roosevelt in 1933, it might have gotten even *him* impeached— and yet the people seem willing to accept it. But
looking at the broad indications, I do feel that there is a move to
the right. I've always believed that conservatism is, as I said a
while ago, the politics of reality and that reality ultimately asserts
itself, in a reasonably free society, in behalf of the conservative

position. An excellent example was the race riots of the mid-sixties. Even the participants discovered that those Gadarene experiments were futile.

PLAYBOY: Mayor Daley's celebrated order to the Chicago police to maim looters in the rioting that followed the assassination of Martin Luther King confirmed the feeling of many young people— black and white— that American society places a higher value on property than on human life. Do you think looters should be shot?

BUCKLEY: I reject the notion that a property right is other than a human right— that is, it's not an animal right or a vegetable right. The commitment of the state to the individual is to protect the individual's freedom and property, property being one of the things that materialize from the exercise of freedom and, therefore, in many senses, are the fruits of freedom. So I elect a mayor to protect me and my property effectively, with graduated responses to various conditions. If theft is an aberration— as it is, for instance, in the Scandinavian countries— I would consider a mayor who orders his men to shoot thieves to be absolutely barbaric. But if theft reaches near-epidemic conditions, a different response is indicated. I wish there were something in between simply shouting, "Hey! Come back!" and shooting somebody in the leg. Unfortunately, I fear that when that in-between thing is discovered, liberals are going to come up with elaborate reasons for not using it— Mace being an excellent example.

PLAYBOY: Mayor Daley's shoot-to-maim order, and his handling of demonstrators at the Democratic Convention that same summer, struck many observers as proof of an authoritarian and ugly aspect of America's turn to the right. If you had been mayor of Chicago, would you have handled the protesters as he did?

BUCKLEY: No. I've been pretty well satisfied that it was a basic mistake not to open up Lincoln Park. You simply can't require people to evaporate— incorporealization not being a typical human skill. But with the exception of his ruling on the use of the park, and the workaday tactical errors, I think Daley's resoluteness was justified. Obviously, the excesses of his police were *not* justified, but a lot of Americans were glad the demonstrators got beaten up. They were glad for the commonplace reason— there's a little sadism in all of us— but they were also glad because they knew goddamn well that the chances of the demonstrators' breaking the law with impunity were overwhelming. It was sort of a return to posse justice. If you knew absolutely that Abbie Hoffman and the boys were never going to spend a night in jail— which was a good guess at the time— then people figured, "What the hell, beat 'em up. At least get *that* satisfaction out of it."

PLAYBOY: Is that the way you felt?

BUCKLEY: No. But I understand the feeling.

PLAYBOY: Liberals Carl Stokes and John Lindsay were both re-elected mayor last year. Do these elections contradict your general thesis of a move to the right?

BUCKLEY: No, they don't. Lindsay's re-election is certainly a special case. A perfectly reasonable assumption is that if there had been a runoff between him and Procaccino, even Procaccino might have beaten him. I don't think one can conclude very much of an ideological nature from the event in New York City. In the matter of Stokes, it seems to me that there are a great number of people who practice, for reasons that I applaud, an inverse racism; many Cleveland whites voted for Mr. Stokes precisely because he is a Negro. The idea is that, among other things, it is a good investment in conserving America to remind a population that is always being urged toward cynicism that it *is* possible to rise up the ladder. But I think that Stokes is one of the four or five truly brilliant politicians I've ever run up against, so I'm prejudiced in his favor.

PLAYBOY: Would you practice this kind of inverse racism?

BUCKLEY: Yes. I think there's a very good argument for voting for a Negro because he's a Negro— until such time as it becomes simply redundant to make such a demonstration. I wouldn't vote for a Jew because he was a Jew, because it seems to me that the time has long since passed when it was necessary to demonstrate that a Jew can rise as high as he wants to. This is not the case with the Negro.

PLAYBOY: Haven't you used this argument to suggest that America should have a black President?

BUCKLEY: Yes, I have. I would take great pleasure in the pride that would come to the black community if there were a Negro in the White House. I think it's worth working for.

PLAYBOY: The possibility of a black American President seems remote in a decade that is opening with a widespread crackdown on such militant black groups as the Black Panthers. Do you think there is a campaign to exterminate the Panthers?

BUCKLEY: No. But I think there should be. I mean, obviously, to exterminate the *movement*, even as I favor the extermination of Ku Klux Klanism, though not necessarily Ku Kluxers.

PLAYBOY: Why?

BUCKLEY: Because I am persuaded that the Panthers have solemnly registered their basic goals, which are to rob people, by category, of their rights to life, to liberty, to freedom; and because they are arming themselves for that purpose. Any organization caught—as the Panthers have been caught time and time again—with caches of machine guns and grenades and Molotov cocktails is presumptively guilty of non-Platonic ambitions. Every state in the Union forbids that sort of stockpiling of arms.

PLAYBOY: Where have the Panthers indicated that their basic goal is to rob people of their rights?

BUCKLEY: In their literature. Read it. I don't carry it around. It is as thoroughly impregnated with genocidal anti-white racism as ever the Nazis' was with anti-Semitism. And it makes no difference to the Panthers where on the left-right spectrum the white politician stands. On the death of Bobby Kennedy, the Black Panthers' national newspaper ran a photograph of him lying in a pool of his own blood in the Ambassador Hotel with the head of a pig replacing the head of Mr. Kennedy. The rhetorical totalism suggested here, combined with the doctrinal genocidal passions, suggests to me that whatever was the appropriate attitude toward Goebbels in, say 1930, is appropriate, in 1970, toward the Black Panthers.

PLAYBOY: Doesn't the publication of such a picture, however repugnant, come under the protection of the First Amendment?

BUCKLEY: It does, formalistically; which is why I included actions—the Panthers' stockpiling of weapons—among the reasons why I think their extermination as a movement is desirable. But I would like to note that it is a naïve liberal assumption to think that the Bill of Rights protects every manner of written or spoken dissent. In the heyday of McCarthyism, Professor Samuel Stouffer from Harvard did one of those *Travels with Charley* bits around the country to discover the extent to which the Bill of Rights was an article of practical faith held by the American people. He found out that something like 75 percent of us didn't believe that members of the Communist Party should enjoy *any* rights. Needless to say, he wrote a horrified book about his findings. Now, it is extremely easy for people with an ideologized knowledge of American history to suppose that this is something new, let alone that it is impossible to compose a theoretical defense of it. But it is apparent to me that the profoundest studies of what, for instance, Thomas Jefferson or Abraham Lincoln meant by freedom was a freedom that was severely limited, even theoretically, in the right it absolutely granted to anyone to call for the persecution, let alone the liquidation, of others. When Jefferson said, "Those who wish to dissolve the Union or to change the republican form of government should stand undisturbed as monuments of the safety with which error of opinion may be tolerated where reason is left free to combat it," I am convinced by such scholars as Harry Jaffa that he meant not that we should grant freedom to the enemies of freedom because they are entitled to it but that we should grant freedom to the enemies of freedom because we can afford to *indulge* them that freedom. Accordingly, it becomes a practical rather than a theoretical consideration whether, at any given moment in American history, a particular group of dissenters whose dissent is based on the desire to rob other people of their freedom ought to be tolerated.

PLAYBOY: Are we at such a moment in history—when we can't afford that freedom to a few hundred out of 200,000,000 Americans?

BUCKLEY: Quite possibly. I don't think the Panthers are in a position to take over the country, any more than the Klan was. But the Klan deprived particular people in particular places of their effective freedom. So have the Panthers, by the use of the same weapons: intimidation and, it is now alleged by one or two grand juries, both murder and conspiracy to murder. So I say: Let's do to them what I wish we had done to the Klan fifty years ago.

PLAYBOY: When you say that we should not tolerate a group of dissenters such as the Panthers, what do you propose we do about them?

BUCKLEY: Society has three sanctions available for dealing with dissenters of this kind. There is the whole family of social sanctions; if they don't work, we then have legal sanctions; if the legal sanctions don't work, we are forced to use military sanctions. As an example of the social sanctions, I give you what has happened to Gerald L. K. Smith, the fierce anti-Semite. Would Smith be invited to join the sponsoring group of the Lincoln Center? If he gave a $1,000 contribution to the President's Club, would he be admitted as a member? No. Gerald L. K. Smith has been effectively isolated in America, and I'm glad that he has been. After such an experience as we have seen in the twentieth century of what happens— or what can happen— when people call for genocidal persecutions of other people, we have got to use whatever is the minimal resource available to society to keep that sort of thing from growing. If the social sanctions work, then you have the Jeffersonian situation, in which libertarian rodomontade is onanistically satisfying— a society in which the least possible force is the effective agent of that society's cohesiveness. I would like to see people like Bobby Seale and Eldridge Cleaver treated at least as badly as Gerald L. K. Smith has been. But no: They get applauded, they get invited to college campuses, they get listened to attentively on radio and on television— they are invited to Leonard Bernstein's *salons*— all of which makes rather glamorous a position that, in my judgment, ought to be execrated.

PLAYBOY: They also get jailed, exiled and even shot.

BUCKLEY: Cleaver was jailed for committing rape, which Gerald L. K. Smith hasn't done, so far as I know. And he was wounded after a shoot-out with Oakland police. Huey Newton was convicted of voluntary manslaughter. A gang of them are up now for murder and conspiracy to terrorize. Now, I'll grant you this: I have not been satisfied that the killing of Cleaver's buddy in that particular battle in Oakland— the young man who walked out of the house in his shorts and T-shirt— was justified. The policeman who killed him may have panicked, as others of us have done, with less tragic consequences, to be sure. But he wasn't acting on orders from J. Edgar Hoover, whose sins, if there are any, are explicit rather than implicit. But to return to my point, if I may, about the attention lavished on such people: The same, to a certain extent, was true of George Lincoln Rockwell, who got an extensive ventilation of his views in this magazine. For as long as that kind of thing happens, you encourage people to consider as tenable a position that in my judgment ought to be universally rejected as untenable. The whole idea of civilization is little by little to discard certain points of view as uncivilized; it is impossible to discover truths without discovering that their opposites are error. In a John Stuart Mill-type society— in which *any* view, for so long as it is held by so much as a single person, is considered as not yet confuted— you have total intellectual and social anarchy.

PLAYBOY: On the other hand, by publishing an interview with a George Lincoln Rockwell, one might encourage him to expose the untenability of his views and thus help discredit both himself and his philosophy, even among those who might previously have been sympathizers.

BUCKLEY: I acknowledge the abstract appeal of the argument, but I remind you that it can be used as an argument for evangelizing people in Nazism, racism or cannibalism, in order to fortify one's opposition to such doctrines. The trouble is that false doctrines *do* appeal to people. In my judgment, it would be a better world where nobody advocated tyranny; better than a world in which tyranny is advocated as an academic exercise intended to fortify the heroic little antibodies to tyranny.

PLAYBOY: If the evils of a particular doctrine are so apparent, what harm is there in allowing someone to preach that doctrine?

BUCKLEY: What is apparent to one man is not necessarily apparent to the majority. Hitler came to power democratically. It's a nineteenth-century myth to confide totally in the notion that the people won't be attracted to the wrong guy. George Wallace, not Nixon or Humphrey, got the highest TV ratings. Take, once more, the Panthers. There are, I am sure, hundreds of thousands of Americans who would like to hear a speech by Eldridge Cleaver. One reason they would like to do so is because they like the excitement. Another is that they like to show off. People like to show their audacity, their cavalier toleration of iconoclasm— it's the same kind of thing, in a way, as shouting "F--- Mayor Daley" in a loud voice in the middle of a park in Chicago. Moreover, the views expressed by Eldridge Cleaver, *et al.*, have not been proscribed by settled intellectual opinion, because, thank God, we have not experienced in America the kind of holocaust that Caucasians visited against the Jews in Germany. I contend that it is a responsibility of the intellectual community to anticipate Dachau rather than to deplore it. The primary responsibility of people who fancy themselves morally sophisticated is to do what they can to exhibit their impatience with those who are prepared to welcome the assassination of Bobby Kennedy because that meant one less pig. Their failure to do that is, in my judgment, a sign of moral disintegration. If you have moral disintegration, you don't have left a case against Dachau. If you don't have that, what *do* you have? Make love not war? Why?

PLAYBOY: Do you think that a more concerted police attack should be launched against the Panthers?

BUCKLEY: I would support a full legal attack, with the passage of new laws, if necessary, as we have done in other areas. For instance, I don't think we have enough legal weapons against people who push heroin. People who are practiced in the profession of trying to halt the flow of heroin see themselves as engaged in a losing fight— primarily because by the time the agent can gain entry to the home or apartment where he suspects there is a stash of heroin, it has been flushed down the toilet. The so-called no-knock provision of the President's new crime bill was written precisely to overcome that problem. Now, I know— everybody knows— that that provision is capable of abuse. But I think a libertarian ought always to ask himself: What is the way to maximize liberty?

PLAYBOY: In what way does the no-knock law maximize liberty?

BUCKLEY: Directly. In *Manchild in the Promised Land*, Claude Brown identifies heroin as the principal problem in Harlem— *not* housing, *not* education, *not* discrimination, *not* the absence of economic opportunity. Heroin. If the heroin traffic in Harlem were brought under control, we would see— in his judgment— a dramatic drop in crime and a lessening of those restrictions on freedom that accompany a high crime rate.

PLAYBOY: Would you disagree with former Attorney General Ramsey Clark's contention that eliminating poverty is the key to reducing crime?

BUCKLEY: I would. Drug abuse and crime both have to do with the state of the ethos; and the ethos is not a function of poverty. Consider Portugal or Ireland: Poor people don't necessarily commit crimes.

PLAYBOY: A few minutes ago, you referred to the moral disintegration of some Americans. Would you make that a general indictment— applicable not only to those who tolerate the Panthers but to most Americans?

BUCKLEY: Yes. The most conspicuous attribute of the twentieth-century American is his self-indulgence. In a marvelous book called *The Odyssey of the Self-Centered Self*, Robert Fitch traces the principal concerns of civilization through the past 200 or 300 years; our concerns were, he says, first predominantly religious, then predominantly scientific, then humanistic—and today are essentially egocentric. I think that ours is an egocentric society. The popular notion is that there is no reciprocal obligation by the individual to the society, that one can accept whatever the patrimony gives us without any sense of obligation to replenish the common patrimony—that is, without doing what we can to advance the common good. This, I think, is what makes not only Americans but most Western peoples weak. It comforts me that that also was the finding of Ortega y Gasset.

PLAYBOY: How does the increasing social awareness and involvement of young people fit into your thesis?

BUCKLEY: I don't say that somebody who spends the summer in Mississippi trying to bring rights to black people is primarily self-centered, although such a case could be made concerning some young people and by using less intricate psychological arguments than, for instance, the liberals fling around to prove that we are all racist. I'm talking about the general disease of *anomie*, which is the result of people's, by and large, having become deracinated, suspended from any relationship to the supernatural and prescinded from the historical situation. A lot of them retreat and think about themselves, even *exclusively* about themselves—the drug people—the dropouts, formal and informal. Certain others venture into utopianism, which, as I've said, necessarily and obviously breeds frustration and despair, conditions that some of them prefer even to drugs. But the lot of them, I think, fail to come to terms with the world, fail to come to terms with the end of life. They have absolutely no eschatological vision, except a rhetorical sort of secular utopianism. A related phenomenon: When I was last on the Johnny Carson show, he announced to his mass audience, "Well, after all, the reason the Soviet Union arms is because *we* arm," the implicit axiom being that there is obviously no difference between them and us. What makes it possible for the man who has the largest regular audience of anybody in the United States—not excluding the President—to say blandly something like that is testimony to wave after wave in the successful intellectual offensive against epistemological optimism—against the notion that some things are better than others and that we can know what those things are.

PLAYBOY: Do you think this moral relativism is at least partially a consequence of the decline in religious belief?

BUCKLEY: Yes. In orthodox religious belief. It's a commonplace that there is no such thing as an irreligious society. The need for religion being a part of the nature of man, people will continue to seek religion. You see the Beatles rushing off to listen to the platitudinous homilies of that Indian quack, Maharishi-what's-his-name, but they'd rather be caught dead than reading Saint Paul. Young people who have active minds tend to be dissatisfied with the ersatz religions they pick up, and yet so formal is the contemporary commitment to agnosticism— or even to atheism— that they absolutely refuse to plumb Christianity's extraordinary reservoirs of rationality. I doubt if you could get one of these kids, however desperately in search of religion— who will go to any guru, who will even talk to *Joan Baez* and attempt to get religion from *her*—to read *Orthodoxy* by Chesterton or any book by C. S. Lewis.

PLAYBOY: Perhaps orthodoxy— lower case— is at fault. Many young people would say they think Christ was a great man; they might even know a good deal about Him. But they are appalled by Saint Paul's horror of the body and of sex.

BUCKLEY: I'm sure that among the vast majority of students, the knowledge of Christ is superficial and that the *only* thing they know about Saint Paul is that he was "anti-sex." In fact, Saint Paul's anti-sexuality was, I think, a mode by which he expressed the joys of asceticism, the transcendent pleasure of the mortification of the flesh. By no means is this distinctive to Christianity. In fact, Christianity in its formal renunciation of Manichaeism took a position concerning the flesh that is far more joyful than, for instance, that of the Buddhists or of a number of other religions.

PLAYBOY: One of the reasons many people have difficulty accepting your religion, Roman Catholicism, is that they have been convinced by experts that there are soon going to be more people on the globe than the earth can support, yet the Church does its not-inconsiderable best to prevent the spread of birth-control information. Do you also take a serious view of the population problem?

BUCKLEY: Yes, I do. I think it is the second most important problem in the world, after ideological communism.

PLAYBOY: Then the Church's position on birth control distresses you?

BUCKLEY: No. It is not established by any means that the influence of the Church is very direct on the matter of the increase in population. It happens that the birth rate is the greatest where the Church has no influence: India, for instance, or Nigeria. It is impossible to establish a correlation between the birth rate in Latin America and the prevailing religion on that continent. The Catholic position on birth control is, therefore, something against which we agonize rather more theoretically than practically.

PLAYBOY: What do you think we can do, then, to keep the population down?

BUCKLEY: Get people to stop reading *Playboy*.

PLAYBOY: Very funny. What's the real answer?

BUCKLEY: Well, the real answer is to make sure that people who don't want more children and who have no religious scruples against the use of birth control paraphernalia are aware of how they can get and use them. My own assumption is that we are moving toward the discovery of a chemical that will prevent conception, that will be generally dispensed— perhaps in the water supply— and can be readily neutralized by any woman who desires to do so.

PLAYBOY: Should the U.S. volunteer birth-control information and devices to such overpopulated nations as India?

BUCKLEY: They don't need any more information. They can get it from the *Encyclopaedia Britannica*. As to giving them the pill—sure, if they ask for it.

PLAYBOY: Do you have any other sexual opinions that might shock your bishop?

BUCKLEY: I didn't give you a "sexual" opinion. I don't know that giving free pills to India is heretical. Would American rabbis object to free pork for India? Heresy? I don't think so. I happen, for example, to favor the legalization of private homosexual acts committed between consenting adults and of prostitution. The second is the more important. Legalizing prostitution would provide a ready outlet for pubescent lust and greatly facilitate the hygienic problem, pending the domination of the appetite and the restoration of morality. Also, it would cut down the profits and power of the Mafia, the existence of which enrages me.

PLAYBOY: How else would you combat the Mafia?

BUCKLEY: By making gambling—but not gambling debts— legal.

PLAYBOY: Advocating the legalization of gambling, prostitution and homosexual acts between adults puts you in agreement with most liberals. Do you also agree with them in the area of censorship? Would you defend the right of the state to, say, stop performances by Lenny Bruce?

BUCKLEY: I'm troubled by that problem. By the way, do, please, try to remember that the conservative opposes unnecessary legislation. I've written about the censorship dilemma. Obviously, a perfectly consistent, schematic libertarianism would give you an easy answer—let anybody do anything. Including cocaine vending machines. But a libertarianism written without reference to social universals isn't terribly useful. Here, I think, is where the science of sociology becomes useful. If sociology suggests that societies don't survive without the observance of certain common bonds, certain taboos, then we can maintain that in the long run, we diminish rather than increase freedom by protecting people who violate those taboos. Having said that, let me add that I'm perfectly well aware that this particular argument can be abused by people who want a narrow conformity. But once again, let's reach for an example: When *Salvation*, the rock musical, was produced in New York City, the reviewer for *Time* magazine listed the things that it takes to make a successful rock musical nowadays. It has to be dirty, anti-American and anti-religious. Under the last category, he said: It will no longer do to attack Protestantism, because Protestantism has become so etiolated as to have no potential for shock. You can't shock anybody by making fun of the dogma of the Bishop of Woolwich. Second, it can't be anti-Jewish, because the playgoing community on Broadway tends to be heavily Jewish and the Jewish people hold that certain things should be held in reverence. For instance, no jokes about Buchenwald can be made in New York City. Therefore—attack the Catholics!

There's still a certain amount of awe in the Catholic religion, but the Catholics are a politically unorganized group in New York City and you can get away with ridiculing them. So, the writer gives the audience the iconoclast's thrill, but safely: They're not going to lose at the box office. Now—should society in general defer to the specially pious concerns of significant groups within that society? We extend certain protections against public affronts. For instance, the courts recognize a limit to what a storekeeper displays in his window. But what about his shelf? Or the stage? Is it right to have laws forbidding, let us say, a comedy based on what happened at Dachau? I know all the theoretical arguments against it, but there's a tug inside me that says that society perhaps has to maintain the right to declare certain kinds of aggressions against the venerated beliefs of the people as taboo. This is a codification of grace, of mutual respect.

PLAYBOY: Would you admit that the tug inside you to ban certain kinds of irreverence may be irrational?

BUCKLEY: Yes— absolutely. But there is a place for irrationality. Many of the conventions of any society are irrational. The obsequies shown to the queen of England, for example, are utterly irrational. Oakeshott has made the demonstration once and for all that rationalism in politics— which may be defined as trying to make politics as the crow flies— is the kind of thing that leads almost always and almost necessarily to tyranny.

PLAYBOY: Can you give us a specific way in which society might suffer from a comedy— however tasteless and debased— about what happened at Dachau?

BUCKLEY: Yes. You can hurt a people's feelings. A people whose feelings are hurt withdraw from a sense of kinship, which is what makes societies cohere. Moreover, a society so calloused as not to care about the feelings of its members becomes practiced in the kind of indifference that makes people, and the society they live in, unlovely.

PLAYBOY: But if a taboo has to be maintained by force of law, is it still a taboo?

BUCKLEY: It depends. Some taboos are codified, some aren't. Some laws protect what isn't any longer taboo. I don't think Lenny Bruce would be arrested today in New York, the movement having been in the direction of permissiveness in the past four or five years. The question really is: Do we— or do I, I guess— approve of the trend, and I'm not so sure that I do. A society that abandons all of its taboos abandons reverence.

PLAYBOY: Doesn't society abandon something even more precious by attempting to preserve that reverence by force?

BUCKLEY: Again, it depends on the situation. If you have a society that is corporately bent on a prolonged debauch— determined to wage iconoclasm *à outrance*— then you've got a society that you can't effectively repress. I mean, you have a prohibitive situation. But if you have a society— as I think we still do— in which the overwhelming majority of the people respect their own and others' taboos, the kind of society that, say, forbids a lawyer from referring to Judge Marshall as a nigger, or Judge

Hoffman as a kike, then it isn't much of an exertion on the commonweal to implement such laws as have been on the books in New York for generations. My final answer to your entire line of questioning is ambiguous: If you ask simply: Does the individual have the absolute right to do anything he wants in private contract with another party? then my answer is: No, only the presumptive right. A sadist cannot contract to kill a masochist. John Stuart Mill reduces the matter of sovereignty to the individual's right over himself. The state hasn't the right to protect you against yourself—which is a good argument against my being required to wear a helmet when I ride my Honda.

PLAYBOY: Doesn't Mill's dictum against the state's right to protect you from yourself also argue for the abolition of most drug laws?

BUCKLEY: Does it? Take heroin. Except under totally contrived circumstances, there is no such thing in America as a person inflicting purely on himself the consequences of taking heroin. If a man goes that route, he deserts his family—if he has any; he becomes an energumen who will ravish society to sustain the habit, and so on. Most important—as far as I'm concerned—he becomes a Typhoid Mary of sorts. I know that I'm using a metaphor, but I can defend the use of this particular metaphor. We know from serious studies that heroin users desire to communicate the habit to other people and often succeed in doing so.

PLAYBOY: Do the same arguments apply to marijuana?

BUCKLEY: Not really, or not so severely. The first and most obvious thing to say about marijuana is that the penalties for using it are preposterous. But I don't believe that it ought to be legalized yet; the consequences of its use have not been sufficiently studied. It seems crazy to me that in an age when the Federal Government has outlawed Tab, we are wondering whether we ought to legalize marijuana. Now, it may be that marijuana is harmless, although at this moment, I am persuaded by those scientists who emphatically believe the contrary. It may be that we would be much better off persuading everybody who now drinks whiskey to turn on instead. But we don't *know*. Some scientists say that middle-aged people who take marijuana risk special dangers because they have gradually concatenated their own quirks, latent and active, into a moderately well-adjusted human being. Psychotropic drugs can shatter that delicate equilibrium. Conversely, it is speculated that marijuana can keep some young people from making the individual adjustments they need to make. Some scientists claim that prolonged use of marijuana wages a kind of war against your psyche, the final results of which are not easy to trace.

PLAYBOY: Your attitude toward grass typifies your agreement with middle-class Americans on some issues. Are there any contemporary American middle-class values that you *dislike*?

BUCKLEY: You'd have to make me a list of them. If ostentatious forms of material achievement are a middle-class value, I don't much like them, though I wouldn't go out of my way to evangelize against them; we all have our little vanities. I am told that in certain big corporations, it is unseemly for the junior V.P. to own a more expensive car than the senior V.P., and absolutely *verboten* for his wife to have a mink coat if the wife of the senior V.P. doesn't have one. But who *does* approve of Babbittry? Not even Babbitt. He merely practiced Babbittry. The middle-class values I admire are husbandry, industry, loyalty, a sense of obligation to the community and a sense of obligation to one's patrimony. When Winston Churchill died, Rebecca West said that he was a great affront to the spirit of the modern age because he was manifestly superior. I said in introducing Clare Boothe Luce, when we did a TV program in Hawaii a few months ago, that her documented achievements are evidence of the lengths to which nature is prepared to go to demonstrate its addiction to inequality. It is a middle-class value to defer, without animosity, to people of superior learning, achievement, character, generosity.

PLAYBOY: To whom do you personally feel inferior?

BUCKLEY: Millions of people, living and dead.

PLAYBOY: Who among the living?

BUCKLEY: To begin with, anyone who knows more than I do, which would be millions of people— or hundreds of thousands of people— right there. I also feel inferior to people who regulate their lives more successfully than I do, to people who are less annoyed by some of the petty distractions that sometimes annoy me, to people who are more philosophical in their acceptance of things than I am.

PLAYBOY: Does that includes Mrs. Luce?

BUCKLEY: She's much more talented than I am.

PLAYBOY: Norman Mailer?

BUCKLEY: Much more talented than I am. Now, there are

certain things in which I am Mailer's manifest superior. Politically, he's an idiot. And he's botched his life and the lives of a lot more people than I've botched, I hope. On the other hand, he's a genius and I'm not.

PLAYBOY: Among other contemporaries, how about T. S. Eliot?

BUCKLEY: You're talking about birds of paradise now. Like Whittaker Chambers. I make it a point to seek the company— intellectually, above all— of people who are superior to me in any number of ways, and I very often succeed.

PLAYBOY: To whom do you feel superior— and why?

BUCKLEY: To those who believe that they are the very best judges of what is wrong and what is right.

PLAYBOY: Would you please name names?

BUCKLEY: Would you please expand your printing facilities?

PLAYBOY: As long as the discussion has become personal: To what extent has your feud with Gore Vidal developed into a publicity stunt from which you both have benefited?

BUCKLEY: In my case, at least, to no extent at all. I don't see how one profits a) from being publicly libeled or b) from walking into a situation in which one pays legal expenses several times the value of anything one earned after industrious work preparing for television programs or doing an article.

PLAYBOY: Would you care to add anything to what you said about him on the air during the 1968 Democratic Convention and in response to his subsequent comments about you?

BUCKLEY: No.

PLAYBOY: Why did you agree to appear with him in the first place?

BUCKLEY: I agreed to appear in November of 1967 because I thought I could use the forum effectively to advance the conservative viewpoint. I was informed in April that Vidal had been selected to appear opposite me. My alternatives then were to break my contract or to proceed. I decided not to break the contract, even though Vidal was the single person I had named as someone I would not gladly appear against.

PLAYBOY: You have been publicly active for nineteen years. How successful do you think you have been in advancing the conservative viewpoint?

BUCKLEY: Very successful. That success has come primarily through the instrumentality of *National Review,* which has the second highest circulation of any journal of opinion in America.

It repeatedly furnishes the reading public with the very best conservative thought, whether philosophical, critical, strategic or social. It has had the effect of consolidating the conservative position, causing many people to abandon— however unhappily— their resolution to dismiss the conservative alternative as anachronistic, superficial and inhuman. I don't say that *National Review*, or something like it, would not have been created had I not been around; it most certainly would have— in fact, I only midwifed it— but I'd say that the mere fact of having done so renders me, as midwife, very successful.

PLAYBOY: Which failures of the conservative movement in the past ten to twenty years most distress you? The fact that Goldwater didn't get more votes than he did?

BUCKLEY: No, not at all. It was a foregone conclusion that he wouldn't get many votes from the moment Kennedy was assassinated. It's very hard to explain to militant pro-Goldwaterites like myself that in a strange sort of way, an inscrutable sort of way, voting against Goldwater was explainable as a conservative thing to do. The reason I say that is because a nation convulsed in November of 1963 as ours was reached for balm, for conciliation, for peace, for tranquillity, for order. To have had three Presidents over a period of fourteen months would have been dislocative beyond the appetite of many conservatives. Now, this doesn't mean that I side with those conservatives who voted against him— I happen to be more adventurous than some conservatives— but I can respect their point of view. In any case, that was not by any means my idea of the great disappointment of the sixties. That was the failure, on the whole, to verbalize more broadly, more convincingly, the conservative view of things. The conservative critique has been very well made, but it hasn't got through with sufficient force to the opinion makers. It is still hard as hell to find a young conservative with writing talent. That distresses me deeply. Most of the people who write the really finished essays in the college newspapers are liberals, New Leftists. I don't know exactly why and I'm vexed by it, but there were only a dozen— or fewer— conservatives in the sixties who have become writers of some achievement.

PLAYBOY: Personally, what do you expect to do during the next five years? Do you plan any more political candidacies?

BUCKLEY: There was a lot of pressure on me to run against Goodell. By the way— I haven't told this before to anybody, but what the hell— I had decided back in 1967 to run against Bobby Kennedy in 1970. I reasoned that Johnson would be re-elected and that Bobby would go for President in 1972. He was, in 1967— as, indeed, later— the symbol of left opposition to Johnson. I resolved to challenge his politics in the Senatorial race. When he died, I abandoned any idea of running for Senator in 1970. Along came Goodell— and the pressures on me to challenge him. The principal moral allure was that it was something I deeply wanted *not* to do. Quite apart from the sort of inertial disadvantages of running against Goodell, and the gruesome prospect of campaigning, I had to face the fact that I would automatically be stripped of those forums to which I had gained access. No more thoughtful television programs, no more columns— because it has now been more or less agreed among American editors that they won't carry a column written by a practicing politician. I think of Galbraith's adage: The Senate is a good place to be if you have no other forum. If I were Senator from New York, it isn't at all clear to me that I'd have more influence than I have today, with my various outlets.

PLAYBOY: Did running in the 1965 mayoral race in New York strip you of those forums?

BUCKLEY: Yes and no. In the first place, it was a local contest and I never wrote about it in my columns. The television series was postponed precisely on account of my running. Another thing: It was sometime after 1965 that many newspaper editors reached their decision to embargo writer-politicians. They faced the problem directly when Senator Goldwater, a columnist, ran for President, lost, resumed his column and ran for Senator in 1968.

PLAYBOY: How would you feel about running for a seat in the House?

BUCKLEY: God, no. Not unless I can have all the seats simultaneously.

PLAYBOY: If there were a conservative Administration in this country— say, if Ronald Reagan became President— would you be tempted to accept a high post in the Administration?

BUCKLEY: No. In the first place, I don't like it much. In the second place—

PLAYBOY: Don't like what much— Washington?

BUCKLEY: That's right.

PLAYBOY: Cabinet meetings?

BUCKLEY: I don't much like any kind of meetings. Besides, I have no reason for supposing that I'm a skillful administrator; I may be or I may very well not be. But the kind of thing that I am practiced in requires considerable freedom of expression, and freedom of expression is obviously something you need to be very continent about when the point of the thing is to advance the collective endeavor.

PLAYBOY: With or without your own involvement in an official capacity, are you optimistic about the conservative movement in America?

BUCKLEY: I am, mildly. There has been some encouraging de-ideologization of politics in the past twenty years. When I went to college, Henry Wallace was still able to grip a lot of people with hopped-up visions like the nationalization of the steel industry. We've watched the experience of England since then and studied nationalized industries elsewhere, and *no* one will go to that parade anymore, no one except the types who squat in the fever swamps of ideology. The collapse of the poverty program as a Federal enterprise strikes me as significant. It strikes me as significant, too, that Patrick Moynihan got up at an A.D.A. meeting a year or so ago and said, Let's face it, gang, conservatives know something intuitively that it takes us liberals years of intellectualizing to come up with— namely, that the Federal Government can't do everything it wants to do. Peter Drucker, who is certainly not considered a conservative fanatic, says now that the only things the Government has proved it can really do competently are wage war and inflate the currency.

We've seen what's-his-name, that nice guy Kennedy sent down to South America to screw things up— Richard Goodwin— predict in *Commentary* that the great struggle of the seventies will be over the limits of state power. Which is exactly what conservatives wanted to fight about in the thirties. We've seen Arthur Schlesinger call a couple of dozen Kennedy types into his apartment for a daylong "secret" seminar— nobody was supposed to know about it, but *I* knew about it— in which they reconsidered their enthusiasm for executive power, because executive power, it turns out, can be administered by the likes of Lyndon Johnson! These are pretty encouraging indices. They suggest to me that there is a wide concern over the survival of the individual in the machine age and over the limits of Federal and executive power. They may, in turn, stimulate a curiosity about the on-

Inveighing We Will Go : 64

tological role of the state. That is conservative territory, but admittance is free.

PLAYBOY: Even if you don't intend to run for office again, do you plan to keep writing?

BUCKLEY: Yes. We've kept an alternative landing field in operation, you see. When the liberals fly in, thirsty, out of gas, they'll find it in full working order— radar OK, bar open, Coca-Cola and coffee on the house. We know it's necessary to assimilate the experience of the modern age. Cardinal Newman said in a related contest— between the logical positivists and the conservatives— that one of our great challenges is constantly to incorporate new experience, so as not to leave ourselves with a piece of brittle lace, the touching of which would cause it to crumble.

PLAYBOY: Don't most dogmas, theological as well as ideological, crumble sooner or later?

BUCKLEY: Most, but not all.

PLAYBOY: How can you be so sure?

BUCKLEY: I know that my Redeemer liveth.

II. Is Nixon One of Us?

August 1, 1971

The scene is the White House, May, 1969. The guest of honor is John G. Gorton, Prime Minister of Australia. He stands in the receiving line next to the President, who himself introduces the guests, after they have been presented to him by the chief of protocol. It was my turn, but the lady just ahead of me had caught the special attention of Mr. Gorton, who ventured beyond the formal greeting and was speaking to her. Mr. Nixon, finding an unanticipated second or two on his hands, leaned over and whispered to me, his eyes on the Prime Minister, *"He's one of us."*

I will listen patiently to those who say that what Mr. Nixon says is usually programed for the situation. But not always. This wasn't. It was utterly spontaneous. The Prime Minister of Australia, the President of the United States, the editor of *National Review,* members of the same fraternity. What fraternity? I recalled, as I worked my way into the dining room, a story my father told me about a bumptious young journalist who, late in the reign of Porfirio Díaz, startled protocol by plunking himself down next to the President of Mexico in the Pullman car from which periodically the President would augustly emerge to open a new dam or review a regiment or survey the results of an earthquake in the provinces. Always the corner of the presidential car was occupied by General Díaz, the balance of it by journalists and courtiers. Having sat down, the young man turned to the dumbstruck President and said, genially, *"Qué tal, compañero!"* President Díaz's answer was deep frozen. *"Compañero de qué?"* he asked icily. The young man's reply made him a national hero. *"Pues . . . Compañero de viaje!"* Just so, I might have gone back to President Nixon and asked: Was the Prime Minister a companion—"one of us"—in the sense that we were all three male and over forty years of age? Or because we would all be eating, that night, food prepared in the same kitchen?

Clearly Mr. Nixon was not revealing himself to me as a *National Review* conservative; and certainly he was not suggesting that Mr. Gorton was one. I settled down to an understanding of what Mr. Nixon had meant to communicate even before the after-dinner toasts made it plain. Mr. Nixon introduced Mr. Gorton to his guests as someone who "knows the great role that his country can play, that ours must play, and who has that courage that we all admire so much— the courage to speak up when sometimes it might be perhaps more politic to say nothing, or at least to say something else."

Mr. Gorton more than returned the compliment. He was very, very explicit. He looked across the great dining room over the heads of the three hundred guests to the portrait of Abraham Lincoln, and recalled what it was that Lincoln had had to stand up against during the stress of his Administration. If Lincoln had failed, the Prime Minister said, "there would be no United States today. I think," he went on, "that we will stand together in the future as we have in the past. I hope that this will be true. It has been true and I believe it will be true." And, magisterially, he closed, "And for our part— speaking for Australians— *wherever the United States is resisting aggression, wherever the United States or the United Kingdom or any other country is seeking to insure that there will be a chance for the free expression of the spirit; wherever there is a joint attempt to improve not only the material but the spiritual standards of life of the peoples of the world, then, sir, we will go waltzing Matilda, with you.*"

Nixon meant to say to me: Gorton is an anti-Communist. That used to mean a great deal in America, and it still means something. It is, of course, the source of Richard Nixon's strength with the American right. We have known him as an anti-Communist. Anti-Communists can feel one another's presence. Although it bore no national political fruit, small but important achievements were registered over the years by anti-Communists who worked together, in *ad hoc* associations, in pursuit of special objectives: Socialists, conservatives, labor union leaders, professors: they had the tie in common of acknowledging Communism as the principal philosophical-strategic threat of the century. Richard Nixon might, in identical circumstances, have leaned over and said to the Socialist scholar Professor Sidney

Hook: "He is one of us," and Mr. Hook would not have thought the President guilty of that ugly modern sin against which the kids rail: co-option.

The question a great many American conservatives are asking themselves these days about Mr. Nixon is, "*Is* he one of us?" Or is there nothing left of— us? Or— a third possibility— does the bond of anti-Communism simply not mean anything anymore? Strange, if that should be so; it was Mr. Nixon who, in the aside, invoked the bond as recently as in May of 1969. He has been President of the United States ever since. Has he, while in office, presided over the liquidation of the anti-Communist communion?

"Barry Goldwater found out you can't win an important election with only the right wing behind you," Mr. Nixon said to me, in 1967, driving through Central Park to a television studio. "But I found out in 1962 that you can't win an election without the right wing." Mr. Nixon had undertaken, during that season, to visit occasionally with leaders of the American right wing, because Ronald Reagan had just been elected Governor of California. In those days it was not generally accepted that Mr. Reagan would make a bid for the Presidency. Richard Nixon knew that Reagan would; or, more exactly, he proceeded on the assumption that pressures would eventually prevail on Reagan to enter the race. And he knew, instantly, that Reagan was a threat.

"Any new face on the Republican scene who wins the governorship in California by a million votes is a significant contender," he told a half-dozen of us, in his New York apartment, in December, 1966. "And on top of that, Reagan has a national following." The American right, almost all of it, never anticipating a serious bid by Reagan, agreed to go with Nixon until he lost a primary. But Richard Nixon doesn't lose primaries. Accordingly, he arrived at Miami with the support of John Tower, Strom Thurmond, Barry Goldwater, *National Review,* and *Human Events.* Against these icons, Ronald Reagan could not successfully appeal; not to a conservative constituency, which is what the majority of the delegates at Miami Beach were. There are those who believe that with the defeat of Reagan in Miami Beach, the American right changed permanently. And ˙that, sensing this, Richard Nixon went busily to work undermining the structural positions of the right.

The most incisive funeral service was intoned by L. Brent Bozell, the editor of *Triumph* magazine, not long after Nixon's inauguration. In an open letter to American conservatives he said, "Historians will differ as to the moment when the movement you lead"— Mr. Bozell had announced himself as a separated brother of the conservative movement—"ceased to be an important political force in America. But there will be no one to dispute that it was all over by November, 1968, with Nixon's victory. This is because (1) Nixon in 1968 was your man, and (2) Nixon in 1968 had repudiated you. He was your man in the sense that whatever remained of your energies was committed to his election, and whatever remained of your hopes was committed to the success of his Presidency. He had repudiated you in the sense that he had pointedly and recognizably rejected every distinctive feature of your movement: that is, everything that set it apart from other political forces in the country. He had rejected everything that gave it an identity— or, more to the point, a *being*. And since he did this with your full knowledge and thus with your implied assent, he was free to ignore you upon assuming the Presidency; and you were powerless to affect his future course."

Mr. Bozell is too wise to insist on an authoritative definition of conservatism, but he plausibly argued that it is not difficult to enumerate what it was that "came on" to the country as conservatism "since it acquired an identity and shape after World War II and the Roosevelt years. . . . For this purpose [the conservative movement] can be reduced," he summarized, to four historical attitudes: antistatism (as represented by Hoover and Taft); nationalism (as suggested by the name of General MacArthur); anti-Communism, and constitutionalism, "which has never had a single champion of the stature of the others, but which may be recalled by thinking of Bricker, or more recently, Thurmond."

And what happened? Bozell, the ex-conservative, put it more wholeheartedly, and more indiscriminately, than most people would who still think of themselves as conservatives: "On every front where your program has confronted secular liberalism's, you have been beaten. Consider your campaigns against big government, against Keynesian economics, against compulsory welfare; your defense of states' rights and the constitutional prerogatives of Congress; your struggle for a vigorous anti-Soviet foreign policy; your once-passionate stand for the country's flag and her honor." To which dirge Mr. Bozell might have added, if he had been writing two years later: Consider your stand against Communist China; your opposition to unbalanced budgets; your resentment of Supreme Court decisions that transfer the First Amendment into an antireligious instrument of bolshevik ruthlessness. And— a criticism of the Nixon Administration strangely unreported— consider the mysterious added difficulty of doing business. The businessmen who deal with the Federal agencies— with the S.E.C., the F.C.C., the F.D.A., the C.A.B., the F.T.C.— have been scratching their heads with a wonder that turns now to exasperation, and even to fury, about the inexplicable difficulty of *doing business* under an Administration that is philosophically "pro business."

It all adds up, and the reports of disaffection, which peaked with the announcement of Mr. Nixon's forthcoming trip to Peking, are everywhere. Recently Kevin Phillips wrote about it. It was Phillips, who, at age twenty-eight, wrote *The Emerging Republican Majority,* published in 1969, a vervy volume of political statistical analysis which informed Nixon and his advisers that the *Zeitgeist* was turning sharply, that if they desired to be opportunistic, as well as holy, here was a rare historical opportunity: they could serve their mundane interests no better than by taking a heaven-blessed turn to the right, that being the direction which the trendiest vector of American politics was grooving towards. Mr. Phillips' analyses were widely shared, however glumly, by some of Nixon's critics, who calculated, after adding the Wallace vote to the Nixon vote, that American public opinion, in the four years between Goldwater-Johnson and Nixon-Humphrey, had gone through a sea change; and that into the foreseeable future the politics of the majority of Americans would be "conservative," loosely defined.

Messrs. Scammon and Wattenberg, in their own book, *The Real Majority,* appeared to validate Phillips' thesis. It is not doubted that Mr. Nixon sculptured the Congressional campaign of 1970 on the assumption that Phillips *et al.* were correct. He held up— as the symbol behind which the country would unite in protesting— the unruly, anarchic, iconoclastic college student; and although the luridities were assigned to the Vice President to express, Mr. Nixon himself campaigned against licentious youth as not unnatural expressions of the kind of thing that happens when liberal ideology reaches maturity.

The results of the election were ambiguous. Some of Mr. Nixon's conspicuous friends and epigoni won. But some lost. The Phillips/Scammon/Wattenberg thesis, while it was not exactly discredited, has been sent back to the factory for debugging. It isn't known whether the President is still attached to it. Meanwhile, Mr. Phillips has publicized in his syndicated column evidence of dissatisfaction with Mr. Nixon by the American right. He cited a meeting in mid-June in Washington of young conservatives who were heavily involved in the 1968 Nixon campaign who are nowadays asking themselves whether they should do it again in 1972; a meeting at *National Review* of other conservatives, wherein there was related discussion; the expressed dissatisfaction of representatives of the American Conservative Union, of *Human Events*, of Young Americans for Freedom; Southern fractiousness, expressed by Clarke Reed, Mississippi G.O.P. chairman and leader of the Association of Southern Republican Chairmen; the pressures on J. Daniel Mahoney, chairman of the New York State Conservative Party, to deny to Nixon the party's endorsement in 1972 (an ironic turn— in 1968 the Conservative Party sought to endorse Nixon, but Nelson Rockefeller refused to permit it, and was able to have his way only because of his unchallenged dominion over the Republican electors). In short, the pressures mount against him by the same right wing whose backing only a few years ago Mr. Nixon acknowledged as indispensable.

What happy state of affairs might Mr. Nixon achieve for which American conservatives would concede that our diplomatic *détente* with Red China was indispensable? Well, the Vietnam war could end, with marginal pressure for its ending detectably Chinese. Nothing like the Russian role in ending the war against Japan, thank you. The Taiwan Government is approached by Peking: Peking will agree to a plebiscite. If the Taiwanese elect to join Mainland China, that is as it will be. If they elect otherwise, there will be official recognition by China of the independent Taiwanese state. As a gesture (the treaty is pretty much meaningless), China agrees to sign the antiproliferation treaty. China agrees to stop provisioning the insurgents in Laos and Thailand— and actually does so; and further agrees to recognize the *de facto* Government of Cambodia. A miracle? But it is reported that Mr. Nixon is "elated." A hardheaded man, why should he be elated by less than a miracle?

How does Mr. Nixon view the situation? Probably with considerable calm. What Richard Nixon doesn't know about politics isn't easily knowable. To be sure, he doesn't know, at this point— nobody does— how his fortunes will be affected by the diminished enthusiasm of some of his backers. It is clear from the Administration's hostility to proposed reforms designed to reduce the sums of money spent on political campaigns that he believes that dollar controls will work to the disadvantage of his own candidacy. If one projects the figures from 1968, his calculation is sound. But the dollars that were sent to Mr. Nixon in 1968 in such profusion were the fecund donations of a people who thought that Mr. Nixon would accomplish a great deal; which, sad to say, he has not (put aside, for the moment, whether he could ever have accomplished what they expected of him). How will they respond this time around? Their disappointments are keen, their misgivings in some cases conclusive. How does Mr. Nixon arrange this datum, in his strategic distribution of the problems at hand?

I would suppose that he is taking careful account of the uses he will get from the rhetoric that predictably will be used by the opposition. Take Senator J. William Fulbright, so solidly situated in Democratic esteem. On April 4, 1971, he delivered a speech in which he more or less equated the pretensions and ambitions of the United States of America with those of the Union of Soviet Socialist Republics. His words were: "We, too, keep a fleet in the Mediterranean, which is a good deal farther from our shores than it is from the Soviet Union; and our main objection to Soviet 'influence' in the Arab countries is that it detracts from our own. Were it not for the fact that they are Communists— and therefore 'bad' people— while we are Americans— and therefore 'good' people— our policies would be nearly indistinguishable."

They were not widely publicized. President Nixon will surely publicize them, and their implications— and should— as the thoughts of the principal Congressional spokesman on foreign policy of the Democratic party, now that Lyndon Johnson is officially discredited and Hubert Humphrey has slid into a set of positions which forcefully and eloquently contradict the positions he so forcefully and eloquently championed during the sixties (poor Mr. Humphrey; if only he would learn occasionally to speak *other* than forcefully and eloquently).

Senator Muskie, by current measurements, has moved sharply left, racing, with difficulty, to catch up with the Reichian leftism of Senator McGovern, who would begin the greening of America— or such is the impression he leaves— by simply ignoring the existence of malevolent governments, peoples and, for that matter, mosquitoes.

Senators Harris and Kennedy blur in the mind as occupying positions roughly in the same area, with only Senator Jackson standing out as— to use the word Lyndon Johnson and Richard Nixon would use— a realist in foreign policy. The chances that Senator Jackson will be nominated are slim. The chances that he will be nominated and that his nomination would not beget a strong national left party are negligible. So: if Jackson should be nominated, Nixon would profit enormously by Democratic defections— we might as well think in terms of 10 million votes to the left party, bearing in mind that this year is the coming-out year for the kids, and they are likely to be frisky. If it is other than Jackson, Mr. Nixon will have great opportunities to suggest how dramatic are the differences between himself and his policies, and those of the Democratic candidate.

Inasmuch as said differences are not likely to be arresting in matters of domestic policy (the Democrat would hardly campaign on the promise to run up a greater annual deficit than Mr. Nixon's $25 billion) the national debate, give or take such interesting, but politically nonsexy questions as wage and price controls, is likely to revolve around very serious, very grand questions of foreign policy. It is here, I expect, that Mr. Nixon will seek to make his bid for the enthusiastic support of the American right. On this important matter, I am not so sure that he will be able to prove he is one of us, or that he will find, at the stretch, that he has enough time to make his demonstration.

The fact is, the kind of confidence in America and American institutions that made Woodrow Wilson the idol of an epoch in twentieth-century, liberal American history is, well, dissipated. It is said of Mr. Nixon that he is the "last liberal," the last Wilsonian; and indeed one hears in the exchange of toasts between Richard Nixon and John Gorton the accents of Wilsonian chauvinism (as we would nowadays call it). The conservative critics of Woodrow Wilson, over the years, opposed what was then called "interventionism," not because they doubted that American habits (self-rule, private property, regulation by competition) were superior, but because they doubted the capacity of America to force-feed these habits on other countries, and the prospects for any foreign policy based on cultural imperialism.

The Second World War brought American conservatives face to face with the reality of the Soviet Union, and they changed their view to the extent of acknowledging that the responsibilities of America now included heavy international involvement in the affairs of the world. The difficulties of framing an appropriate rhetoric have not been solved (as one can see by studying the rhetoric used by Prime Minister Gorton at the White House where, in order to avoid using the word "Communist," he found himself using generic Wilsonianisms). But the position was— is— roughly as follows: that America's responsibility is to intervene where necessary to prevent a crucial aggrandizement (here and there there would be differences on whether the aggrandizement was crucial or merely incremental) in the power of realistic potential aggressors: in brief, the Soviet Union and China. The American left nosedived, during the sixties, into an anti-Wilsonian position only in part because they had freshly experienced American powerlessness. Mostly it was because the assault on American institutions had made fashionable a kind of international egalitarianism ("Who is to say they'd be worse off under Communists than under the Americans?").

The question is now truly planted: Is what we Americans have so markedly superior to what the Soviet Union has as to warrant (1) the expenditure of $80 billion per year on the military, and (2) a foreign policy based on an explicit preference for the risk of nuclear war, over against submission? I register my unclassified opinion that this is the important datum of the sixties in America. It was the decade in which an important minority of Americans, who exercise extraordinary influence in the academy and in the opinion-making community, asked themselves the question: Is it worth it? Are atomic submarines, and ABM's, and hydrogen bombs, and Minutemen, and orbital satellites— are they all worth it, given what we know about the corruption of America, as we have learned about it from our priests and poets and professors? No single datum establishes this opinion as conclusive in the intellectual world, but it is suggestive to note that when the question was asked of upperclassmen at Yale in 1963—Would you fight a nuclear war rather than surrender to the Soviet Union?—the answer was Yes, 78 percent. The same question, asked of Yale students in 1970, got the answer Yes, 37 percent.

Now Mr. Nixon cannot be suspected of even crypto-membership in this legion, notwithstanding the subtle hold of his native Quakerism upon him. In formal terms he is—quite the contrary of the pacifist—a continuing disciple of Woodrow Wilson, though one is safe in assuming that the attachment is primarily sentimental (clearly, Mr. Nixon would not dream of volunteering in such open-end crusades, as, say, John F. Kennedy trumpeted in his celebrated Inaugural Address: "In the long history of the world, only a few generations have been granted the role of defending freedom in its hour of maximum danger. I do not shrink from this responsibility—I welcome it"). But Mr. Nixon, on the other hand, would not hesitate to answer the question that divided Yale undergraduates along with the minority; and Mr. Nixon is not likely to forget that the views of the minority of Yale students are the views of the majority of their elders, to whom Mr. Nixon will be appealing, in 1972, on rather basic terms.

Now it is not by any means predictable that the election contest of 1972 will present the nation with an Allen Drury-type choice between a candidate who is unwilling to surrender to the Soviet Union, and another whose positions, soritically examined, add up to surrender. The debate will more likely be on the matter of emphasis—priorities, they call it—with the Democrat stressing the unfeasibility of the ABM, the recidivist cold warism of Richard Nixon, the selling of the Pentagon, the discreditable provenance of the Vietnam war, the arrogance of U.S. foreign policy—that kind of thing. Richard Nixon will find himself obliged to come forward with very candid estimates of American power, projected out over the next few years. I say *obliged*, not because the Democratic candidate is likely to come forward, from the left—as John Kennedy did to an earlier Nixon, as Nelson Rockefeller did during the same season—charging that the Republican incumbent was insufficiently committed to American military predominance. No, the revelations—the scandals—will this time around come from deep within Mr. Nixon's own Administration, and unlike John Kennedy's synthetic missile gap, these will be altogether authentic.

Notwithstanding the stylishness of divulging state secrets, it probably will require nothing more than careful deductions to document America's otiose nuclear deterrent. Indeed, Melvin Laird has said it, for those who listened closely and were willing to suppose— even as one can stretch the imagination to suppose that J. Edgar Hoover is *really* concerned about crime rather than about the aggrandizement of the F.B.I.— that Laird is concerned about American security, rather than about the selling of the Pentagon. It will then be Mr. Nixon's task to explain why, in Year 4 of his Administration, we find ourselves in such jeopardy as he did not advertise, in Year 3— let alone in Year 2, or Year 1— we would find ourselves in unless we repaired the balance. If Mr. Nixon comes forward saying, bluntly, that his program for— if you like— American rearmament could mean the difference between life and death for America itself, could mean the difference between the continued independence of the Middle East and of Western Europe, and their satellization by the Communist powers, he will have the American right. The whole of it. Even if there are those members of it who will wonder bitterly why, during his first three years as President, Nixon didn't warn us with Churchillian tenacity about our progressive incapacity to cope, satisfactorily, with the crystallizing authority of Soviet arms.

The quicksilvered domestic considerations will be continuingly difficult to pin down. Richard Nixon never came on as a counterrevolutionary, not really; notwithstanding the chiliastic rhetoric with which, like other candidates (great societies, new deals, new revolutions) he announced himself. Did anyone really expect that Richard Nixon would dismantle the welfare state? The postulates of state welfarism have been ratified and reratified in every national election from 1936 on.

His dalliance with and insecure instrumentation of interventionist fiscal economics reflects nothing more than the regnant confusion among economic theorists, and the acquiescence even by free-market economists in the proposition that it is a political necessity to talk imperiously to the economic seas, even though we all know that the President sits on the throne of King Canute.

Respecting constitutional reform—what does a strict-constructionist President do, having had two of his nominees rejected, and the two whom he did appoint acquiesce in some of the dogmas (forced segregation, forced secularization) which by then had become institutionalized? Perhaps President Barry Goldwater would have launched gamy constitutional amendments, limiting the control of the courts over local school boards and their decisions on busing and church schools. But not Richard Nixon. He tried in his own way. An honest try. He failed. He never said he would go further than he did.

Sometimes American conservatives act as though Richard Nixon was guilty of the defeat of Barry Goldwater. That is unrealistic, and conservatives have prided themselves on being realistic. That leaves them—leaves us—continuing to dream, and does nothing to deny us our paradigmatic responsibilities. But Mr. Nixon isn't involved with paradigms, and probably isn't interested in them; and the probability is that the American right will have understood that, well before November of 1972: provided there is no suspicion—none at all would be tolerated—that Mr. Nixon has been taken in by the other side's reveries, the reveries that are based on the notion that the leadership of the Communist world suddenly stepped forward, as after a speech by Billy Graham, to submit to prefrontal lobotomies, after which they returned to duty at Helsinki, and other pressure points in the world, to push SALT through to international peace and harmony, to tranquilize their legions in Vietnam, Egypt, Chile, West Germany, and Madagascar, whose name I mention only to meet the anapaestic challenge. Richard Nixon will have to collapse that superstition, if the suspicion widens, as it is now doing, that he indulges it; and the tactical question is, how long can he postpone doing so, before the American right comes to the conclusion that he is not one of us?

III. Mr. Nixon's Long
March to China

Preliminaries

April 30, 1971

The extraordinary development involving China is a psychological blow to those who believe that tenacity in Vietnam is indispensable to the stabilization of Asia.

The position of Lyndon Johnson and Richard Nixon (and of course of their Secretaries of State and Joint Chiefs) has been the domino theory. If South Vietnam were communized by force, the resistance in Cambodia, Laos and Malaysia would cease. Surrounded, Thailand would change governments, and vote in one whose foreign policy was the instrument of China. The pressures on Indonesia's hundred million would be insupportable. Next, of course, the Philippines, who could not easily breathe in that iron lung, as a Western-oriented enclave. South Korea would logically be next, once again through the satellization of its policies. Then time for the big one, Japan. If the United States made it plain that it would not live up to its commitments under SEATO, then Japan's choice would be to cooperate with the nearby great power, or go it alone. Do you really believe all of that domino theory business, someone asked President Nixon at the Governors' Conference a year ago? The President snapped back: Ask the dominoes. Indeed.

But now the famous Ping-Pong development. It has weakened an indispensable plank in all the scaffolding. The reason why Mr. Nixon is exchanging pleasantries with Red China is, although not spoken, quite clear: China is different from the China which was annealed into its present condition through two decades of aggression, torture, convulsion, and xenophobia: the China which was the main threat to the dominoes. It isn't clear whether he intended exactly to call attention to the difference, but in effect he did so when two weeks ago at the American Society of Newspaper Editors dinner Mr. Nixon was asked why, under the circumstances, we don't go ahead and recognize Cuba. We had a flash of the Old Nixon. Because, he fulminated, Cuba is determined to be a bad neighbor, determined to encourage a hatred of America, determined to disrupt hemispheric relations.

One can only assume that, if Mr. Nixon was thinking rigorously, he no longer believes as much about China. Granted, he hasn't yet recognized China, but he leaves us now to believe that that is mere formality, that it will depend on this or that document of understanding, perhaps some such thing as Roosevelt got out of Litvinov, who solemnly promised to abandon all efforts at subversion, a promise that must have caused roars of laughter in all of those offices in the Kremlin engaged at that moment in slipping the subversion into high gear.

What does that do to the domino theory? Nothing. But it does a great deal to those who believe in the domino theory. Because they have suddenly been asked to believe that we should think of Red China as merely another Soviet Union. I happen to think that is quite bad enough, but in fact the Soviet Union has not overrun any new country, nor has it (yet) satellized the politics of any contiguous country since the Czechoslovakian coup of 1948. And China has not taken any new territory since Tibet, if you don't count a little gob of India. Why then is it necessary to contain China by fighting a surrogate war in Southeast Asia?— many Americans will suddenly wonder. If Mr. Nixon and Chou En-lai are prepared to settle their differences at a negotiating table, why not let the Southeast Asian thing run its course? We are beholden, in a way, to the South Vietnamese people, yes; but we are not beholden to them except in a grander context which presupposes that if we let them down, little by little a whole tier of nations will become instruments of an enemy bent on the destruction of the United States.

I do not, myself, doubt that Mr. Nixon is playing chess with China. But he should be reminded that there are lots and lots of spectators who will not only be surprised by some of his moves, but dismayed. And if and when he is in a position to cry "checkmate," he may look around him and find that there is nobody left there to applaud.

July 16, 1971

Concerning the evolving drama of Mr. Nixon's trip to China, a few observations:

1. If Mao Tse-tung had "free elections" in Mainland China tomorrow, it is altogether possible that he would achieve 99 percent of the vote even if immunity were granted to dissenters. The reason for this is apparent from the reports on China that have come flooding in since the authorities there raised the curtain to a few athletes and journalists last spring. China seems to have killed or otherwise disposed of the incremental objector, so as to have achieved the society of the perfectly misled. No doubt it is true, as a Bolshevik hack once blurted out, that when all the world is covered in asphalt, one day a crack will appear, and through that crack, a blade of grass will grow. There no doubt stirs, in a Chinese breast or two, the seed of defiance: but it is not the kind of thing that any longer threatens the regime. It is as safe from being taken over by people who desire liberalism, as the American Legion is safe from being taken over by Communists.

Even so, we are hardly absolved from the moral question. One could visit the slave markets of Charleston, South Carolina, in the early part of the nineteenth century, and find total docility, from which it did not follow that slavery was a happy estate. It is written that among the best educated, most sensitive Jewish intellectuals in the cremation camps, a torpor and desensitization arose and, drugged by pain, starvation, and desperation, they turned animal-like, obsequious towards their captors, jealous and prehensile towards each other. When the liberators came, those who were left did not know, in at least one recorded case, whom to applaud. Their indecision wasn't an indication of anything other than the triumph of terror. Terror in China, largely cloistered from public view, has produced Chinese Man: and it is before this audience that Richard Nixon proposes to exhibit himself.

One thinks of the forthcoming elections in South Vietnam, and of the critics of President Thieu who are already busy discounting those elections, insisting that they will not yield a government which is "responsive" to the will of the people. What is their quarrel with the government of Mao Tse-tung? Do they hope that

Mr. Nixon will ask Mao to form a government responsive to people who have not been ground out by cookie cutters from his Book of Thoughts? Will the Americans for Democratic Action ask Mr. Nixon to demand that China invite Chiang Kai-shek back from Taiwan, to form a coalition government?

2. No, the moral argument is of course put permanently in abeyance. The critics of South Vietnam, which introduced rudimentary democracy fourteen years ago, are, like the concentration camp inmates, silent, and smiling, and unctuous, when they address Mao Tse-tung, or Chou En-lai. Their sins are not only forgiven them, they are not remembered.

All the restraints one thinks of as decent in suddenly fraternizing with the killers are forgotten: and it becomes basely clear that what matters isn't so much whether a government is vile in its provenance, in its practices, in its ambitions, as whether it is powerful. If it is powerful enough, American Liberals will preen like schoolboys before a headmaster. I am waiting for one of the progressive legislators who are congratulating Mr. Nixon to answer simply the question: Was Franklin Roosevelt derelict for not traveling to Nazi Germany to be convivial with Adolf Hitler? If they answer that Adolf Hitler could be ostracized because he did not have enough thunderbolts truly to terrorize the world, one replies that he had enough to be the cause of the death of 25 million people during the Second World War; and anyway, if the accumulation of power is the excuse for otherwise unjustified behavior, why weren't they urging us, over the past twenty years, to act in such a way as to prevent the Red Chinese from accumulating all those thunderbolts?

3. Why has Mr. Nixon neglected this dimension of the problem? Only a few months ago, asked by a reporter what excuse did we have left to continue to ostracize Fidel Castro, Mr. Nixon drew himself up and delivered some anti-Communist boilerplate on the evil behavior of Castro. The evil behavior of Castro! By Maoan standards, he is Florence Nightingale.

In 1939, the world was stunned, as it was stunned last week, by the announcement of a Soviet-Hitler pact. The Soviets had been merchandising the Nazis as their principal enemies for six years, and vice versa. Suddenly: a pact.

One year and ten months after that pact, the two nations went to war, the reversal of feelings suiting the convenience of Hitler (and for that matter Stalin). But meanwhile, the two countries totally reversed themselves and accordingly even Stalin's fellow travelers totally reversed themselves on the question whether the United States should go to the help of England.

The moral of this historical reminiscence is that Nazi-Soviet pacts are precisely possible between governments which are run by Nazis and Soviets. Free countries require preparation. Require, in this case, elaborate reasons and public discussion for suddenly turning as Mr. Nixon has done. Ah, but his motives are perforce secret, and Machiavellian. No doubt they are the former, for as long as the New York *Times* permits it; and we must agree that they are intended to be the latter (either that or the President is certifiably mad). What makes him think that he can manipulate the nation, as Hitler and Stalin did? Because the public is hell bent on appeasement at this moment, he can probably get away with kissing the bull on the nose. But then when he gets around to making his move, and needs the strong military tools, the indomitable public mood, the tenacious public opinion: how is he going to come up with it? Who will believe him? Why should they believe him? Do you see what I mean?

September 10, 1971

In Latin America, particularly in Chile and Mexico, the rage is an interview, just published, between a Mexican journalist and Chou En-lai. Julio Scherer García, the editor-manager of *Excelsior* published in Mexico City, spent two and one-half hours with Chou, whose penetrating monologue, obviously delivered to a keen listener, cuts like a blowtorch through Western fatuity.

It is rich and long, full of interesting bits and pieces. Chou tells us, for instance, that "the truth of the assassination of President Kennedy has not yet been revealed." The Chinese Communists do not desire to turn China into the center of world revolution, he says. On the other hand, he admits that China would help out national liberation movements. "Why not?" Chou commented, slipping into English vernacular. And then elucidating, in a style that is vintage Oriental Paradox: "The destiny of every nation is the responsibility of its people. We oppose aggression, intervention, subversion, and outrage. But we support national liberation movements."

There is even a flirtatious dalliance with the big lie. "Legal punishment in China is administered through work and re-education. Few are imprisoned, even fewer executed. We do not believe in the effectiveness of execution. We do not restrain power through killing." This datum will unfortunately fail to revive several dozen million Chinese corpses.

Mr. Scherer asked, "Does China see any future for socialism through election?"

Chou: "We do not believe in struggle by the parliamentary method. We do not conceal our views. We have not seen any cases in which any country has succeeded in expelling the forces of aggression from abroad or in attaining complete national independence and real, authentic democracy through parliamentary practice. The Latin American nations won their national independence through armed struggle. Unfortunately in the twentieth century aggressive forces have again infiltrated these countries."

Chou then garbled something President Nixon said out in Kansas City recently . . . "The decline of the British Empire has proved [the inadequacy of parliamentary democracy]. Even Nixon recognized on 6 July 1971 in a press conference that twenty-five years ago it would have been impossible even to imagine that U.S. prestige would have fallen as low as it now is. As he contemplates the twenty years since the end of World War II, the United States has suffered such loss of prestige throughout the world that even the President indicates his surprise. The origin of these problems, the lack of prestige, we know well: It is due to the attempt of the United States to dominate the world."

"The Premier is looking at the clock," Mr. Scherer's notes disclose. "It is clear that the interview is coming to an end. He is almost standing. . . ."

Scherer: "How is it possible for the champion of anti-capitalism, Chairman Mao Tse-tung, and the champion of anti-communism, President Richard Nixon, to meet? Why does China accept its mortal enemy in its own home?"

Chou: "Because the United States has imposed a blockade against China and has demonstrated hostility to it for 22 years. The Geneva and Warsaw talks at the ambassadorial level have lasted for 16 years without results. Now Nixon wants to raise the level of the negotiation, and he knocks at our door; why should we not open it?"

Scherer: "Do you believe Nixon would come to China if he felt the trip would not benefit him?"

Chou: "There are two possibilities about his visit to China. If the negotiations succeed, the people of the East and of the entire world will benefit. This is the main thing. Now then, if the trip is not successful, President Nixon will unmask himself. If he arrives in Peking without wanting to resolve problems the entire world will see this and comment on it. We can assert only this: China does not traffic in principles, nor do we sell out *our* comrades-in-arms, never."

Scherer: "But does the United States?"

Chou: "Draw your own conclusions. I think they are very clear. [Chou chuckles]."

The Trip

January, 1972

En route. Everywhere we turn, we come upon the logo of this voyage. "The Visit of President Richard M. Nixon to the People's Republic of China." It is thus emblazoned on our baggage tags, stationery, rucksacks. At first it puts you off. But if you sit down and doodle, asking yourself: what is a self-effacing way to say it, answers leap not instantly to mind. It is, after all, a visit. The U.S. principal is, after all, the President of the United States. And there is no getting around it that his name is Richard M. Nixon, or that his destination is—CAUTION. It may appear stilted that every time one alludes to the area in question, one speaks of it as the "People's Republic of China." Actually, it is not only proper but reassuring that we continue to do so. You see, we recognize a government which is called "The Republic of China," and that government sits in Taiwan. Strictly speaking it is bad form to visit a territory of a government you recognize, which territory is in mutinous contention with the recognized government. Thus one would not, a few years ago, have dispatched the Queen of England to Biafra. And if one had done so, one would have avoided designating it as a visit to Nigeria. Accordingly, the constant references to PRC were, one supposed, diplomatic appeasers, for the benefit of Chiang Kai-shek. About the last he would get.

Even so there is the narcissistic overtone, which mocks republican tradition, reminding us of the distance we have traveled since Benjamin Franklin and Thomas Paine, the exemplar and the ideologue of republican anti-pomp. There is Bonapartism in the air in these parts— Lyndon Johnson would not have ventured to a Bar-B-Q without the Presidential seal engraved on his blue jeans, and there is the beginning, in Nixon's court, of Transylvanian chrome. After all, it would have sufficed, for purposes of communication, to refer to the "Presidential Visit to the People's Republic of China," leaving it to our grandchildren to reach for the almanac to remind themselves who was President of the United States at the Peking Summit, and to their grandfathers to hope that the almanac in question will be written in English, rather than Chinese.

The omens were not good. For instance, we were required to land at Shanghai before going on to Peking. Why? Shanghai is four hours from Guam, less than two hours from Peking. The ostensible reason for landing there was to pick up a Chinese "navigator." Nobody on the U.S. team thought to object that our regular navigators could home in on Peking all by themselves, and if absolutely necessary, could have got a little help from the Strategic Air Command. No, the gentlemen Chinese had something symbolic in mind, which they did not, typically, divulge. The history-minded recalled that the emperors of yore required that visiting nabobs pause well outside the confines of the capital to sue for permission to go further.

And then, it was somewhere along the line suggested that the Presidential party plop down in Boeing 747's, which would have made unnecessary, for instance, the use of two 707's for the press. A frozen no. As it is, we were permitted only to put down in the sleek American jet, after which we were made to travel (to Hangchow and Shanghai) in one of theirs (made in Russia). Another bad omen: we were allowed to carry off the aircraft only a single suitcase. Why? You figure it out. I can understand being told to bring only a single suitcase to the Normandy landing. Hardly to the capital of a nation of 800 million people, a very small percentage of whom would be distracted by the necessity of carrying a few dozen extra bags. Hardly the way to get off to a good start with Walter Cronkite, I mused.

Aboard the plane, on the endless trip, we read, mostly. Theodore White, the gifted old China hand, renowned now for his series on the making of American Presidents, was ecstatic at the prospect of revisiting old haunts, and of justifying his early optimism about the vector of Chinese Communism. We tease each other. He looks up from his pile of clips from time to time, offering me anti-Red Chinese tidbits in return for anything favorable I can supply him from my own pile. At one point he beamed. "I have a clip here that says the Red Chinese have killed thirty-four million people since they took over. What will you offer me for that?" I rummage about and offer him the clip that says the Red Chinese have reduced illiteracy from 80 percent to 20 percent, but he scoffs, like a pawnshop broker. "Hell, I have that one." I scrounge some more for pro-Chinese Communist data and finally tell him, disconsolate, that I can't find one more item to barter for his; and he smiles contentedly at his tactical victory. But has he lost the war?

Peking. The press speculated feverishly over the astonishingly spare reception given to President Nixon at the airport. He himself had only a few minutes' notice that he would come out of Air Force One onto an all but desolate scene. He went through the gaunt ritual with the kind of smile you wear when you congratulate the man who beat you in the election. They stood there at attention during the playing of the two national anthems, Mr. and Mrs. Nixon, Chou En-lai, Rogers, Kissinger, the lot of them, like wax figures in Mme. Tussaud's museum, and one felt the jolt of surprise that, the music over, they should have come to life, to march on bravely, in the silence— no music, no applause, no bustle, no crowd-roar— to review the honor guard, dutifully there to do its listless bit. The motorcade swung on determinedly, fifty minutes into the heart of Peking. The only crowds were towards the end of the journey, in the thick of the central city. And they weren't Chinese ogling to see the President of the United States, but Chinese en route, at lunch time, from one side of the avenue to the other, stopped by police until the procession went by. That would appear to have been the single concession of the governors of the People's Republic of China: they did not make President Nixon stop for the red lights.

We joked about it, at the press table. One correspondent, reflecting on the tumultuous public reception recently given to Haile Selassie, reminded us that, after all, the Ethiopian government is older than the American Government— *absit invidia.* A second wondered whether the Western press hadn't underestimated the success of the Cultural Revolution. "Maybe the Chinese we saw are all there are left?" But through it, Chou's shaft had penetrated. There was Wounded Pride in the air. Everyone knows that in a totalitarian country the size of the crowd tends to be a decision of the masters. But Nixon had seen crowds reach up, piercing the screen of official impassivity, to touch his hand. It was so in Poland in 1959, when he was Vice President and hundreds of thousands of Poles, defying the official chill, cheered and cheered and cheered. Nothing like that would happen to Nixon, not even after the benediction later in the afternoon from Mao Tse-tung. He never, anywhere, caused a public ripple.

It wasn't so much that the people were hostile to him, though they had every right to be after a generation's saturation bombing, as that they were indifferent to him, somehow tuned out; leaving these matters, as they had been taught to do, to their masters, who could be trusted to advise them when it served the purposes of the People's Republic to cheer lustily, as they had done for the Lion of Judah. We were, after all, among people who have not yet been informed that an American astronaut walked on the moon in 1969.

After Mao Tse-tung gave Nixon an audience, the official atmosphere flushed out. That night I espied Personal Diplomacy. Everyone could see Richard Nixon in the large banquet hall, seated alongside Chou at a round table of a dozen or so dignitaries, but I saw him best, not alone from the advantage of being seated only twenty yards away (the correspondents were strung out alphabetically). I watched him through binoculars, after his remarks, raising his glass to toast Chou En-lai and the three or four Chinese officials seated at his table. Then— to the astonishment of everyone and the consternation of the Secret Service— he strode purposefully one by one to the three surrounding tables and greeted Chinese official after Chinese official, his face red with the sweat of quite genuine idealism, bowing, smiling radiantly, touching each individual glass. He looked altogether noble, flushed with the righteousness of great purpose, and the two dozen Chinese— old generals, commissars, politicians— were quite visibly startled, first at being approached at all, then at being wooed so ardently.

Kindly make no mistake about the moral courage all this

required. It is unreasonable to suppose that anywhere in history have a few dozen men congregated who have been responsible for greater human mayhem than the hosts at this gathering and their spiritual colleagues, instruments all of Mao Tse-tung. The effect was as if Sir Hartley Shawcross had suddenly risen from the prosecutor's stand at Nuremberg and descended to embrace Goering and Goebbels and Doenitz and Hess, begging them to join with him in the making of a better world. Never mind the difference, that the latter were convicted butchers, aggressors, and genocide-makers, and the former, by the narrowest quirk of the Cultural Revolution, are not: all that that difference reminds us of is that history is indeed the polemics of the victor.

We *were*, after all, in Peking. And among the pamphlets distributed to the American press in the hotel corridors' literature racks is a speech by Mao Tse-tung less than two years old. "While massacring the people in other countries," goes this particular thought of Chairman Mao, "U.S. imperialism is slaughtering the white and black people in its own country. Nixon's fascist atrocities have kindled the raging flames of the revolutionary mass movement in the United States. The Chinese people firmly support the revolutionary struggle of the American people. I am convinced that the American people who are fighting valiantly will ultimately win victory and that the fascist rule in the United States will inevitably be defeated." Moreover, in contemporary Peking, you cannot pass by a monument without staring into the face of Josef Stalin. That was the backdrop of Nixon's performance.

On top of that, there was the morning's performance at the airport. If charity covers the Big Lie, here was charity's test. Mr. Nixon began his speech by thanking Premier Chou for his government's *"incomparable hospitality."* At the hands of an ironist, that statement would have brought down the house. With Mr. Nixon, one merely scratched one's head; nervously. He went on to pull out every stop.

— He quoted Mao.

— He said that he wished the United States and China might undertake a "long march" together, which fawning historical reference was as if Chou had said that China wanted to find itself side by side with America the very next time we face the rockets' red glare.

— He talked about things like equal dignity for the people of the nations of the world, to the premier of the largest totalitarian country in the history of the world.

— And then . . . and then, he toasted Chairman Mao, Chou En-lai, and the whole lot of them. I would not have been surprised, that night, if he had lurched into a toast of Alger Hiss.

Premier Chou was more cautious. He had begun the day with a snub, he would end it with condescension. Behind him in the huge hall the flags of the two countries hung grandly— the usual business, at state banquets. Except that the U.S. flag was just a little smaller than the Red Chinese flag. Proletarian subtlety. Then, not a word from Chou in acceptance, if that is the word for it, of Richard Nixon. He didn't even say that Nixon is an *amiable* running dog. The stress, always, was People to People, it being Communism's theoretical insistence that the American people are okay, but their leaders are awful, and something of a lacuna in Communist theory just how it came about that Okay People elect fascist, warmongering leaders.

There was not a word, in Chou's speech, which would have earned him a demerit in Communist theology class. Came the toast: "I propose a toast"— to President and Mrs. Nixon? No. ". . . *to the health* of President and Mrs. Nixon." The difference between toasting someone, and toasting someone's health is, well, noticeable. (Two banquets later, at Hangchow, Nixon slid unobtrusively into the more cautious formulation.) And, finally, Chou toasted "to the friendship between Chinese [*sic*] and American peoples," which sentiment flirted not at all with heresy, friendship among all peoples being a postulate of Marxist dogma. The implications were not— are not— immediately apparent. But watching the face of Chou through the binoculars, one could not help but reflect that the fissured smile of the airport had broadened, as it might have done on the face of his hero Stalin, when the boys got together to toast peace, dignity, and self-determination for all peoples, back at Yalta.

Every day the correspondents were given a choice of a half-dozen Chinese Communist achievements to witness, and it soon occurred even to the best-disposed among us that our affable hosts had lost sight of the critical perspective. It has after all been a very long time— fifteen? twenty years?— since reporters in any force have been permitted to visit China. Totalitarian societies are very good at hiding things like concentration camps, Liu

Shaochi's, and material misery. Why are they so poor at hiding ideological infantilism? Perhaps because it is like hiding grass. But I mean, there was the President of the United States and his moderately cosmopolitan staff, plus all of us, seated in the ballet hall, a new building which, incidentally, makes the Lexington Avenue subway look like Disneyland. Would we view a Chinese classic? A modern classic?

It was a thing called *The Red Detachment of Women,* which is China's *Gone with the Wind* or, better, *Uncle Tom's Cabin.* The synopsis was printed and given to each of us. It was as if at a White House conference of African presidents, we had taken them over to the Kennedy Center to see a ballet of Li'l Black Sambo. I quote exactly.

The heroine, Ching-hua, is the property of a "despotic land-lord" who (Act I) gives orders to one of his "running dogs" to sell her. She is mercilessly beaten, escapes, and is retrieved by two Red Army men who feel "profound proletarian feelings" towards her. They embrace her (Act II) into a Red Detachment of Women where she is warmly received by "the soldiers and villagers whose class feelings for her are as deep as the sea." During a liberation maneuver against her former slavemaster she goofs (Act III) out of an excess of zeal, and is warned (Act IV) that "only by emancipating all mankind can the proletariat achieve its own final emancipation."

I feel quite sure that, at this point in the ballet, Richard Nixon was prompted to poke Pat under the seat, but between him and her was seated Madame Mao Tse-tung, who is the iron patroness of this kind of thing—it was her resentment of an opera insufficiently servile to Maoism that touched off the Cultural Revolution in 1965; and anyway, one might as well have frolicked across the body of Ana Pauker, as across Chiang Ching. In Act V, our heroine's principal Red protector is overwhelmed by the Kuomintang, but when he recovers consciousness, "he stands rock-firm and faces the pack of bandit troops in righteous indignation." Only (Act VI) to die "a heroic death with the fearless heroic spirit of a Communist" but not, you will be glad to learn, until after he has managed (at not inconsiderable operatic length) to "denounce the diehard reactionaries." At which point the marines move in, and "the broad revolutionary masses flock to join the Red Army amidst resounding battle songs." The last sentence in the synopsis is a modest thought for today: "Forward,

forward, under the banner of Mao Tse-tung, forward to victory!"

The muse ringing in our ears, the next morning we visited Peking University, probably the most shattering single experience of the journey because one had the sense of participating in a running show trial. Our host was the active head of the campus, who got his advanced degree in physics from the University of Chicago in 1926, which solved the language problem, right? Wrong. The poor derelict, whose English had been previously ascertained to be as good as Eric Sevareid's, spoke through an interpreter. Because the room was full of Red Guard thugs, and it was obvious that they desired to hear his answers so that, if necessary, they could later on correct him for ideological irregularities.

Cautiously, during the question period, we probed the circumstances of his and his university's humiliation, without of course exactly letting on. We knew that he knew that we knew that he was reduced to puppetry, but better a puppet alive, than to stand rock-firm and face the pack of bandit troops. Someone asked him what had been the errors of Peking University before the Great Proletarian Cultural Revolution caught up with them, and he replied that the errors, partly his own responsibility, had been to imitate Russian universities by forgetting the imperative of proletarian politics and lending itself instead to the cultivation of an academic elite. Translated, that means Peking U sought excellence. How had he learned the exact nature of his delinquencies? A "Mao Thought Propaganda Team" came to the university in the fall of 1968 and stayed on a whole year. After they left, the governing of the university was turned over to a "revolutionary council," of which this wretched man had become the spokesman, surrounded by brachycephalic peasants who, knowing only how to praise the thoughts of Chairman Mao, need know aught else, in order to correct the venerable professor.

We puzzle that our hosts should have proudly invited us to view contemporary Chinese Communist academic life. One recalls Evelyn Waugh's Azania, where the young black prince, incompletely educated in Western habits, gave a state banquet for two very British ladies come to inspect the local situation in behalf of the Royal Society for the Prevention of Cruelty to Animals. In his toast, the prince solemnly averred that, in Azania, they worked industriously to devise means of being cruel to animals, that they had not yet achieved English standards, but that they were every day making progress.

There came the long lull, when the sight-seeing became routine, the banquets had piled upon each other, twelve courses every time, toasts and more toasts, and the speculation became razzled on just what Nixon and Chou would finally come up with— something grainier, we hoped, than the soapsuds we had been fingering for days now. I remember the cartoon in *Punch* after the summit conference in Washington between Sir Anthony Eden and President Eisenhower. The artist depicted Eden in long tweed skirt and shawl sitting contentedly on a bench in front of the White House, Eisenhower in knickers and sport coat; holding hands. The caption summarized the Joint Communiqué: " 'Darling?' 'What, darling?' 'Nothing, darling. Just darling, darling.' "

Time, meanwhile, a little time, to pause over some of the mannerisms of the principals. Chou's own, distinctive tics, we are unfamiliar with, but one notices that his government is given to approaching all problems numerically. When, for instance, it was observed years ago that the revolution continued to tolerate those unclean elements, Chairman Mao promulgated the Four Purifications Movement, among whose accomplishments was the repeal of the premature Three Freedoms and One Guarantee. The Maoists were historically scarred by the Fifth Extermination Campaign Chiang Kai-shek had mounted against them in the thirties, which of course they survived by citing the proberb "One spark can consume a hundred miles of prairies." The Five Principles first enunciated by Chou at the Bandung Conference way back in 1955 were reaffirmed at the banquet given for Mr. Nixon, notwithstanding that the Cultural Revolution has eliminated the Four Olds (old ideas, old culture, old customs, old habits), some time after withdrawing from the Hundred Flowers, whose blooming was a mistake, as recognized at the Eight Great Rallies of the Cultural Revolution, which was precipitated by Madame Liu's misdirected modification of the Ten Conditions on Agriculture in her (totally inadequate) Later Ten Conditions on Agriculture.

Mr. Nixon would not likely, at proclamation-time, herald the Seventh Day Principles of Nixon-Mao, but we knew that he would certainly call the agreement the most momentous document since the Ten Commandments. We were right.

Mr. Nixon had just come from visiting the Great Wall. Undeniably, the Great Wall is the greatest wall in the history of the world. Absolutely no doubt about it. But look what the Great Wall did to Mr. Nixon. "[The Great Wall] is a certain symbol of what China in the past has been and of what China in the future can become. People who could build a wall like this certainly have a great past to be proud of and a people who have this kind of a past must also have a great future." Mr. Nixon floats through that kind of thing without ever having to face the difficulties of it, as he would unquestionably have to do if he were a member of the House of Commons. The trouble with the statement is a) the China that built the Great Wall, not many generations after Socrates drank the hemlock, is only dimly related to Mao's China, if you discount the fact that the Emperor Ch'in and the incumbent both dispose of slaves; b) the whole emphasis of Mao's China is to forget, not remember, China's past; and c) anyway, people who have a great past *don't* necessarily have a great future, *e.g.,* Portugal. The statement was therefore inaccurate, maladroit, and anti-historical: But who cared?

And then the ballet of the night before, said Mr. Nixon, was "very dramatic— excellent theater [C+ would have been a generous rating], and excellent dancing [B] and music [C—] and really superb acting [B—]. I have seen ballets all over the world, including the Soviet Union and the United States. This is certainly the equal of any ballet I have seen." Bullsticks. It is not the equal of any ballet Mr. Nixon has seen. Oh dear. One has the feeling that if Mr. Nixon, in his second term, having decided to patch up our difficulties with the Devil, travels down to conduct a summit conference, he will tell Charon that he has used ferries all over the world, but that Charon's is absolutely the equal of any he has ever ridden on. . . .

The moment came. If we assume that Henry Kissinger exacted from Chou En-lai the promise that he would not take the occasion of President Nixon's visit to China to dilate on the depravities of the United States and its foreign policy, then you would not have been surprised, sitting in the packed mini-auditorium that served us in Shanghai as the press room in which the joint communiqué was distributed to the ravenous press, that the Chinese section of the communiqué employed civil language. It is not known how much this ordeal of self-restraint cost our hosts, whose public rhetoric has for so many years now been tuned to the running-dog mode. It is as if, suddenly, you asked Arthur Rubinstein please to play his recital on an atonal scale.

Still they managed it. And, at the other end of the communiqué, Richard Nixon, having surrendered on the principal point, nestled into the clichés in which all statesmen can relax. In particular Western statesmen, because U.S. types, when we talk about democracy, national sovereignty, justice, and individual freedom—however we allow for significant differences in the practice—have in mind something not altogether different from democracy, national sovereignty, justice, and individual freedom. While the other side, recognizing the uses of these distinctively Western ideals, uses the language a bit ill-fittingly, but so doggedly now that the intellectual slouch is no more remarkable than the bagginess of the trousers of Mao-man.

The eyes raced over the communiqué—Presidential Press Secretary Ronald Ziegler would seconds hence enter the room to answer questions (we did not know that it would be Kissinger who would answer them), and it was required that we become instantly familiar with the rather verbose statement, the end-point of the endless week: this was our summit, and we could not dawdle. The gentleman on my right, august representative of the New York *Times,* quickly got the point. "Score one for them, zero for us," he whispered. Except that New York *Times* dispatches do not do that kind of thing, he played, later in the press room, with the lead: "President Nixon departed from China today, leaving Taiwan behind."

Henry Kissinger, who more closely than any man in living memory superintends Presidential foreign policy, was visibly nervous, his wisecracks (he is genuinely witty) edgy and forced. When the inevitable question about Taiwan came up he was as ready for it as the bride to answer: "I do." It is very difficult, he said, to talk about—he couldn't call it a "country," since it was precisely this point that our hosts were contending. To call it an "area," on the other hand, would have been a little unfeeling. So he referred to It, throughout, as an "issue," which, indisputably, it is. He said that because of the particular sensitivity of the Issue, he would say what he had to say one time only; that he would not return again to the Issue, no matter how elliptically or ingeniously other questioners in the room might approach the subject. The fact of the matter, he said, is that the President's annual World Report, issued only a month ago, reiterated the United States Government's determination to stand by the mutual defense treaty with Taiwan. "Nothing has changed on that position."

Of course, everything had changed, and everyone in the room knew it, including Kissinger, although it is true that his understanding of public communications is anomalously underdeveloped. Mr. Nixon had caved in: he would mention, in the communiqué, Vietnam and Korea, but there would be no mention of U.S. fidelity to Taiwan. *Inclusio unius, exclusio alterius.* The rest was summit boilerplate:— professions of faith in peace and national sovereignty, anti super-power talk, and of course the talk about future talk.

Four years ago Henry Kissinger, before joining the staff of President-elect Nixon, evaluated Defense Secretary Clark Clifford's attack on President Thieu on the matter of the shape of the negotiating table in Paris. He said to a friend, "If the United States slips the rug from under the Thieu government, the word will go out among the nations of the world that it is perhaps risky to be an enemy of the United States. But to be its friend is fatal."

Veni, Vidi, Victus

Shanghai, February 28, 1972

Here is what the Chinese gave up: 1. They consented to traffic with representatives of the government of the United States even though the United States still recognizes the government of Taiwan. 2. They performed routine rhetorical exercises on the themes of world peace and national sovereignty, thereby disappointing a few Berkeley sophomores and African fundamentalists who believed that Maoism would never equivocate on the primacy of its international revolutionary mission. When the New York *Times'* reporter asked Kissinger: What has the United States accomplished that wasn't already accomplished by Ping-Pong? Mr. Kissinger, nettled, recited Chinese obeisances to the good international life. He might as well have cited the Soviet Union's guarantee of civil liberties as listed in its constitution.

Here is what the United States gave up.

1. With all the world poised to consider one point above all,

namely the integrity of the United States' commitment to Taiwan, we issued a communiqué in which the Red Chinese asserted and reasserted their absolute right to conquer Taiwan, which is what it comes down to; while we uttered not one word on the subject of our defense treaty, not one word on the applicability of our principles of self-government and independence to the people of Taiwan. That staggering capitulation, for all that Kissinger sought to distract from it by citing President Nixon's World Report which last January reaffirmed our defense treaty with Taiwan, was the salient datum in the week that changed the world. All Asia will understand that whatever the mandarin niceties of the President's World Report, at the crunch Nixon didn't dare to risk a social breach in Peking, and the implications of such a breach, merely to reassure the people and the government of Taiwan—notwithstanding that, on announcing last summer that he would go to China, Mr. Nixon guaranteed that he would not jeopardize the best interests of our "friends." Since uttering those words, Mr. Nixon has seen the expulsion of Taiwan from the United Nations, and now the expulsion of Taiwan from the Presidential catalog of nations in Asia whose independence he is prepared to affirm even while in China. I recall the toast President Nixon made to Australian Prime Minister John Gorton, as someone who has "the courage to speak up when sometimes it might be perhaps more politic to say nothing, or at least to say something else."

2. We have lost—irretrievably—any remaining sense of moral mission in the world. Mr. Nixon's appetite for a summit conference in Peking transformed the affair from a meeting of diplomatic technicians concerned to examine and illuminate areas of common interest, into a pageant of moral togetherness at which Mr. Nixon managed to give the impression that he was consorting with Marian Anderson, Billy Graham and Albert Schweitzer. Once he decided to come here himself, it was very nearly inevitable that this should have happened. Granted, if it had been Theodore Roosevelt, the distinctions might have been preserved. But Mr. Nixon is so much the moral enthusiast that he alchemizes the requirements of diplomacy into the coin of ethics; that is why when he toasted the most merciless chief of state in the world, he did so in accents most of us would reserve for the president of Switzerland. When Mr. Nixon, as he regularly did, made reference to the outstanding differences between our two

"systems," he made it sound as if, after all, there are those who prefer gingham to calico.

3. Mr. Nixon has almost certainly adjusted American politics in such a way as to compel almost the whole of the Democratic Party to the position that we need to dump Taiwan, or to use the historical formulation, to let it fall without appearing as if we had pushed it. Previously that had been one of the aberrations of Senator George McGovern, who collects them. Last week, Senator Fulbright took it up. Now, in the communiqué midwifed by Richard Nixon, the Chinese list the independence of Taiwan as the principal obstacle to the "normalization" of relations between China and the U.S. And Richard Nixon, by his heroic actions of the past week, clearly puts normalization as the highest objective. The analytical deduction will necessarily occur to Democratic Presidential candidates, and the arguments will have been made for them by Richard Nixon. All of this might take a few years to transact, in America. But in Asia, they will have got the signal. Mr. Kissinger spoke to the press about the "basic objective" of setting "in motion a train of events and an evolution in the policy of our two countries." That was brilliantly accomplished. We should certainly know, by now, the direction in which we are headed. No wonder that they took to toasting, in the People's Republic of China, with increasing ardor, the health of Richard Nixon.

A reporter seated at the table with me in Hangchow, after listening to Mr. Nixon's toast to Mao Tse-tung, whose revolution he had just finished bracketing with George Washington's, leaned over and said: "That should dispel the last suspicion that there is a trace of ideological conviction left in Richard Nixon."

He wasn't suggesting that Nixon is not committed, within the United States, to the usual ideals— self-government, a private sector, a bill of rights. Merely that he is utterly indifferent to whether these ideals are practiced elsewhere in the world: indeed, that he apparently cares not at all if these ideals are persecuted in other parts of the world. (How far, far away Nixon is from being the "last Wilsonian" that Garry Wills thought him to be, a year or two ago!)

There is the school of thought that says we should go out with our Marines and make the world safe for democracy. The soldiers in that school are very few, and tatterdemalion, and there are volunteers only when freedom in Israel is jeopardized. There is the school at the other extreme, which is quite simply indifferent to the practices of other governments—the school in which Richard Nixon has apparently enlisted. In between there is the main army, composed of those who, while not prepared to go to war merely to relieve an oppressed people, are prepared to distinguish between those governments that make an effort, however clumsy, to acknowledge the role of the individual, and those others that make the individual the objective of their extirpative passions.

Because we are a people of conscience, unsuited to cynicism, it became necessary—indeed it was inevitable—that very soon after Ping-Pong we should discover the virtues of Red Chinese society. James Reston, quicker even than anyone expected, opened that particular dike with a testimonial to Maoist society which would have been appreciated by a settlement of Franciscan brothers. "I'm a Scotch Calvinist," Mr. Reston said. "I believe in redemption of the human spirit and the improvement of man. Maybe it's because I believe that or I want to believe it that I was struck by the tremendous effort to bring out what is best in man, what makes them good, what makes them cooperate with one another and be considerate and not beastly to one another. They are trying that." Next came the celebrated articles by Professor Ross Terrill, the Australian Sinologist who traveled extensively in China last summer, a writer of great literary skill whose two very long articles, published in the *Atlantic*, have been by far the most influential documents on China of this season. I didn't come across a correspondent who had not seen and fondled them.

The articles in question are extraordinary because, with the rather important exception that Mr. Terrill treats not at all the subject of Maoist terror or Maoist slaughter, he does not, really, hide anything. It is as if Owen Lattimore, traveling through Siberia with Henry Wallace, had reported not that the Soviet Union did not maintain concentration camps there, but that the Soviet Union did indeed maintain them, in great profusion, but that even so, Soviet life was ardently to be cherished.

It is important precisely because Terrill is a departure from the school of apologists of which Lattimore, Walter Duranty, and Joseph Davies were conspicuous practitioners, to savor his arguments, to finger the texture of his appreciation of Mao's

China. Important not only ad hoc, but because here is the way station to Orwell.

Everyone who knew Shanghai then, and knows it now, remarks the transformation. Indisputably, and by anybody's measuring rod, there are improvements. Twenty-five years ago, in Shanghai, the street-cleaners would begin the day by picking up the corpses of people who, since the previous day, had died—of cold, or famine, or exhaustion. There are no casual corpses in Maoist Shanghai, no beggars, no dope peddlers, no prostitutes, no gambling, no night life, no racetrack, no fun. Ah. Terrill is defensive about the grayness of modern Shanghai, and he exercises himself on the subject by discussing the famous Bund— the fabled waterfront, formerly the fashion and play center of the city. Now, in the old way, there is no Bund, and no role for the Western visitor to the contemporary Bund. "Yet the fact that [the Western visitor] is nothing as he wanders unheeded proves that what was once a preserve where he felt his authority now belongs to the Chinese people. And there is an obvious, to some people moving, egalitarianism in the social relationship of these streets and parks. Of course it is 'dull' for the spender or the adventurer. Justice is not necessarily exciting, and it is the face of international and social justice which smiles behind the blandness of the Shanghai Bund."

Now it is quite true that during much of the nineteenth and twentieth centuries, the white man was king in China, which was carved up by the major Western powers into spheres of interest in which the extraterritorial agencies exercised control even to the point of running their own courts and post office. And let us grant that the situation was ripe for change: grant, even, that it had begun to change well before what the Chinese Communists call "Liberation," October 1, 1949, the date when, having vanquished the armies of Chiang Kai-shek, Mao established the People's Republic of China.

But even under the British and the French, the usufructs of the Bund were not denied to Chinese on the basis of the color of their skin. They were available on the basis of the ability to pay. It is at the very least incomprehensible what it is that Terrill means by the phrase "justice is not necessarily exciting." At worst he is saying that justice is an attribute of Maoist China. To say that, on the morning after the Cultural Revolution persecuted, tortured and killed hundreds of thousands, perhaps millions, of Chinese for alleged inconstancies to Mao, is effrontery. Mao's victims are exactly the counterparts of the tortured victims of Josef Stalin, best described by Solzhenitsyn, and counted by Robert Conquest. He must mean kicking out the foreigners. But were the foreigners guilty for all those corpses lying in the streets? Who is guilty, now that the foreigners are twenty-five years gone, for the corpses that continue to line the streets of Calcutta? Of socialist Calcutta? On the other hand where are the corpses in uncolonized Taiwan, where the annual income is five times that in the People's Republic of China?

Professor Terrill disdains comparative figures. He likes discrete Chinese figures. "Some statistics by province, supplied to me by Revolutionary Committees, show why the worker is better off than in the recent past. Take Shensi. The value of fifteen days' industrial production in the province equals that for the whole year of 1949. The value of industrial production in 1970 was double that of 1965. At Liberation, there were twenty thousand pupils in the Middle Schools of Shensi. Today there are 710,000 (population has about doubled)." In 1949, China had fought a civil war for four years, following a war fought against the invader Japan during the previous seven years, which followed a civil war of ten years fought simultaneously with a war against its own warlords. One old China hand commented, "For every mile of railroad track the Nationalists laid down after the [Second World] War, the Communists would tear up two miles of track. How can you blame the Nationalists for a lack of progress?" And Mr. Terrill neglects to mention that between 1965 and 1968, though there may have been 710,000 students in the Middle Schools of Shensi, there were zero students in colleges in Shensi or elsewhere, the entire college system having been closed down by the Red Guards. So it goes with the statistical game. Always the assumption is that you can compare the tons of steel manufactured today, with the tons of steel manufactured during the last year that Nicholas II ruled Russia. How would Russia fare today if you extrapolated the progress it made between 1900 and 1914? Terrill reminds us that after the War, China was "prostrate." So was Japan prostrate; and Formosa and West Germany. Not only prostrate like China, but defeated, unlike China, which was on the victorious side. In Japan, per capita income is $1,800, in Formosa, $800. In China estimates vary, from $100 to $140. The typical wage is $1 per working day. Socks cost $2.50. White cotton shirts, $4. Foot-operated sewing machines, $75. Bicycles, $75. Food and shelter are extremely cheap (how could it be otherwise?). The day before leaving, we visited the Friendship Store, where the Chinese goodies are. There were no Chinese in that vast store, at least not on the buying end of the counters. Social justice is drab indeed. A young CBS cameraman with five small children fussed about, making his purchases. At lunch he told me: "I dropped $525 in that damned store. My thirteen-year-old boy wanted a jade Buddha."

Terrill, as I have said, makes no bones about freedom's end. "Turning back towards the hotel, I pass a Protestant church—its closed gates bearing the banner, 'Carry through the Cultural Revolution to the end.' "

Sometimes he tries to explain it. "Wherever I walk, there is a People's Liberation Army man with boyish grin and fixed bayonet. 'Back the other way.' Well, it is a sensitive area. . . . There was, in sum, an openness and a practical root to nearly all the restraints that met me in China." Terrill does not explain the practical root of the refusal of any news vendor to sell him the morning papers. Meritocracy? "Another PLA [army] officer, a tough, cheery man who confessed his total ignorance of medicine, was head of a Peking hospital." Cultural freedom? "I found cultural life far more politicized. . . . Public libraries, and museums too, are closed. Churches are boarded up, empty, and checked with political slogans. In 1971 you simply do not find, as you could in 1960, segments of social and intellectual life around which the tentacles of politics have not curled." Propaganda? "In Shensi, with a population of 25 million people, 100 million Mao works were distributed during the Cultural Revolution." (It is one of the minor benefactions of Providence that since Lin Piao became an unperson, all copies of Mao's works carrying Lin's introduction, which is to say virtually all extant, have had to be recalled.) Freedom for the fabled worker, in behalf of whom the whole colossus exists? "I inquired of the spokesman of the factory Revolutionary Committee. 'Can a worker transfer work by his own individual decision?' I might have asked if the leopard can change his spots." A broad education? "At PKU [Peking University] I saw the English class which was reading and discussing Aesop's fables. . . . They received me with clapping—though few, I found, knew what or where Australia is." Coercion as an aspect of daily life? There is the lacuna I have mentioned, that Terrill is silent about the bloody Caesarian section that brought about Mao-man. Still . . . "Though force remains the ultimate basis of any state, control of the people in China is more nearly by psychological than by physical coercion. It is no longer simply 'Communists' on one hand and 'Chinese society' on the other. A merger has occurred at many points— a new kind of tao (way) emerges. This makes possible a Dictatorship by Idea (rather than by force). It is not like Poland or Hungary, where the Communists are a blanket spread over the body social. This may be what gave me an impression in China of pervasive yet light-handed control." (I learned, while in Peking, that the Chinese authorities had specified, in advance of Nixon's arrival, that nothing should be sent out by foreign reporters relating to the intensive preparations being made by the advance televison and satellite teams, a proscription which was honored with the trivial exception that a correspondent from Reuters sent a paragraph reporting on two Americans who, having contracted pneumonia, were sent to a hospital in Hong Kong. The authorities, reaching for means of expressing their displeasure, suspended for forty-eight hours the delivery of the little sticks of candy that are placed every day on the bedtable of hotel guests. The Reuters man, though mightily amused, confessed that he felt keenly the psychological force of this deprivation.)

And Professor Terrill summarizes. "People ask 'Is China free?'— but there is no objective measure of the freedom of a whole society. . . . Study of China suggests that the revolution has been good for workers and peasants but problematic for intellectuals. It is hard to go on from there and make over-all value judgments that are honest. First, there are so many gaps in our knowledge of China that it can be like judging America on the basis of Kent State and Angela Davis' case (I know this because I used, before I came here, to judge the United States mainly by its spectacular lapses). Second, our experience has been so different from China's. Not having plumbed the depths of brokenness and humiliation that China did in the century following the Opium Wars, we cannot know the corporate emotion that comes with the recovery.

"Yet at one point we and China face the same value judgment. Which gets priority: the individual's freedom or the relationships of the whole society? Which unit is to be taken for policy and moral judgment alike: the nation, trade union, our class, my cronies, me? This is the hinge on which the whole issue turns. Professor Fu . . . did not make his own decison to take up the problem of insect pests—it was handed him. Is that wrong? The writer, Kuo Mo-jo recalled, cannot now do books for three thousand or at most eight thousand readers, as Kuo used to in Shanghai in the 1930s, but must write for the mass millions—and he's judged by whether he can do that well or not. Is that wrong?" Surely the corporate good is to be preferred? "Capitalism opens the door to tyranny of wealth: Chinese Communism opens the door to the tyranny of a corporate design." As long as human beings are free to use the language, they will find elegant excuses for depriving other human beings of their freedom.

Terrill is merely B. F. Skinner, operational. A brave man, in such an essay, to allude to the "tyranny" of capitalism.

It is in a season that receives cordially the theoretical works of B. F. Skinner and the journalism of Ross Terrill, that Richard Nixon is operating, toasting Chairman Mao, who by material standards has yet to do for his country as Adolf Hitler did for his. Somehow the generic incantation, which used instantly to collapse such analyses—*Mussolini made the trains run on time*—doesn't have its ancient power to restore instantly the focus. The reason is that the West, so far gone these days in a rare combination of satiety and self-abuse, is indifferent in part to freedom, in whole to the cause of freedom. By contrast the Chinese Communists are not indifferent. They are proof against Western derision because they know what they want, are utterly outspoken in their consecration to human debasement as a means of achieving Communism, lucid and unswerving in their designs, insouciant to the resentment we used to feel at the corruption of the terms that used to designate our ideals: justice, liberty, individual rights, government as the servant of the people. Richard Nixon—his glass raised high to Mao Tse-tung, toasting to a long march together, he and we, likening our two revolutions to each other, landing at Andrews to impart the information that the Chinese people greatly esteem their government—may yet emerge as the most flexible man of the century, perhaps even as the most deracinated American who ever lived and exercised great power.

The haunting philosophical questions temporarily aside, there is the practical question of the future of the island of Taiwan.

Over the years, Chiang Kai-shek has steadfastly maintained that he is the lawful head of the government not only of the province of Taiwan, but of all of Mainland China.

For a long time we indulged him the title of chief of state of all of China. Partly we did this out of sentiment, even as we recognized exile governments during the Second World War. Partly we did it thinking it just possible that Mainland China's government would collapse, as once or twice it came very close to doing.

But the situation is now irrevocably changed. Even if the next Cultural Revolution should succeed in deposing Mao, it will not restore Chiang Kai-shek. So that Chiang, growing old, lives by a fiction in which he is all but isolated. Meanwhile, that fiction serves the purposes of his enemies.

"The United States," said the joint communiqué issued in Shanghai, "acknowledges that all Chinese on either side of the Taiwan Strait maintain there is but one China and that Taiwan is a part of China. The United States Government does not challenge that position. It reaffirms its interest in a peaceful settlement of the Taiwan question by the Chinese themselves. With this prospect in mind, it affirms the ultimate objective of the withdrawal of all U.S. forces and military installations from Taiwan. In the meantime, it will progressively reduce its forces and military installations on Taiwan as the tension in the area diminishes."

Now it can be seen not only that the contradiction closes in on Chiang Kai-shek, but that the United States is making gleeful use of it. As long as Chiang maintains that the two territories are one, who is the United States to disagree? And if they are one, it will in due course be plain that the dog should wag the tail rather than vice versa. We have a defense treaty, on the basis of which it continues to be strictly a matter between Taiwan and the United States how many troops we desire to keep on Taiwan territory. But we have, with China, a joint communiqué in which we pledge ourselves to Chou's Five Points, one of them noninterference in internal matters. The lowering paradox finds us, already, promising the Mainland that we will reduce our military mission in Taiwan. And in the United Nations, Taiwan has only the standing of a mutinous province, an Asian Biafra.

The time has come for the government of Taiwan formally to secede from China. The instrument of secession would be at least as eloquent as our own Declaration of Independence. More, really, because however hateful King George was, he was the soul of toleration, by Mao's standards. George Washington and his fellow secessionists had not had an experience of independence from Great Britain. By contrast, Taiwan has governed itself for twenty-three years, disturbing not the peace of the world, indeed earning the admiration of all who have come to know it, for its economic progress, for the slow but steady enlargement of democratic institutions, and for its devotion to its own independence.

Granted there are Taiwanese who resent Chiang Kai-shek and his government of Mainlanders. But even there, there has been a considerable shift of sentiment from fifteen years ago, when the Mainlanders occupied almost all the positions of responsibility. Although there are Taiwanese who will continue to resent Chiang's government (there were Americans who opposed the Declaration of Independence), there are very few Taiwanese who would elect to be governed by Peking.

Accordingly, the stage is set. It is difficult to see how the United States, or for that matter any other country whose politics are not dictated by Communist capitals, could fail to recognize, instantly, the independent country of Taiwan. Even the Communists acknowledge— formally— the right of revolution, and the rights of independent states. And Taiwan would be nothing less than that— an independent state, de facto and, now, de jure.

One wishes that one could instantly assume that the United States would welcome such a development, as releasing it from a dilemma. At the present moment our posture towards Peking is too slavish to be absolutely certain even of that. But what alternative would we have?

That is, to the extent one can find solutions, the current solution for the Taiwan problem. It would be a sign of health, and ultimate patriotism: a gesture of devotion to the people who have sheltered him during the past twenty-three years, if Chiang were now to make this concession to reality, and this contribution to order and hope for what is left of his people.

IV. The Eastern Front

A Million and One Nights in Soviet Russia

December, 1970

It wasn't so long ago (children) that one simply didn't travel to Russia as a routine thing. Years and years ago distance was the thing—it is 1,500 miles from Paris to Moscow, and historical accounts of the distance leave permanently in mind how long it took, how hard it was, and how unprofitable the journey for the most publicized nineteenth-century traveler from Paris to Moscow, who barely made it back, leaving most of his army behind. More recently, the casual traveler was simply not permitted to go to Russia: Tourism was one of those few, blessed subjects upon which V. I. Lenin did not pronounce, and therefore the presumption—during the twenties and thirties—was: No. To enter Stalin's Russia, you had to be a journalist, preferably friendly; or a scientist who knew the multiplication tables better than whatever Soviet scientist pleaded for permission to get you in; or Paul Robeson. After the War, it was much the same until after Stalin died; and then, little by little, the curtain was shiftily parted, and a trickle of disinterested Americans came in. By disinterested, I mean Americans who went there other than to make cold war—for instance, the gang of performers who went there to do *Porgy and Bess*, accompanied by Truman Capote, who wrote memorably about that trip for *The New Yorker*. I wish I had been there when the articles, translated, were put before the relevant commissars. It must have astonished, and maybe dismayed them, that Capote had such a very good time—*verrry* suspicious. Visitors to the Soviet Union are unpredictable, the Russians have every reason to believe. During the last days of the War, Henry Wallace, only a month or so before F.D.R. replaced him as Vice President, had traveled to Siberia with Owen Lattimore at his side, to report that he had not seen any of the fabled, and therefore presumably fictitious, concentration camps. A prominent American industrialist had been over there and reported exuberantly that, you had to hand it to Russia, there were *absolutely* no labor-union problems over there.

Anyway, on into the fifties, the Soviet Union decided to encourage tourism, and the program for tourists was laid out, as diligently as a Five-Year Plan, and as dreamily. Insofar as the idea was to lay claim to an appropriate share of the tourist dollar, the program—like the Five-Year Plans—failed. There are many reasons for that beyond the obvious ones, beyond distance, beyond ideology. I had read about what it was to travel in Russia, felt I knew something about it when Frank Shakespeare called and asked if I would travel to Novosibirsk as a member of the United States Information Agency's delegation to inspect the opening of our exhibit there, on May 12. Frank Shakespeare is an old friend of mine. He is the head of U.S.I.A. and known in chic circles primarily as the Bad Man in Joe McGinniss' book *The Selling of the President*. The thesis of that book is that Frank Shakespeare, formerly of CBS, conspired with one or two other expert television cosmeticians to sell Richard Nixon to the American people. The book is a glorious performance, and I wouldn't have missed it for the world; indeed, would as gladly have read it if it had been written about Hubert Humphrey, whom the ingenuous author ingenuously conceded it might just as well have been written about. Anyway, we are to be very suspicious about Frank Shakespeare, McGinniss suggests, because during the Presidential campaign—just imagine!—Shakespeare exclaimed to another Nixon aide when the news of Russia's armed invasion of Czechoslovakia came in over the wires, that no one had the right to be surprised, that being the kind of thing Russia tends to do, when in doubt. It is utterly consistent that such a Red-baiter should have suggested to Mr. Nixon that he appoint me to serve as a member of the U.S. Advisory Commission on Information. I have to confess that, like the rest of the world, I was unaware of the existence of said commission on the evening when Mr. Shakespeare tendered me on the President's behalf an invitation to join it, subject—to be sure—to confirmation by the Senate. Duties? They are prescribed by law: The commission must report periodically to the Congress and to the President on the activities of the U.S.I.A. Salary? Zero. (That, you understand, is what makes it prestigious.) Perquisites? No-vosibirsk, every now and then. And, of course, access to extremely interesting people. The five-member commission ("not more than three of whom shall be from any one political party. . ." wrote the wary Congress in 1948) meets once a month in Washington. We have dinner on Sunday night with whatever VIP from the State Department or wherever drew the shortest straw, then no-nonsense meetings beginning at 9 A.M. Monday, and stretching through lunch (with another VIP), into the late afternoon. The chairman of the commission is Dr. Frank Stanton, the president of CBS, who is the most efficient and the most hospitable man in the entire world— it is he, I think, whom I would call if I were head of the Bureau of Standards, and I suspected that my normative yardstick had shrunk— or grown: He would know what to do about it, how to do it genially, and, if necessary, how to break the news to the scientific world. I visited with Dr. Stanton (he is a Ph.D. in psychology) before accepting the appointment, in order to raise a few questions, among them whether joining a Presidential commission mightn't mean a conflict of interest as a journalist. Nonsense, he said— after all, by statute at least two members are from a different political party from the President's, presumptively dedicated, therefore, to his political undoing.

So I accepted, was taken in to chat with President Nixon (his desk is very neat, as is his mind, have you noticed?). I enjoyed the visit, beginning with the cozy tour of the surrounding rooms, in which Shakespeare and I whiled away the few minutes it took the President to finish with the Queen, or whoever. The Cabinet Room is directly adjacent to the Oval Room, and I observed that just under the President's chair are three call buttons, after each one of which is written the name of one of Mr. Nixon's aides, should he need any one of them to come in quickly during a Cabinet meeting. Frank told me that the three buttons survived from the days of Lyndon Johnson, but that in those days they were marked, respectively, PEPSI-COLA, DR. PEPPER and SPRITE. President Johnson apparently did not conceive the necessity of needing mere mortals to nourish him. The President was very very cordial, and said one or two things which I would have been reluctant to disclose in any case, but which at this point I would disclose only on my deathbed, confident that no one would at that point very much care. Because, as they say, security-wise, you can call me Sealed-Lips Buckley, after what I went through. The

President having appointed me, weeks and weeks went by, during which the Federal Bureau of Investigation went after me; during which I received telephone calls and letters from girls and boys I had not seen for years and decades, advising me that they had been visited by the FBI, who had asked whether I was a reliable citizen, and really and truly anti-Communist. I remember thinking, after one old friend who had served with me on the *Yale Daily News* twenty years ago called to tell me that *his* FBI inquirer had asked whether Mr. Buckley would be willing to sign a loyalty oath, that if the FBI declined to clear me, I would at least have consummated the greatest imposture of the generation. But, in due course, the FBI, William Fulbright, and the Senate of the United States having cleared me, my "commission" came in. I studied it carefully. It is an impressive scroll, standard for all Presidential appointments, high and low. There is the printed form, and four blanks, which permit a fine holographic rendition of (1) your name, (2) the office to which you have been appointed, (3) the duration of the appointment, and (4) the space that is introduced by the printed words, "in recognition of . . . " after which, in my case, was written, "his integrity and ability." I found that altogether satisfying, quite content with the President's apparent knowledge of my integrity and ability. . . . But then I found my mind wandering. What was the inventory of honorifics from which these two qualities had been selected? *Numero unius exclusio alterius,* my mother used to say to me. If I was singled out for my *integrity* and my *ability*, what was I by inference *not* being singled out for! A few months later, I was in Saigon, listening to Ambassador Bunker, who was interrupted and called out of the room. My eyes strayed and I spotted, in the corner of his office, *his* commission. I rushed over and looked at the corresponding blank—and read, "in recognition of his integrity, ability, *and prudence*." The FBI had found me out.

Who else would go to Novosibirsk, and what was the purpose of the trip? I asked Frank Shakespeare. Frank Stanton, Jacob Beam (the U.S. Ambassador to Russia), Kempton Jenkins (U.S.I.A. area director), Shakespeare, and I. The purpose: to inspect the exhibit at Novosibirsk and, in general, U.S. cultural and educational activities in the Soviet Union. Would it be a good opportunity to poke about a bit and learn something about the Soviet Union? *Ideal,* said Frank Shakespeare, among whose charms is his enthusiasm, which would ignite waterlogged wood. I signed on.

London. Urgent message to call Lou Olom, staff director of the Advisory Commission. I got through to him, a few hours before the flight to Paris, where I was to convene with the Novosibirsk delegation, and go on to spend one night in Moscow, then on to Asia. The Novosibirsk opening is off, said Olom. The Russians, he explained, had informed the embassy that it would be "at least" a week before it could open, because of an unforeseen scarcity of electricity and sanitary facilities. The inference in Washington, he told me, was that the Soviet Union was looking for a way to react feelingly to a speech delivered a few days before by Premier Kosygin denouncing the United States' "invasion" of Cambodia. The Communists' scanning device having come about 360 degrees looking for a way to blip their displeasure, the handiest thing they could come up with, of a nonconvulsive nature, was our innocent little opening at Novosibirsk. But, true to their own fashion, the Soviet officials would not admit that they had staged an official act of petulance, whence the story about the shortage of electricity ånd sewage facilities.

It was marvelously handled, I was to learn a few days later in Moscow. Monday, May 11, is a holiday in the Soviet Union, celebrating Victory Day. At exactly 5 P.M. on the preceding Friday afternoon, a Soviet official from Novosibirsk, telephoning from the office there that handled (pursuant to the cultural exchange agreement) the Soviet end of the U.S. exhibit, left a message with the U.S. Embassy announcing the postponement. At this point the American dignitaries were homing in on Paris from various parts of the world, where they would assemble for the afternoon flight to Russia on Sunday. The embassy, trying to assimilate the meaning of the postponement, called back to ask for a fuller explanation. No answer. The ambassador then took over—Jacob Beam is a veteran, who may *sound* like Mr. Smith come to Washington, but who at the cockpit of the Pentagon on X-Day would be indistinguishable from John Wayne—and *he* called the Foreign Office. No answer; same excuse—national holiday. Undeterred, he tracked down a responsible official at his home. Said Russian promised instantly to telephone to Novosibirsk, to find out what was going on, and to call back. He did so, to report—his voice heavy with surprise—that, in *fact*, there *was* a shortage of electricity in Novosibirsk.

Now that, friends, you will understand as a real diplomatic

crisis. The *Russian* in Moscow reports to the *American* in Moscow that, incredible as it may seem, the *Russian* in *Novosibirsk* is telling the truth! Diplomacy has its limitations, and one cannot imagine Ambassador Beam, for all that he is a man of disarming candor, informing the *Moscow* Russian, huffily, that he does not believe a word of what the *Novosibirsk* Russian said, that what is more he, Beam, is from Missouri, which in any case he is not, having graduated from Princeton after a happy boyhood spent in Kent, Connecticut.

It transpired that the electricity required to service our little educational exhibit in Novosibirsk came to a daily total of 100 kilowatts. Novosibirsk is an industrial center of over a million people, so that the Russian cavil about the shortage of electricity is something like New York's Carnegie Hall canceling a scheduled concert pleading that it could not furnish the electricity necessary to illuminate the piano player. The shortage of sanitary facilities was even less convincing, inasmuch as no new facilities were in fact added during the week in which the exhibit was held in suspense, not to mention the unspoken Soviet assumption that no Soviet citizen worthy of his fatherland was likely to tarry at an imperialist exhibition long enough to run up against the necessities of nature.

Under the circumstances, the ceremonial opening was permanently canceled. One cannot deploy Shakespeare, Stanton, Beam, and Jenkins, like a mobile, by merely moving everything up a week. But Buckley had the week clear, and decided to proceed to Russia, and allocate the time that had been reserved for Novosibirsk to Moscow and to Leningrad. I proceeded, after consultation with Shakespeare in Paris, to Orly for the nonstop flight to Moscow, on a Japan Airlines flight that would, after dropping down at Moscow, proceed to Tokyo nonstop. I traveled with Larry DuBois, from *Time* magazine, who hadn't been to Russia either, and came along to see the action, if there was to be any. I had been briefed in Washington, and would be briefed again in Moscow, on how to keep out of trouble in Russia. No sex (the cameras are ubiquitous); no drunkenness (beware the mickey finn); no compassion for the stranger who approaches asking would you please mail this letter to her daughter when you reach New York (entrapment); no rubles bought in Paris (where you can get them at, approximately, seven for one versus the one-for-one official rate); no provocative ideological literature (even if it is for your own use)— a novel by Solzhenitsyn is not the ideal thing to carry in your briefcase, unlikely as it is that it will be confiscated on the spot (other things might ensue). I read, on the plane from Paris, Andrei Amalrik's *Will the Soviet Union Survive Until 1984?*— and dutifully left it aboard the plane, even though I had not finished it. At just about that time, Amalrik was taken in by the KGB.

I should at this point admit that for years I have husbanded a little skepticism about the horror stories one hears of as routine in Russia. I know, I know, that the Soviet Union has done everything from exterminating millions of recalcitrant little farmers, to instructing Alger Hiss on just how to smear Whittaker Chambers. But people whose lives revolve around the civilized seasons find it hard to believe in the particulars of the institutionalized Orwellian state. There are all the familiar historical cases. . . . The gentleman is on his way to the Hotel Metropole, and an old man gives him a sheaf of papers— would he please read them when he gets a chance? He is just entering the lobby when he receives the packet, so he nods— pleasantly (as who would not)— stuffs it into his pocket, and before even turning around, he is seized by the KGB and charged with espionage. The incident would have been as newsworthy, in Russia, as a prostitute's arrest for communicating venereal disease— except that the gentleman was Professor Frederick Barghoorn of Yale, the President of the United States was John Kennedy, the Premier of the Soviet Union was Khrushchev, the historical situation was halfway between Kennedy's high point of strength (October, 1962) and Khrushchev's downfall (October, 1964): And the United States chose to make an international issue out of the victimization of poor Mr. Barghoorn, who was presently released by the KGB. You can't win them all. But they win a lot of them. I was told about a recent case, an English M.P., a lovely fellow, brimming over with the milk of cultural exchange, who dutifully undertook at a ceremonial lunch to match his Soviet hosts drink for drink, toast for toast, beyond the point when, his vision having blurred a bit, he could notice that the Russians who were now raising their glasses of vodka were not in fact the same Russians who had excused themselves a few moments before to use the sanitary facilities. They were what we imperialists call Ringers, and they drank heartily, until the point of conviviality was reached beyond which our English friend could not express himself except by lurching forward to the only window in the little banquet hall, and there relieving himself of every good wish he had so ceremoniously ingested in honor of mother Russia and her contemporary leaders. By utter coincidence, exactly across the street, an amateur Russian photographer happened, together with telescopic lens, to focus on the guilty, sick Englishman, whose plight he instinctively recorded, which photograph, quite naturally, the Soviet press published widely, suggesting, ever so delicately, the incontinence of the typical English official visitor to the Union of Soviet Socialist Republics.

So you believe one particular story, because you believe the man who told it to you, because he is all professional and is not there to waste your time nor to titillate you; but, mentally, you reason that it *must* be yet another exception. You pick up a book, late in the evening of your third night in Moscow. It is called *Message from Moscow* and is signed, "An Observer." It is published in America by Alfred Knopf (hardly a Russian-baiting firm), and the author is a student who after three years of graduate work over there has taken careful stock of what it's like everywhere, all the time, in Russia. He doesn't reveal his own name, because he fears to implicate his friends. About himself he divulges only that he is a socialist (he might be British, or he might be American). On one point only is he absolutely impatient, and that is towards those who disbelieve the lengths to which the Russians routinely go to effect their repressions. You are never absolutely secure, he says; not in the classroom, not in the grocery store; not even in bed with your occasional distraction. That book, so very understanding— so very sympathetic— is the skeleton key to life in the Soviet Union these days. It is a book that cannot be disbelieved, and it taught me, as I went through its pages, how impossible it is for an American to compete with someone like the Observer who wrote this book, who stayed three years in Russia, speaking the language fluently, untouched by any initial ideological hostility. What a curious Western tradition it is, that we should all of us try to say better what we cannot by the nature of the case hope to say one half so well as that gentleman over there, who has written a book which nobody has read, to speak of.

Moscow. The airport (which, along with military installations, you are forbidden to photograph. Especially you must not photograph bridges. *Never* photograph a bridge. Don't even bring along with you a picture of your favorite bridge back home). The terminal we landed at is strangely unmenacing in appearance, and would be thought inadequate as the municipal airport for, say, Bridgeport, Connecticut. There is Muzak (or radio, I don't know) and I hear "Home on the Range." The American brass are there, and they slither me through. I had completed the Customs Declaration Form, answering No to the question, Did I have with me "gold, silver, platinum, metals of the platinum group, coins, bars, unwanted scrap, precious stones, pearls, and articles thereof."

The drive into Moscow. It is Sunday, late afternoon, during the equivalent of the Western weekend rush hour. I didn't count, but I am certain we did not see twenty passenger cars along the 25-mile route. It was a Vlaminck sky, dark gray, white white. At the little gate of Spaso House was the guard supplied by the Soviet Union— by common acknowledgment, he is a member of the KGB. (Fair enough. Ours probably report to the FBI.) He saluted us through, and I got out into the enormous, oddly-structured town house completed for a Moscow industrialist in 1917 (1917!), and used by us as an official residence ever since F.D.R. sent William C. Bullitt as our first post-Czarist ambassador, Maksim Litvinov having promised him that Russia would absolutely honest Injun give up subverting the world. Mr. Beam, tall, white-haired, crew-cutted, fluent in East European affairs, bookish, old-Southern in hospitality, married late to a chatty, amusing, handsome, iron-willed, super-large-hearted former employee of Voice of America. The circumstances were embarrassing, because a dinner had been laid on for the entire delegation. Now arrived at Spaso was not the whole egregious delegation, but a single member of it, with no plans for Novosibirsk, and five unscheduled days— unscheduled also for the ambassador and his wife, who had planned to be with us in central Asia. I suggested delicately to an aide that under the circumstances I remove myself and bunk down elsewhere after the first night; but the ambassador would not hear of it, and I have to admit that I was very pleased, for all the obvious reasons, but primarily because the Beams are perfect to come-home-to and to discuss with, informally, that day's vicissitudes (the last night I spent with them the staff was out, and we did TV dinners in the kitchen). After dinner that first night, with the deputy chief of mission, the head cultural officer, the aide-de-camp, and their wives, I asked whether the Voice of America got through in spite of the jamming, and the ambassador trudged out his great big portable Zenith and diddled with it, Mrs. Beam told him he was doing it wrong, here, let her try it, the deputy chief of mission said try holding it up, this way, pointing west, which the ambassador did, tapping the aerial with his finger, while Mrs. Beam, her face concentrated as though she were Arturo Toscanini's acoustics engineer, fiddled with the tuning dial. A few words were finally deciphered, but they sounded like enjambments, and were garbled testimony to the effectiveness of Soviet jamming, resumed after the Czechoslovakian invasion, after five years of noninterference. But the jamming, it transpired, is effective only in parts of Russia, and there is a lot of evidence that V.O.A. gets through. At Novosibirsk the U.S. Russian-speaking guides were, some of them, on temporary duty from V.O.A., and their voices were recognized by many Russian visitors to the exhibition who, the jamming notwithstanding, were regular patrons of V.O.A. broadcasts.

At this point I could contain myself no longer, and begged to be excused in order to lay eyes on Red Square, a mere ten minutes away. It was only ten at night, and I set out to meet Larry DuBois. He had had a typical experience, going from the airport to the hotel where he had reservations only-they-never-heard-of-him, on to a second hotel, which Yes, they had a room for him when-he-telephoned-from-the-first-hotel, but No, when he got there ten minutes later they had-no-record-of the ten-minute-old telephone call. At this point in desperation he had called the residence, and the cultural-affairs officer, the Magnificent McKinney Russell, who speaks a Russian which is at once fluent, seductive, and imperious, took hold of DuBois at the other end of town like a crippled aircraft, and, by a series of soritical telephone calls, guided him down gently to the Hotel Metropole, where I picked him up, and from there we walked excitedly the 200 yards to Red Square.

Moscow is at latitude 55 degrees, abreast roughly of Copenhagen, so that during the late spring the day yields grudgingly to the night, and at 10:30 we could still make out the Prussian blue in the sky, giving the background for the golden domes and spires of the Kremlin, where at Ouspensky Cathedral seventy-five years ago, young Nicholas the Second was crowned Emperor of Russia, and the people, in an excess of enthusiasm, stampeded over each other during the attendant festivities, killing hundreds of celebrants. Their grandchildren, in *their* enthusiasm, line up day after day, by the thousands, to walk into the tomb of Lenin, who, through his minister Sverdlov, executed the Czar and his Empress and their children and, subsequently, every Romanoff he could get his hands on. They do not stampede, the contemporary pilgrims, because the queues in the Communist world are orderly, except where, as in East Germany not long ago, and in contemporary Cuba, the frontiers abut upon another world and give easy access to it, in which case the queues are quite uncontrollable, so much so as to require, finally, huge walls, and paralyzed airports, and gunboats foraging among the fishing boats for human cargo, to stanch the flow of pilgrims who yearn to get away from the world shaped by the little bald fanatic whose mortal remains are scarred so very much less than the world he had a hand in shaping.

But in Red Square, even as four hundred years ago they worshiped Ivan the Terrible, they file into the squat, austere mausoleum on the terrace of which, 20 feet higher, we can see the inscrutable officialdom of Red Russia lined up on ceremonial occasions, the Kremlinologists of the world dangling over them with their calipers, to measure the telltale differences that might suggest who is closer today, who is further removed, from the power to catapult the world into one more war, the final war, perhaps. Behind Lenin's tomb is the wall of the Kremlin, on the grassy side of which the heroes of the Soviet Union are buried, or in any case memorialized, the least of them first, on the northern end of the wall, whose names are written on stone slabs. Then, proceeding south, the greater figures, who merit bronze busts and pediments. Directly behind Lenin's tomb is the simple slab beneath which are the remains of Josef Stalin, removed from alongside Lenin soon after his anathematization in the late fifties. But Stalin is gradually rising from the dead. Only a month or so after we dallied over his perfunctory slab, a bust sprouted up from the ground— an enterprise which could not have required less official attention than the launching of a Soyuz moon-landing. Just this year, the Soviets managed to publish an official history of World War II without once mentioning Stalin after 1945— one of those breathlessly humorless accomplishments of which they are so singularly capable, reminding us again and again and again of the undeniable vision of George Orwell. But the hagiolaters will not be forever denied, as witness the unobtrusive rise, by the Kremlin wall, of the likeness of Stalin, which like the beanstalk is likely now to grow week-by-week back to full trinitarian status with Marx and Lenin. For one reason because a mid-position on Stalin is, historically and morally, like coming to rest in mid-air between the diving board and the water; for another because communism, or whatever you choose to call what it is that they practise in Russia, cannot easily allow for a ruler who, preaching Lenin, proceeded to misgovern for twenty-five years. Irregular performances by bad Popes well after the consolidation of the Church are one thing. But you cannot announce that Saint Paul was after all a liar, a thief, and a lecher, without subverting Christianity. So, in due course, they will preach that Stalin the Prophet was despised only by the despicable. And the injustice will be rectified, most congruently, by Stalinist dispositions of the incautious, anti-Stalinists, who are, ever so quietly, nowadays running for cover (try to tease a condemnation of Stalin out of a Soviet official next time you come across one at a diplomatic do). Red Square is brilliantly illuminated, and the people stroll about it, the natives who find it a convenient place to stroll; the out-of-towners, who gawk, and take pictures, and crowd about the tomb to see the sentinels replace each other, strutting to and from their posts, stiff-legged and proud of their illustrious burden.

The next morning I spent at the embassy, listening to cultural and educational officials, and then yet another go with Security. There were two of us at that session, I and a bearded professor, a Sovietologist headed for Novosibirsk to stay there for the duration of the exhibit, in order to answer the questions of the visitors. I heard again what I had heard in Washington, plus also that the Russians were brilliantly informed on the passage of dope through their country. A little while back an airliner originating in Istanbul stopped at Tashkent to refuel, before going on to Copenhagen, and New York. Three young American passengers did not bother even to leave their seats, since the stop would be for only a few minutes. But Soviet agents went into the plane, called them out, searched them and found hash, and turned them over for sentencing to three years' hard labor. All of the huffing and puffing by our embassy has sprung only one of the three. Other countries in Europe are doing exactly the same kind of thing. I reminded Security, and he agreed, though neither of us had heard of anybody being pulled out of an airplane in a country he was visiting only for the purpose of picking up fuel. Anyway, I said gravely to the bearded American professor, under the circumstances he had better not pick up any junk at Novosibirsk, and he stiffened with rectitude, smiled nervously, and, duly briefed, went on to Novosibirsk—which did open, a week after the scheduled day.

The ambassador told me that he had laid on a biggish lunch with Soviet officials in anticipation of the full American delegation's being there (we would have gone after lunch to Novosibirsk). As it now stands, he said, er, it isn't obvious how many of them will show up. In other words, those Russian officials who *had* accepted, had been invited by the ambassador to lunch with the ambassador, with Frank Shakespeare (head Government-propagandist), and Frank Stanton (head capitalist-propagandist), just to begin with.

Now, in the two or three hours before lunch, we had in miniature, the entire spectrum of possible Soviet diplomatic responses. Possibility (1) was that *all* the guests would cancel, Kosygin having in his anti-Cambodia speech given the signal that the freeze against America was on, the subsequent postponement of Novosibirsk serving as a baton-rapping signal to the entire Soviet orchestra. In that event, the dozen guests had before them two alternative ways of expressing themselves. Either, (*a*) they could telephone in their decision not to attend the lunch, on the explicit grounds that they did not believe it appropriate, during this bloody chapter of American imperialism in Indochina, to proceed with the normal social-diplomatic amenities: or (*b*) they could telephone in to the embassy and advise that unfortunately there was a crisis in the Urals, or that they had to go to work on the sewage system in Novosibirsk, or that their mother-in-law had suddenly passed away: communicating to the ambassador the same message, but in a significantly different way. *I.e.,* if form (*b*), rather than form (*a*), was used, it suggested to the diplomatic corps that the anti-Cambodian response was not to include any formal interruption of diplomatic contact; whereas form (*a*) would have suggested that precisely such an interruption was a part of Soviet strategy.

Then there was possibility (2), that one-third, or even one-half, of the scheduled guests would telephone in, giving this-or-that excuse for their sudden change in plan. Nothing there of grand diplomatic import, particularly if it was limited to one-half. All that that would mean, then, was that the big shots involved considered it beneath their station to appear at a luncheon which had been raided of its premier celebrities, leaving only— well, me.

Then (bear with me if you will), there was possibility (3), wherein the guests, by their unanimous presence at the luncheon, might accomplish two purposes at once, if indeed it were desired to accomplish them, namely, (*a*) to suggest that there was absolutely no complicity between the shortage of electricity in Novosibirsk, and Soviet foreign policy in general; and (*b*) to suggest that the acceptance of the ambassador's invitation to lunch had had nothing whatever to do with any Soviet curiosity concerning the person of the head of the United States Information Agency, or the head of the Columbia Broadcasting System. To do otherwise would be to suggest that they cared enough about U.S.I.A. and CBS to cause either the presence of their managers at lunch to be the reason for accepting an invitation, or their absence to be the reason for canceling their previous acceptance— all of this being, well, beneath the level of attention that attracts Soviet dignitaries of that category. Get it? You may believe that that kind of thing went out with the fan flutters of Madame de Pompadour, on the basis of which the court knew who was in and who was out. You would be wrong.

Anyway— if the suspense has not done you in— they were all there, except for one gentleman who telephoned in a legitimate excuse. It is interesting to speculate, in the Russian context, what it is that constitutes a "legitimate excuse." The very best excuse is to die. Accidentally, if possible, though the chances of that, in Russia, are poor to middling. Another good excuse is to be sent suddenly abroad. Third best is a grave illness in the family. Next is a summons by the Kremlin. But that becomes attenuated, because a summons to the Kremlin can be understood as a summons not to go to the ambassador's party.

Anyway— as I remember— this gentleman gave a moderately good excuse; *i.e.,* his reason for not coming fell somewhere between dying, and being summoned by the Kremlin. And so, at 1300 Moscow Mean Time, on May 11, I walked down from my room into the great reception hall of Spaso and, for the first time in my life, found myself surrounded by officials of the Soviet Union, each of them with a drink in his hand. *"This is Mr. Buckley, Mr. Sverzablydyczky." "How do you do, Mr. Sverzzzsky, so nice to see you." "How do you do, Mr. Buzzky, so nice to see you. Are you enjoying Moscow?" "Oh yes, yes, are you enjoying Moscow?"* (NONE OF THAT, BUCKLEY,— I stopped myself.) *"I mean, are you enjoying the weather in Moscow, Mr. Sverzzzsky?"* And so on, right around the room, and then lunch is called. The gentleman on my right is the most important of all, and the gentleman on my left only a little less so. The Right gentleman had accompanied Kosygin when he traveled by car from the United Nations to meet President Lyndon Johnson at Glassboro. He reminisced about the trip, and I ventured that it must have made him feel homesick to find no traffic on the New Jersey highway, but we let it pass, let it pass. The gentleman on the left was afflicted with a fine sense of humor, which he turned on uniformly, on all matters, except of course that he would never turn it on at the expense of the Soviet Union. I mean, if you had said to him, "Didja-hear the one about what was the most important historical event of 1875? Lenin was FIVE YEARS OLD!!!," he *might* have laughed, but there was enough ideological steel there to cause you not to go in for that kind of thing, so we talked about his avocations, the most important of them being canoeing, of which he is a total addict. Canoeing. Hmm. That made him a Canoeist. I told him that not long ago Prime Minister Trudeau of Canada had been accosted, while moving through a crowd, by a lady who, seizing his lapel, asked him, "Is it true that you were once a Communist?" Trudeau had answered, "No, madame, not a *Comm*unist, a *Ca*noeist*" —* and proceeded there and then to relate to her, at a length most distracting to his bodyguards and appointment-keepers, his last experience with the sport, canoeing down some Canadian river or other. "How long is that river?" my companion asked. I don't know, I said: *very* long. "Well," he smiled, "the river *I* went down on my last vacation was eighteen hundred kilometers long— the part I traveled— and not one human being did I see the whole length of the passage!" I told him that that was quite extraordinary, which it certainly is, promised to send him James Dickey's novel *Deliverance*, and we agreed that we both looked forward to our meeting tomorrow, at the "U.S.A. Institute," which is a fairly-new, Kremlin-sponsored organization, composed of scholars, journalists, scientists, and diplomats— 150 of them in all— whose job it is to concentrate on the United States of America, for the benefit of the Soviet Union. I asked him how many would be present at the session scheduled for me, and he said a half dozen or so, a half dozen being exactly how many in fact were there, when I arrived at the haughty mansion that the fabulous Prince Bolkonsky, introduced to the non-Russian world by Leo Tolstoy in *War and Peace*, once lived in, and dominated.

In between was fairyland. . . . Viola, from Intourist, took us everywhere, to the Armory to see the treasures, beyond the imagination of, well: me. There, also, are the Fabergé Easter eggs, given to Alix by Nicky, one of them with tiny paintings of all the Romanoffs; another containing a miniature of the entire Russian railroad system, with even a little locomotive that putters, or once did, along the tracks. . . . Where does Khrushchev live?, I asked Viola. He lives in an apartment house, said Viola. I know, but *which* apartment house? The same apartment house that Molotov lives in. Would you take us by that apartment house? Why? We Russians respect the privacy of private people— after all, Khrushchev and Molotov are private people. I know, I just have a private historical curiosity. Come on, Viola. Well, she relents, as a matter of fact, that is it over there— she points to the Bernard Baruch Metropolitan Life Insurance Company Urban Renewal John F. Kennedy Lower Upper Middle Income Plaza, which is mostly laundry hung outdoors, and television antennae. I wondered what would happen if one entered the building, looked under "Khrushchev" and pushed the elevator button. . . . But that is the kind of thing, in the Soviet Union, you will always wonder what would happen if you did it, because such things simply don't happen. I do remember the American a few years ago (a wonderful young man, as uninhibited as Silly Putty) who sailed into the Lubyanka, beamed at the startled man at the desk, "Hiya folks, I'm Charles Wiley from New York, and I thought I'd sure like to take a tour around this here prison!" and off he went, smiling, and waving, and using his three words of Russian, going further than anyone before him had gone, whose destination was this side of the crypt of Amontillado, until, finally, the resources of the Union of Soviet Socialist Republics mobilized themselves and, dumbfounded but firm, led Charles Wiley back to the street, and presumably returned to tell their grandchildren about the crazy American.

The phone rang early in my room at Spaso. *Pravda* had published that morning an extensive and extraordinarily bitter attack on the U.S.I.A., on Frank Shakespeare, and on myself, calling us all "werewolves," right-wing extremists, etc. A translation would be made available to me before my meeting with the U.S.A. Institute, and indeed it was. It was remarkable primarily for its stylelessness: It was nothing more than ideological boilerplate, though as I say, rather more bitter than that kind of thing tends to be: enough so to raise the eyebrows of the embassy people.

I asked my friend DuBois to join me, and took along a tape recorder, having been told by the embassy that the week before, Theodore Sorensen, campaigning for the New York Senate seat of Robert F. Kennedy, had taken along *his* tape recorder (Sorensen lost in New York, and it is not known how he did at the U.S.A. Institute in Moscow, though historians should note that there *is* a tape). I was cordially, if formally, greeted— certainly I was not made to feel like the werewolf described that morning in the official paper— and found myself seated opposite a table at the center of which was my Stakhanovite canoeist friend of the day before. I asked if he minded if I recorded our conversation. Well, he said, as a matter of fact, the U.S.A. Institute's proceedings were off-the-record affairs, and he would just as soon I didn't use the tape recorder, unless I absolutely insisted on it. Well, I said, not at all, not at all, if it would make you uncomfortable, let's just forget it, as I shoved the little machine away from us, on towards the center of the table. Well, he said, beaming, I suppose you are left only with your one hidden recorder? The two men to his right laughed, and the two men and a girl on his left laughed, and Larry and I laughed, and I said, Well, you see, you underrate Yankee ingenuity, because I have a mike not only here (I pointed between my neck and my collar) but also here, under my right lapel, and here, under my left lapel. We all laughed, and I remember wondering whether some X-ray machine or other would quickly inform the chairman whether I was making a bourgeois joke, or was maneuvering from Bondian desperation. . . . Anyway, the conversation ensued, for two and one-half hours. The usual things. With one or two interesting and not altogether expected emphases. The Chairman-Canoeist began with a ritual denunciation of our move into Cambodia, in which his Rockettes concurred (I do not mean to suggest other than that they were extraordinarily bright, and learned, and resourceful in their arguments: merely that they played together like the Budapest String Quartet), and I replied, Look, let's save time, the United States, belatedly, is treating the Cambodian frontier like the geographical fiction you people have been treating it as, ever since the war began; so what is the point in accusing us of escalation, simply because we behave like you?

We traversed the frontiers of the cold war, at military, political, and even— ever so lightly— at philosophical levels. What interested them most, however, was— clearly— Economics. Only a week or so before, Henry Ford had come to town. The Soviet Union was after him to build a great big truck complex, and the reception given to him was, by all reports, the most fabulous since Marco Polo arrived in China. The Soviet big-cheese car is called a Zil, and they have probably managed to produce about five and one-half of them, every one of which (or so it seemed) was put at the disposal of Henry Ford II, the capitalist-exploiter whose favors they so much wanted. They put him in the poshest dacha in town, and everything went for him smooth as can be, so anxious were they that he should go along on the matter of the trucks. To be sure, when one of his daughters who was traveling with him decided to buy a $4,000 stole, she found that the seller wanted cash, c-a-s-h, and the poor girl spent the rest of the afternoon signing 400 ten-dollar traveler's checks. But anyway, the chairman wanted to know how I could account for the *stupidity* of those Americans who opposed Henry Ford's setting up a truck plant in the Soviet Union when, after all, if *we* didn't, all the Russians would have to do was invite *any* old other country to do the same thing, like say Japan, or Italy, or Germany, or France, or England— and what would *that* do to our balance of payments? I murmured something about Americans' resentment of the number of trucks currently being sent by the Soviet Union to North Vietnam, which are in turn used to bring down ammunition to kill Americans with, whose parents might, under the circumstances, look darkly at the prospect of the Ford Motor Company's supplying the Soviet Union with those trucks it was short of, on account of its commitment to North Vietnam— get it? I was dealing with enormously sophisticated people, and of course it gradually became clear to all of us— but it would have been very impolite to recognize the hovering enthymeme, which was— is— that just any old country can *not*, in fact, supply Russia with what the Ford Motor Company could supply it. A few days later, in Leningrad, I heard the news that Henry Ford, back in Detroit, had said No, he would *not* build the new plant in Russia, under the circumstances, the circumstances (unspoken by H. Ford) being, of course, the Vietnam war. I thought of my friends at the U.S.A. Institute, and the blast they would surely receive the next day from the Kremlin. *Who, if not the U.S.A. Institute, is supposed to know the mind of Henry Ford? Why permit Russia to be embarrassed, if it was all that obvious he would say no? What in the hell do you people down there leading those posh lives and drinking cocktails with all those visiting Americans think you're up to?* Well, I reflected, at least the bum steer hadn't come from me. . . .

It was time to go to a lunch at McKinney Russell's with a few journalists, two of whom (*Time*, CBS) were expelled from Russia a week or two later, for venial sins of intellectual curiosity. I found them all very resigned about Soviet Russia. Henry Shapiro, of UPI, lives even now in the same apartment he bought from Eugene Lyons in 1935. Eugene Lyons! (Whose book, *The Red Decade*, brought more fellow travelers to share in his disillusionment with communism than any other book of the period.) In Moscow, if you are truly settled down there, you must be careful, very careful, very very careful. Shapiro— wise, learned, amiable— is a fixture, and wants to go on living in Moscow. A few days before, Kosygin even mentioned him (teasingly) by name at the appearance at which he denounced Richard Nixon. But Shapiro cannot mention Brezhnev by name, teasingly.

Another glittering afternoon and evening, a trip to Zagorsk, the spiritual home of Russia, where one of the three surviving seminaries continues the hapless production of a dozen priests per year, like eyedropping holy water into hell. The Bolshoi ballet doing *Don Quixote*. Blinis at the Metropole (in the restaurant reserved for clients who come forward with non-Russian currency: There are such restaurants everywhere, and PX-type stores, and they do to the Russian people what Jim Crow did to the Negroes); and then the midnight train to Leningrad. We sat, Larry and I, in my little compartment and offered Scotch whiskey to William Jay Smith, America's poet-in-residence at the Library of Congress, who had been invited over to read his poems and to visit with Soviet poets, and kept wondering where he could find

Brodsky, who is in disrepute. Everybody is vague about where Brodsky is. The trouble was, we could not hear each other very well because the radio was playing right into my compartment from a unit high on the wall. I had reached to turn it off, and found that you don't turn off the Russian radio when Central Planning has decided it should be playing: Nor do you control the volume—there is no control, no ON-OFF switch. But a half hour after midnight it did go off and we could then hear each other better—as could, presumably, the KGB. The next morning at exactly 6 A.M. the radio resumed with music the brassiness of which makes it easier to understand why so many Russians take vodka before breakfast. I went to brush my teeth, and noted the stewardess, sitting in front of a large samovar of tea next door to the bathroom. I smiled, said "Tea, please, *spasibo*," totally exhausting my knowledge of Russian, and she gave me such a glare of ferocious resentment as froze me in panicked perplexity. I rushed back and asked the poet, who knows Russian, whether the sounds "Tee pleeze" add up, in Russian, to a dirty word, and he said no, not that he knew of, and just then she appeared, and, incredibly, plunked a cup of tea down in front of me on the little collapsible table. DuBois asked her, or rather gestured to her, manufacturing a most effusive smile, whether he too might have a cup of tea, and damned if she didn't do to him *exactly* what she had done to me: Yet, a few minutes later she was back, plunking down a cup of tea for *him*. Woody Demitz from the embassy, a young, experienced, Russian-speaking diplomat doing werewolf-tending duty, explained to us that many Russians are just that way, particularly in their professional dealings with people. Two nights later, I remember, we *could not* get anyone at either of two large restaurants to take our order—pleas, bribes, threats, availing us not at all. *There is no available sanction*, I was told. Tips are officially proscribed, but on the one hand they are routinely expected, and on the other, they simply do not amount to enough to influence the behavior of a waiter who is predisposed, whether by the Russian climate, or by the Russian political system, to—simply—resent clients or patrons. There isn't enough to buy in Russia, with that extra ruble or two that the waiter can get in tips. In Moscow when taxis are scarce the way to get attention is to raise your hand, concealing in it an American dollar bill. A few such bills and the native can enter the foreign-currency stores, and buy a few of the goods unavailable to mere ruble-earners. It is not easy to describe the concerted neglect of the interests of the consumer of which the Russians are capable; and it is necessary to know, when traveling in Russia, that the reason for this neglect isn't merely the vaunted xenophobia (though there is that, and sometimes one can taste it); but rather a lost tradition of service. You, the tourist in Russia, are indistinguishable, as far as the waiter is concerned, from the native traveling salesman or housewife. You must, all of you, be countenanced—because that is what is ordered from on top: That is one's *job*. All of you are a general inconvenience, and there is no point whatsoever in going through the motions of welcoming the patronage. (Obviously, there are exceptions, even as one comes across polite cabdrivers in New York.) Personal relations are altogether different.

Nina, for instance, who met us so coldly at the Intourist office in Leningrad; yet by the time we had opened the doors of the car, she was and would continue to be (except on the one occasion when she was provoked ideologically) marvelously hospitable and obliging, even when we offered her, for lunch from my tuck box, caviar and potato chips, having determined that we would never again willingly set foot in a Russian restaurant. Yes, she confirmed, this was the Square where the Revolution began. Over there—yes, stretching all the way down along the river—is the Winter Palace, the formal residence of the czars during the two centuries that St. Petersburg was the capital of Russia, up until the Revolution. We will go through it, the parts that are open to tourists, in just a few minutes, don't be impatient, she clucked. Over there, on the river, is the gunboat, preserved as a national monument, that fired the shot that triggered the Bolshevik takeover. You can see the fortress where Lenin's brother was imprisoned, but you can't quite see over to the fortress where he was hanged. Over there—we cruised—is the great town house of Prince Yussoupov where he and his friends murdered the monk Rasputin, just before New Year's Day, 1917, throwing him finally (he was harder to kill than King Kong) into the river, right in front of the house, and causing the shudder that, some of them say, finally demoralized the royal family which, a few months later, lost its power. The Winter Palace was never physically touched by Nazi hands, because although the Nazis besieged Leningrad for nine hundred days they never penetrated the city's defenses: This was where Russian civilian heroism ran the longest

course, even as, at Stalingrad, military heroism saved the city—
the same heroism, said Nina, the same people. Do you realize, she
asked, that this was a city of three million people when the War
began and I was a little girl, and when the War was over, the city
was a city of less than one million people? But the Nazis, failing to
get into the city, satisfied themselves by wrecking everything
outside it, the whole complex of summer palaces of the czars, for
instance, and then shelling Leningrad, doing great damage to the
Winter Palace. The treasures of the Palace were packed up and
sent away to the Urals before the Germans came, but some of
them were found, many were damaged. We walked into the
palace and the experience was breathtaking. I mean, there isn't in
the West anything on the scale of the Winter Palace. Versailles is
a Petit Trianon. The rooms, many of them reconstructed, are
quite literally perfect, and the taste unblemished, the conspicuous
exception being the fabulous throne room, where a chauvinist's
lackey replaced the throne itself with a post-War map showing in
mosaic the territorial reaches of post-War, prehensile Russia. The
jewels, a collection of czarist baubles, outmatch in vulgarity and
in beauty anything of the sort anywhere, and suggest the
emotional reason for the contrasting drabness of the Bolshevik
costume, indeed, for the drabness of Soviet art—the diabetic
imperative. The architecture in the Winter Palace, and in the
summer palaces, is mostly Italian in provenance. The czars no
more thought to insist on Russian architectural or decorative pre-
eminence than, say, we would think to insist on American pre-
eminence in camera lenses. The scale of the thing—ridiculous
and sublime—reflects the expanses of Russia, the lateral
terrestrial infinity, the vertical complement of which was expressed in the Middle Ages by the height of the holy spires of the
great cathedrals of France and Germany, which could not go
higher only because of the dumb limits of contemporary science
which already were strained to exuberant lengths. But building
sideways there is no restriction, which is why for instance the
Winter Palace simply goes on and on and on, and although I did
not take measurements, I warrant you could walk from one end
of the White House to the other fifty times before going the
length of the Winter Palace; before reaching, if you started at the
other end, the auditorium where, on the night that it was storm-
ed, Georges Enesco from Rumania, young, talented, glamorous,
gave his scheduled violin concert, before a severely diminished

house of aristocrats, who reseated themselves about him—less, one supposes on reading about it, because they sought the *Gemütlichkeit* that was otherwise unavailable in so large an auditorium, than because they thought, *noblesse oblige*, to console the artist against any suspicion that the plebeian irregularities outdoors in any way suggested a straitened appreciation of his art, or an unseemly abbreviation of Russian hospitality.

There is no American installation in Leningrad, but there is an agreement in principle to permit the opening of a consulate there, in return for a Russian consulate in San Francisco. There are many altogether respectable American legislators who resisted the idea of more Russian consulates in the United States, though even if one supposes, as it is perfectly reasonable to suppose, that a Russian consulate in San Francisco would be devoted to the elaboration of the art of subversion, surely the practice of that art, in the San Francisco area, would be an exercise in supererogation? Leningrad—like San Francisco—faces the sea; and on the weekend we were there, the streets—more accurately the restaurants and the foreign-exchange bars—were clogged with Finns, coming in with markkas in their jeans, taking the three-hour bus ride to get away, would you believe it, from the comstockery of their own surroundings, I speak of teenagers, blond blond blond, hippie, long-haired, jaded in appearance, fourteen-year-olds asking for dry martinis *very* dry (they are not served booze in Finland, at their age), qualifying to travel about in the spots where Russian youth are excluded, because they do not have non-Russian bread. They sweep in and sweep out during weekends, a visigoth children's invasion, cool, bored, unconcerned, except for sensual gratification. If it were physically possible (you get the impression) for these young Finns simultaneously to smoke marijuana, drink martinis, and copulate on the barstools of the foreign-exchange bars, that is what they would most assuredly do, on Saturday nights. The only thing they would not ever neglect to do is, to return to Finland, when the weekend is over.

We told Nina how sad it was that we had so little time, but she did not repine; she is used to *givens* in any situation, whether it is the scarcity of food during the Nazi siege she survived, or the ebb and flow of tourist traffic, which could leave her overworked for weeks, or under-utilized for months: She was at one point sent to

Indonesia for two years where she dutifully learned Indonesian, having kissed her husband good-bye as stoically as a whaler's wife at Nantucket two centuries ago. We drove finally to the summer palaces at Tsarskoe Selo, an hour's drive, and she led us to Catherine's Palace, once again endlessly magnificent, only a dozen rooms restored, but exquisitely. I asked if I might visit Alexander's Palace, just down the road, because it was there that the last czar and his czarina made their home. She resisted, as Viola had resisted in Moscow when I asked her to take us by the Lubyanka; but she did not make a point of it. Yet when the car stopped, outside the garden, 200 yards from the tatterdemalion columns, in design not unlike the White House's, on the informal side of the palace, she did not get out of the car, a gentle act of symbolic resistance that could hardly be assigned to lassitude, since she is surely the most energetic cicerone in Europe. So Larry and I got out, and roamed across the yard-high grass, ambling towards the great columns through which, when Woodrow Wilson was President of the United States, the czar and czarina and their four girls and little hemophiliac son would stroll from the garden into the house, whose apartments were mostly living quarters, but which provided public rooms for the ministers who regularly waited upon the imperial presence, on the implicit understanding that the parliamentary devices that had grown up during his reign were, notwithstanding the explicit language of the con- stitution to which the czar had acquiesced, nothing more, really, than the democratic sufferances of an emperor who had been crowned the Autocrat of Russia. When he arrived at Tsarskoe Selo from the German front, after the storming of the Winter Palace, he had abdicated his throne en route. And in the next few days, walking through the columns into the garden, he could not suppress the habit of raising his hand to return the salute of what had been his imperial guard, which had surrounded the garden with adamant loyalty over the stormy years. That guard was gone, replaced by carefully selected revolutionary soldiers who would as soon have saluted the czar as take an oath against vodka. The head of the detachment insisted that the very large garden in which the czar and his family were used to strolling should for reasons of security be ruled off limits, except for the two or three acres through which we now ambled; and Nicholas, seeking exercise, decided to bicycle around the remaining pathways; whereupon the guards, it is recorded, entertained themselves by wheeling around suddenly and poking sticks into the czar's bicycle wheel, causing him to catapult over onto the ground, whence he would lift himself, silently, deliberately, unreproachfully, remount the bicycle, unminding of the taunters, who for half such an aggression would thirty days earlier have been knouted and hanged; and head back toward his family, so as not to interrupt, by any melodramatic defiance, the grisly end that awaited them all, sixteen months later, in the cellar at Ekaterinburg, where they would be shot down, on orders from Moscow, already beginning to practice the trade in which it would become proficient: ordering the executions of royal families, dissident ideologues, small landowners, prisoners of war, hundreds, thousands, millions. I thought, as I walked through the grass, towards the gutted palace, that it is all no more difficult than understanding the men who tumbled the czar's bicycle, an act, under those circumstances, as exhausting of the resources of human cruelty as would be the signing of the order to eliminate a million kulaks in order to prove a large institutional point. At the veranda a soldier appeared, his dress as shabby as the palace he guarded, to say that we had already wandered too far. No matter, there isn't anything left there to see, because these apartments, where the last Romanoffs lived, so intimately, so devotedly, have not been restored, and they do not lie on the Intourist route. I wonder why the government doesn't raze Tsarskoe Selo, but of course they have always shown that certain caution that many iconoclasts show: Thus, at Leningrad, they convert the cathedral of Kazan, where the czars prayed, into an "Institute of Religion and Atheism"; but they do not tear it down, whether for reasons of husbandry, or because they believe that the profanation of a cathedral is high-class revolutionary piquancy. I think there is a third reason, which is that the Russians, even the Communist Russians, cannot practice wholehearted Orwellianism; *i.e.,* they cannot induce themselves to *destroy* that which they disapprove of (unless it is a human being). They sublimate it (as with the Kazan Cathedral); or ignore it (as with Tsarskoe Selo); or profiteer from it (as with the crown jewels one pays to see). But you do not simply *destroy* it, for some reason; a reason the understanding of which would leave us better understanding the Soviet Union, and hence the world.

The next day—the last day—Nina took us to yet another

summer palace, Peter's pad, to which we had intended— it is on the Finnish Gulf— to travel by hovercraft, that being the way one travels there nowadays; but it was the opening day of the season, and she feared that the water traffic would be too heavy, so we went by car, arriving at the fabled gardens through which one could hardly move for the people— surely ten or fifteen thousand were there— who came to rejoice in the fountains, and to line up (approximate waiting time: two hours) to enter the palace. Some of the fountains were designed to tease the children, and any grown-up in the mood for that sort of thing. A hidden spout would go off at unexpected moments, dousing the trespasser, rather like the electric rod at Coney Island. We were agreeably surprised that Nina, after quietly talking with someone, led us past the head of the line into the apartments, again artistically perfect, again reconstructed inch-by-inch from the ruins left by the Nazis. I told Nina that she obviously had plenty of *blat*, and she turned on me, strangely suspicious— where had I picked up that word? (It is, I gather, high Russian idiom for "pull," and I had got it from the book *Message from Moscow.*) I thought to intensify the mystery and said to her, "Tolsti taught me the word." "Tolsti" is what one *doesn't* call Tolstikov (first secretary of the Communist Party of the Leningrad region and, according to some, the most ambitious neo-Stalinist in Russia); except in situations of utter security, which are ex officio never reached by Americans talking to Intourist guides. Nina's reaction was both cautious (she really *didn't* understand how I could come on to the existence of Tolsti, or *blat*, not somebody who had proved himself as ignorant as I had done during the two days we had spent together); and amused— how exhilarating it is to see the ingenuous foreigner traipse so lightheartedly over such dangerous territory, because the foreigner didn't know about the land mines.

But her curiosity was contained, and she went back to explaining the works of art in the palace, her mastery of which, like her mastery of Russian history, was altogether extraordinary. That afternoon she took us through the Kazan Cathedral to survey the Museum of Religion and Atheism, which is as impartially devoted to religion and to atheism as the Museum of Natural History is to supernatural and natural history. Among the exhibits, all of them calculated to document Lenin's point that religion was an instrument of repression— raising the gullible question, Why did Lenin neglect to exploit the possibilities of religion as a mode of repression? Answer: He didn't— was a chestful of instruments of torture, labeled by the exhibitors as having been commonly used during the Inquisition. When I asked, kitchen-debate-wise, whether they had been borrowed from the Lubyanka Collection, Nina was most firmly displeased with me, and I was not able to jolly her out of that displeasure; so I acknowledged the tastelessness of my remark, and, of course, it was, in a way— in that context— the remark of a bully. One does not make light of the doctrine of tran-substantiation with an altar boy. But, as we drove back to the hotel, we were friends again, and I asked if she would like to have me send her any books when I got back to New York. Well, she said, yes, she would, though she doubted that I would in fact remember to send them, just as she doubted that Larry would remember to send her any of the pictures he had taken of us. "They always say they will, but they never do." I asked her what books she wanted, and she did not hesitate. She wanted *Peyton Place, Hotel, Valley of the Dolls,* and *The Carpetbaggers.* I promised her that I would send them, and Larry interposed jocularly to ask Nina whether she would like to have my own book, *The Governor Listeth,* and Nina said bravely that she did not know that I wrote books, but that she would certainly like to have my book, that she only hoped that it was not as biased as Harrison Salisbury's book about the siege of Leningrad, and I assured her that it was ten times as biased, and she smiled, and we pulled into the hotel. Her handshake was purely professional. I hoped to find a trace there of that tingle that distinguishes from the purely perfunctory experience, but I must admit that I did not. Whether, after she has read *Valley of the Dolls, Peyton Place, Hotel,* and *The Carpetbaggers,* she will acquire that sensitization our Esalen types preach of, which might have permitted us to embrace across the Iron Curtain, I cannot say; I would say only this, that I do not know what other books one can honorably recommend in the circumstances: What would you and I read, or want to read, if we were born and brought up in Leningrad? Solzhenitsyn's *Cancer Ward* sells there, in the black market, for 80 rubles, which is one-third Nina's monthly pay. But there are other reasons against reading Solzhenitsyn in Russia, even if it were known that one could do so with absolute safety. *Nina does not want to be troubled*; and I would not want to trouble her, not unless the prospects of success were assured, or at least reasonably assured. "We waited for years for the American Army," a Polish intellectual told me a few days later— (in Poland, by contrast with Russia, they all sound like Lenny Bruce)— commenting on the recent visit of our astronauts. "And when it came, there were just three of them."

Communism Under the Poles

Bucharest, June 4, 1970

A cosmopolitan Frenchman observed over a century ago that there is no joy to match that of leaving Russia— however much you may be drawn to it; however resigned you may be to returning there. The sensation endures. It might be argued that in the age of Gogol the sensation was a slur on Mother Russia. In the age of *Pravda,* it is as undeniable as hunger and sex. No man physically or psychically normal can fail to experience the sense of liberation. Even if only to land in Poland.

Poland! Poland has simply given up on the matter of achieving any kind of independence as a result of its own exertions. To the west of it is East Germany, still dominated by Ulbricht, the Stalin-lover. Even farther away is Czechoslovakia, the light that failed. To the southeast, to be sure, is Rumania, with its extraordinary defiance of Russia (Rumania was the only satellite to dare to denounce the invasion of Czechoslovakia). But Poland, where it sits, hasn't got a chance. There is a fatalistic acceptance here of her national impotence. It was back before the flowering of Napoleon that she became an object for the satisfaction of the polygamous appetites of her neighbors. It was only for a period as brief as the vision of Wilson that she resumed self-government, which she has not seen since Molotov and Ribbentrop signed the pact that showed the world how much in common were the worlds of Lenin, and the worlds of Hitler.

So, Poland doesn't fool around protesting Soviet foreign policy or any such thing. What does happen in Poland is that a few attempts are made— successfully— at giving Polish citizens an intimation of the kind of life it is possible to live out from under the shadow of the Soviet Union. No, not free speech. No, not freedom of the press. No, not political freedom. No, not freedom of travel. It is most accurately described as— a freedom to edge towards these things without the certainty of the guillotine; which, if you are certain of it, causes you spontaneously to repress whatever impulse you feel towards self-expression.

In Poland, you can move about the country more freely than in the Soviet Union. By the way, Poles find it easier to get permission to travel— to be sure, on professional business— to America, than to travel to the Soviet Union. In Poland you can talk not only to intellectuals but to Party functionaries, on the implicit understanding that you both revile the Communist system; and not even protocol is breached. The anti-Soviet cultural impulse is altogether unrestrained.

A closer observer in Warsaw puts it this way. The most convenient way of classifying the Poles, he says, is in four categories. One, the utterly convinced Communist. Two, the willing— the happy— whore. Three, the unwilling— the unhappy— whore. Four, the true opponent. Poland is run by a very few Ones, a lot of Twos, and a great number of Threes. The Fours are there, but they have no influence, except in their tight little circles, and such power as they have they do not, obviously, elect to display. So that what you have in Poland is a government for which the Soviet Union makes every decision as regards foreign policy, which does not countenance any expression of corporate resistance; but which finds it inexpedient to crack down, in the way that the Soviet Union would crack down with gusto, on certain manifestations of intellectual mobility.

For instance, you have the Church. It flourishes. The pressures are of course there, but so were they there when the King executed St. Stanislaus in the eleventh century. A few journals are tolerated, for instance a highbrow Catholic journal, which although it doesn't criticize the oligarchy, nevertheless laughs, covertly, at the ideological pretensions of Communism, which only the Number Ones take seriously. The Number Twos keep their eyes open for signs of excessive exuberance among the Number Threes, but on the whole they let things go, and letting things go means that students can talk frankly to each other without fearing a Soviet axe; that tourists can talk to Poles without risking their eternal stigmatization; that a visitor can open his window in the morning and feel that he knows now, with certitude, what is the difference between Purgatory and Hell.

Tito the Elder

June 6, 1970

The government official, whose spoken English is better than most American professors', explained excitedly what is happening in Yugoslavia— the trends towards political and economic decentralization, towards intellectual (if not political) freedom, the nervous elation of national independence. His enthusiasm was altogether genuine.

"Of course," he said, "I have to admit that there *is* opposition to our program." What kind of opposition? I asked. "Well," he said, "there is opposition from the statists, who think that our departure from Stalinism is wrong; and there is also opposition from those who think that we are not moving fast enough in the direction we're going."

I leaned forward in the chair and asked excitedly: "Which of the oppositions would you classify as your left wing, which as your right wing?" "Why," he said thoughtfully, "the statists— the Stalinists— are our right wing, and the impatient are our left wing."

I find that a fascinating commentary on the extraordinary thing that is happening in Yugoslavia. The ruling class, under what is now an avuncular Tito (as distinguished from the Tito who not so long ago used to like to tell the lightning bugs when to shine), is discovering the extraordinary benefits of economic and bureaucratic freedom. Agriculture is largely de-collectivized; the six constituent republics exercise real power; scientific knowledge circulates freely; the frontiers are open; only 20 percent of the GNP is appropriated by all the governments combined. The result is that the standard of living has soared.

But it is very untactful, in Yugoslavia, to press upon the exuberant managers the formal point that what they are slowly doing is discovering the extraordinary uses of the free market. There isn't, really, anything much to be gained from such ideological I-told-you-so-ism. The Titoists refer to their system as "socialist" at every opportunity. So what? Moreover, it is evidence of their terminological integrity that they should think of the Stalinists in their midst as representing the "right" wing, while on their left— those who urge even greater economic and political freedoms: *i.e.,* those who in America would be thought of as Goldwater conservatives— are their left wing.

It is important, in Yugoslavia, to understand that Tito greatly desires to go down in history as having midwifed a brand-new social form, or if you like, synthesis. He desires his name to become an eponym: for a dreamy social arrangement which is on the one hand wonderfully productive economically, free intellectually, and yet socially cohesive. He was for years and years a most fundamentalist member of the Communist apparatus, and he cannot stand, in his later years, to abandon the old liturgy, never mind that what is going on in Yugoslavia is as far removed from what goes on in the Soviet Union as Hong Kong is removed from Peking. "We are halfway towards where we want to go," the seasoned and enthusiastic editor of the Party journal— *Kommunist*— told me. "Where do you see yourself as having arrived after you have completed the journey?" I asked. "It is a never-ending journey," he said. "In that case, you haven't come halfway," I ventured primly; he agreed, a formalistic concession. I did not tell him that the ideas he had just elaborated would have qualified him, in America, to serve as editor of *U.S. News & World Report.*

Yugoslavia was a revelation to me. It might not survive, to be sure. The insiders tell you that if the Soviet Union decided finally to move, the Red army would occupy Belgrade after a weekend's work: though to be sure after that, the war against Yugoslav guerrillas would be at least as expensive as the Nazis'. Historically, one cannot forgive Tito the blood he spilled, in behalf of a vision so fanatical, and so useless. But the point surely is that unlike the elderly Stalin, or Mao, he is not now exhibiting what Professor Wittfogel described as "the megalomania of the aging despot."

It is as seemly to be enthusiastic over the contemporary Tito as it was to be enthusiastic over the Dubcek of 1968. You have only to travel from Russia to Yugoslavia— or for that matter from Rumania to Yugoslavia— to rejoice at what you see happening, and to admit most happily, that however defective the reasoning of the Truman and Eisenhower Administrations might in fact have been, in fact it is, providentially, paying off.

It may be that we do not deserve a significant part of the credit, but it is absolutely, unquestionably true, that America's policy of encouraging Titoism in Yugoslavia (if you rule out the liberationist alternatives that were available to us after the war) has served us. Served us, as beneficiaries of an East European showcase of the relative advantages of relative freedom—a fox in the bosom of Soviet ideology. And, above all, served the Yugoslavs, who can look with pity and scorn at the hideousness of those who are condemned to continue to live according to the gospel of Lenin and Stalin.

V. Winding Down The Wars

The Cambodian Incursion

May 5, 1970

Much of the criticism that has come in of Mr. Nixon's Cambodian declaration is of the assertion that America must not become a second-rate power. Mr. Paul Harvey, for instance, the Midwest broadcaster whose following is very great among people who have tended to back Mr. Nixon's Vietnam policies, broke absolutely with the President on this one. "Mr. President," he intoned, "I love you." Pause. " — But you are wrong." Mr. Harvey then informed the President that it isn't worth it to be a first-rate power if the cost is to be as high as is suggested by his decision to fight in Cambodia; and besides, he said, the mothers of the United States cannot bear enough male offspring to sustain United States' efforts on such a scale as is being suggested.

Others, in their own way, are saying one or another variation of the same thing. Senators Fulbright, Hatfield, and Proxmire. The whole, it would seem, of the American Academy. And surely Shelley Winters will be heard from. The implicit challenge is to the assertion that America needs to be a first-rate power.

That is a central question, strangely unexamined. We look about us and recognize that there are a great many second-rate powers which are somehow muddling through this century. They have their preoccupations— one thinks, for instance, of the English; but they have also their domestic felicities. And they are not called upon, anymore, to fight extensively in far-off lands, or to bear the brunt of everybody's animadversions who feels that if he were President of the United States, the world would be so very much more congenial. The joys of being a second-rate power are very considerable. We tasted them fully during the nineteenth century. It would be totally desirable if every power in the world were a second-rate power. But unfortunately, nature decrees that there shall always be at least one first-rate power. And just because the United States steps down, should it ever elect to do so, it does not follow that so would the Soviet Union. Or Red China.

It isn't mere bombast that Mr. Nixon is talking. What he said in his well-structured speech wasn't that it is fun to go and die for the good-old glory of a good-old first-rate power. He wasn't King Harry at Agincourt, bringing the fighting blood of his countrymen to an elated boil. He does expect, and is entitled to expect, that thoughtful Americans understand what it is that happens when a power climbs down from greatness in a world where other nations, of hostile disposition, will inherit the position of primacy.

It wouldn't greatly matter if we became a second-rate power yielding, let us say, to Great Britain, which was a first-rate power during the nineteenth century, providing with her navy the shield needed for our brilliant gestation. But if we lose now it is the Soviet Union that we will lose to. And the Soviet Union desires to preside over a world which is quite horrible to contemplate; desires, by whatever means, to extend the Soviet system, recently described by a correspondent of the New York *Times* as the "greatest assault ever mounted on the human spirit."

What is happening in Indochina is a contest of wills. Ours has been bent on establishing that a modest, nonaggressive alliance continues to be tenable in a remote part of the world, suggesting that our other alliances, in closer parts of the world, will also prove tenable. The enemy is bent not only on simple aggression, but on proving that the United States cannot dispatch a responsibility she willingly and intelligently entered into. If the Communists establish that the United States cannot do that, then, and as of that very moment, the United States abdicates as a first-rate power. Humiliation, of course: but we can endure humiliation. The French did, after all. But the French were spared worse humiliation— by the presence of a friendly first-rate power in the world— the United States. Let those who wish to abandon Mr. Nixon at this moment force themselves to say: What will make us convincing, tomorrow, when, facing the Mideast, we tell the Soviet Union that we desire a balance of power there, the survival of Israel? What prestige will we bring to the Organization of American States when we discuss the virtues of stability in Latin America? The advisability of continuing America's responsibility for the Panama Canal? What, a very few years after our collapse in Asia, will our partners in Europe think when the Soviet Union presses its advantage, and elaborates its Brezhnev doctrine to authorize, say, the occupation of West Germany?

These are questions to which manifestly Richard Nixon has given very great thought, and if he prevails, history will owe him a great debt. If he does not prevail, he has nevertheless earned the great debt from those bound together in spiritual unity against tyranny.

Hysteria

Warsaw, June 2, 1970

I think I like diplomats. I was in the room when the news was brought to our ambassador to Warsaw, Mr. Walter Stoessel, that the Chinese had canceled their scheduled talks, in protest against Cambodia. His reaction was that of a manager informed that his store had run out of peanut butter. Well, order some more. Well, wait for the Chinese to change their minds. If they want to, they will; if they don't want to, there's nothing we can do about it. Some of the boys in Moscow, at the Soviet's U.S.A. Institute, tried to work me up into a dudgeon over our action in Cambodia, and it was wonderful to see their feigned indignation when, in fact, you knew that what they really wondered about was our stupidity at not having done the same thing long ago. Look, I said, the border of Cambodia is a geographical fiction as far as you people are concerned. Why do you find it deplorable that we should treat that border in exactly the same way that you do? They changed the subject, and started talking about MIRV's.

News in this part of the world is very difficult to get, because of course you can't buy non-Communist newspapers. What you hope to get, from somebody at an embassy or from a journalist, is a not-too-old copy of *Time* or *Newsweek*.

I got the May 18 *Time* in Warsaw the day I observed the calmness of our diplomats, and it was like a plunge into hysteria. It is one thing to hear the Communists rant and rave about things in general, something else to hear it done by the editors of the most prominent American newsweekly. You would have thought, on reading this issue, that Richard Nixon had launched a pre-emptive nuclear strike against North Vietnam.

The tone is at once fustian, self-pitying, and apocalyptic. The response to Cambodia "mocked" Nixon's "unfulfilled promise to lead the nation" "forward together"—as though B's response to A's leadership is necessarily A's fault. Nixon's calculations concerning the domestic response to Cambodia proved to be "dangerously wrong": once again, the planted axiom being that it was Nixon's fault that the Kids, or *Time* magazine, should have become hysterical. Cambodia "has already destroyed far more American resources of morale and cohesion than any North Vietnamese supplies could be worth"—a sylleptic confusion exposed by asking the question, *What* resources of morale? If a nation goes crazy because we do a militarily obvious thing, where was the morale we suddenly lost?

The Kids, by contrast, are treated by *Time* as a cross between St. Francis of Assisi and Immanuel Kant. "They filled the warm evening with the refrain of the John Lennon mantra: 'All we are saying is give peace a chance.' " Ah, the sweet innocence of youth. "Some of the less inhibited youngsters stripped and went wading in the nearby Reflecting Pool." The reference is to a dozen great big post-pubescents whose anxiety over Cambodia caused them to strip nude and frolic in a wading pool at the center of the central part in the capital city of the nation, poor youngsters.

President Nixon's efforts to establish a little direct contact with the uninhibited youngsters is treated with open scorn. " [Nixon's] discussion rambled over the sights of the world that he had seen—Mexico City, the Moscow ballet, the cities of India." Those who, by contrast, capitulated to the Kids, are dealt with matter-of-factly, not a trace of editorial annoyance showing. "Oberlin College President Robert Carr simply canceled final exams, gave all his students credit for their courses and turned over the campus to antiwar planning."

The official reaction of the National Guard would not have been treated differently in *Ramparts* magazine or for that matter *Pravda*. "Tom Hayden turned up and tried to blend the war, the Black Panthers and the Kent State murders into one rhetorical attack on the U.S." Murders! Not "murders," understand: murders. In the same magazine that a couple of issues back spoke decorously of the "alleged" murder of Rackley by the Black Panthers. The unofficial reaction of some anonymous Americans is portrayed as sadistic and brutalitarian: "I'm getting to feel like

I'd actually enjoy going out and shooting some of these people, I'm just so goddammed mad," is a specimen.

On the background of Cambodia there is some very bad reporting ("Henry Kissinger was also said to have dissented and took pains to deny the rumor" but was careful to tell his friends who remonstrated with him, " 'I want you to understand that I hear you' ").

And embarrassingly premature doom-talk. "When President Nixon announced two weeks ago that he was sending U.S. combat troops into Cambodia he hoped to achieve two major goals. One was to force Hanoi into meaningful negotiations. The other was to reassure America's allies that in a crisis the U.S. would not be 'found wanting.' On both counts, he not only failed but failed disastrously." For one thing, only people under the age of eight expected that Hanoi would instantly respond to Cambodia by coming to the bargaining table; for another, anybody over the age of eight knows the uses of heroic rhetoric.

The historic event proved to be not Mr. Nixon's decision to cut off the supplies in Cambodia, but the panic of some Americans whose urbanity and sense of perspective is the keel of the republic.

Laos and Vietnamization

February 9, 1971

Everybody is storming the doors of the White House endeavoring to find out just what is going on in Indochina, what exactly are we up to. It is significant that there are no reports of newsmen besieging President Thieu in Saigon for answers to these questions. And why not? What is Vietnamization, anyway?

Fifteen months ago, back from a trip to that area, I wrote that Vietnamization will not work unless the term embraces the devolution of political as well as military authority to the government of South Vietnam. The reasoning behind that analysis is as simple as that nobody in the world would pay any attention to South Vietnamese troops slipping over Laotian or Cambodian boundaries, except that that area of the world is predesignated as a great theater of big-power confrontations. As long as China and the Soviet Union are provisioning one side, and the United States is provisioning the other side, any action that appears to tilt the situation towards escalation constitutes big news. As we all know, headlines not only reflect major events, they cause major events: and many great intransigencies have directly resulted from the news' provocation of a major power.

What if there were no headlines? That, really, is the direction towards which we must move. Pre-Nixon, the situation was as follows: the Russians and the Chinese arm the North Vietnamese who reach outside their own borders to wage guerrilla war against South Vietnam, and, less directly, against Laos: while dominating the foreign policy of Cambodia. The United States provisions the South Vietnamese and sends a half-million Americans to help with the fighting. But—a very important but—the United States forbids the use of any troops, whether South Vietnamese or American, to be used outside South Vietnam's borders. No amphibious landings in North Vietnam, no expeditionary force to sever the Ho Chi Minh trail, no Dieppe raid on Sihanoukville. The war goes on and on and on.

Enter Nixon, and the concept of Vietnamization, by which little by little the Vietnamese will replace American soldiers. Then the Cambodian venture, using native and American troops, followed by Mr. Nixon's promise—fortified by Congressional resolution—that U.S. troops will not again venture outside South Vietnam.

Now all of this is easy enough to understand, except that the entire world continues to believe that the White House is running the entire war, and is responsible for every decision being made in the war. That may be true, though one doubts it. The President and military staff of the Republic of South Vietnam are not children, and they have been known in the past to resist pressure from the United States. The question is the extent to which the White House is cooperating with a true Vietnamization of the war. At this point, it should be President Thieu answering the questions of the reporters. The position of the United States government ought to be that we are continuing to help supply the government of South Vietnam, whose purposes are defensive; even as the Russians are supplying the armies of North Vietnam, whose purposes are aggressive. But that it is being left strictly up to the South Vietnamese military how to conduct the war.

As we begin to persuade the world that we are disengaging from the tactics and strategy of the South Vietnamese military, we slip quietly out of the headlines, for the simple reason that foreign troops drawn osmotically into Laos in defense of their own country make a very small headline if they are South Vietnamese, and a very large headline only if they are American, or if they are being directed by Americans. Sure, Russia and China will continue to rant about the forces of imperialism, even as they step up their aid to the North Vietnamese imperialists: but it would clearly mean the localization of the war, because the world community would not doubt that the South Vietnamese were engaged in doing the militarily obvious thing in the pursuit of their own security. But the entire show is given away when the White House and the Pentagon behave as though it were quite natural that the reporters should expect to get the news from Washington.

February 13, 1971

— *Lam Son 719*

The news is that the military operation against Laos, which was originally called Dewey Canyon II, is now called Lam Son 719, and the symbolic meaning of that change in terminology is crucially important. It suggests what should all along have been suggested, namely that the operation is a South Vietnamese operation, not an American operation. That it would not be feasible except for the logistical and air support of the United States means simply that we have a veto power over extensive South Vietnamese military activity, even as the Soviet Union has a veto power over extensive North Vietnamese military activity. So what?

But now consider, in the light of this move towards a convincing Vietnamization, how strange, indeed how inexplicable, some of the reactions that have come in. Georges Pompidou, for instance, is quoted as saying, "I deplore the events in Laos and I condemn them, and with me, so does France." By Mr. Pompidou's reasoning, French forces struggling to liberate the homeland in 1944 and 1945 should have stopped at the borders of Belgium and Germany, rather than press forward to victory. It is altogether unclear why it was correct for France to fight her enemy, Nazi Germany, in Africa, Italy, the Lowlands, and indeed into Germany itself, but wrong for South Vietnam to move into

Laos to defend itself against the use of that nation as a corridor for hostile enemy troops.

Mr. Pompidou went on to say, "There can be no military solution. The solution can only be political, thus negotiated." When politicians speak that way, one has the feeling that their descent into cant suggests that not even they take seriously what they say.

A stone's throw from the presidential palace, in Paris, negotiators are beginning the third year's effort to find a political solution to the chaos in Indochina. Suppose the North Vietnamese were to take another year? Or another two years? Or another ten years? What are South Vietnamese supposed to do in the meantime? Visit Gay Paree?

Political solutions, more often than not, are reconciliations based on military realities. The military reality in Indochina is that the political solutions to which the North Vietnamese agreed in 1962 respecting Laos have been utterly ignored. The reason why has not been so much the military weakness of Laos and South Vietnam, as the restrictions placed upon Laos and South Vietnam by the United States Government. It is as though we had said in 1944 that we would help the exile government of General Charles de Gaulle to liberate France, but that Nazi forces surrounding France must not be touched.

The intransigence of the negotiators in Paris is a direct result of their belief that the military situation in Indochina argues a strategic usefulness of obduracy. The South Vietnamese desire a political solution too. They are less adamant in such matters than leaders of all-Western struggles. The men Mr. Pompidou grew up admiring, in whose war he fought gallantly, were demanding things like unconditional surrender. The South Vietnamese, with considerable restraint, have not said that they aim once and for all to remove from Hanoi the militant imperialists who have soaked Indochina in blood during the past ten years. They merely ask that the United States grant them, and that the community of nations applaud their use of, the fundamental military mobility consistent with international law to deprive the enemy of the use of a neighboring state for the purpose of mounting continued aggression against the independence of South Vietnam.

The absence of any reaction that can be compared to that against the Cambodian operation is heartening, and precisely it is explained by our understanding that South Vietnam should not be expected to inherit *our* political incumbrances which, because we are a great power, attach to any operation, the apocalyptic overhead of potential great-power collisions. So that Operation Lam Son 719 it is, and must hereinafter be thought of as being.

The news should come from Saigon, not Washington; to the extent possible, Saigon should begin to use mercenaries— Sons of the Flying Tigers— in order to diminish the formal participation of United States armed forces. And those who desire the long-sought-for political solution should cheer the news that, finally, military action is proceeding of the kind that precipitates political solutions. This is going to be a long one, but the moves are exactly in the right direction.

The Fear of China

March 2, 1971

It is hard to understand the implied psychology of the headlines. THIEU HINTS AT INVASION OF NORTH VIETNAM is a *scare* headline. The words, and indeed the ensuing text, are arranged in such fashion as to suggest to the reader that a clearly undesirable development may well take place. An examination of the psychology behind that assumption tells us what is wrong with the Vietnam operation.

Contrast such headlines as appeared in other historical circumstances. CHURCHILL VOWS TO PURSUE NAZI AGGRESSOR INTO GERMANY. Or, ALLIES ESTABLISH BEACHHEAD IN ANZIO. There was universal cheering, not only because the headlines suggested that the initiative had moved to our own side, but because the prospects of peace were accordingly advanced.

The ambivalence in the existing situation is for two reasons. The first, though not the foremost, is the long-since-identified professional pride that has been invested in the dogma of South Vietnamese military incompetence. If the government of President Thieu were to succeed in taking the war into North Vietnam and requiring the enemy to negotiate a peace, many political and journalistic reputations would be severely wounded; and if vanity can cause wars, as everybody agrees is the case, why shouldn't we agree that vanity can be the cause of prolonging wars?

But for the majority, the ambivalence has to do with Fear. Fear of the giant, Red China. Concerning this fear, two observations.

1) It has been a widely used argument by American doves that NVN's independence of Red China is a real independence. Obviously it is at the sufferance of Red China, even as the independence of Albania is at the sufferance of Russia: but it is independent just the same. By that one means that the war policies of the North Vietnamese are determined by the North Vietnamese, not by Peking.

Now this independence is partly the result of Ho Chi Minh's historical afflatus, and partly the result of the heavy participation of the Soviet Union in the aggressive efforts of the North Vietnamese. To the extent that the latter is the cause of it, there is bound to be, and indeed we know that there is, tension of a certain sort between China and NVN, which flows naturally out of the tension between the Soviet Union and Red China.

Provided that the United States troops were not themselves engaged in a military action against North Vietnam, what is it that would cause China to enter the war? Mrs. Nguyen Thi Binh, the chief Viet Cong delegate to the peace talks, says that China is after all a "paternal and a socialist neighbor," and implies that that itself would be sufficient to bring China into the fray. To which the objection is: why hasn't it been sufficient to bring China in before now?

After all, NVN's position is that there is only one Vietnam, that the southern part of it has been imperialized by American troops. So why did not China come in during 1965? And why have not Chinese troops moved south directly against what is left of the free government of Laos? Since nothing would be more preposterous than to suppose that the South Vietnamese were entering North Vietnam in preparation for an assault on China, what is the reason for supposing that China would react now, if she did not react to the landing of American troops in South Vietnam in 1965?

And then 2) suppose that the analysis is incorrect? Suppose that China does then move? How is South Vietnam any the worse off? If South Vietnam's struggle for independence is foredoomed by great-power considerations, the sooner South Vietnam finds that out the better. If Chinese soldiers are needed to protect

North Vietnam against retaliation from those upon whom she is aggressing, let that fact stand out. If the South Vietnamese are supposed to endure endless aggression . . . because they are forbidden to move against the source of that aggression . . . because China might enter the war: why not find out? How will they be worse off? Mr. Nixon, it seems to me, perfectly captured the realities of the situation when he said in answer to a question on February 17, "I would not speculate on what South Vietnam may do in defense of its national security. South Vietnam will have to make decisions with regard to its ability to defend itself."

Calley

April 6, 1971

The reaction to the conviction of Calley has greatly surprised everyone, and is directly responsible for the President's sudden intervention, springing Calley from the stockade pending the final disposition of the case by military review boards, the Supreme Court of which is the Commander-in-Chief himself. It appears that the mail is altogether lopsided, 100-to-1 in favor of Calley, and that is a vexing datum, inasmuch as Americans do not usually rally to the cause of someone who, it has been determined, aimed a rifle at old ladies and little children, and killed them.

A few observations: 1) The American people are very well aware that a diligent effort is being made to discredit the military. They sense, moreover, that the effort springs from other than mere technical dissatisfaction with the performance of the military. It is one thing to say that General Westmoreland is incompetent because he assured us over and over again that the Vietnam war was on the verge of being won, dozens of thousands of casualties ago. It is another to scoff at the military in what amounts to generic terms, and that is the kind of criticism that is being leveled.

It is the fruit of a cultural assault, of which Dr. Strangelove was a historical landmark, and CBS's *The Selling of the Pentagon* a recent expression. In between is the running contumely, the closing down of ROTC chapters in the fashionable colleges, the decline in re-enlistment, the chaos surrounding the draft laws.

All of this is not merely the derogation of an American institution: it is the derogation of the institution that is supposed to defend the republic against foreign enemies. So that without exactly realizing why, many Americans view the conviction of Lieutenant Calley as an elaboration of the attack on the military. And they view the attack on the military as a vote of no confidence in the society the military is supposed to defend.

2) It is, moreover, widely suspected that Calley is a "scapegoat." The word is being used loosely: too loosely. Properly used, a scapegoat is an innocent who is singled out to receive the punishment that should properly be visited elsewhere. Calley's situation is not such. In the first place, there is apparently no doubt that he did what he was accused of doing, never mind for a moment whether the circumstances were extenuating: he did kill twenty-two people whom he had no reason to kill. But the courts-martial are not over: his immediate superior is about to be tried, and so is the immediate superior of his superior. Whether it will reach on above the brigade level one cannot at this point be certain, but already, there is hardly evidence that the case is being ended with Calley as scapegoat.

3) To the extent that the public is outraged that Calley should be singled out for court-martial, one needs to urge reflection. It is true that only one man out of perhaps five hundred is stopped on the highway for speeding. It is the luck of the draw, and one feels a twinge of bitterness when it happens to oneself, knowing of all the others who got away, and are even now speeding along happily above the speed limit.

But are we really prepared to believe that what Calley did in South Vietnam was routine? I do not doubt that there are other living and unnoticed American soldiers who have taken innocent lives illegally. But surely one should await the evidence, before presuming that the American military has become so calloused and cruel and irresponsible as to make My Lai massacres altogether workaday phenomena?

The point about My Lai surely is that it is an aberration— an atrocity. Not that it is the victimization of only a single man who happened to be caught speeding. Those Americans who protest the Calley verdict thus indiscriminately are unwittingly allied with others who are desirous to believe that Calley is a typical product of the American womb.

4) As regards the question of ultimate responsibility, the public is entitled to be confused. We hanged Admiral Yamashita after the Second World War, and if we applied rigorously the logic of that execution, we would have a case for hanging General Westmoreland. That would be preposterous and cruel. So that we learn, gradually, what some people knew and warned against in 1945: victors' justice.

We are overdue for shame in our complicity in the Nurem-berg-Tokyo trials, the chaotic legal and moral implications of which were spotted by Senator Robert Taft, and celebrated by John F. Kennedy in *Profiles in Courage.* But whatever we do to amend these doctrines, it is inconceivable that we should come up with new rules of war that permit to go unpunished such an act as Lieutenant Calley was found guilty of, and I for one am proud of a country that makes such activity punishable by imprisonment or death.

The Shifting Positions of Arthur Schlesinger, Jr.

May 11, 1971

Every ten years or so, I meet with Professor Arthur Schlesinger, Jr., in public debate, an experience I always find instructive, which is to say nothing of what Mr. Schlesinger must find it. This time around hostilities began early, when Mr. Schlesinger, making his way aft to the economy section of the New York-Boston flight, paused briefly to tease me for sitting, typewriter on my lap, in the first-class section. I retaliated, after we were under way, by asking the stewardess to deliver a package into which I had rolled a cigar, with the notation: "Arthur: This is my con-tribution to your last meal." After we landed at Boston, Professor Schlesinger told me and our hosts that now he knew what was wrong with conservatives, they smoke such lousy cigars. I replied that we were given no choice by those who bungled the Bay of Pigs.

I confronted Mr. Schlesinger, during the debate, with the resolution of the Americans for Democratic Action, which called for the impeachment of Richard Nixon. He told the crowd he knew nothing about the resolution, although he did not contest that he continues to serve as vice chairman of the ADA: and managed to make it all sound as though I had made up the resolution. Tricky Arthur. Returning to the reception hall after the debate, the professor's captivating elderly mother turned to him and said, "Arthur, really, I do not believe that it is sensible to try to impeach President Nixon. To begin with, you would have to get all the facts absolutely straight. . . ." "But Mother," Arthur said impatiently, "I had nothing to do with it!" "Even so," said Mrs. Schlesinger, the widow of the famous historian, lest her point be lost, "it really isn't a good idea, Arthur." I took pleasure, on bidding Mrs. Schlesinger good night, in telling her that I knew her son Tom, and that if you threw him in, you came out with an acceptable average among her two sons.

Mr. Schlesinger spent, as I expected, much time in the fashionable denunciation of the Vietnam war. In anticipation of which I had poked around and culled a few statements concerning that war, which as an amateur historian I make available. It is, for instance, surely relevant to note, the week after the prestigious ADA decides to impeach Richard Nixon, the plank of the Democratic Party platform on the subject of Vietnam. The Democratic candidate, Mr. Humphrey, ran on a Vietnam plank, approved by the delegates in Chicago in the summer of 1968, that said:

"Our most urgent task is to end the war in Vietnam by an honorable and lasting settlement which respects the rights of all the people of Vietnam. . . . We reject as unacceptable a unilateral withdrawal of our forces which would allow that aggression and subversion to succeed." It is perfectly honorable to change one's mind. But it is surely something less than that to go about asking to impeach a Republican President because he seeks to implement the plank of the Democratic platform of two and a half years ago.

There are those who will say that the Democratic plank at Chicago was substantially different from true Democratic sentiment at Chicago, because Mayor Daley ran the show. That is of course a hobgoblinization of what happened in Chicago: after all, Hubert Humphrey is grown up, and if he had objected to the formulation, he was free to express his differences. But what was being said during that general period about Vietnam by the opposition: by Arthur Schlesinger, for instance?

In 1967 his views were solicited for a book of opinions on the Vietnam war. He wrote: "It seems to me meaningless to ask whether one is 'for' or 'against' the American intervention in Vietnam. That intervention, for better or for worse, is a fact. The real question today is whether one is 'for' the immediate termination of that intervention or 'for' its continuation until a negotiated settlement can be achieved. On this question, I am for a negotiated settlement."

And wait, there is more: "Obviously the Vietcong and Hanoi will not negotiate so long as they think they are going to win. Since a military stalemate is the self-evident and indispensable precondition to negotiation, the continued presence of American troops is plainly necessary."

Does that make Arthur Schlesinger, vice chairman of an organization that wants to impeach Richard Nixon for believing exactly the same thing that Arthur Schlesinger was preaching two or three years ago, a hawk? An ex-hawk? A repentant hawk? An incomplete ex-hawk? Hear what Mr. Schlesinger went on to say, concerning Laos. . . .

I am opposed to unilateral withdrawal, Mr. Schlesinger wrote, for several reasons, among them: "the effect it would have in neighboring countries, especially on the gallant struggle of the Laotian neutralists under Prince Souvanna Phouma to maintain their independence. Also I find something distasteful about those sitting in ease in Europe and America who would righteously hand over a country to a tough Communist crew on the ground, evidently, that, though they wouldn't much like Communism for themselves, it will be just great for the Vietnamese."

Yes indeed, Mr. Schlesinger was pretty emphatic on these points those days. Later in 1967 he wrote, "No serious American . . . has proposed unilateral withdrawal." Question: Is Senator McGovern a serious American? He proposes exactly that. Are Mr. Schlesinger's colleagues in the ADA who want to impeach Nixon serious Americans? Indeed (Mrs. Schlesinger: Please leave the room, dear), is Arthur a serious American?

The Pentagon Papers

June 29, 1971

Concerning the unfolding drama of the Pentagon Papers, a few observations:

1. The general naïveté is distressing. Conservatives, who distrust government and rail against the aggrandizement of it, precisely do so because they know how government tends to operate, how government saps social energy, and distorts ethical norms. But to expect that government will operate otherwise than it does is quite simply unrealistic. One can simultaneously disapprove in the abstract of a particular practice, while recognizing that the practice is essential to the performance of a particular duty. For instance lying.

General Eisenhower, who by contrast with his successors was our Albert the Good, quite simply "lied" when asked if the airplane that had been brought down over Soviet Russia was an American spy plane. A day or so later, when it was obvious that the lie would not be digested, President Eisenhower's assistants morosely admitted to the truth, and whiff! there went the Spirit of Camp David which had been bottled only a few months before.

So it goes with the Pentagon Papers. The principal complaints have to do with government dissimulation. Governments must dissimulate. The wag who defined a diplomat as someone sent abroad to lie for his country was not a caricaturist, but a candid photographer. Everybody knows that totalitarian governments lie to the people. Not everybody knows that democratic governments lie to the people. Only we do not call it "lying" — for a very good reason. We feel, in our pores, the ethical difference between, let us say, a Khrushchev who insists that he desires democracy for Hungary, which is why he sent the tanks to Budapest; and an Eisenhower, who said he knew nothing of spy planes over Russia, when what he wished to do was to protect government secrets the accumulation of which was designed not to give the United States such power as is necessary to crush Freedom Fighters in Budapest and in other capitals of the world, but to give the United States such power as is necessary to restrain Russian tanks from rolling over Freedom Fighters in other capitals of the world.

2. The Pentagon Papers reveal that there was considerable

pessimism in official Washington during 1964, which pessimism Lyndon Johnson and the State Department suppressed the expression of. Now I ask you, is that to pass as A Revelation? If so, then we should have up for perjury the football coach of South Indiana State who tells his players during the half that he KNOWS that in the second half they are destined to mow down Notre Dame.

It is sometimes the business of government to reveal how bad is the situation. But not often. That is why, on a famous occasion, Franklin Delano Roosevelt said that the only thing we had to fear was fear itself. That was an epigrammatic way of saying that he, Roosevelt, would take a cultivatedly optimistic line, because he was temperamentally optimistic. When he said those words, about the American economy, said economy looked a great deal worse than even the military situation in Saigon.

3. The pity of it is that people are not going to read the Pentagon Papers— well, to begin with, they're not going to read them at all. Second, they are not likely to understand them in a worldly way. Unlikely, for instance, to know that these papers, so solemnly midwifed, are nothing more than memoranda expressing attitudes, contingency plans, encyclopedic lists of alternative approaches to particular problems, routine exercises in the necessary dissimulations of government. What they may breed, however, is such a demoralization as will translate itself into a cynical suspicion of the essential vitality of democratic mechanisms. That is why we must concentrate, concentrate hard, on what the papers actually reveal, and ask why it is that, already, we go about so shamefaced.

The New York Times Papers

July 17, 1971

The quotations, most of them, are strewn about, and diligent researchers, knowing that they are there to be found, could round them up. To spare them the trouble, here they are, in a size suitable for framing:

"Fortunately, the new Vietnamese rulers are dedicated anti-

Communists who reject any idea of neutralism and pledge themselves to stand with the free world. . . . If the new regime succeeds in identifying itself with the aspirations of the people, it will have taken a long step toward repulsing further Communist inroads throughout Southeast Asia."— Editorial, "Opportunity in Vietnam," New York *Times,* November 3, 1963.

"The goal of American policy in Indochina, as we have repeatedly declared, must be the creation of a situation in which those agreements [Geneva, 1954 and 1962] can be truly effectuated. This implies an end to the subversion supported by North Vietnam and Communist China in Laos and South Vietnam.

"The chief obstacle to such a settlement at the moment is undoubtedly the belief of Peking and Hanoi that they can win control of the entire area by continuing their present tactics. The use of additional American military and economic resources to disabuse Mao Tse-tung and Ho Chi Minh of such illusions is entirely justified."— Editorial, "War Against China?" New York *Times,* June 21, 1964.

"The United States joined battle with the Vietcong guerrillas in the rice paddies of South Vietnam two and a half years ago for two simple but impelling reasons:

"1. The United States is the only Western power capable of meeting the Chinese Communist challenge for hegemony in Asia.

"2. The United States wants to demonstrate to the rest of the world that this country has both the desire and the ability to defeat the Communist strategy for expansion— a formula composed of guerrilla military tactics and political and psychological action that Peking refers to as the 'war of national liberation.' . . .

"The fall of Southeast Asia to China or its denial to the West over the next decade, because of the repercussions from an American defeat in Vietnam, would amount to a strategic disaster of the first magnitude."— Neil Sheehan, New York *Times,* August 16, 1964.

"Washington . . . is not morally free, for example, to carry the air war into the populous areas of North Vietnam, where the really important strategic targets are located. Nor is it morally free to abandon the people who have committed themselves to the battle in South Vietnam and who will be at the mercy of the Vietcong if we pull out.

"Even more important, it is not free to submit to the triumph of the Communist guerrilla techniques without making them pay dearly in the process, for if they succeed in Vietnam, nobody dare assume in Washington that the same techniques will not be applied in all the Communist rimlands from Korea to Iran." — James Reston, New York *Times,* April 25, 1965.

"The *Times,* of course, later changed its mind as it is entitled to do, but its story of how we got into Vietnam is misleading without mentioning the standfast mood of the nation in that period— a mood to which the New York *Times* contributed more than its share." — Howard K. Smith, *ABC Evening News,* June 23, 1971.

"The editorial was entitled 'Breach of Security,' and it denounced an article 'purporting to tell what went on in the executive committee of the National Security Council. . . . The secrecy of one of the highest organs of the United States has been seriously breached. What kind of advice can the President expect to get under such circumstances? . . . How can anyone be expected to advance positions that may be politically unpopular or unprofitable? Does no one in Washington recall the McCarthy era and the McCarthy technique? . . . The various positions of the members of the NSC taken during deliberation must remain secret. . . . The integrity of the National Security Council, and of the advice received by the President, is at stake.'

"The article that inspired the New York *Times* to this burst of righteous indignation was a *Saturday Evening Post* piece on the Cuban missile crisis by Charles Bartlett and this writer. . . . It contained no word from any NSC paper, or from any other secret document." — Stewart Alsop, *Newsweek,* June 28, 1971.

Thieu and Democracy

September 16, 1971

The concern of our leaders for the state of South Vietnamese democracy shows that the old Wilsonian virus continues to run in our veins. It is partly the fault of Lyndon Johnson and (less so) Richard Nixon. Mr. Johnson was forever talking about how it was America's goal to secure the right of the South Vietnamese to have a government of their choice, and there are echoes of the same kind of thing in the Presidential rhetoric of his successor. In point of fact, Mr. Nixon was telling people long before he became President that the United States had no business in South Vietnam except insofar as our presence there related to American security, and it is of precious little bearing on American security whether President Thieu runs against one or a dozen opponents.

It was a dozen candidates (by the way) that Thieu ran against the last time around, and of course the critics were dissatisfied with that performance. They kept saying that he was a minority president, which is true: so was Abraham Lincoln and so, for that matter, is Richard Nixon. If you have enough contenders, the chances are that the winner will come in with a plurality instead of a majority. But then the White House sent over some observers from the American academy, who came back and reported that the election had been run fairly, in the sense that the votes had been fairly counted. The exclusion of candidates who were judged to be unqualified in a time of civil war because they failed to declare their solidarity against the enemy was not held to be a democratic travesty. Winston Churchill, in England's hour of crisis, would not have shared an election with a Quisling. In fact, Mr. Churchill's government simply did away with national elections during the War.

It is extraordinarily disappointing to admirers of Senator Henry Jackson that he should at this point come forward to say that if he is not satisfied that President Thieu is re-elected as the result of an authentic democratic exercise, he will "rethink" his support of our venture in Vietnam. There may be reasons enough to rethink our venture in Vietnam, but democratic scruple is hardly one of them. The South Vietnamese electoral tangle is mystifying to men of occidental orientation, but we ought to make an effort to understand. We are dealing with a country whose total experience with democracy is younger than that of an American eighteen-year-old. We are talking about a country ravaged by disorder, tumult, inflation, terror.

The question that Senator Jackson should be asking himself is: What outcome would least likely result in the undoing of the agonizing effort of the past four years? That is the only moral— and intelligent— question to ask. If the re-election of Thieu is the likeliest event to bring stability and insure the independence of South Vietnam, that is the goal we should desire above the others. The others, it now appears, are disruptive campaigns in which personal ambitions enhance the enemy's subversive leverage. Big Minh, a popular figure who withdrew from the race, eight years ago conducted the assassination of the incumbent President, a development we now accept as an overture to the chaos that precipitated American involvement. Marshall Ky, for all his talk about patriotism and duty to the country, would rather embarrass South Vietnam and jeopardize its chances of surviving, than participate ignominiously in the kind of political charade which— just to give an example— is routine in the enlightened state of Mexico, every five years.

Professor Harry Jaffa wrote hauntingly a few years ago, in an essay on the historical meaning of civil liberties, that "No American statesman ever violated the ordinary maxims of civil liberties more than did Abraham Lincoln, and few seem to have been more careful of them than Jefferson Davis. Yet the cause for the sake of which the one slighted these maxims was human freedom, while the other, claiming to defend the forms of constitutional government, found in those forms a ground for defending and preserving human slavery."

It is such an analysis as this that we need to meditate. Is the prospect under a re-elected Thieu, running without formal opposition, better than the prospect of a Thieu government undermined by an American government which is overwhelmed by the kind of scrupulosity identified centuries ago by theologians as a moral excess that lapses into sinfulness?

One notes sadly that the U.N. is getting into the act. The commentary in the current issue of a journal of opinion is apt: "Let's face it. There's something unsatisfactory about an election in which there is only one candidate, and so we hope that U

Thant will instantly urge fair and unrigged elections in Albania, Algeria, Argentina, Bolivia, Brazil, Bulgaria, Burma, Byelorussia, Congo (Brazzaville), Congo (Kinshasa), Cuba, Czechoslovakia, Ethiopia, Greece, Guinea, Haiti, Hungary, Indonesia, Iraq, Jordan, Kenya, Kuwait, Libya, Malawi, Mongolia, Morocco, Nepal, Nigeria, Pakistan, Peru, Poland, Portugal, Rumania, Rwanda, Saudi Arabia, South Yemen, Spain, Sudan, Syria, Thailand, Tunisia, Ukraine SSR, USSR, United Arab Republic, Tanzania, Yemen, Yugoslavia and Qatar. Don't forget Qatar, U."

The Extraordinary Patience of Mr. Nixon

May 29, 1971

It is hard to describe the reaction to the dramatic announcement of Mr. Nixon with respect to the SALT talks. The reason why is that what the President said is not easy to understand. Indeed an understanding of the technical complexity of the SALT negotiations is, quite simply, beyond the layman's powers, and for that matter beyond the powers even of some scientists. That's the kind of thing that happens when variables and coefficients of variables come into play. It is unlikely that you can find even a skilled layman who can give you immediately the answer, say, to such a question as: What if the United States offered to limit the ABM defenses around its MIRV-equipped Minutemen? Indeed if such a proposal were made at Vienna, Russian negotiators would go back to their hotel and think about it. As much time is given to very special chess moves. This is a very special chess game.

A few observations: 1) It has been the assumption of American Conservatives that as long as Richard Nixon is President, American security is something we do not need to worry about. Granted the details are complicated, and beyond the reach of the common understanding; still— Richard Nixon will simply not let us down. Why? Because Mr. Nixon, whatever you say about him as a practical politician, is undeniably a patriot. And a patriot simply would not preside over the liquidation of America's nuclear deterrent, America's nuclear deterrent being generally understood as something in the absence of which America is— nothing.

2) President Nixon's strange silence, during his Presidency, on the general subject of strategic deterrents suggests (to his friends) one of two things. Either that he has an ace up his sleeve— a new weapon, or a concept of a new weapon which could be put on the drawing boards and got into action in plenty of time before the Soviet Union becomes too imperious. A second possibility is that Mr. Nixon is enjoying the waters of Vienna because he figures that the Soviet Union has got to come forward with disarmament proposals that are agreeable to us, the economic strain of its own armament effort approaching intolerability.

3) Although one cannot rule out either of the two points as underlying the public nonchalance of the Administration, still there is anxiety. And that anxiety, at this moment latent, is likely to be aroused in the weeks and months ahead. It is to deal lightly with it to suggest that that anxiety could determine such questions as Mr. Nixon's re-election. That anxiety festers because,

4) It is increasingly apparent to the American body politic that the conjunction of the great political, moral and philosophical pressures of the past half dozen years comes down on the White House in such a way as to encourage the superstition of detente. We are nowadays behaving vis-à-vis our brothers on the other side of the Iron Curtain as if they were altogether amiable political adversaries. I doubt, to give a silly example, whether a reform Democrat in New York City could be persuaded to utter words against the Kremlin that could compare in sharpness with the routine denunciations of, say, Mayor Daley of Chicago.

Now the significance of this datum is that Mr. Nixon, as a political centrist, is inevitably influenced by the intellectuals' emphasis upon negotiation, disarmament, detente, the disdain of nuclear superiority and of defensive missiles. He has gone further than a Richard Nixon unburdened by such pressures would have gone— sitting around, waiting for evidence of the Soviet Union's bona fides, fiddling, to use the phrase, while Rome burns. Another way of putting it is: the preternatural patience Mr. Nixon has shown in his dealings with the Soviet negotiators is inconceivable in the absence of the national disposition to: do anything, except face the facts of life.

The facts of life are that Mr. Nixon is sitting in the White House while the Soviet Union is accumulating a first-strike capability.

If he has an ace up his sleeve, the time to show it is soon. If it isn't there, he might lose re-election, which is a minor consideration up against what he, his children, his children's children stand to lose.

The Expulsion of Taiwan

An Address to the China Conference

October 29, 1971

I

We meet in circumstances most of us regard as bitterly sad. We all became accustomed to the reality of Mainland China. We grew, even, to acknowledge that the men who won the revolution in China after the Second World War embarked on a revolutionary course which was totalist in its ambitions: to remake man, no less. The usual practices by which accountants measure the cost of social enterprises seemed somehow inadequate. The learned debate among the necrologists is over the question whether ten or fifteen or fifty million human beings have been executed in the course of giving flesh to the thoughts of Mao Tse-tung. The ghastliness of it all was on such a scale as to cause us to become almost clinical in our consideration of it, like the harried doctor who threads his way insouciantly through the corpses that line the streets of a city in the final throes of a deadly plague. We felt we could maintain our balance only by indulging a little counterrevolutionary vision of our own, namely that the government of Chiang Kai-shek would recover the Mainland: even as, on coming across the story of Anne Frank, the occasional reader experienced that sense of personal indignation which brings him to feel that by rushing personally to her aid, he might, somehow, save the legions destined to die in the extermination centers.

Well, Chiang did not recover the Mainland, the government of Mao Tse-tung did not fall, and the West didn't have the stomach to make it fall; and soon it became the fashion to allege that we were ignoring the largest country in the world by our failure to extend to it diplomatic recognition. Such in fact are the paradoxes of diplomacy, that we more conspicuously notice a nation by declining to recognize its government, than by recognizing it: we are more acutely conscious of Cuba, which we do not recognize, than of Guatemala, which we do. Still, along the way the assumption was stimulated that the government of Mainland China was co-equal with the people of China, a point our formal diplomacy tends gravitationally to accept, causing us sometimes to move from professions of friendship for the Chinese people, on over to professions of friendship for the Chinese government, without the ceremonial pause that, ideally, would acknowledge the hypocrisies to which international protocol so often drives us.

Mr. Nixon's decision to accelerate the trend towards recognition of the revolutionary government was no doubt motivated by his conviction that the people of China cannot, A.D. 1971, reasonably hope to overthrow their oppressors. Or— worse— that the New China Man is the successful product of twenty years of Mao; that he has been successfully transformed; that, like the citizens of the Soviet Union who dumbly cheered Stalin, descendants of those citizens who implored Ivan the Terrible to resume his throne: that they are too far removed from hope to know even how hope is defined. It is here and there argued that Mr. Nixon's decision to go to Peking did not in fact midwife the expulsion of the representatives of the one government, and the admission of the representatives of the other government. And indeed it is true that before Mr. Nixon's announcement, there had been erosion. Still, if it wasn't cause-and-effect, history will assign it that relationship; and symbols being so often more memorable than facts, let us accept the symbols: that the new reality is that we accepted the government of Mao Tse-tung as dominant over Mainland China, and the United Nations did too, extending the logic to incorporate Taiwan: who says A, must say B. Even so, one supposes, we would eventually have accepted the government of Pétain and Laval as dominant over France, if it had lasted there twenty years.

But the experience of this week leaves us with the burden of meditating on one or two things. The first is the United Nations. The second is our attitude towards it. The third is our relationship with the deposed government.

II

The general elation over at the United Nations was most graphically expressed when after the vote defeating the United States on the important procedural point, the delegate of Tanzania stepped forward to the podium and danced a jig. The elation had less to do with the substantive point: it doesn't really matter that much to the delegate of Tanzania, who in any case has to share the General Assembly with one hundred and thirty other nations, whether one of those one hundred and thirty is or isn't Formosa. The jig expressed that special delight one feels on beating a giant. We, of course, are the giant in the situation, and although there was a giant and a few middleweights lined up against us, still it was the first time that the United States, premier economic and until very recently premier military figure in the world, went down to inglorious defeat: on a resolution sponsored by Albania, a little, reclusive country composed primarily of rocks and serfs, with here and there a slavemaster, whose principal export is Maoism. And, of course, the backdrop was perfect: the skyline of New York, metropolitan hearth of the giant who was felled by a coalition led by Albania, which tallied the vote of Byelorussia as the equal of France's and England's, and weighed the principles of the United Nations Charter, well, not at all.

The trouble with fantasies is that they do not endure, not in the real world. Inevitably, when a collection of nations comes together to frustrate the will of a large, powerful, and independent nation, the frustration boomerangs. If membership in the United Nations is greatly worth having, it is because the United Nations has much to offer its members. Foremost— as projected by its architects— is power and prestige. The power of the United Nations depends very heavily on the extent to which its determinations are accepted as binding by those nations of the world which are themselves powerful. Insofar as the United Nations engages in activities that reveal its weaknesses (say, its failure to bring peace in India); or that reveal theoretical hypocrisy (for instance, its insistence on universality alongside its refusal to recognize Rhodesia); or its capricious politics (the expulsion of Taiwan); it diminishes that which made membership desirable in the first place. It is as if everyone wanted to go to Harvard because Harvard had so fine a reputation, and gradually Harvard begins admitting everyone who wants to go to Harvard.

What happens is that gradually Harvard loses the reputation that made it desirable in the first instance.

Actually, it has been quite a while since first it became apparent that the United Nations had no clothes. Its highwater mark was the Korean War, when we dressed up our soldiers as agents of the United Nations and went along with the act. But soon after that—very soon after that—we were confronting, in connection with events in Poland, in Hungary, in Tibet, on the Sino-Indian border: all over the world, the military and moral powerlessness of the UN: and shrewd international specialists, like Professor Hans Morgenthau, were warning that it is important to remember that "the United Nations is a procedure, not a policy." It was inevitable that the UN should become primarily an instrument of manipulative politics, through which to cause, among other things, embarrassment—the embarrassment in the most recent instance, of the United States. It makes a difference when *we* are singled out for humiliation. The UN's condemnation of Israel a few years ago made no difference at all to Israel, because Israel is profoundly convinced of the correctness of its policies. The condemnation of China as an aggressor made absolutely no difference to China because China, like Russia, like Herbert Marcuse, insists that such condemnations as are directed against its activity are expressions of bourgeois morality: indeed, they are likelier to collect condemnations, as proof of their effectiveness, than be embarrassed by them.

But this is not true of the United States of America. We care very deeply when we see done primarily in order to embarrass us, manifest injustices; committed by an international body of which we are a founder, serve as principal underwriter, and in which we are an active participant. We care enough to do something about it. We cannot refound the UN, removing the utopian gleam from the eyes of its architects. To alter substantially our subsidy is interpretable as an act of petulance which, for all that there is actuarial and spiritual justification for it, somehow makes us ill-at-ease. The answer is to revise the nature of our participation in the United Nations, which is as inevitable as the movement towards midnight in Cinderella's clock. They danced a jig on taking Moscow, in 1812, but, little by little, they discovered that there was nothing there.

III

Back in 1945, critically-situated Americans dreamed of an evolving world federation, the inevitable result of a nuclear politics. The form such a federation would take was never clear, but it was hoped that the United Nations organization would prove adaptable. Into its composition the architects injected strains of prudence and reality, as also strains of idealism and egalitarianism. Thus the Security Council would guard the essential interests of the essential powers. And the General Assembly would have authority in matters of great consequence, but mostly in areas in which it was given explicit scope by the Security Council— areas where the moral force of the international body needed harnessing in order to advance the stated objectives of the UN, which are the objectives of Eagle Scouts.

A few years after its inception we discovered, hard on the experience of prolonged Soviet intransigence, that the Security Council was all but immobilized by the veto. It was then that we moved (successfully) to give more authority to the General Assembly, which emerged in the decade of the fifties as the primary focus of attention. During the same decade, and in the next decade, membership in the General Assembly multiplied, with the end of colonialism in the non-Russian world. And a feeling of collegiality grew among the nations of the so-called Third World, which is happiest left loosely defined, though it is not inaccurate to say about them that they tend to exercise diligently the luxury of not having to share the burden of international stability. These nations dominate, numerically, the United Nations. And they move, in decisive blocs, to serve the interests of major powers on matters that, for reasons grave and trivial, suit, episodically, their fancy. They are grown accustomed to a moral-sociological rubric which is altogether infectious, causing for instance the American delegate, Mr. Francis Plimpton, to proclaim proudly a few years ago that colonialism was dead— to say so in a chamber in which thirteen nations metronomically do the bidding of a single state, the alternative being to lie down to receive its tanks and infantry; in a chamber in which the meaning of the word "racism" consolidates as— an unfriendly act by any white man against any nonwhite man; and democracy is something the absence of which is deplorable only in Spain, Portugal, Greece, Taiwan, and South Vietnam.

Even so, the United Nations has its uses, and the United States would be mistaken recklessly to withdraw from it. But in weighing our relations with it, we should bear it in mind that we are (and let us always be) a square country, which believes in the rules of the game. It has not occurred to us, since Adams defeated Jefferson in the election of 1796, to do other than accept the verdict of the voting majority. The General Assembly of the United Nations, as we have just now seen, has the raw power (in effect) to admit to membership the de facto governors of Mainland China, and to expel from membership the de facto governors of Taiwan. In virtue of our having participated in that vote we feel particularly uncomfortable because— somehow— we know that we will resist its sacramental corollary— discontinuing our own relations with Formosa. We acknowledge that the General Assembly has the right to act as it did, but we recognize also that in virtue of our active participation in a procedure that permitted the result we have seen, we have become involved in a process that has caused a great injustice, and one which is, moreover, intolerable in the light of our continuing strategic commitments.

I call on the President of the United States to instruct his ambassador to the United Nations to cease, beginning immediately, to vote in the General Assembly. To argue there, yes; to listen, yes; to plead; to explain; to cajole, threaten, conciliate, yes; to vote, never. Because to participate in the vote, given the American ethos, is psychologically to involve ourselves in the outcome of a vote and this we cannot— as the only major world power concerned with ethical considerations— agree to do. Just as our official position at this juncture towards Taiwan cannot be defined by the action of the General Assembly, so on future occasions— predictably— we shall have to make our own policies, removed from recommendations of the General Assembly which come to us with parliamentary conceit. We should, accordingly, try to free ourselves of the psychological shackles that imperceptibly inhibit us— for so long as we participate in that vote. Loose those shackles, and we can continue to participate in the affairs of the United Nations, having calmly described the nature of our relationship to it. If the United Nations wishes to expel from membership all nations that resist domination by those other nations the United Nations at any particular moment desires not to offend, why let it do so: but let it not understand itself as engaged in writing the moral law, or in making pronouncements which have presumptive weight in the chancelleries of the world: or, most particularly, in this chancellery. By a word, the President of the United States could effect the great reconciliation between the theoretical and the actual. If he does not give that word, he will have lost an opportunity for penetrating leadership.

We are a neat people, who desire an orderly relationship with the UN, whence the need for Presidential action. Lacking executive punctilio, we will nevertheless know, intuitively, how to proceed. Soon, very soon, the parliamentary decisions of the United Nations will affect the policies of the United States about as much as decisions of the National Student Association, in solemn body assembled, affect the American academy.

Meanwhile we must cherish Taiwan, which is the West Berlin of China. It was to that island that a tired, bedraggled, dispirited group of refugees, under the leadership of a man already old, but of flinty spirit, fled from a shipwrecked nation, and addressed themselves to the enterprise of bringing order and a measure of freedom to fifteen million people. We in America helped them. Nowhere was our help more productive. In twenty years, they contrived a standard of living second only, in Asia, to Japan's. They did this while nourishing the culture of their ancestors, adapting it, stressing those qualities in it of patience and fortitude, of stoicism and resignation, of emphasis on the spirit, which have given Taiwan that special presence which will survive Chiang Kai-shek.

That small country is abloom with promise. We are bound to it by a treaty which the gates of the United Nations shall not prevail against. It is a far cry from becoming the capital province of all of China. But it is the repository of the hopes and dreams of those Chinese in whose breast lingers the seed of resistance to the furies of Maoism: which is to say, in every Chinese, because it is given to man, without exception, to be attracted to that which distinguishes him from other species: to love and compassion, to idealism, to freedom and dignity.

And so, while Mainland China struggles in its endless ordeal against human nature, the little island of Taiwan must grow, and prosper; making its way towards that estate which the Charter of the United Nations describes, in those resonant phrases which appear today so hollow and mean, like the language of the Constitution of the Soviet Union, which charter once presented itself to a credulous world as embodying the human condition we seek to achieve. The people of Taiwan may feel lonely today, and isolated. But they should know that they are the more conspicuous for their loneliness and their isolation, and that in the years and decades to come, their separated brothers on the Mainland will look all the more wistfully to Taiwan's government in consideration of what it has done for its people, and permitted to its people; and all the more puzzlingly to that august derelict in New York City that took pleasure— so momentary, so obscene— on that gray autumn day in 1971, from encouraging the slavemasters, and humiliating the little band of brave and faithful men who for twenty years, as members in good standing of the United Nations, sustained the vision of a better life for the people of China; and who now, rejected by the United Nations, will continue to sustain that vision— because they are alone— all the more proudly, all the more hopefully, all the more grandly.

VI. Elsewhere

A. Latin America

Allende Wins

September 19, 1970

Concerning the situation in Chile, a few observations:

1) It is not true in the formal sense that for the first time in history a nation has voted itself into communism. In order to do that, it requires that a majority of the people should vote for the Communist candidate. Far from getting a majority, Dr. Allende received this time around an even smaller percentage of the votes than he received in 1964, about what Barry Goldwater got in 1964. To conclude that because the Chilean Congress is likely to respect precedent by voting in as president the man who won the plurality of the votes, therefore it follows that a free nation will have voted itself into communism, is disjointed. The proper way to put it is that democratic mechanisms abound which make it possible for someone who has won even a small minority of the vote, to take power.

2) Although it is certainly true that the strength of Dr. Allende is a tribute in part to Communist propaganda, in part to the shortness of the historical memory, in part to the collapsing strength of the Catholic Church, it is also testimony to the substantial superstition that the Social Democrats (in Chile they call them Christian Democrats) are the worst enemies of the Communists. On that myth we have been brought up, and over and over and over again, our postwar thought-leaders have urged us to deal with the "progressive" governments of Latin America, Italy, and Germany. In Italy, a few years ago, the progressive government made a deal with the hard socialists who in turn made a deal with the Communists. In Germany, the fighting socialist anti-Communist mayor of Berlin became the head of the Social Democratic party, and then the prime minister,

whereupon he made a treaty with the Soviet Union the consequences of which may make Munich look like Custer's Last Stand.

The critical date is October 24. We should bear in mind that Chile's Congress is under no constitutional compulsion to name Allende. He needs about twenty votes, and they would only come from the Social Democrats. Unfortunately, the vote is by secret ballot, and the party will not therefore accept official responsibility for the impending act of treachery. But the world will know that it was Social Democrats who made possible the Communists' taking power, and the world will be sorely vexed.

3) In Chile there are three television networks. One of them is controlled by the Communists. A second by an unholy combination of left-Marxists and Catholics. The third by the state. So that when Allende takes power, he would automatically take control of the only important broadcasting facility not already dedicated to revolutionary communism.

4) It is amusing to hear a few liberals vesting their hopes in the army. Surely— they are saying, having for generations scorned the uses of an army in Latin America— surely the army will stage a coup, and prevent the Castroization of Chile? It is not certain by any means that the army will come to the aid of the country. To do so now would alienate a great number of people who harbor illusions about what communism will bring. Bear in mind the hundreds of thousands of Viva Castro's that on New Year's Day, 1959, were shouted out by Cubans who a year or two later were fleeing to Miami on anything that would float. Coups are better scheduled when it is certain that the people will be grateful to the liberators.

Under Chilean law, the president has almost total powers to advance whomsoever he wants to head the various branches of the military. Now hear this. Under Chilean practice, every officer who is senior to the man who is advanced, is compulsorily retired. That means that by elevating the right captain, say, President Allende could retire the whole senior military, and thus diminish the threat to his regime.

5) Although there is a qualitative difference between democratic leftism and communism, it is a fact that approximately 65 percent of the voters voted against the Right, whose conduct, from all reports, was pretty stupid. Even so, what now happens to the old saw (one of Bobby Kennedy's favorites)

that a people have a right to live under communism, if that is their desire? Do the Chileans (just over one-third of them) have the right to impose a Castro-style dictatorship on the rest of the country? Such an absolutization of democracy is for children. It recalls the wry comment on African democracy, One Man, One Vote, Once. Because the prospects are, under Allende, for dictatorship, and for the end of the rights of the dissenter. And unless one is prepared to suspend one's allegiance to human rights, one's allegiance to democratic rights needs to be delimited. The humane, liberal obligation of the Chilean Congress is to spare the Chilean people rule by Allende: that is the true democratic imperative.

The Role of Communications

October 17, 1970

I intend to visit Chile a month or so from now, even as I wish I had had the wit to go to Havana a month or two after Castro took power there; because one likes to form one's own impressions of what it is like when a people has opted for the extinction of liberty.

Much of what has happened in Chile has been written about— the poverty, the insouciance of the oligarchs, the bad manners of American businesses. What has not been widely noticed is the role played in the election by Communist propagandists. A role that tends to confirm the importance of communications in the making of foreign policy.

I have here, thoughtfulness of a correspondent, a list of activities undertaken by the Communists during the year before the election. Bear in mind that Chile is a country of only nine million people.

1. Soviet and East European films, both features and documentaries, are shown regularly in commercial theaters. There are, besides, private showings, in embassies, clubs, binational centers, etc. Both the Soviet Union and Czechoslovakia sponsor these films on television.

2. The Soviet Union publishes a picture magazine, especially edited for Chilean consumption, whose circulation is ap-

proximately ten thousand. The Chilean-Soviet Cultural Institute publishes a monthly bulletin, a four-page review of cultural news, taken from the Russian Novosti News Agency.

3. The Communist Party of Chile produces a bimonthly theoretical journal, *Principios*. In addition, the Party publishes *El Siglo*, a daily newspaper. The Socialist Party (whence Allende issues) is extreme Left, pro-Cuban, and pro-revolutionary. It produces *Punto Final*, a biweekly journal of opinion with a circulation of about ten thousand, and its own daily newspaper, *Ultima Hora*, with a circulation of twenty thousand.

4. A publishing company called Sociedad Impresora Horizonte publishes a cataract of pamphlets, magazines, and books. A typical publication was *Diary of Che Guevara* in 1968.

5. During 1969, the Soviet Union, Cuba, Czechoslovakia, and Poland participated in trade fairs or in single exhibits, including cultural and technical exhibits. The Chilean-Soviet Cultural Institute sponsored an exhibit of over five hundred Marxist books contributed by the USSR. One exhibit was devoted totally to "Yankee Aggression in Vietnam." Cuba's exhibits included one on the theme, "Che Guevara Lives Forever."

6. Communist news agencies available in Chile come in from Communist China, Cuba, East Germany, and Russia. Obviously if Brezhnev burps, it will be reported in Chile.

7. In 1969, the USSR broadcast 73 hours to Latin America. East European Communist countries, 84 hours. Communist China, 28 hours. And Cuba, 163 hours. These figures are *per week*.

8. Officials of the Soviet Embassy made available program-tapes to provincial radio stations. Antofagasta Station carried a weekly program produced by a Chilean student at Lumumba University. The Communist Party conducted a regular program on a Santiago station and on six provincial stations.

9. The Communist front groups were active. They include, in Chile, the World Peace Council, the World Federation of Trade Unions, the International Student Union, the Women's Federation, the International Organization of Journalists, and the Latin American Solidarity Organization, whose nominal president is—Allende.

10. There are fourteen societies for friendship and cultural relations with the Soviet Union, two for Cuba, others for East Germany and Czechoslovakia.

11. In 1969, 205 Chilean students were trained in the USSR and East European countries.

12. So far as Communist information and cultural centers, libraries and reading rooms are concerned, there is the Chilean-German Democratic Republic Cultural Institute in Santiago as well as in other cities; there is the Chilean-Polish Cultural Institute in Santiago; and the Chilean-Soviet Cultural Institute in fourteen cities including Santiago. The Yugoslavs also have a cultural institute in Santiago. The most active centers are in San Antonio and Santiago. They disseminate propaganda and cultural information. The range of activities is wide and includes lectures, films, graphic art exhibits, student exchanges, pamphlets, concerts, *English teaching*, folk dance classes, ballet, news bulletins, etc.

13. In 1969, the USSR participated in poetry and ballet; the Czechs also performed a ballet. The Soviet poet Yevtushenko recited his poems in Chile.

In 1969, the Congress of the United States diminished the appropriations for the United States Information Agency.

Along the Andes

— *Pulling Away:*

Bogotá, Colombia—January 23, 1971

Journalists who leave America for a protracted period of time (in my case ten weeks) are usually so hard-pressed to arrange their affairs that they do not have time to pause over the meaning of their departure. I arrived at Bogotá after six hours in the air, and discovered shortly that the first Ambassador from the United States, Mr. Richard C. Anderson, came here in 1823, with wife and child, after a journey of just less than five months, that being how long it took.

It is a strange and altogether critical sense of security that attaches to the American citizen who is away from his country, traveling in lands that are torn by political passions. A friend who spent years in Chile was asked what would he do if Chile went Communist, and his reply was altogether straightforward. I am, he said, no further away from the little house I and my wife own in Bethany, Connecticut, than ten hours, on Braniff Flight 815.

Americans who travel abroad are able to flaunt that final in-souciance to the foreigner who asks provocatively what will we do if the country we visit becomes communized, or otherwise totalitarianized? Why, what we do is go home. That is what "going home" of course means, and it is a wonder that the meaning of the American experience is so very hard to grasp.

A few days before leaving New York, I stood before three thousand college students, engaged in debate with a professor who described America as a land "dedicated to death." The audience cheered. Carried away, the professor explained that the reason Kosygin and Nixon smile when they shake hands is that they have more in common than anything that separates them. He went on to elucidate that the reason the United States is dedicated to death, is because high profits come from death-dealing.

All the rest was foreplay and the students reacted ecstatically to the revelation. It was futile to give them the detumescent facts, such as that Roosevelt and Churchill also smiled together with Stalin, that the stock market leaps up with joy at any indication that we are approaching peace in Vietnam, that Nixon the killer has reduced by two-thirds the weekly casualties in Vietnam. That is to get in the way of the singular pleasure so many people get from savaging the United States. Every impiety gives pleasure, which is no doubt why Moses thought it necessary to enjoin us to honor our father and mother. The kick one gets nowadays out of surrealistic criticisms of the United States is— is what one finds oneself thinking about, as the gangway goes up, the engines roar and you fly away.

A Frenchman has written a book, with the rather sacrilegious title, *Neither Marx nor Jesus*. His point, after what one gathers from the press is a little impartial iconoclasm, is that the United States is undergoing a genuine revolution, of the kind that is most welcome. And that the reason why is that the United States is truly mobile. His thesis would appear to harmonize with that of Charles Reich who in *The Greening of America* takes the metaphor of Adam Smith, who explained that an invisible hand moves in economic affairs in such a way as to produce the best possible solution via the free marketplace.

One gathers from Reich that the equivalent of the invisible hand is working culturally in America, such that the long hair, the marijuana, the student power, the bell-bottomed trousers, the free sex, the indifference to authority: all these are combining together to bring about a greening of America. Thus the Frenchman also believes that America's nervous system is the one truly malleable social force in the world, and that we are working our way quite rapidly into a new and different kind of society, free of Marx, and free of Jesus. It is indispensable to the evolution of such a society that we should be displeased with America as it is.

America, one gathers, is Walter Mitty, but with the powers of the Wizard of Oz to realize instantly the shape we would have ourselves be. We must be a society without the Pentagon, but with no fear of foreign pentagons. Without racism, but with total freedom. Without unemployment, but with total economic freedom. With free sex and no bastards. With booze and no hangovers. With order, but without authority. With God but without divine encumbrances. And the question formulates, as one travels over Cuba, and towards Chile: Who will, in deference to the revolution these gentlemen seek, repeal history? David Hume, who sometimes sounded like the village atheist, said in repudiation of miracles, that he would sooner believe that human testimony had erred, than that the laws of nature had been suspended.

As I reach Latin America, I like to think that, a few nights ago, listening to the cheers that were awarded to the professor who indicted America, my ears betrayed me, rather than that the voices I heard were engaged in betraying a country that, for all its faults, has permitted us so very much: permitted us the dream that the nations I am now visiting have struggled, so unavailingly, to realize.

— Colombian Uncertainty:
Bogotá, Colombia— January 26, 1971

They are wondering, in Bogotá, whether the Nixon Administration has a "South American Policy." It is generally agreed that the Alliance for Progress was— a failure. That is to say, the policy towards Latin America enunciated so grandly by President John F. Kennedy can be seen to be related historically to Allende, even as the Versailles Treaty can be seen as related to Hitler. This does not mean that Woodrow Wilson's schematic visions required Hitler, any more than the New Frontier's required the communization of Chile. Merely that although Mr.

Wilson and Mr. Kennedy had quite contrary intentions, what in fact happened, was a) Hitler, and now b), Allende. Mr. Wilson's intention was to make the world safe for democracy, a vision he pursued by grand designs. Mr. Kennedy's intention was to graduate South America from reaction, to which end he launched a program designed to strengthen the hand of progressive-democratic governments, which, in Chile, led to the first democratic victory for an avowed Marxist.

Colombia is both distressed and awed by what happened. Distressed, because the leaders of both major parties in Colombia recognize that the Chilean way is not likely to produce any desirable result. Awed, because it simply isn't plain that it will prove possible, in the crucial years ahead, to resist the forces that are now convulsing Chile. The idea of the Alliance for Progress was to make economic aid available to democratic leaders in South America, such as to catapult the economies of these nations forward at a pace sufficient to satisfy the electorate that democracy plus reform is the best way out of the doldrums.

What happened in Chile hurt most, because we have regarded Chile as the exemplar of progressivism. It is as though the child on whom we devoted the most attention and care had decided, upon finishing graduate school, to embrace cannibalism. Now the first thing to learn about Latin America is that everyone there shares a single resentment: namely, that Americans tend to lump the whole of the area together. We tend to assume that there is a homogeneity that binds all the countries in South America to a common destiny. On this point, Latin Americans speak fiercely. They ask, for instance, why it is that we do not treat Europeans in the same way. We do not, in fact, assume that that which holds true in England also holds true in Italy, or Finland. Why, then, should we take it for granted that if Chile went so far berserk as to elect a Marxist president, it should follow that Colombia might do the same thing?

And yet, even as one agrees that there are enormous differences— racial, temperamental, cultural, historic— between, for instance, Colombia and Brazil, still we realize (as do South Americans) that there are sympathetic vibrations, such that one cannot, in thinking about Colombia, simply dismiss the Chilean experience, or for that matter the Cuban experience. The diplomatic imperative is on the one hand to recognize the in-dividuality of Latin American countries, while coping with the great historical tug which, expressing itself in Cuba and Chile, inescapably affects the destiny of, for instance, Colombia.

President Pastrana has been in office only a few months. He is, officially, a Conservative. He is the last of a series of presidents who, by covenant, agreed to alternate executive power. It is as if the United States had agreed in the late fifties, that in order to terminate a civil war, we would so arrange it that every odd year the President would be a Democrat, and on even years, a Republican, and that meanwhile, Congress should be exactly divided between Republicans and Democrats. That may be a good way to end a civil war, but it is of course no way to achieve strategic internal harmony. It is rather like wage-price controls. What happens is that the forces of the market insist on political distinctions, so that the differences between individual members of the same party are now at least as significant as differences between members of different parties.

And now the leaders of Colombia, face to face with the end of the Liberal-Conservative agreement in 1974, are girding for a showdown. There are two great magnetic fields affecting Colombian politics. One of them is Chile. Chile is the symbol of the success of iconoclastic-leftist demagogy. The other pole is: the United States. We are the symbol of total diplomatic ineptitude, combined with brilliant empirical success. *I.e.*, the United States, without a "South American Policy," is the country that has solved as many of the social problems as ever have been solved on the face of the earth, by rejecting Marxism. Chile is the country which, embracing Marxism, suggests to the voting masses of Latin America an exciting alternative, never mind Cuba, never mind Russia, never mind China.

The problem for Mr. Nixon is virtually insoluble. What more can he do? The Alliance for Progress didn't work, and in any case we continue to spend, in Colombia, about as much money ($100 million per year) as we did under Kennedy-Johnson. Probably Mr. Nixon should dish up some rhetoric—very important. Rhetoric satisfies urgent human needs, particularly where form means so much (Colombian peasants who would not be able to answer the question whether Kennedy was President of the United States or of Sears Roebuck hang his likeness on their walls).

It is overdue for Mr. Nixon to say something about Latin America that lifts the spirit, even as we acknowledge that the lonely fight against leftist-demagogy is their fight, that we can help them, but cannot save them.

There is a protocol in Colombia (and for all I know elsewhere) that drinks must not be served until the president arrives at the party. It is said that any diplomat violating this rule during the reign of President Lleras, even if he was hours late, would have been bounced out of the country the next day.

His successor is not that way at all, and even if he is fifteen minutes late, he expects his hosts to give the guests the means to ease the agony of his absence. Even so, President Pastrana, a member of the Conservative Party, is very much in command of his government, although he does not enjoy the advantages of so many other chief executives in Latin America, of dominating the Congress, or of doing away with it altogether. So that he is not in a position to count on an acquiescent Congress to enact all his reforms.

Dr. Pastrana asked me how did I account for the American Government's surprising refusal to renew for the customary length of time the coffee pact, on which the economies of Brazil and Colombia depend. I murmured something about that being Congress' decision, not Nixon's, and he sighed, recalling that soon after he went to Washington as his country's ambassador a few years ago, he found himself wondering why he had not been accredited to Congress, rather than to the President.

What Dr. Pastrana desires is a series of measures aimed at bringing employment and contentment to the dispossessed, whom he identifies as, primarily, the urban population. He cites the doubling of Bogotá's size every three years, by families fleeing the countryside for lack of employment, or for fear of guerrillas, or both. He feels that unless something is done quickly for the ghettos that surround the five major cities of Colombia, turmoil may come at the general election of 1974, when the voters are released from the seventeen-year-old pledge to alternate the presidency between the two major parties.

President Pastrana says that democratic tradition in Colombia is very strong, that during the one hundred and fifty years of its independence, only three times has the government been illegally overthrown— and then, he tells you with a trace of a smile, only for four years each, as if the democratic rhythm of the people overwhelmed the prehensile resources of the despot.

In anticipation of a demagogic campaign in 1974, President Pastrana has implemented an agricultural reform law which is the despair of its victims, who insist that *they* (as in Peru) will include not only the landowners, but the peasants. In Chile, there are fifty or sixty thousand landowners. In Colombia, there are over a million: so that (they claim) the dissolution of the farms means a formalistic rural socialism, which will dissolve the viable units— much larger than the few hectares each peasant is destined to get— which are necessary to finance the heavy machinery without which Colombian agriculture cannot compete on the world market.

In this vexed situation, the United States Government finds itself, primarily through the Agency for International Development, supporting by various moral and financial disbursements the public sector. On top of that, Colombia is a signatory to the Andean Pact, along with Uruguay, Bolivia, Chile, and Peru, by which the most productive enterprises in Colombia shall become, depending on the classifications, anywhere from majority owned to wholly owned by Colombians.

Now there are as many versions of the meaning of some of the escape clauses in the pact as there are lawyers in Bogotá, but it is generally agreed that it will discourage foreign investment. Why, Colombians will ask wistfully: and one finds oneself explaining, with no little embarrassment, the laws of economics, and depending on whether the conversation has been genial (almost always), or distempered (once or twice), one doesn't remark, or else one does, that there isn't after all any reason for Americans or Germans or Dutch to send capital to a country many of whose own citizens are sending capital (yes, illegally) to Florida and Switzerland.

There is the shadow of state socialism, and the remoter shadow of Chilean communization. Even so, Colombia is one of the best bets in Latin America. It is basically conservative, basically democratic, basically enlightened. The ghastly guerrilla wars of the fifties are behind her. Her resources (Colombia is as large as Oklahoma, New Mexico, and Texas combined) are extraordinary. With a market for her exports, the control of her incredible population rise, and resistance to the socialist alternative, she should make it.

— *The Left-Military of Peru:*

Lima, Peru—January 30, 1971

The generals who took over the government of Peru in 1968 ousted President Belaúnde Terry and shipped him off to Spain, an indignity personal and constitutional which, except for the unpleasant aspects of the incumbent government, struck many Peruvians as a nice exercise in poetic justice, inasmuch as Belaúnde Terry himself became president after a military junta had ousted his constitutionally elected predecessor.

That sort of thing happens quite often in these parts. A junta within the military, coming to the conclusion that the democratically elected government is leading the country to perdition, takes over. Rather amiably, incidentally, or at least by the standards of the French and the Russian revolutions. With the Castroite exception, people in Latin America don't tend to get killed, merely exiled; and often they turn up again, a few years later, and not unusually they have another go at politics. But this particular whirl by the Peruvian junta has worried a lot of Peruvians who in years gone by have sighed their way through coups d'état with the fortitude of a father enduring the long adolescence of his daughter.

This group, instead of doing the usual business of restabilizing the republic, is on to something. Ideology. The generals actually want to govern Peru in pursuit of a social vision which, when it is explained to you, leaves you deeply embarrassed. Not because it is a bad social vision (few social visions are), but because it fails to account sufficiently for the obtrusive realities. One of these is that wealth cannot be created by an act of will. Another is that the lure of utopianism can be a formidable political instrument: and the generals who govern Peru are holding out visions of affluence which can only have been rivaled by the letters that the ecstatic Pizarro addressed to Charles V when he started to rake in the gold that the Incas were using, like whitewash, to decorate their public buildings.

The generals, this time around, turned sharply left, which of course accounts for the difference in the Eastern seaboard liberal attitude towards them, which is formal but pleasant—in sharp contrast to the freeze that President Kennedy imposed on the junta in 1962. To begin with, land reform. That reform has temporarily delighted the *campesinos:* though as in Colombia, and in Chile, there will be a hangover, caused by the shortage of tools and experience, and in the case of Peru, the need to begin to repay, in bits and pieces, the money through which, theoretically, the bondholders who used to own the land will get a little compensation.

A general who is a member of the junta and an enormous enthusiast for the undertaking explains that, to be sure, about 60 percent of the capital needed by Peru will have to come from abroad. Will it be free capital coming in? Well, he said, you need to understand that capital is "cold," and therefore much of it will have to come, in the first instance, from government, or government-supported enterprises. What if the governments don't come in and help? They will have to, he said confidently— to avoid South America's turning towards "extremism." But, the visitor noted, U.S. government capital went into Chile as though the President of the United States intended personally to atone for the avarice of the *conquistadores,* and what did it avail the United States? Peru, said the general, is different. In Peru, communism can never come, because for us, "the axis of life is the human being."

What will eventually induce private capital? The reasonableness of the government's regulations, the general explained. Look, if you want to start a match factory for $2 million, you put up the $2 million, we will let you take out the first $4 million in profit, and then you will have to sell— not give away, sell— 51 percent of your match factory to Peruvians: and then— forever— you can have 49 percent of the profits. He looks up as pleased as Plato must have done on finishing the last sentence of *The Republic,* and one felt it almost discourteous not to plunk down $2 million on the spot.

It is a complicated thing the generals have undertaken, and the danger is not only the economic naïveté, but the ongoing attrition on other institutions that may not be robust enough, next time around, to save Peru from a most awful letdown. Liquidate the power of the middle and upper classes, of the Church and the landed class, of the managers and factory owners, and what you end up with is: Bolivia. The hope is that before too long the generals will once again yield power, in order to escape the fate of Frankenstein. Meanwhile there will be a scarcity of matches.

— *Chilean Ferment*

Santiago, Chile— February 4, 1971

The brand-new hotel here, in mid-season, has twenty-three guests today, which means that five hundred beds are empty. Tomorrow, sixty of them will be occupied by a Cuban delegation. "And they probably won't pay their bill," a young Chilean businessman, busily engaged in disengaging from Chile, remarked in his emptying office, the files packed up, phonograph records in cartons, as he mused on how he will raise the money to pay his debts— he has sold everything except his little beach cottage in the ten weeks since Salvador Allende was inaugurated as president, but there are no buyers. There are lots of beach cottages, and very little cash.

A professor, himself a socialist, explained that for reasons he could not put his finger on, he had found himself early that morning pecking away at his own typewriter, instead of relying on his perfectly competent secretary, who would be at his service a few minutes later. Somehow he did not want to share what he had to say in that letter with someone whose sympathies were, in all matters, with the Allende government.

Another scholar is trying very hard to master the art of intrigue. He could write you a book tomorrow about some of the great intrigues in European history, but he never knew such a one as his department is engaged in. You see, the balance of power is in the hands of the cook. I kid you not. The university system in Chile has for years and years been dominated by a senate of sorts in which everyone is represented, professors, assistant professors, students, maintenance men; and yes cooks. The difference is that under Allende the politicization of everything is such that great consequences ensue on the littlest vote. In this case, the question is whether the department will more or less formally establish itself as a revolutionary arm of the Communist-Socialist-radical coalition that rules Chile. The cook is in favor of it. The professor in charge is against it, pleading that any such marriage must be at the expense of the integrity of the department's scholarly calling. He was supposed to have finished a book months ago, but he has not begun it. How can he, when he needs to spend the time to muster a majority sufficient to overcome the political dedication of his cook?

Another professor, young, soft-spoken, freshly returned from several years in Germany where he did his doctoral dissertation on the artist's idea of the New World during the sixteenth and seventeenth centuries, looks you straight in the eye and tells you goddamit it is a bloody slander to allege that the Allende government is engaged in persecuting *El Mercurio,* the leading opposition daily. You are told the same thing by government functionaries, who include lawyers, ideologues and playboys, and you pay them little heed, even as, a world and a half away, you would pay little heed to a representative of the Rockefeller administration in New York who insisted, say, that Rockefeller had no differences whatever with Mayor Lindsay.

But the professor is something else, because he genuinely believes it to be so that the Allende government is innocent. It goes as follows: *El Mercurio* (government spokesmen will tell you) is simply one enterprise in a complex of enterprises dominated by a single family, and over the years the business fell into lax habits. Good government (of the Allende type) is charged with enforcing the laws. One such law holds that the Edwards Bank, an arm of the enterprise, had no business underwriting a particular transaction without sufficient collateral. As for *El Mercurio*— why, all the government is attempting to insure is that, like other enterprises, it has paid its taxes. All of this against a background of: a) frozen credit; b) price control; c) wage increases by government decree; d) the flight of capital; e) the withdrawal by the government of official advertising in the newspaper; f) harassment by a union controlled by the Communist Party; g) the arrest of a prominent executive through the resuscitation of an old dormant law. There is no question in the minds of the managers of the Edwards enterprises that eventually they will all be exonerated of any substantive wrong-doing. There is considerable question whether, by that time, *El Mercurio* will still be publishing. Exit the axis of opposition to the Allende government.

What is interesting—mark this well—is that the young professor, and so many other idealists like him who support so avidly the revolutionary government, will not admit to any knowledge of what, in fact, is taking place in Chile. *They don't believe it.* What they believe is the purity of the government's purpose. You sit and listen, and a great literature of the past generation runs through your mind. The excuses made by the professors who, early in the thirties, backed Hitler. The solitary ruminations of Nikolai Rubashov, who decided to submit to the fictions of Stalin's prosecutors rather than ground the Communist balloon by tying it to the earth with a strand of truth. Allende isn't Hitler, or Stalin. But his supporters are of the breed of the supporters of Hitler and Stalin. They will not credit the evidence which every day accumulates before their eyes. There are reasons historical, cultural, ideological and even moral, which account for their blindness. Meanwhile one begins to understand what Albert Jay Nock meant when he wrote in his journal that he thought someday to address himself to the question: How do you establish that you are slipping into a dark age?

We have climbed almost to five thousand feet, rising rung by rung up the thermals that lift fitfully from the foothills of the lower Andes that peter down to the outskirts of Santiago, a joy for those who love to glide. The pilot behind is unconcerned with the violent wrenchings of the little sailplane that spurts up as he keeps banking it over sharply, to stay in the upstream. He is constantly talking, while he maneuvers to stay in the geyser. "When Allende was voted in," he says, "I decided to split. So I called my accountant and I said to him, Tell me exactly how much money I am worth. A few days later he told me. You are worth, he said, one hundred and fifty thousand dollars."

"Well," he said, diving down now to escape the spiral, and beginning a long glide toward Los Curros, where the national observatory is, and Allende's private residence (we must turn away, by regulation, before reaching a bomb-dropping relationship to it), "I sat down and asked myself a few questions. I said, Look: I own a membership in this gliding club, where I am a part-time instructor. I have my little business. I have a small airplane. I go fifteen times a year to ski at Portillo, with my wife and son. I have a sailboat at the lake. We have two cars, a swimming pool and a house. Where else can you have all of that with capital of only one hundred and fifty thousand dollars? So— I decided— I'll repose my faith in the army."

Chile, by the way, is not the ideal incubator of Marxist revolution. There is spectacular poverty, but among a very small percentage of a population, which, by the way, is almost wholly literate. The more general poverty is urban, not rural. Only 20 percent of Chile's nine million people work the land. As one historian has noted, if you need to draw a picture of the quintessential victim of Chilean economic torpor, it wouldn't be the land-serf, struggling to make do with a few cents per day; or the miner out of a novel by Émile Zola, exhausted and dehumanized by the demands of an encroaching industrialization. Rather it is the shop clerk, poorly paid, bored, apparently immobilized, suffering from inflation, high overhead, a politicalized environment within which his enumerated rights (and, oh, how they love to enumerate the rights of the people. Our Bill of Rights would serve only as a cheese tidbit introducing the Rights of the Chilean People) are meaningless, unless he happens to know somebody who knows somebody who is a judge, or a member of parliament.

This is not to say that the situation is frozen for the salesclerk. The last three presidents of Chile came from utterly humble backgrounds, as incidentally did Pablo Neruda, revered in Chile as a combination of Voltaire, William Shakespeare and Frank Sinatra, whose amorous verse is overpoweringly beautiful, and whose tendentious verse (Neruda is a lifelong Communist) is as fulminatory and galvanizing as *La Marseillaise*. The thing of it is, not enough Chileans conceive of rising up the ladder—except through politics. "Thus politics becomes the substitute, for the young Chileno, for almost every avenue of social or material advancement a young American might consider: a substitute for the professions, for industry, for the army, the arts; even the Church."

The Chile of this moment, halfway between Allende's inauguration and the municipal elections of April, is composed of roughly three lots of people. The first are those who are wildly excited by the revolution. "They speak and write like John Reed fifty years ago, talking about the Ten Days in Russia That Shook the World": and it is important to remember that revolutions *can* be fun, particularly for those for whom the alternative is merely another day in the shop. Second, there are those—like the glider-sportsman—who feel that they have few practical alternatives, and just enough of a stake in the country, whether material or romantic, to edge them over towards a decision to stay—and to hope that the legalistic tradition of Chile, or if not that, the army, "or if not that the Catholic Church, or the anti-Communist tradition of the people," will singly or together restrain the Allende government.

And then there are those who are in the active opposition.

They are, technically, a majority of the parliament, and a majority of the voters. They want to stay and fight. But the odds in their favor diminish. There is the persecution of the principal opposition newspaper, *El Mercurio*, and of the publishing house, Zig Zag. The blackout of opposition on television, which is owned either by the government, or by government-oriented universities. There are twenty-nine radio channels, of which only three are antigovernment, and there is a question how long they can hold out. Allende swears there will be elections (parliamentary) in 1973, and (presidential) in 1976. By that time, however, elections may prove to be as significant as Mexico's, where the embarrassed party in power, as secure as Queen Elizabeth on the throne, practically has to subsidize the opposition, in order to put on the periodic charade. The differences however are considerable, because the economic program of Mr. Allende, unlike that of Mexico's PRI, is based on chimera. And when that happens, it eventually transpires that you cannot eat chimera. And when *that* happens, the government is either overthrown, or else it rules by the lash.

A few rules of the game. 1) In Chile, the word "Marxist" is used with extraordinary latitude, primarily because it isn't a term of abuse, so that people don't mind if, by mistake, you call them Marxists. A "Marxist" in Chile can be anyone ranging from Norman Thomas to Leon Trotsky. 2) Allende is a Marxist, but not a "Communist," if by Communist you mean, on top of the obvious things, someone who believes in a) subservience in international affairs to the Soviet Union; and b) the *elimination* of the private sector. Recently Allende repeated, for the tenth time, that he will not subordinate his foreign policy to any other country's (and I believe that that is his intention); and, in an interview with a left-wing Peruvian paper, that he seeks to nationalize only 120 out of the 35,000 business enterprises in Chile (in contrast, say, with Castro, who eighteen months ago nationalized even the kiosks).

Now that is a little disingenuous, because in Chile, the 121st largest company is probably engaged in selling goldfish. Still, the attitude is revealing, but the crunch comes by considering what in fact the Allende government is headed towards.

It should be recalled that even before Allende, the government was "socialist" by any common understanding. The government, pre-Allende, owned major companies, and controlled a number of others; controlled prices; set wages; restricted the movement of capital; and dominated all the most active labor unions.

The Allende enterprise is described by students of the subject in Santiago as a venture in "post-Keynesian structural economic rearrangement." The idea is this: If you have a country which is under-industrialized, you need to do two things simultaneously. 1) You need to provide the capital with which to industrialize. 2) You need to create a consumer demand (a "felt" demand, they call it) for the production of the new industrial plant.

Now—the reasoning goes—if you simultaneously control a) credit, and b) the labor unions, why can't you simultaneously a) lend to industry (which of course has been nationalized) the money it needs to expand its capital plant; while b) stuffing money into the hands of the workers, so as to leave them with a surplus which can be used to buy up the production of your new industrial plant? To be sure, there is the time lag. Ah-hah. The time lag is coped with by virtue of two assets. The first is the splendid surplus the government now has (over $350 million U.S.), which is the result of the high price of copper over recent years, plus U.S. aid; and second, the powers the government enjoys to keep the national currency (the escudo) protected against disdainful handling by the hard currencies. If the government says: the escudo shall trade at fifteen to one dollar, and anyone who trades it higher will be sent to jail, you have a potent instrument. Today you can buy escudos at 30-1—so much for the market's confidence in Mr. Allende. An economist-journalist, meditating on the Allende plan, commented: Well, maybe it will work. If it does, all we'll have to do is tear up every economics textbook ever written.

The trouble of course is that notwithstanding that the Allende government enjoys certain important, and altogether adventitious advantages (for every cent that the price of copper rises, Chile benefits by $23 million per year), inflation is going to take over internally. And the trade unions will be the first to see through the chimera—by demanding wages that stay ahead of inflation.

But insofar as they succeed in getting them, the felt demand for the products of the new industrial plant wastes away because the workers are left, substantially, with only living wages. It is at this point that the government will need to act: to repress the demands of the workers, to devise the means of importing what the manufacturers need in order to increase production; to look beyond the resources they now enjoy on account of their diminishing trade surplus: and to wonder where, where, will they get the hard currency.

By economic inducements? Impossible. The essential commitment of the country is against privately owned capital, and anyone investing in Chile today is better off buying the Brooklyn Bridge. Therefore? Political inducements? The United States is not likely to be interested. Europe and Japan, eschewing ideology, and essentially unaffected by what has gone by, are keeping their eyes open for economic opportunities. But Chile isn't likely to offer many, in its tatterdemalion state, except such receivership as Chileans, whether for or against Allende, would not accept. Russia? There is the possibility, and notwithstanding Allende's nationalism. But Russia would only be interested in Chile if it proved that to rescue Chile would be grievously to hurt the United States: and it is this relationship that now concerns us.

What can the United States "do" about Chile? On the one hand it would be pointless to look out for, let alone to manufacture, reasons for a confrontation—nothing would more quickly serve the purposes of the Allende government, which can count on Chilean nationalism above all things. On the other hand, it would be foolish to subsidize in any way Chile's venture into a kind of autarkic socialism. In Lima, a calm observer of the Chilean situation remarked that if Chile succeeds, you can forget about the rest of South America—every country there will take the Chilean road.

Now this doesn't, unfortunately, mean that the reverse is true— that if Chile fails, so also will socialism fail as a lure for other countries. Even as Castro is thought to have done it wrong in Cuba, others will come up in the years ahead with careful studies showing how Allende went wrong, busting to try it themselves. There are no permanent victories, Burke said; even as there are no permanent defeats.

But such is the general demoralization that some Americans are actually asking, "What interest does the United States have in

Latin America? Why should we be concerned? Why should we do anything at all?"

Ten years ago John F. Kennedy's Inaugural Address, promising that Americans would endure any sacrifice to contain the enemies of freedom, was toasted from the Washington *Post* to the *New Yorker* and back, as the essence of the American chivalry. On the tenth anniversary of that address, references to it are almost uniformly embarrassed: America has gone out of the business of defending other countries against totalitarianism, certainly if it is home-grown, and not impossibly if it is imported: Vietnam was our last, embittered, Hurrah.

But it pays to dwell on what are the consequences of a nationalistic, exploitative, tortured Allendeism, spread throughout Latin America. If we intrude in Latin America, we will make enemies. If we hold ourselves aloof from Latin America, we will make enemies: very simply because we co-exist with countries that haven't made it. It is the application of egalitarianism to international affairs. The very few wealthy people in Chile (and in Peru) are the lightest of burdens on these countries. Take away everything they have, give it away to the people, and you get one Roman candle each. A young lawyer was present when Adlai Stevenson, touring Latin America a few years ago, said to President Alessandri that, really, he thought it only right to take the land owned and worked by Chilean *hacendados,* and turn it over to the people. To which President Alessandri is said to have replied, "Mr. Stevenson, before I would be inclined to take from Chileans what they own, and earned, I would find it more reasonable to take from Americans what they own, and earned."

Now that has been done, and the question is whether the passion for redistribution will be confined within the political boundaries of individual nations. President Allende says that he will not "export" his revolution, but President Allende is already disdained by his left-wing as a compromiser who does not understand the nature of the grand international undertakings of which he is purely a temporarily useful instrument. He is the wave of the immediate, not the strategic future. And although it is comfortable to suppose that the United States can graze contentedly in its own pastures on through the years ahead, without regard to what happens elsewhere, the dynamics of world politics are against it. We will earn the respect of the rest of the world because it admires us or because it fears us: or the rest of the world will show us what happens to great powers that moon about in solipsistic reveries.

The safest thing to do is also the generous thing to do. It is to try to help those nations that are skeptical about the Chilean way. Not— needless to say— by sending down the Marines. But by encouraging the leaders of the resistance to Allendeism. By giving them the information and technical advice they need. By inviting them to the United States, to examine the other way. By publicizing the failures of Chile, and of Cuba: and for that matter of China, and the Soviet Union. This is not a pentecostal solution, shining with flame and fire and baptismal conversions. It is a way; an approach, requiring patience, ingenuity, self-confidence. An American graduate student, doing his dissertation in Santiago after two years in the Peace Corps, tells me he wishes that those students in America who want to politicize the universities might spend a few weeks at the University of Chile. He reflects that the Peace Corps was good for him, even though it didn't accomplish very much for the Latin Americans he was supposed to help. There being no other silver lining around, one wonders whether the Chilean experience mightn't, at least, be helpful to America?

Cuba Is Denounced by the Intellectuals
May 27, 1971

Sixty American and European intellectuals, among whom the most conspicuous are Jean-Paul Sartre, Susan Sontag, and Alberto Moravia, have sternly protested the humiliation of the poet Heberto Padilla by Fidel Castro. Indeed their remonstration is so firm that a French expert on Latin America, M. Marcel Niedergang, comments in *Le Monde* that— in the paraphrase of the New York *Times*—"the letter marked the effective break of European, United States and Latin American intellectuals with the Cuban regime that they enthusiastically supported in the 1960s."

Heberto Padilla is a youngish man who elected to stay in Cuba after Castro took power. His mother, his father, his brother, and his sister took off, and settled down in various parts of the United States, where they have not been tortured once, so far as the record shows. Mr. Padilla, a gifted poet, began to give expression to his reservations about Castro's Cuba, and in due course he was detained. Thirty-eight days later, a "confession" was issued over his signature, in which the poet described himself as ignoble, unjust, cowardly, treacherous, and untruthful. Thirty-eight days to secure a confession of that sort suggests that Fidel Castro may even have advanced Josef Stalin's art. What Castro cannot do with the sugar harvest, he has succeeded in doing with Cuban poets.

As for the intellectuals, the letter of protest suggests that what offends them most is that Castro should have betrayed their confidence in him. The broken body of Heberto Padilla is a rebuke to their self-esteem.

Now, ladies and gentlemen, it becomes very important to bear in mind that we are talking now about people who consider themselves the brightest in the whole world. Jean-Paul Sartre simply takes it for granted that the intellectual history of civilization is a pretty straight line from Aristotle to himself, with perhaps a gregarious pause along the way to acknowledge Copernicus and Hegel. Susan Sontag summarizes her world-view with the observation that the white race is the cancer of history, and is no doubt especially troubled to have to criticize a member of the Third World. Moravia is a Communist. Miss Sontag is too young, but Moravia and Sartre have been around for years, apologizing for the Communists. Along with Miss Sontag and others, they had repeatedly proclaimed Castro's revolution as— the words they use now in their reproachful letter—"a model in the realm of socialism."

About the time they first began uttering those words in behalf of Castro, a small magazine in New York, hearing that a Cuban journalist, Ernesto de la Fé, was about to be executed by Castro, sent a young reporter down to interview him. A cable to Castro's office elicited a reply, of which the following are excerpts. The date was May 4, 1959:

"Dr. Castro already answered your ambiguous question. . . . He said de la Fé was the Paul Goebbels of Cuba . . . Ernesto was a paid informer, a crime which carries the death penalty in war. . . . Since de la Fé is a Fascist and a traitor, can he be anti-Communist? I think not. He uses that banner to cover up his own crimes. There is very little difference between any Fascist and any Communist. A skunk by any other name would still. . . . Your defense of Ernesto de la Fé puts you in quite a spot. Since you are defending a Fascist and a traitor people will wonder whether you actually hate Communism or merely use that banner for ulterior motives." (Signed) Dr. Juan A. Orta, Director General.

It isn't known whether Ernesto de la Fé is alive or dead. Dr. Orta, presumably, has long since been shot, imprisoned, or liberated, for the sin of equating Fascism with Communism. But the rhetoric, away back in May of 1959 when Castro was affecting to be non-Communist, was revealing enough for junior clerks to get the message. But not for Nobel Prize winners to get the message. One would think that in tribute to the future Padillas who will be seduced by the political advice of such as Sartre, Sontag and Moravia, they would, as an act of contrition for having helped Castro entrench himself in power, publicly renounce any future role as political advisors to a world so substantially tyrannized by their political inability.

B. What Is Israel?

Jerusalem, February 3, 1972

It is much easier to talk here about the Mideast problem than it is in New York City. One gentleman, for instance, on whose judgments Israeli security heavily depends, told me most calmly that he does not in the least blame the Egyptians for being hostile to Israel in the light of the events of the past twenty-five years. And a best-seller here by Amos Elon— *The Israelis, Founders and Sons*— savors the abundant ironies: that Israel, spawned by nationalism and persecution, should now find itself the instrument of the persecution of a minority which is historically blameless of harming the Jews; and threatened by a bitter nationalism which Israel had a hand in catalyzing.

So? So there is something called "Israeli intransigence." Mrs. Golda Meir rolls the phrase on her tongue, and asks: "Isn't it better to be alive and intransigent, than dead and accommodating?"

There are rumors here that the old warrior is getting ready to make concessions which will affront some of her supporters as a fissure in the great wall of intransigence; but the concessions will most likely be formalistic: better jaw jaw than war war, Churchill is forever quoted as saying, and he was half-right. The Six Day War of 1967 did not settle anything permanently, but the kind of jawing that preceded it was spiritually exhausting because the hostile Arab world had Israel at bayonet point, threatened by the Egyptians in the Sinai and in the Negev, by the Jordanians in the Jordan valley, and by the Syrians in the northeast, at the Golan Heights. Now, occupying all these areas, Israel can afford to jaw, unafraid of a blitzkrieg's putting an end to a republic in which are congested more human dreams—spiritual, social, and political—than in any area of the world of comparable size.

Israel isn't going to risk her survival on *anybody's* say-so. "American President after President has made guarantees to Israel," Mrs. Meir will tell you, "and I put a lot of faith in the word of an American President. But I know how the world works. There isn't any American President who is going to give me command of the Sixth Fleet. I was in New York during the invasion of East Pakistan. You call the U.S. ambassador in desperation. He calls the State Department. The State Department calls the White House. The White House calls the UN ambassador. I watched it all on television when I was in New York. Malik making long speeches. The Chinese laughing. Everybody talking. Days go by. Israel could be dead in days. Look at East Pakistan."

The thing to avoid, I do not tire of repeating, is historical moralizing. Otherwise you will run the danger of sounding like one of those dreary Mensheviks who palsied every conversation for fifty years by going on about what might have been done to make the Russian revolution go right, and who was at fault. The point is: Israel is at war with nations which made war on Israel. Now Israel is in operational command of territories which were used to wage war against her. Israel isn't going to give up those territories in response to plausible and exquisitely symmetrical proposals that spring out of the mind of Mr. Jarring, or Mr. Rogers, or even Buckminster Fuller.

They are resourceful polemicists, in these parts, and one of them reminded me that it was twenty-five years before the U.S. returned Okinawa to Japan, and that on the occasion of doing so, our Secretary of State remarked that the return of captured territory is "very rare," but that the Japan of today is different from the Japan of Pearl Harbor, which is quite true; but of course the Egypt of today, though different from the Egypt of 1967, is not quite that substantially different.

Israel will take her own measure of the developing situation in Egypt, and — in the description of one Israeli official — will look for a "process" to begin, not an "act" to consummate, reconciliation. I cannot help but meditate on how much better off we would be if we had used the same yardstick in our dealings with the Soviet Union.

Not all the resolutions in the world will move Israel. Only experience will. Peering over the barbed wire at the Suez Canal, at an Egyptian soldier on the opposite shore, I asked the lieutenant whether they ever waved at each other. No, he said. "But it's better than a year ago, when we cursed at each other." That's progress, in these parts.

I asked Mrs. Golda Meir why she does not call more pointedly to the attention of world Jewry the threat posed by the relative military weakening of the United States and by the post-Vietnam nonchalance with which we are being urged to regard our mutual defense treaties. She replied that although it was unquestionably her own conviction that these trends were threatening, nevertheless it would be unfitting for her to presume to speak to all the Jews of the world concerning political matters. But, I said, you are chief of the government of Israel, and Israel is more than merely a state, is it not? "It is and it isn't," Mrs. Meir explained; vexedly, because she wrestles, every day, with the two Israels.

There is Israel the formal state. She is the head of its government, and as such she must observe the conventional protocols, and one of them is that you do not permit yourself to instruct people in other countries, whatever their ties to your own, on how to analyze the international political situation.

On the other hand, of course, Israel was conceived by its most conspicuous founders as something more than merely another state. More, even, than a homeland for the Jewish people who had been bereft for so many centuries "through a historical catastrophe — the destruction of Jerusalem by the Emperor of Rome," as S. Y. Agnon put it on accepting the Nobel Prize in 1966. The founders, in the words of Amos Elon, sought "a safe haven for Jews, and a new paradise to boot. A kingdom of saints, a new world purged of suffering and sin. . . .

"In this," Elon sighs, "they would fail. . . . Modern Israelis are motivated by self-interest and the brutal realities of power. The early pioneers were dreamers: their innocence gave them great strength; courage came from inexperience. Modern Israelis are likely to be weakened by hindsight."

What then is Israel? The question is eternally disputed—what is it that defines a Jew? To which question the accepted answer has come to be: To believe oneself to be one. By the same token Israel is whatever the individual Israeli believes it to be. Some continue to think of it as the crucible for a truly just and egalitarian society. Others think of it primarily as the most exciting contemporary example of the historical reaches of human willpower. (Murray Kempton muses that for all that we are supposed to have entered the age of superpowers after the Second World War, historians of the future will spend most of their time talking about Israel and North Vietnam.) Still others think of Israel as having lapsed altogether into conventionality.

The founders were mostly socialists, but socialism is not a fighting faith here. I have not heard it put better than by Mr. Shimon Peres, the talented Minister of Transportation and Communications. "By and large, those in the world who placed freedom above equality have done better by equality than those who placed equality above freedom, have done by freedom." This is a statist country, but I expect that any country would be, which came into being under such duress as Israel did, and which needs, in order to defend its sovereignty, to continue, into the indefinite future, as a garrison state. But one does not run into the kind of faith in socialism which was matter-of-factly accepted a generation ago. Even the spirit of the kibbutz flickers, and it is hard to attract young people to them. Religious idealism was never dominant, and the civil sway of the church is explicitly resented, even if it is implicitly approved; even as the lapsed Catholic of a dozen years ago would find excuses for not eating meat on Friday.

Whatever happens, Israel is the home of shrines. Secular and political—what is there to compare with Israel's single-mindedness since 1947? (And can the most devoted secularist reason that it is lacking in spiritual substance?) And, of course, the religious shrines. The Western Wall, where they come to weep. The pilgrims from every country in the world. I saw yesterday two dozen American Negro women, at the sub-terranean cave in the Church of the Nativity. Their preacher spontaneously delivered a little homily, and led them, then, into song. I remembered Whittaker Chambers' words about the rise of the spiritual among the Negro people—"the most God-obsessed (and man-despised) since the ancient Hebrews. Grief, like a tuning fork, gave the tone, and the Sorrow Songs were uttered." There, at Bethlehem, holding each other's hands, they sang "Little David, play on your harp," and one senses why the term Judaeo-Christian came to be hyphenated.

C. Involve Ourselves in India?

December 16, 1971

Now Senator Kennedy proposes that President Nixon assume the moral lead in effecting a reconciliation between Ulster and Ireland. This proposal ought to remind us that the Presidency of the United States tends to be primarily a political office, rather than a solomonic one—better suited as a conduit of power, than of moral wisdom. So that what Senator Kennedy is really proposing is that the United States involve itself in the Irish struggle, and the question is: why? Why on earth? We were foolish enough to involve ourselves in England's dispute with Rhodesia, from which involvement we got nothing, zero: Why should the United States get into the Irish picture?

And then there is India-Pakistan. The preferences of Richard Nixon are pretty plainspoken. Over the years, and not-withstanding Pakistan's dalliance with Red China, he has found Pakistan a more reliable ally. India, on the other hand, is probably the world's mother lode of moral hypocrisy and that gets to itch, you know. Nehru interrupted his lifelong moral trance in order to decline to join those nations that protested Khrushchev's invasion of Hungary in 1956. A few years later he interrupted it again to wage war against Goa, which he gobbled up without once pausing in his running denunciations of imperialism.

Now his daughter, fired by the glory of it all, hurls India's thunderbolts at East Pakistan and, quite obviously, everybody is relishing the whole thing, paying no attention whatsoever to the United Nations which in peaceful times they laud as the principal deterrent of aggression: and so on.

On the other hand, the repression by West Pakistan of the insurgents in East Pakistan staggers the mind for the brutality of it. Ten million refugees. Torture and bloodletting on a truly genocidal scale. Surveying the quarrel between Pakistan and India, one understands emotionally the macabre suggestion by one observer that the United States should send arms to both sides.

Still, what are the interests of the United States in the matter? Clearly, as a member of the community of nations, we desire to see a ceasefire: because ceasefires are generically desirable. On the other hand, as a practical matter, we obviously are not going to get a ceasefire from India now, any more than the United States, Britain, and France would have obliged the world with a ceasefire on the eve of our crossing the Rhine in the closing days of the Second World War. We feel the imperative to recommend a ceasefire in the Security Council of the United Nations, notwithstanding that previous resolutions during the past hectic fortnight have been vetoed by the Communist principals, who have begun shouting at each other with such force that the Chinese representative found himself addressing the Russian representative as "Mister" instead of "Comrade."

The rhetoric is for the U.N. The cool eyes of the Administration are no doubt studying the conflict in terms of the strategic interests of the United States. Clearly the indebtedness of the Indians to the Soviet Union is crucial. So crucial, that India's foreign minister is even moved to deny it, stressing that India will always be independent, even of Russia. No doubt the great naval facilities along the sub-continent will, after the smoke settles, belong all the more substantially to the Russian fleet. But the Indian Ocean is becoming a Russian lake as it is, and we are not going to war on Pakistan's side in order to reverse the irreversible.

If Red China intrudes on the side of Pakistan, which is altogether unlikely, we will have a first-class, though almost certainly non-nuclear, war; one in which the Russians and Chinese would almost certainly respect each other's frontiers and boundaries: even then, what would we get out of intervening? It is sad but true that sometimes history gives us situations which are not only necessarily resolved by the use of force, but best resolved by the use of force. If two parties opposed—in the Congo, for instance, or in Nigeria: or in the Indian sub-continent—are absolutely intransigent, what other solution is there than that they must trade blows, and come to terms by *force majeure?*

The counsel of the Kennedy people is very confusing these days. On the one hand they decry our discharging in Southeast Asia our formal commitment; on the other, they are asking that we involve ourselves in a situation, as in Ireland, in which we have nothing whatever to gain, except a diminution of Richard Nixon's vote next November, which is the likeliest objective of Edward Kennedy. It isn't a call to isolation to remind oneself that the impact of local wars greatly increases insofar as it is calculated by the belligerents that the United States— and Russia, and China— must involve themselves. We should stand by Pakistan with our grain and our blood plasma: but that's all. We are entitled to stay home for this one.

New Delhi, January 29, 1972

— *New Delhi: The Smoke Settles*

The mood here is triumphantly anti-American, and it suddenly occurs to you that there is very little America can do which is quite so much appreciated as giving a people a good excuse for being angry and condescending towards America. Hating America is fun. In India it has been an exhilarating experience, a great catharsis. I cannot imagine that India would be as pleased with herself today if the United States had backed her during the war with East Pakistan, instead of— to use the celebrated word— "tilting" towards Pakistan.

No doubt about it, U.S. policy during the nine-month crisis was inept. One Administration spokesman, well situated to see all the contours, muttered privately that the best that could be said of it is that, finally, the White House transformed a catastrophe into a defeat.

The Indians arrange their arguments as follows:

— The Pakistan government launched a program of genocidal proportions upon discovering, after the elections of December, 1970, that the majority of the inhabitants of East Pakistan desired, in effect, to separate their state from the governing state of West Pakistan.

— The United States has patronized Pakistan over the years, ever since in the fifties Pakistan agreed to serve as the central-Asian link between SEATO and CENTO, the tiara of treaties stretching from New Zealand to England that crowned the diplomacy of John Foster Dulles. Therefore, it was distinctly America's responsibility to put pressure on the Paks to stop their killings and to yield to the verdict of the Eastern plebiscite.

— Meanwhile, the pressures on India progressed towards intolerability. Ten million refugees flowed out of East Pakistan, causing great dislocations in the neighboring Indian states.

— Then (so the story goes), early last December, the Pakistani air force initiated an action which could only be considered as an aggression on Indian territory. That left the Indians with no feasible alternative than to launch their "war of liberation." To have done this was noble enough— after all, India had nothing to gain except the relief that would result from repatriation to Bengal of refugees. Moreover, the military campaign cost almost 10,000 Indian soldiers' lives. To do all this while the United States was yapping at their heels, sponsoring anti-Indian resolutions in the United Nations, bringing an aircraft carrier into the Indian Ocean, and conducting highest-level meetings at which Henry Kissinger, speaking for the President, actually moralized against the Indian position— well, it was too much to bear.

The narrative is of course incomplete.

The Pakistani repression was hideous and flatly indefensible. The scale of it is not yet certified. A lady, allegedly well informed, told me that the Paks had killed three million people in East Pakistan between March 25 and liberation day on December 17. I hope and pray that she exaggerates, and I thought to ask her how come Mrs. Gandhi, on her official visit to Washington in November, did not call public attention to the scale of the horror: Indeed, who did call attention to it?

A second point. In the post-Vietnam world, the government of the United States is less given than previously to asserting itself in disputes involving other nations.

And then, isn't it likely that the White House had perforce a larger set of considerations to consult than the old Muslim-Hindu rivalries— when, for instance, it moved the carrier *Enterprise* to the Indian Ocean? There are those in India who fancy explanations for this maneuver— and indeed for the whole "tilt" of U.S. policy— as that Richard Nixon, lonely and climbing his way laboriously up the great ladder in the middle sixties, was treated perfunctorily while visiting in India, majestically while visiting in Pakistan. For this he summons the *Enterprise*? To remind Indian royalty that they once had treated him as a poor boy?

There have got to be other explanations, if we are willing to assume that the President of the United States and his closest advisers are not mad. Such explanations have to do, of course, with the implicit American guarantee that Soviet client-states will not be free to develop into licentious juggernauts, when fueled by victories such as the Indian army enjoyed in East Pakistan, lurching hither and yon, like cargo come loose in the hold of a freighter. "Express News Service, Patna, January 17. Defense Minister Jagjivan Ram said here today that . . . the prime minister, with her 'strong flair for correct judgment,' had told him soon after the surrender of the Pak forces in Dacca that she desired to announce a unilateral ceasefire. Mr. Ram confessed that at first he was doubtful about the soundness of this move, particularly because arrangements had been made to rush troops from the Bangladesh sector in the western theater of war 'for the final kill.' " There you have it.

It was an intellectual, not Gunga Din, who told me, his eyes alight, that this was the first real war that India had fought, that the others didn't really count because they were primarily factional, or unsuccessful, for reasons which are now extraneous. This was the war that India won, against the Pakistanis, without any help from the United States. What happened, he explained, was that after the humiliations of 1962, when the Chinese Communists easily had their way during the great border dispute, it began to dawn on India that the age of Nehru was passing.

In due course Nehru died. A close study of the failures of the Indian army in 1962, and of Indian diplomacy, suggested the wave of the future. And, when tested last December, the Indians proved victorious.

It was a conclusive military victory. The implications of it, as they are understood by Indian enthusiasts, are immense. India (you will hear) is the fourth major power on earth, after America, Russia and China. Far more important than Japan, because— as someone put it— Japan's umbilical cords are too easily cut. India, with her enormous population (550 million), her natural resources, and her strategic situation, can't help, particularly now that she has been annealed by the December victory, emerging as a great power. How lucky that she had the wit not to sign the nuclear anti-proliferation treaty!

That was a highbrow talking. Listen to how it comes through as rendered by the cheering section. The cult of personality is hard at work in India. Listen.

"How . . . did this miracle— for no less it was— come about? Can that frail, modest little lady of New Delhi conceivably play Chanakya to Morarji and Yahya, Nixon and Mao, alike? Or can there be a hidden deus ex machina, god from the machine, somewhere behind all this political skill and diplomatic strategy?

"The answer is simple and uncomplicated. Yahya blurted it out when he referred to his formidable adversary as 'THAT WOMAN!'; and Mujib acknowledged it when he saluted her as India's 'magnificent Prime Minister . . . who is not only the leader of men but also of mankind.' "

Mankind is a whole lot to be the leader of, but as by now we have guessed, it isn't a bird, or a plane, "It is Indira Nehru Gandhi, alone and herself, who accomplished it all. For Indira is Gandhi plus Nehru: Jawaharlal's sense of history, foresight and idealism mixed with the Mahatma's wisdom, acumen and capacity for ruthless action— a formidable combination."

Last year, after twenty-five years of independence and socialism, with a population of 550 million people, India produced as many automobiles as the United States produced in 1908. The roadworker down the street from where I write, is working an eight-hour day for three rupees, or 36 cents. The annual per capita income is approximately $75 per person. After years of socialized effort, this monstrously large nation exports less than Formosa, whose population is about 2-1/2 percent of India's. If you want to buy a motor bike in India, all you need to do is amass $750 and wait ten-twelve years.

Those who take comfort by remarking that all that deprivation has served to finance great spiritual and intellectual progress, are unconvinced by the figures. Seventy percent illiterate: An international record of nonviolence framed by Nehru's refusal to condemn the Soviet invasion of Budapest, his own military annexation of Goa, and Mrs. Gandhi's refusal to heed the cease-fire petition of the General Assembly when asked to stay her hand in East Pakistan. What about India's silence on the purges and repressions in Russia?

The scale of it all, and the contradictions, overwhelm. Socialism in order to achieve progress: yet the growth in per capita income was negative during the years 1965-1969. And since then, it has risen only exiguously. Socialist Nirvana.

Culturally, the country is wobbly. Intensive nationalism, under Nehru, caused them to give up English as a required language in the schools, and the estimate is that five years hence, even as lingua franca, the English language will cease to serve, irreversibly: after all, only 3 percent of the population handles it now. There are 14 other languages, and Hindi, the principal of them, is spoken by only 25 percent. Television is only in New Delhi, has not yet spread. Xenophobic economics frightens away many potential investors. The accumulated difficulties of poor India, so put upon by history and nature, explain, a little, the special, elated meaning for her of the dramatic events of last December.

D. Ireland

Belfast, July 16, 1970

— Northern Ireland's Paisley

The Reverend Ian Paisley is just one of the problems of Northern Ireland; indeed it is by no means predictable that were he to depart this vale of tears and go on to a Paradise absolutely free of Roman Catholics— free even of God, if it should prove that He too is a Roman Catholic— the situation in Northern Ireland would clear up; although there is no doubt that it would improve. When Cardinal Segura, scourge of Seville, died a dozen years ago, an American tourist asked his guide what had been the result of the absence of so imposing a presence. She replied, devoutly, that upon the Cardinal's death, he and Seville had passed on to a better world.

The thing of it is, about Paisley, that Paisleyism is more important than Paisley, and would most likely survive him, although the virulent weekly transfusions would at least be interrupted. The Reverend Paisley is the head of an organization called the Free Presbyterian Movement, which is the principal mechanism in Ulster for sublimating anti-Catholicism into a) pro-Christianity; b) pro-the reigning Unionist Party; and c) pro-the formal attachment to the United Kingdom. As I say, if Paisley were to go, or (as some wags suggest will inevitably happen, that being the way the Mother of Parliaments muddles through), were he to retire from the sectarian wars in order to become the Earl of Paisley, P.O. House of Lords, Paisleyism would survive, even if it would suffer for the lack of so theatrically gifted a spokesman.

I mean, when you sit down at 11:30 A.M. on a Sunday, at the Church of the Martyrs, the bright new edifice (one of Dr. Paisley's thirteen churches), and wait anxiously for his appearance, you know that the good Lord, in His altogether inexplicable toleration, is about to present you with something quite special. He hoves in, middle-aged, hulking-tall, all-baritone, telling you that Jesus Christ is profaned by the gaggle of Romanists who stand between Him and the Word, as transcribed, immaculately, by Ian Paisley.

The Rev. P. has a rather informal theological education, having received his Doctor of Divinity from Bob Jones University in South Carolina. Dr. Paisley can hardly be said to have invented anti-Catholicism in Northern Ireland, that having been invented by a shrewdish denominationalist history going back four hundred years: but he does his gifted best to give it life; so that, on Sunday, July 12, the anniversary of the Protestantization of England by William of Orange, he is there to remind the flock that any weakness shown towards the Catholic minority in Northern Ireland (a half-million people, out of one and one-half million) is a weakness towards the blandishments of the devil.

You listen to him for an hour, and if you are at all disposed in that direction, you leave girding your loins to resist any and all of the demands which, in Northern Ireland, have come to be known as the demands of the Civil Rights Association, the demands, crystallized beginning only in 1966, forty-five years after the partition of Ireland, that the Catholic minority in the North be given a one-man one-vote relationship to the government; and that they be given equal consideration when it comes to housing and jobs and civil service.

Between 1966 and today, the Unionist Government capitulated: and the civil rights have been progressively granted, although they will not go into full effect for another year or so. But the passage from effective disfranchisement to first-class citizenship has thrown the country into psychic terror. Psychic because, notwithstanding the infamous rioting and the rhetorical bloodshed, in fact one notices a steady graph up towards genuine equality.

There are many residual difficulties. One of them is that although the ruling party, the Unionists, will privately confess their loathing of Paisley, they do not know what to do about Paisleyism. The Reverend Bigot not only got himself elected to the House of Commons in the last election, he very nearly beat the Prime Minister, Captain Terence O'Neil, in the election of 1969.

Paisley has become an eponym for: Resist Equal Rights for Catholics, and Remember That the Catholics Really Want a Unified Irish State. So that although during the church service you notice that the parishioners who exult in the phlogistonic rhetoric (Burn! Burn! Burn! Set Fire to Your Hearts for Gee-zuss Krrayesst!) are mostly middle-class, middle-aged fellow travelers of anti-Catholicism, still, in the brand-new university at Coleraine, you will find the graffito in the men's room: Paisley Forever. This much is safe to say: if Paisleyism triumphs, Northern Ireland will disintegrate.

— And on the Left, Bernadette Devlin

The symbol on the other side is Bernadette Devlin. In fact they are not really complementary. Paisley comes through as the bitter-ender, who desires a tightly-controlled, London-oriented, Catholic-hating Northern Ireland; Bernadette Devlin as the Joan of Arc of Catholic emancipation.

In fact Paisley would dissolve his allegiance to the Queen (he is a Member of Parliament) in a minute, if by doing so he could fashion a viable, independent Northern Ireland. And Bernadette Devlin cares nothing for Catholicism— or Protestantism, or the Queen, or Parliament (she too is a member): she cares for "socialism." Because it is socialism—she profoundly believes— that will rescue Northern Ireland from its quandaries. I say profoundly believes with caution. She is only twenty-three, and every year or so since attaining political consciousness, she has come to believe profoundly in slightly different goals, although she appears recently to have become semi-permanently arrested by "socialism," nestling down comfortably in left radicalism.

Miss Devlin does not, however, preside over the organized opposition. There are others. Mr. John Hume is the Catholic reformer who beat Mr. Eddie McAteer, the longtime leader of the opposition in Northern Ireland, in the last election. McAteer, surely the most quietly charming and eloquent man in the English-speaking world, wants, simply: union—with the Irish Free State. John Hume believes that union is a) unachievable at the moment, and b) wouldn't in and of itself accomplish anything very much. Here he agrees with Bernadette, the residual difference being this, that Hume believes that no progress of any sort makes sense which is not evolutionary; which is to say, non-violent. Whereas Bernadette, although she sometimes exhibits a little caution in speaking about it, more or less gives you to understand that the Northern Ireland situation is so impossibly ossified that only a good bloody revolution will shake it loose.

Miss Devlin—have you noticed?—is now an international heroine of the revolutionary community. Immediately after her precocious election to Parliament in 1969, she delivered a razzle-dazzle speech in the House of Commons which really turned the revolutionary set on. In due course she discovered that she was in fact influencing nothing more tangible than whether a new post-box should be set up in one of the towns in her constituency.

At that point Miss Devlin decided to ventilate her problems in the United States, which she did, appearing on the usual television programs, and receiving the key to the city from Mayor John Lindsay of New York, who gave it to her as automatically as he'd have given one to Lady Macbeth, if she had represented herself as a dedicated anti-colonialist, without regard to race, color, or creed.

But the American tour, and the sparkling autobiography that came after it, were not enough to keep Miss Devlin in an adjusted relationship with her iconoclastic muse. So, a few months later, she gave Mr. Lindsay's key to New York City to a surrogate, with instructions to hand it over to the Black Panthers, so as to register her solidarity with the oppressed class of Americans.

Miss Devlin, symbol of radical Catholicism in Ireland, is a very sprightly, attractive, literate, amusing woman, who however cannot think her way out of a paper bag, as readers of her book will quickly discover. Her solution for Northern Ireland is: social-ist revolution. What socialist revolution has accomplished for anybody, anywhere, she carefully refrains from telling us, pleading her innocence of parliamentary or historical politics. She gets "lost," she confesses, when she reads about the differences between the Mensheviks and the Bolsheviks. That is a little bit like getting lost in understanding the differences between the Nazis and the Democratic Socialists.

Poor Miss Devlin, she is in jail at this moment, having incited to riot, or whatever they call it in Northern Ireland. And, of course, her incarceration was yet another cause for a riot, such riots as have been plaguing a land that should be so sanguine, the Catholic civil rights reforms having got through; so optimistic about the future, notwithstanding the demagogy of Paisley, or the puerile socialism of the endearing, high-spirited Bernadette.

— The Future

I came away from Ireland convinced of the bona fides of the principal officials of the governing party, notwithstanding its refractory record on the matter of extending elementary rights to the Catholic minority. The thing to remember, if you can, is this: that the Catholics have won their war, and that in due course they will be exercising their civil liberties, and this means a good many concrete things, for instance a greatly reduced Protestant majority in the Stormont, which is what they call the Irish Parliament; and, in local centers of dense Catholic population like Londonderry, political control, which in turn means greater access to public housing, that kind of thing.

But that war for equality having been officially won, there is the old miasmic war left undissipated, namely the religious antagonisms— suggested by the name of Paisley— which will not necessarily reduce now that the Catholics are first-class citizens. The reasons are various. For one, there is unemployment in Northern Ireland, approximately 7 percent, and as much as 17 percent in the small industrial center of Londonderry. There is a widespread fear that as Catholics acquire political power, Protestants will lose their jobs; or, if you like, their job preferences. There is the strategic fear that the Catholics, who already exceed one-third of the population, will in due course become an oppressive majority and perhaps the agents of coercive unification with the South.

Then there is the bitter Paisley Protestant movement, which regrets the reforms already made, and will labor unremittingly to stoke the fanatical fires. And of course the great historical overlay of religious animosity, suggested by the answer given to one perplexed visitor who asked an Ulsterman why the talk was always of "Catholics" and "Protestants." "Aren't there any *atheists* in Ireland?" "Yes," the native explained, "but you see, there are *Catholic* atheists, and *Protestant* atheists."

One hesitates to prescribe for other people's countries, but here is mine for Northern Ireland. It is generally agreed that but for the English military presence over the Orangemen's weekend, there would have been a lot of bloodshed. Paradoxically, the potential for a good life has never been better: economic opportunities are great; industry is most hospitably greeted; there is a skilled and abundant labor force; there are tax and other benefits given to the foreign investor—the constituents are all there for material and social progress. But the thing of it is that a) fanatical Protestant sectarianism, as with Paisley; and b) the sort of undifferentiated Catholic-socialist fanaticism of Bernadette Devlin and Eamonn McCann, maintain, under existing arrangements, a convulsive leverage on Irish affairs.

Paisley cannot be ignored, because his voice is very strong in the Stormont. Paisleyites are Ulster's Fedayeen, and they have to be controlled, or else they will control. Bear in mind that the population of all Northern Ireland is equal to that of Atlanta, Georgia. And Paisley is a very big figure, as are the two or three Bernadettes.

Now if England is going to have to a) maintain order in Northern Ireland because the Irish can't do it by themselves; and b) subsidize Northern Ireland with all the welfarist benefits that now inure to Ulster in virtue of her membership in the United Kingdom, then surely it would make sense to abolish the Stormont, until things settle down? There is no equivalent parliament in Scotland, or in Wales: why should there be in Northern

Ireland? Abolish the Stormont, and you abolish the leverage of Paisley. Paisley's ranting anti-Catholicism, practiced in Westminster, will bring only yawns; ditto the ideological cadenzas of Bernadette.

The British, then, can superintend the evolution of the new Northern Ireland, with civil rights for everybody. In due course manifest destiny will make itself felt— but only after ten or twenty years of practical experience with pluralism. And then, if the two Irelands should want to fuse, an unfrightened Protestant population will know that they will not suffer at the hands of Dublin. Or, if the experience with England is especially satisfactory, the North Catholics may find they have developed stronger ties to England than those to the South that were officially severed in 1921.

It is not easy to visualize, in the current heat, an alternative based on the reconciliation of altogether antagonistic forces. Dublin's policies are affected by Northern pressures, and the stability of the South depends on stability in the North: a stability which depends, at this point in history, on reducing the leverage of the fanatics. I do not see how that can be done other than by England.

E. England

London, October 22, 1970

— *The News in London*

Today's newspapers endeavor to give all the news. The *Daily Mirror's* American reporter advises that before being admitted to do a story on a sexual resort in Southern California, he was asked to prove his "sincerity" by, er, consorting with the wife of the owner-director, which he said he did, "twice." The *Daily Telegraph* confirms that every Englishman will do his duty, twice if necessary, no matter what the pursuit. "By command of the Queen, the Lord Hamilton of Dalzell (Lord in Waiting) was present at Heathrow Airport, London this morning upon the departure of the President of Zambia and bade farewell to His Excellency on behalf of Her Majesty. By command of the Queen, the Lord Hamilton of Dalzell (Lord in Waiting) was present at Heathrow Airport, London this evening upon the arrival of the President of Pakistan and welcomed His Excellency on behalf of Her Majesty."

That's a lot of Heathrow in one day for poor Lord Hamilton, but it was certainly worth it to get the President of Zambia out of the country. The President of Zambia— one Kenneth Kaunda— had come to town to instruct the Prime Minister, Mr. Heath, on South African policies. They had had dinner at Number 10 Downing Street, and that dinner is the talk of the town. There are several published versions of what went on, my favorite naturally being the most garish.

I have had a special place in my heart for Mr. Kaunda ever since learning, a year ago, that I am not allowed to set foot in his country, my offense having been to publish— as a matter of fact, to republish— the remarks of Dean Acheson denouncing America's boycott of Rhodesia. I have never been persona-non-grata'd before, at least not by entire countries, and since on the whole it is a lot more fun to be forbidden from going to Zambia than to go there, I think I'd have egged Mr. Kaunda on if I had been hiding behind the curtains at Number 10, as we call it here.

It is everywhere agreed that the dispute was over the projected sale of arms to South Africa, Kaunda's point being that to do so would outrage black Africa, and cause the dissolution there of the Commonwealth. Heath's point being that he has not been elected Her Majesty's First Minister in order to take orders, on matters affecting English security, from nattering nabobs of negativism. One story goes on to say that Mr. Heath turned to Kaunda and said, Look, buddy, do *we* bring up the fact that *your* country is trading every day with South Africa? And via Rhodesia at that? Eh? Mr. Kaunda at that moment called for his retinue and his limousine, and went back to the hotel, and was next seen by Lord Hamilton of Dalzell (Lord in Waiting) at Heathrow. Mr. Heath, meanwhile, has got himself a lot of sympathy. He points out that the arms he proposes to sell to South Africa are only useful against enemy sea power, and would not likely be used for the purpose of anti-black repression unless the navies of Zambia,

Tanzania and Kenya develop into a major flotilla of aircraft carriers and battleships, for the sake of an amphibious landing on South Africa. The purpose of the armament is to guarantee the freedom of sea lanes, which the Soviet Union is increasingly dominating.

That dinner party shares the front pages with the news from Canada. When Mr. Trudeau gave himself the War Emergency Powers, I was under the impression that the British press would attack him quite unanimously, inasmuch as the assumption is that war emergency powers are for use in war emergencies.

To begin with, consider what Trudeau actually said. "There are a lot of bleeding hearts around who just don't like to see people with helmets and guns." He said that without once quoting Baudelaire, and Mr. Agnew could not in fact have said it better. "All I can say," Mr. Trudeau went on, "is go on and bleed." Here Mr. Trudeau sounded like the late Westbrook Pegler. He was not through: "But it is more important to keep law and order in the society than to be worried about weak-kneed people."

Enough. But Pierre Trudeau using the rhetoric of Lester Maddox has not frightened the English, who ask their brother Canadians to do to the separatist organization what they would never permit the Americans to do, say, to the Black Panthers. "Much will depend," says the *Times,* "on the speed with which the police can now seize the terrorists and smash their organization" — *smash* their organization. And the *Telegraph,* "The Prime Minister has acted with a vigor and determination which any democratic leader must show when presented with a direct conspiracy against the state. . . . The Canadian government has as a result suspended most of the rules — and rightly."

Not that it should have surprised anyone. The Canadian government spent the late forties vigorously prosecuting a Communist spy ring, suspending the rights of everyone in sight; and most of the fifties, criticizing the horrors of McCarthyism. The English don't fool around. *Salus populi suprema lex.*

But historical perspective is not lost. A correspondent, who may just be one of those Englishmen who have not paid their annual television licensing fees, writes to the *Times,* "Sir: Extract from an advertisement placed in the *Evening News* by the Ministry of Post and Telecommunications:

" 'Our vans can not only tell if you are watching TV, but what you're watching and in which room you're watching it,' and there are still fourteen years to go!"

Fourteen years until (you don't need to specify these things in England)— 1984.

— Understanding Enoch Powell

Close your eyes and ask yourself about whom it would be appropriate to say: "He is guilty of the most abject disloyalty. . . . He has finally sealed his own doom as a serious politician. No one will listen to him again on any subject of national importance. Racialism and McCarthyism have been rolled into one lurid conspiracy theory." That was the pronouncement— by the *Guardian* of London— on Enoch Powell. In punishment for the same speech that evoked that blast, Mr. Anthony Lewis dispatched a column to the New York *Times* under the heading, "The Smell of the Beer Hall." Mr. Lewis cited, from the controversial speech of Enoch Powell, his references to the enemy's being "invisible," to the danger being "from within," to the use, by the enemy, of techniques which are "devilishly simple, yet devilishly subtle."

Enoch Powell is not widely known in America, except to the few who remember that it was he who, two years ago in a speech heard round the world, suggested that England should not only end its policy of admitting immigrants from the Commonwealth, but should undertake ingenious schemes for inducing its resident immigrants to leave the country. What he meant, in practical terms, was of course colored immigrants, there being no white immigrants (net) coming into the United Kingdom these days. His explanation of his proposals was, if not convincing, at least plausible. What he said was this: It is the job of the politician not to seek to alter human nature, but to guide public affairs in such a way as to deflect human nature from collision courses with reality. What I predict (said Mr. Powell) is that at the current rate of immigration, England will at the turn of the century become 15 percent black. And that will cause racial strife, unemployment, and cultural atomization.

Even at the time, the critics of Mr. Powell divided into two groups. The reluctant majority conceded that something had to be done to close the gates of immigration (the Socialist government introduced a bill checking the flow of East Indians from Kenya); and the minority who although they recognized that there could not be, anywhere, any country without any immigration laws whatever, turned furiously on Enoch Powell insisting that his dire prophecies themselves inflamed the social situation: by predicting racial animosity, in effect he midwifed it.

After his famous speech, Mr. Powell was dropped from the shadow cabinet by Mr. Ted Heath, who is now the Prime Minister. It was widely hoped that Mr. Powell would lose his own seat in the General Election, but far from it. It was during that campaign that he made the speech that caused the *Guardian* and the New York *Times* permanently to proscribe him.

I asked Powell what "invisible enemies" he was referring to, and what were the "devilishly simple, yet devilishly subtle techniques" by which the enemies of Great Britain thought to bring down the country. I expected something rather concrete, and was both disappointed and reassured to find that Mr. Powell was referring to nothing more than the kind of thing we in America hear all the time. The enemies, and the techniques, are a) those who hate English (read American) society; and b) those who use English freedoms (read American freedoms) to increase their leverage against their country.

The question—the interesting question—is, why should Powell be treated as feverishly as he is being treated? Is it his rhetorical invidiousness? (A detractor says that he refers to white children as "babies," to black children as "pickaninnies.") Is it his obvious appeal (like George Wallace's) to the racist? Is it the implicit threat in his program physically to expel colored immigrants? Is it his (some say) zestful anticipation of a program of forced expatriation?

The problem is vexing to English conservatives who have greatly admired Enoch Powell. He particularly confounds his critics because he does not have the background of the demagogue (although in England the learned demagogue is not an unknown phenomenon, witness Sir Oswald Mosley).

Enoch Powell was a professor of Greek at age twenty-five. He is a published poet and historian who knows ten languages. And he is a resolute champion of the free market.

One listens to him, and wonders: Are there vibrations there, uniquely audible to finely tuned British ears, that suggest—danger? For myself, I am undecided. Or put more fairly, having observed him only twice I have not sensed that danger that others sense. Would I say as much if I were a black immigrant living in England? Certainly not, inasmuch as it is obvious that inducements to emigrate are, at the margin, indistinguishable from pressures to emigrate. He continues, on the whole, as an enigma, and the great social and philosophical debate over the question whether it is always virtuous to tell the truth, may one day rage over his head.

VII. Law, Order, Violence, Repression

Hysteria and the Omnibus Bill

February 12, 1970

The feverish opposition of Mr. Tom Wicker to the omnibus anti-crime bill ("the greatest threat in many years to American liberty") reminds one of many things, general and specific. Specifically, it reminds me of the heat turned on particularly in New York City, but also throughout the country, against the repeal, in 1966, of the Civilian Review Board set up by John Lindsay to review charges against the police. It was predicted by champions of the board that its dissolution would bring black-white chaos.

When those arguments did not prevail and it seemed clear that New Yorkers would vote overwhelmingly to eliminate the board, someone discovered a "sleeper clause" in the proposed amendment. That sleeper clause, defenders of the board insisted, would have the effect of removing policemen from any kind of effective supervision. Eliminate the Civilian Review Board, they said, and you will get not only chaos, but also you will have constituted a new privileged class— policemen.

Well, the voters came down two to one against the board. Three years later, people have all but forgotten that it ever existed. There is no chaos attributable to its absence. The Civilian Review Board in Philadelphia meanwhile was yawned out of existence. And nobody in all of New York has come up with the "sleeper clause" as a device for mulcting special privileges out of the law in order to immunize policemen.

Now Mr. Wicker and the others are, once again, up to the same kind of thing. Listen. If the House passes the bill the Senate has overwhelmingly favored, we shall have "limited the Fourth Amendment, eroded the Fifth, threatened the Eighth and in numerous other ways combatted crime by assaulting constitutional rights." What, he asks, will the legal community do about it? "Rely . . . on the Supreme Court to rectify it years from now, if ever, and only after untold damage to individuals at the hands of the state, after further demonstrations of this kind of 'justice' to young people, many of whom already believe American ideals are a fraud?"

Now, if I were a young people, strolling at night through the streets of Washington, D.C., I would most emphatically believe that the preeminent ideals of America were fraudulent, because those ideals have to do with the guaranteeing of personal liberties. If I saw murder, loot, mugging, rape, and the merchandising of heroin, I would doubt either the ideals of this country, or the competence of the government to give such protections as is its principal reason for being.

I remember the poignancy of a scene in Truman Capote's as yet undistributed television special on capital punishment. A middle-aged man, a psychiatrist, talks about having personally prevented the lynching of a young man who raped and killed his only daughter. He did so confident that justice would be officially dispensed to the killer. Now, a dozen years later, a pack of lawyers having played Sardines with the courts, the killer goes unpunished, and the mother, a gentlewoman of great sensibility, has begun to despise our society, and even her own husband who trusted it.

Mr. Wicker speaks about the "untold damage to individuals" that will be done by the bill. Speak to me of the untold damage you do to a heroin ring when you bang down the door and catch them pawing over the private enterprise version of chemical warfare. Speak to me about the untold damage that will be done to a defendant who is denied bail (maximum, 60 days) by a judge who surveying the record finds that in the past three years said defendant has been guilty of or implicated in one-half-dozen muggings. Isn't it likelier that the untold benefit to other individuals than the criminals is the object of the omnibus bill?

Mr. Wicker is paying the penalty now of the fanatical extension of the Bill of Rights over a decade or two, such as to have made it, in the words of one prominent New York City judge, "ludicrously difficult to legally prove plain guilt." Mr. Wicker's appeal to latter-day attitudes concerning the majesty of the Bill of Rights should extend back further into history, to the Federalist

Papers— in which Hamilton warned against the dangers of legal impotence. Unless the government has certain powers— to, *e.g.*, detect and convict the lawbreaker—"we shall be obliged to conclude that the United States will afford the extraordinary spectacle of a government destitute even of the shadow of constitutional power to enforce the execution of its own laws."

Notes from "Victims" of Repression

March 28, 1970

There is absolutely nothing like the indignation of the New Left when one of its practitioners is physically prevented from doing what he desires to do or— still worse— when he is caught, tried, and— crowning impudence! punished. *The Leviathan* is a monthly journal published by the New Left, fanatical, moderately literate, overwhelmingly tedious, and worth reading, say once every dozen issues. The current issue is devoted to Repression, and the thesis of the editors (I grant that that is a bit like saying "the thesis of Jackson Pollock") is that the United States is now in earnest engaged in repressing the New Left; that means the New Left is truly challenging the system, and that it becomes important now for the New Left to ally itself formally with the Black Revolution and the Third World.

Now, fanatics' literature is in part interesting because of what they say, in part because of how they say it. It doesn't follow from their saying it that in fact American institutions have finally concerted to repress the revolutionists; but it is interesting that the New Left should be sounding that particular tocsin. And look how they say it. "The murder of Fred Hampton, Mark Clark and twenty-six other Panthers, the legal lynching of Bobby Seale, the imprisonment without trial of hundreds of Panthers around the country, the smashing and looting of Panther offices, the frame-up of Martin Sostre, Ahmed Evans and many other black and Third World militants— all these are not isolated incidents; but part of a systematic campaign to crush black and Third World resistance to imperialism once and for all."

The alleged conspiracy against them is taken to lengths that would embarrass a member of the John Birch Society. For instance, there is "the increasingly political character of the traditional symbiotic relationship between organized repression and organized crime. At the same time as Nixon-Mitchell make a real effort to cut off the supply of the killer weed, the flow of heroin into both black and white high schools becomes a torrent. Coincidence? . . ."

The sensationalizations are of the same order. One young man described how he was arrested and beaten by the New York police for taking part in the demonstration outside the Waldorf-Astoria last December. For some reason, after his initial beating on the streets, he is taken to a hospital where he and his companion are treated. Having gone to the trouble of stitching them up, the police take them to the 17th Precinct — listen, now, if you want to know the kind of rhetorical narcotic on which the boys are feeding — "a torturer's heaven. For an hour, Riley and I were systematically and efficiently beaten by the pigs.

"We were taken into the Squad Room on the first floor. There were about 20 cops sitting and standing around. They put us in a corner. Our hands were handcuffed behind our backs. Our faces were to the wall. There was a metal coat rack and some pieces of wood with nails in them in the corner. We were thrown up against the metal coat rack and the lumber with the nails. Each pig had his special torture. One hit me with his night stick in the calf. Another used a blackjack on my back. A third hit my elbow with a pair of pliers. A fourth took running jumps and kicked me in the back. Another jumped on my toes. Everyone took turns hitting, kicking, spitting, name calling . . ." Upton Sinclair would have thrown up his hands in despair at the perversion of the great tradition of muckraking.

Every article, however, ends on an upbeat, the effect of which is that the Revolution Will Prevail. And there is considerable candor. It is always interesting to read side by side articles that protest repression, and articles that call for law breaking. "The trouble with our reaction," one protester at the Waldorf reminisces, "wasn't that it was too violent — on the contrary, it wasn't violent enough." Another writer asks, why should they observe the law? "According to the honk culture, everything we do is illegal because *they* make the laws. The whole business of definition is really crucial and it's crucial to make people see how it works, e.g., what is the law but some words oinked out by some honk meeting in a building somewhere and conspiring to douche some cultural group that lives differently than the lawmakers?"

Well, it is too early by far to know that repression—the repression of the unlawful—is in fact settled public policy. We shall need to wait before we can say that the mechanisms of our society will work together to prevent revolutionary minorities from conspiring to destroy the freedoms of those who disagree with them. No doubt the recent rash of bomb throwing is an expression of their special indignation at being contradicted. They manage to give the impression, in their literature, that they are truly astonished that the society they are attacking should exhibit, however genially, some of the manners that the New Left has all along insisted are altogether characteristic of the society they now despise for the incremental effrontery of talking back to them.

Excesses on the Right

July 4, 1970

Believing as firmly as I do in the necessity, for reasons practical and symbolic, for what some people call "repression," I feel the corresponding obligation to pass along reports of what would certainly seem to be utterly senseless examples of repression, and what I have in mind is the situation as told me by two observers, in Santa Barbara, California.

It is there, you will remember, that the Kids keep disrupting the campus, so as to make genuine educational activity something that only those skilled in yoga can conduct. It is there, also, that the Kids keep burning down the Bank of America building, for no better reason than that it is a symbol of The (hated) Establishment. And, as one would quite properly assume, it is there that the forces of order have congregated in order to repress the disrupters. What is in question is whether these forces have conducted themselves intelligently. The larger question is whether the individual states of the Union have sufficiently trained riot-control detachments in the art of self-discipline. It is my own conviction that the qualities of firmness and geniality are near-perfectly combined in Ronald Reagan, and that therefore instances of apparently unjustifiable excesses committed by police officials who are unanswerable to him, suggest that all such units are inadequately trained, and that the good policemen are permitting the brutes among them to set the style of counter-rioting repression, even as the good students have permitted the few fanatics among them to set the style for student demonstrations.

Mr. Jack R. Koers, Jr., is a graduate student at Santa Barbara of conservative political disposition. He writes:

"I live in Isla Vista. The entire community appears to be something akin to a war zone. Outside my apartment police officers search the bushes with flashlights and shotguns for people who are dumb enough to step outside their homes. There are ten large dump trucks full of shotgun-equipped deputies. The trucks drive around the otherwise quiet streets at very high speed and fire pepper gas canisters down streets or through apartment windows. There are 30 to 40 patrol cars that scream through the area at speeds close to 70 mph. Their purpose, besides running over dogs, is unknown to this quite terrified observer. I understand, however, that at various times they stop in front of an apartment, kick down the door, and proceed to beat the residents, sometimes arresting them. This happened to a friend of mine last night. His mistake was in displaying a Turkish flag, which the police assumed was sufficient cause for a good beating. This friend used to be very conservative. . . ."

A friend, a young faculty member who voted for Goldwater, writes about a colleague scooped up along with students who refused to disperse when told to do so. "The Los Angeles special forces were brought in. The helicopter turned on its lights, and huge dump trucks full of what looked like Martians arrived to disperse or arrest. Tear gas . . . a horror show. . . . 'Once inside the jail,' my friend reported, 'you are truly theirs. . . . They would line you up against the wall with specific instructions to have your nose only touching it. You can't see a thing, which is the point of it. You can't see their badge numbers. Then for absolutely no reason they would walk up behind you and smash your face up against the concrete wall. The more courageous kids who wouldn't take this, and who yelled, were sent to solitary. Across the way the girls were getting the worst of it. They were even maced. I spent the night. I was allowed one phone call. My wife arrived the next morning at 10:45 with the bail. I was not released until 3:00 the following morning.' A middle-aged insurance salesman, who has voted Republican all his life and has lived in Isla Vista for years, was arrested while standing out on his front lawn. He is enraged. An assistant D.A. who lives in Isla Vista was arrested. He tried to tell the police who he was. They didn't listen. He was booked and thrown in jail. Eight hours later, he was discovered, and curiously all charges were instantly dropped, and the record of his arrest was cancelled. That kind of thing, of course, really warms the kids' hearts."

And—my friend asks—"Are we conservatives to stand back and allow this to happen? Allow ourselves and our system to be outsmarted by a small group of shrewd and utterly immoral madmen from the Left, who exploit police misbehavior and radicalize whole areas? I don't think we can afford the luxury. I think it is up to the conservatives to make the first concession." I agree.

Bearing Down on the Big Boys

April 16, 1970

I have been Kid-watching for the last few days, trying to explore the mood of those who listen and think about the current disorders, the causes and the cures thereof. I have been advancing at the colleges the thesis that precisely what is needed these days, properly understood, is a very solid dose of repression: not in a spirit of vindictiveness, but in the spirit of teaching those who wonder whether the United States is very serious about surviving the current doubts about itself, and about the worthwhileness of its essential institutions.

I have advanced the proposition that the toleration of revolutionary dissent is something that America has traditionally practised (at such times as we have practised it) primarily as a demonstration of our own complacency, not out of respect for any abstract right to revolutionize.

We are engaged in testing in this country, in such proceedings as those against the Chicago Seven, whether the law can stand up against such organized judicial assaults upon it as the bomb throwers and their lawyers are capable of launching. That is the moment for action, bearing in mind the injunction by Hamilton that "the hope of Impunity is a strong incitement to sedition; the dread of punishment, a proportionably strong discouragement to it." It was also Hamilton who observed that the suggestion that mere law, unfortified by force, is "the only admissible principle of republican government, has no place but in the reveries of those doctors whose sagacity disdains the admonitions of experimental instruction."

So, in an age when barbarians plot to drop bombs in department stores, and other barbarians succeed in preventing others from speaking, the time is clearly at hand for what some choose to call repression, what others call a militant defense of the law. Thoughtful students can see the point, but the great tug of their emotional opposition, or so it seems, is their profound conviction that the adults' concern for the law is a selective thing, that we are disposed to enforce only those laws we desire to see enforced, and that we are careful to select our victims from the ranks of the weak and the dispossessed. They have a point.

I think for instance of Governor Kirk of Florida, who has been grandstanding his defiance of the law these days. At this writing, the courts appear to have won, and the Governor has capitulated, under the pressure of a $10,000-per-day sentence. It is good that he should have done so. On the other hand, I did not run into one student who believed that the day would ever come when in fact he would have to put up that $10,000, any more than the postmen and the teachers and the motormen and the air traffic controllers have had to put up the money they have been formally assessed. Do you remember Ross Barnett? He was Governor of Mississippi. He defied the law flagrantly, was threatened with all manner of things. I know not where he resides— perhaps at the Smithsonian Institution. But I do know he does not reside in jail. The government, in order to be convincing, needs to go after some big targets.

I would suggest, for instance, Justice Douglas. It is simply unconvincing to send seven revolutionists who come together in Chicago to jail for conspiring to cause riots, and to maintain on the high court a gentleman who publishes a book in which he suggests that revolution is probably the only indicated course to break the institutional logjam. Mr. Douglas should be impeached, and notwithstanding that Mr. Robert Welch has given impeachment a bad name. The gentlemen who have been running New Jersey have convinced most thoughtful Americans that the law has been, in the past few years, their own warm puppy. Vigorous prosecutions could help here.

There are interesting signs of a crackdown on licentious sedition. The Supreme Court has ruled that a refractory defendant can be bound and gagged. Another court has ruled that a policeman may disperse a meeting that veers towards unruliness. A Grand Jury is investigating charges that students at American University violated the rights of other students by preventing them from engaging in activities of the R.O.T.C. Here is the warp and woof of what the revolutionists, always oblivious to the rights of counter-revolutionists, call repression: what others call the politics of stability. But if we are to be convincing, we must go also after the high and the mighty. Other nominations are welcome.

Impeach Justice Douglas?

April 21, 1970

The Democratic Congressman who had demanded of Republican leader Gerald Ford that he be specific on the matter of why Justice William O. Douglas should be impeached makes a good point — although it is as much his responsibility as Mr. Ford's to concern himself with whether Mr. Douglas has destroyed his usefulness, and Mr. Douglas's book is as easily available to Democrats as to Republicans. And anyway, a précis of Mr. Douglas's book appears in the current issue of a pornographic monthly readily available.

There, nestled among the pudenda, is an article by Justice Douglas entitled "Redress the Revolution," an excerpt from his book, *Points of Rebellion*. Mr. Douglas begins by talking about the generally unsatisfactory state of affairs in America today, including the recent elimination of his favorite trout stream. Then suddenly he finds himself talking about violence, which he concedes "has no constitutional sanctions." This he would appear to regret, because he adds immediately, "but where grievances pile high and most of the elected spokesmen represent the establishment, violence may be the only effective response."

Mr. Douglas reaches abroad for illustrations. He recites tales of horror about life in Guatemala as related by two priests and a nun— ex-nun and ex-priests being perhaps more accurate, since post-Guatemala, they got married. Anyway, Mr. Douglas, who is supposed to be expert on the rules of evidence, passes along the extraordinary news that the Maryknoll priests, "between 1966 and 1967 . . . saw more than 2,800 intellectuals, students, labor leaders, and peasants assassinated by right-wing groups because they were trying to combat the ills of Guatemalan society." An altogether astounding story, as I say. First, that there should have been 2,800 assassinations in tiny Guatemala over a one-year period without anybody knowing about it, second that the assassinations should have been directed against those who sought to combat rather than promote evil; but most ex-traordinary of all, that Guatemalan authorities should have summoned two priests and one nun to witness each and every one of said assassinations.

Mr. Douglas has at this point picked up a lot of steam, and he reports gleefully that the priests advised Guatemalan peasants who approached them, that under the circumstances, it is okay by God to use violence. Under the circumstances . . .

Mr. Douglas moves now to America. Here, he concedes, we do not turn so readily to violence. However, we do run the risk of violence— because the young generation doesn't like the way things are run in America, believing that the entire governing class is run by the special interests.

Now, he explains, the situation was very similar back in 1776.

Then, Americans demanded a restructuring of our institutions. "That restructuring was not forthcoming and there was revolution."

And then, explicitly, the climax. "You must realize that today's establishment is the new King George III. Whether it will continue" — note, that Mr. Douglas would have us believe that the establishment does now exercise the tyrannical practices of George III — "we do not know. If it does, the redress, honored in tradition, is also revolution."

Now what Mr. Douglas has said very simply is that such conditions as legitimized revolution in 1776 now exist in America in 1970. He seems to be saying that George III — the establishment — might well be given, for a little longer, a chance to reverse itself. But that is one man's judgment. Those who — for instance the Chicago Seven — believe that America has been given long enough to change its ways, and therefore advocate instant revolution, disagree with Mr. Douglas only on a matter of timing. What they advocate — violent revolution — is in Mr. Douglas's view, very simply, honored by tradition.

If that is not sufficient cause for impeaching an official of the government who has sworn to defend the Constitution and the execution of its laws, then nothing justifies impeachment. It is quite extraordinary that Congress should have got lathered up over the nickel and dime malversations of Justice Fortas, while sleeping on this one. If Mr. Douglas is not impeached, he may have proven by other means than he intended, that indeed American society is irretrievably corrupt.

Madison, Wisconsin: The Peak

September 5, 1970

Gerald Cohen, a twenty-seven-year-old graduate student at the University of Wisconsin, has been working for his doctorate which he had expected to get about a year from now, but now it will be delayed. For just how long, it is too early to say, because it will take weeks, perhaps even months, exactly to assess the damage done to him by the explosion that all but destroyed the mathematics and physics building ten days ago at Madison, killing one student, and maiming another, destroying several million dollars' worth of equipment, and a dozen lifetimes' scholarly research.

Mr. Cohen is recorded as having said, "It's just stupid—why pick on us? The thing that really galls us is that we don't have anything to do with [Vietnam]—we're just as much against the war as they are."

I suppose under the stress of the circumstances one should forgive Mr. Cohen an inexactitude which, were it committed in the field of physics, would have toppled a skyscraper. He seems to be saying that the blowing up of buildings and the killing of people provided it is established that said people and buildings serve military or paramilitary purposes is one thing, to do that to people who are against the war is another. He is of course quite wrong. Dean Rusk is entitled to the identical protections that William Fulbright is entitled to.

It takes only a moment's reflection to consider what are the consequences of Cohen's Law. If those who oppose the war should feel free in conscience to destroy those who support the war, then those who support the war might, by analogous reasoning, feel free in conscience to destroy those who oppose the war. It would be a dreadful pity if, Mr. Cohen having spent months and months reconstituting his research, a Weatherman faction of Young Americans for Freedom should blow it up again, in punishment for Mr. Cohen's refusal to support the national war effort.

One can hope that he, and his fellow graduate students—and the senior professors who indulge the fanatics who are disrupting the campuses—will recognize that they are, in many ways, victims of themselves, even as the German people were, many of them, victimized by their own early indulgences of Hitler. There are those who, closely observing the inflections of the revolutionary underground press, believe that the revolutionists are themselves slightly awed by the universal dismay that followed the bombing. They are—again, some of them—wondering whether the indiscriminate terrorism of which that bombing was an example is really paying off. After all, nobody at all was mad at Mr. Cohen, or at his colleagues, who were killed or hospitalized; or even at his professors, who were engaged in purely intellectual research.

I am advised that in recent weeks the new heroes of the New Left are the Tupamaros, who recently abducted, and then slaughtered, a United States official in Uruguay. That sounds very good to our revolutionists. After all, the American was held hostage, and his liberty was promised on the condition that the Uruguay government would release fifty political prisoners. When he was killed, what was the world bereft of? Merely an agent of the United States military-industrial colonialist enterprise, so who should mourn his passing? Why not—the thinking goes—kidnap, say, the local CIA-recruiter, hold him hostage demanding, say, freedom for the local Black Panthers who are imprisoned, and then shoot him if they are not released? By doing that, in the style of the Tupamaros, you do not offend the sentiment of—if not exactly Mr. Cohen, those who take Mr. Cohen's reasoning to logical extremes.

The Tupamaros, of course, did not discover abduction as an instrument of revolution or of terrorism. Neither did the North Vietnamese, although it is they who have practised that art most extensively in recent years. And it is they who teach that art in an institute located near Hanoi to students of revolution the world over. Those who continue to cling to the kindergarten superstition that what is going on in South Vietnam is a civil war would do well to explain why the principal sponsor of that war, North Vietnam, bothers to maintain an institute which teaches other Asiatics—and Africans, and South Americans—how to use kidnapping as an instrument of blackmail and terrorism.

So that we can expect a refinement in the art of native revolutionizing, in the months ahead. We shall certainly need a refinement in the art of counter-revolutionizing.

William Kunstler

September 24, 1970

The other day, asked by the moderator at the University of Rochester if I could suggest a measure that would help to bring judicial reform, I answered yes, the disbarment of William Kunstler. Many of the students booed, to whom I replied that they could hardly be booing me, it must be that they disapproved the canon of ethics that binds lawyers in New York State. Either Kunstler must be disbarręd, I said, or the canon of ethics repealed: the two cannot co-exist. The crowd was silent, but sullen, as was Mr. Kunstler, who shared the platform with me.

It was a coincidence that the day before, James L. Buckley (he is my brother, which is also a coincidence), running for the Senate in New York State, called publicly for Mr. Kunstler's disbarment, and asked the other two candidates, Richard Ottinger and Charles Goodell, to join with him in asking the Association of the Bar of the City of New York to take action against Mr. Kunstler.

A still further coincidence is that the evening before the debate at Rochester, I saw a pre-publication copy of the October *Playboy* magazine, which carries a long interview with Mr. Kunstler, some of the racier passages of which would no doubt have been quoted in the letter addressed by James Buckley to the president of the Bar Association, the Honorable Bernard Botein, if James Buckley had read *Playboy.*

On resistance: "It is the role of the American left," says lawyer Kunstler, "to resist rather than merely protest: to resist illegitimate authority." What is "illegitimate authority"? Why, the authority that ordains "the draft . . . any payment of taxes to support the war in Vietnam . . . the domestic and foreign policies of a government that crushes people on every level [he means the United States Government] . . . all the things in this society that tend to degrade and destroy people." In very plain English, Mr. Kunstler says that no American need obey the law.

How, specifically, should we go about breaking the law? Well, take the college situation. "The students can take over [their] college by occupying its buildings." Just plain occupying them? No— the students should occupy the buildings pending the administration's capitulation. If the administration refuses to grant the students' demands, they move one step further. "Another form resistance could take would be the burning down of a particular college building."

This was too much even for *Playboy.* "You condone arson?" Kunstler was asked.

"Yes," said Kunstler, "if a point has been reached in a given situation where the mechanisms of society are not responding to serious grievances."

In plain English that means: go ahead and burn down the building if in your opinion your grievances are sincere, and the mechanisms of society have not appeased you. Speaking for myself, I can count sixty-eight times during the period since my twenty-first birthday, when, applying the Kunstler Code, I'd have felt compelled, personally, to put a torch to the White House.

Can we assume that when the Vietnam war is over, so will Mr. Kunstler's war be over against the U.S.? Not at all. "I would hate to think," he told *Playboy*, "that the war in Vietnam could be the only catalyst for resistance. There is so much more that remains to be resisted: the oppression of black people . . . poverty . . . unequal distribution of wealth, and so on."

Really, our society is surely suicide-bent if William Kunstler is permitted to serve as a *lawyer*. One might as well license a werewolf to practice medicine. Kunstler is a revolutionary. He wishes ardently to politicize all American institutions, and he begins, of course, with the courts. Was the recent mess in Chicago old Judge Hoffman's fault? Don't be ridiculous. "No matter who the judge was, the defendants would have tried to focus on the war in Vietnam, on the issues of racism, poverty, and youth culture," Kunstler now reveals.

There is a case to be made for giving an individual a certain amount of scope for his revolutionary ambitions. There is no tradition whatever for permitting him to work from a privileged position within an institution—our judicial system—which requires loyalty to the processes of law. The disbarment of William Kunstler would serve not only the practical purpose of removing a cinder from the eye of the judicial system, it would mean the affirmation of the legal system by those who are trusted to maintain its standards.

October 12, 1971

The problem of William Kunstler extends now beyond the bounds of legal propriety. But pause there for a minute.

William Kunstler is a practising lawyer, and the question before the house is—ought he to be permitted to practise law? The general assumption is: Why not, it's a free country, isn't it?

To which the answer is that we are a country that seeks to be free, but in order to achieve that objective, it is required that we enforce certain rules, for instance thou shalt not murder, thou shalt not steal. In order to enforce those laws, we set up a court system. That system depends, for its effective functioning, on the behavior of people who play a role in it—judge, prosecutor, defense counsel, juror.

You can make an abstract case for permitting anybody to practise medicine provided that person's client knows full well that he is talking to somebody who never went through medical school. Because the transaction affects, alone, the client himself. But where a trial is concerned, the defense attorney is only one of the moving parts. If he orbits about totally out of control, the result is that the coordination necessary to the approximation of justice is simply impossible. That's why there are rules for lawyers. Such rules as William Kunstler, given to contumely in the courtroom, and to the disparagement of judges and indeed of the system, in that acid-rock rhetoric which is his trademark, consistently violates, contributing to chaos in the courtroom.

The reason (the lawyers will tell you this discreetly) that they don't go ahead and disbar him is not because he hasn't violated the canons of the profession, but because they fear to make a martyr of him. A prudential judgment. The trouble with it is that, widely applied, it is a ticket to immunity. Don't go after the Mafia boss, or you will make him a martyr in the eyes of the Italian community. Don't execute Manson, or you will give rise to a Cult of Manson. Don't exact justice, when the consequences of doing so, carefully weighed, could mean a net worsening of the situation. It doesn't take much imagination to recognize that the results of that line of reasoning include: don't pass civil rights laws, because that will encourage lawlessness in the South.

William Kunstler should be disbarred, or the canons of legal behavior should be pickled and sent to the Smithsonian as antiquarian relics of another civilization. But I pause now not to consider Kunstler the lawyer, but Kunstler the polemicist.

I have reference to an appearance he made recently at Colgate University. He was in good voice. He spoke about Attica. He told the students that the dead there had been "murdered in cold blood in your name and my name." Cold blood? Why would police murder in cold blood eight of their brothers, who were being held hostage?

They were murdered in cold blood by a "horde of racist state troopers." Later, at a press conference, Kunstler, to quote the student newspaper, "supported the idea of prisoners taking hostages to accomplish their goals." Kunstler, in other words, urges the violation of the law, the kidnapping of officials, and presumably, their execution if their demands are not met—the term "hostage" having no other meaning.

About Nelson Rockefeller, Kunstler said that he "deserved to be ruled out of the human race." He called for an indictment of Nelson Rockefeller for murder.

One notes that the rhetoric has become, well, rabid. Rockefeller is a murderer. The state police murderously and intentionally killed not only the prisoners but the guards. All American justice is a travesty. Prisoners should take the law into their own hands. Prisoners should kill guards if their demands are not accepted.

Let madmen be madmen. Eventually the froth turns off the listeners, and the madmen go off to live and sweat in the fever swamps. But I think the time is overdue for sane members of the community, Left and Right, to draw the line. I have not often had appreciative words for Nelson Rockefeller. But out of respect for him, and in protest against the slander of him, I hereby resolve not to share a public platform again with William Kunstler; not until he has shown, by act or deed, the contrition that is appropriate when one assigns evil, murderous, sadistic motives to someone who seeks to do his duty, never mind that he may do it clumsily, or make mistakes. I do not wish Mr. Kunstler to be put in jail, unless that is what the law of criminal libel requires. But I do wish that he should experience the isolation which he has earned from the civilized community.

VIII. The Education
of the Kids

Cambodia

May 9, 1970

The idea of corporate protest is always interesting, and there is a long tradition of it. But as it is developing on the campuses, it becomes at least ludicrous, at most very very dangerous.

It ought to be clear that what is upon us is a national mood. The evolution from collegiate protests over the alleged persecution of the Black Panther Party, to collegiate protests over the decision to move into Cambodia was all but unnoticeable. The students feel like stirring, the weather is right for it (have you noticed that the conscience tends to rest when the climate is cold?), there are incidental benefits (how nice to waive final exams in the name of world peace), and not a little excitement (the morning's newspaper shows on its front page a dozen students' hands outstretched, voting to close down New York University).

A few observations. 1) Everybody's getting into the act will have a desirable effect in one particular respect. When a single college is the focus of attention, the radio, the television, the newspapers and the magazines cover the campus like Verdun, and the whole of the country is privy to the thoughts, counsels, and acts of the dramatis personae. Thus it was in Berkeley a few years ago, in Columbia in 1968, at Yale a fortnight ago. Pretty heady stuff. But now everybody has got into the act. I do believe that if the University of Illinois decided tonight to suspend all future academic activity for the balance of the year, the students could not count on getting a paragraph in the New York *Times*. (Come to think of it, perhaps the University of Illinois has already decided to close down.)

Now since the whole purpose of the walkouts is to stir the adult community, what's going to happen when the adult community fails to stir? The grandest joke of all is the suggestion that academic activity is being suspended in order to permit the students to reflect on the meaning of the Black Panther persecution or of Mr. Nixon's venture in Cambodia.

I propose, in the next day or so, to put on dark glasses and a great big mustache and walk slowly across the Yale campus. To any student I overhear discussing the legal plight of the Black Panthers, I shall ceremoniously award a plaque. For the majority, the suspension of classes is to the stimulation of moral concern as Good Friday has become to church-going.

2) The plight of the true dissenter is unrecognized. I mean, the student who does not believe that United States officials are conspiring to deprive the Black Panthers of their civil liberties, or that Richard Nixon has been transformed into Dr. Strangelove. That student is genuinely forlorn. For the last several years he has comforted himself by the thought that even on campus he is among the majority, an inert majority to be sure. He is no longer confident of that. He hoped, until very recently, that the administration and the faculty of his college would assert themselves, towards a restoration of order and reason.

But it went the other way. Can you think, with the noble exception of Hayakawa, of a single college president who has unambiguously opposed the barbarians? No doubt there are such, but they are very silent about it, or else the press has missed a big story.

What are the minority among the students doing? I know of one case which I fear is not unique. The young man I was told about went out to buy a gun. Because he reasons that the repression that should have been ventured yesterday, back when it might have been done bloodlessly— with suspensions, fines for contempt of court, that kind of thing— is going to turn very bloody today. And he desires to protect himself. Against whom? Against the barbarians on the campus, to be sure. But also against indiscriminate police and national guardsmen. When order breaks down all around you, you are forced back on your personal resources. And in our society, one's personal resources are— a gun.

3) The colleges should, under the circumstances, close down. And the summer should be spent in true meditation of what the consequences are of the breakdown of civil society.

Dear Diary: A Commencement Address

June 23, 1970

Dear Diary: Yesterday, I delivered the commencement address at a very large university in California, and it was something, let me tell you. The campus has a reputation of being pretty calm, I mean compared to some of the others. But they had a lot of excitement just the same this year, and halfway through the winter, the Chancellor had to cancel the black studies program after threats had been made against the administrator of it. And then the morning of the commencement, authorities confiscated 500 copies of the student paper, because it had in it a reproduction of a dirty picture that had appeared in another California college paper, which got the regents into an uproar, saying they weren't going to appropriate any more money for student pornography, the students would have to pay for their own. Free love yes, free smut no, I guess you'd call it.

Anyway, when I got to the Chancellor's office (he is a very nice man, and doesn't give in to the kids when they are wrong, which is very often nowadays, I take it), he told me he wanted me to see a couple of things before the show went on. The first was a widely distributed letter from a student called "Jim" addressed to "Dear Mom and Dad," protesting various things the Chancellor had done. One paragraph that, naturally, caught my eye, said, "William Buckley is going to speak. We asked the Chancellor for permission to let some of our people speak too. He refused. So we have to find alternate [Dear Diary, *you* know that *I* know that the right word here is "alternative"] means of expressing our sense of outrage at the invitation to Buckley and the hatred he sells. So we're going to present ... actions which in themselves are statements against the glib assurance and barely repressed hatred which Mr. Buckley represents."

Then the Chancellor showed me a prepared statement he was going to read at the outset of the ceremonies, about how he had thought of telephoning me a few days ago when he heard there was going to be trouble, asking me whether under the circumstances I would like to change my mind about going, but he decided not to, because to do so would be to admit that his university "no longer had the maturity of a university."

So the program began, three or four thousand people there, and we got through the "Star-Spangled Banner" all right, that was a relief— at UCLA, when the Chancellor was inaugurated a while back, he cancelled the national anthem because he said it would be provocative. Then the Chancellor read his statement, and you could see the troublemakers who were maybe 5, 10 percent, sitting off mostly to one side. Then he introduced the president of the Student Body, a black student who spoke for a very long time, but not loud enough so that the people sitting behind him could hear much of what he said, only we got the drift, things like this was an oppressive community, the Chancellor was very arbitrary, and so on.

And then he said that a few of the students had a presentation to make to Mr. Buckley, and a couple of kids came up on the platform with a largish cardboard box, which obviously had in it something live, because it quivered on the way up, and sure enough it was a little pig. The girl offered me the leash, but I let it slip through my fingers, and the pig went off towards the podium, where the Chancellor was by this time reading the accomplishments of a young man who was standing up there to get his scholarship. But at that moment the pig began to urinate right by the Chancellor, and nobody paid any attention to the student who had worked very hard for a couple of years to distinguish himself— how is that relevant in a modern university? Then my turn came, and I spoke uninterruptedly, if you don't count a dozen students filing out, and one smoke bomb that sort of fizzled off in the wrong direction. Then the degrees were given. Everyone who came up was dressed in cap and gown. Except one girl, getting her Masters, who was dressed in a bikini. She was short, and weighed about 175 pounds, I guess, and I remember thinking, well, no one is exploiting *her*. And one guy, dressed in red undershorts and garters, carrying a banana pie which he presented to the Chancellor and a small American flag, which he later burned, thus contributing to air pollution. They sang the college song, and it was over.

The Chancellor was awfully pleased about it all— after all, nobody had been hurt, the speaker hadn't been booed, or shouted down, in fact he got a standing ovation, there were no obscenities shouted into the mike. As we arrived at the disrobing room, the

Student Body president approached me, stuck out his hand, and said he wanted to apologize about the pig, but that was the only part of his speech he wanted to apologize for. I said unfortunately (obviously under the circumstances I should have said fortunately) the pig-part was the only part of his speech I had been able to make out. I left wondering why he should now be apologizing for something he had done only one hour earlier? It's funny that even an Iron Chancellor and all his men don't really have the power to make a small minority behave, in the modern university, but the small minority has the power to make others misbehave.

Anyway, Dear Diary, there's a lot of us ought to do some thinking about commencement addresses, though as you know, this is the first time I've had any trouble, and I've given a dozen in the last couple of years. You get to wondering though, whether, in the old phrase, you're playing horse to other people's Lady Godiva.

A College Yearbook, Class of 1970

October 13, 1970

An anonymous mischief-maker just now sent me an enormous volume mysteriously called *Nutmeg*. It turns out to be the yearbook of the graduating class of the University of Connecticut at Storrs.

One hundred or so pages after the frontispiece, which consists exclusively of the clenched fist symbol over the caption STRIKE, we reach the section on the "Associated Student Government." Here the editor breaks away from the preceding dozens of pages of telegraphese to describe the ASG— as "the organization through which students express their opinions on academic, community, and political matters. Student clubs sponsored and funded by the ASG range from the Ping-Pong Club to . . . the *Nutmeg*. Perhaps the most important function served by the ASG is that it provides an effective lobby for the elimination of any dissenting opinion.

There is, to judge from *Nutmeg*, only one point of view at the University of Connecticut. One might call it Kidspeak. ￼

Who—for instance—were the speakers who went to UConn during the year? Well, the most conservative was Whitney Young, the affable leader of the National Urban League. On the American spectrum, Mr. Young would weigh in as a Liberal Democrat. At UConn, he must have been invited to deliver the Mark Hanna Oration.

The rest? Well, the black militant from Yale, Kenneth Mills. Sam Bowles, the moratorium-maker from Harvard. At least every Black Panther in the country, and then some. The sodomist-poet Jean Genet. Ben Spock and Allard Lowenstein. Allen Ginsberg, who is delivered to American colleges by the milkman. Froines from the Chicago Seven.

And so on. The editors' idea of art is to split the pictures evenly between cherubic students looking skyward in the hope that America will end its tawdry life and be reborn in innocence, and pictures of unwashed students with heavy beards looking like the self-flagellant orders of the Middle Ages, crushed down by the sorrows of this world. On page five, the student looking heavenward, in turtleneck sweater, wearing three peace buttons, is about eight years old, and just possibly is the editor of this volume. There are one thousand pictures—or is it ten thousand?—of students gathering to protest everything except, one gathers, their yearbook.

The wittiest line in the volume is the sign on the back of a coed, "Support the Mets, Not the War" (you can't repress the kids' sense of humor!). The highpoint in logic is the sign on the back of a student's blazer, "When I die I'll go to Heaven because I've spent my time in Hell"—a metaphysical subtlety that eluded Dante. The graphic highpoint is a student with hair all over himself and an Indian-beaded whatever-you-call-it around his temple, carrying an atlas, for no discernible reason, over his right shoulder; while leaning down, her right hand over his navel, her left behind *his* behind, is an uncombed young girl, with an Indian thing around *her* temple, both of them of course unsmiling, and the caption, "Let the world take notice of student power."

Amen. One would think that President Homer Babbidge would do just that. But the text of the yearbook, which constitutes those telegraphic disjointures I alluded to, includes the following sequence. "Babbidge on leave from campus . . . Babbidge

comes back . . . Nobody knew Babbidge was gone . . ."
So one gathers. On page 92, reproduced full-size, is an order issuing from the administration on May 11. "This is to advise all persons entering this [ROTC] building without permission or legitimate university business, that they are engaged in an improper act. Persons knowingly abusing or misusing these premises should do so only if they are prepared to accept penalties." Pages 90 to 91 are a spread of pictures showing the forbidden ROTC building teeming with students the day after the notice was posted. They used it as a playpen and painted it with Mother Goose-anti-Vietnam art. Needless to say, no students were prosecuted. Because if Babbidge doesn't behave, *Nutmeg* will replace him. Meanwhile, life presumably goes on, at the University of Havana, at Storrs, Connecticut.

Summer Vacation, 1970

August 6, 1970

As far as one can gather, the situation at Powder Ridge was this: the owners of the ski resort there, near the little Connecticut town of Middlefield, casting about for a profitable use to which to put their 300 acres during the summer season, thought to sponsor a weekend rock festival, with rock bands galore, and thousands and thousands of kids, in the style of Woodstock.

That, precisely, is what the neighbors feared would happen, so their representative approached the local judge and convinced him that you just can't have one of those festivals on a mere 300-acre lot, because the kids, and their detritus, spill out over the entire neighborhood and make life hell. Not alone in the active sense, that they wander around naked, make love on the front lawn, introduce the local kids to whatever drugs the local kids haven't yet been introduced to, tie up the roads and, for all intents and purposes, isolate the little village . . .

There are the passive burdens. It is all very well for the entrepreneurs to promise that they will provide all the necessary facilities, but what if they don't? Or what if, as happened at Woodstock and Altamont, more people come than the impresarios had bargained for? Many many more people? Obviously the contingent obligation of the community, in a civilized society, is to drop everything and go to the rescue of the kids. Get them sanitary facilities, doctors, food, water, psychiatrists.

Well, the elders of Middlefield, Connecticut, won their way in the courts, but it was a pyrrhic victory. Because the entrepreneurs were now technically relieved. If there was to be no rock concert, no ticket selling, then their obligations were at an end. Right?

But what happened was that the Kids came anyway. Some of them came because they were confident that at the last minute some court or other would override the lower court—maybe Earl Warren would come out from retirement to oblige? *Something* would happen, something always does, when the Kids' happiness is at stake.

But in fact the courts stuck to their guns, so that when the Kids came—30,000 of them, by one estimate—there *wasn't* anything to do. A couple of fugitive rock bands came in and played, amid judicial harumphing and threats of prosecution. But mostly the children simply wandered around, looking for things to do. Some of them went home, but lots of them didn't. So what *did* they do? Anybody who asks that question without knowing the answer is clearly over thirty, and a threat to progress.

I quote Dr. William Abruzzi, who sort of specializes in tending to the Kids at their festivals. Well, said the doctor, that stupid judge is responsible for what happened. The youths, having "nothing to do," naturally took drugs. As of Saturday, he reported, nearly 1,000 youths had been treated for bad drug reaction. Ten to 20 percent of those suffering bad drug reaction had had "wild, physical, muscular, hostile trips," explained the doctor. Sure, there were token arrests, about 30 of them. It didn't seem to make much difference. "Along the main road to Powder Ridge and inside the garbage-laden ground," reported the New York *Times*, "drug sellers were still openly peddling their wares, including LSD, mescaline, and other powerful hallucinogens." One of the peddlers, picked up by a police infiltrator, had *$13,000* in his pockets.

So there was *that* problem. And, of course, they ran out of food. One resident donated a thousand cheeseburgers, which helped; but it wasn't nearly enough. The water in the local lake is apparently polluted, so it wasn't recommended that they swim there, and it was awfully hot. Some neighbors welcomed them in to use the tap water. A bake shop owner, Mrs. DeVito, opened up her air-conditioned back room, and put out a collection basket into which townsfolk could contribute money to help the children. She marked the basket, "Bread for the Free Kitchen," which shows how quickly she picked up the lingo. Indeed she said that she had learned a *lot* of new words. "Or don't you think so, Dude," she said to a reporter, "or are you on an ego trip?"

One gathers that the drug pushers, who are walking around with $13,000 in their jeans, did not contribute to Mrs. DeVito's bread-basket: and one gathers that the children couldn't afford to pay for their own cheeseburgers, having used up all their bread buying mescaline. An American tragedy it was, at Powder Ridge, Connecticut, over the weekend.

Commencement, June, 1971

June 10, 1971

I dwell on what I have labeled "the skyjacker's leverage," intending to suggest the great handle that the mischievous individual has in our technologized social circumstances. One man with a pistol, or even with a watergun that is taken for a pistol, can commandeer an airplane with four hundred people in it, kidnapping the lot of them and, if that is his bent, destroying them. Professor Dan Boorstin has remarked that one of our difficulties arises from the basic fact that we live in a "flow technology," and all that you need to do in order to hurt somebody is: stop. Stop your car on a crowded speedway, and you may cause fifty cars to pile up behind you. The combination of flow technology, and the skyjacker's leverage, can cause wars— and change the tone of social occasions.

Yesterday it was graduation day at a small, venerable, and altogether dignified college near Washington, D.C. In order to hand out the three hundred-odd diplomas it was necessary that the graduates file by quickly, as their names were called, past the president, who gave each one his diploma, and shook his hand.

One gentleman, looking exactly like Sirhan Sirhan, grabbed the diploma from the president but refused to shake his proffered hand, and the result was as if a blot of ink had fallen on the wedding dress of the bride: there was no erasing the memory of it, and all that it signified in the breach of protocol, and of civil attachments. One, student—needing only to refuse to shake hands. Flow technology.

Then there was the student speaker. He had been elected to perform as valedictorian by the members of his class, with whom he is popular; and he is graduating with high honors. His name is called out and, in academic gown, he walks to the podium. With some difficulty, because he is carrying around his neck two saxophones. *Two saxophones.*

He begins to speak—a normal American voice, unaccented, conversational inflections. He gives the names of the students he is grateful to for this and that. Then the names of faculty to whom he is grateful. Then the names of the thinkers and writers he has read, whom he particularly admires. He then begins his address, which is an examination of the foundations of happiness and wisdom.

After a few moments he announces that he will emit a few tones which particularly please him and are freighted with meaning. This he does, blowing on one saxophone. Then he goes on to blow on the other, whether in order to show the superiority of the second, no one could guess, although it was inevitable that it should be better than the first. Then back to his theme, about how to find ecstasy, and love, and "discipline." The speaker had taken care to insert into every printed program a "schematic" of his talk, designed to give the listener a little help in following the points as he made them. The schematic was conveniently supplied with two-way arrows, explaining the more intricate of the speaker's points.

The several thousand listeners listened most patiently. Indeed they listened achingly: surely, soon now—any minute—they would catch . . . a trace of wit? A flash of humor? An oxymoronic felicity? No, never. He was all bug, no lightning. And it lasted and it lasted, in the hot auditorium. And when he was done, the crowd burst into that nervous applause one hears from parents at their children's piano recitals.

At least the young gentleman was in pursuit of virtue, and his exhibitionism, though embarrassing, seemed to be a part of his offering. And after all, of the seven cardinal virtues he touched on only four, leaving the audience with the scant satisfaction that he had not discovered, prior to the commencement exercises, the remaining three.

At least it was over, at least he hadn't called for killing policemen, or raping Mrs. Nixon, or burning up the college. One takes these things in stride at the academy. The skyjacker's leverage. What can you do? What you do is take the ants out of your pants, and resolve to master whichever one of the mysterious Eastern cults teaches you to turn off, when your brothers insist on making protracted asses of themselves.

Summer Vacation, 1971

July 1, 1971

Two years ago, Woodstock Nation was heralded as the beginning of a new national attitude, whose attributes were: gentleness, spontaneity, and emotional abandon. The theorists went quickly to work, and wove wondrous themes about that spectacular in Woodstock, New York, seeing in it a return to the human purities which had been edged out by the industrial revolution, and the institutional calcification of greed, alienation, and envy. Rock was the great catalyst: against that music, that rhythm, the old inhibitions could not compete. Thus the fairy tale.

Woodstock Nation seems in retrospect to have been something more nearly like Götterdämmerung. The next important festival, at Altamont in California, featured the Rolling Stones, protected by jackboot "bikers" who used their chains, and in one fatal case their knives, to keep the Kids orderly. At Powder Ridge, Connecticut, last summer, it was a fiasco, involving legal injunctions forbidding the congregation, and a corporate pout through the medium of drugs, mostly marijuana and hashish.

At McCrea in Louisiana last weekend *everything* went sour. For one thing there was the heat. External discomfort, which traditionally the hippies ignore, so indifferent are they to inessentials, got them down. As the New York *Times* put it, "The sweltering heat made nudity almost essential," a finding that would surely raise the eyebrows of some of those who work in the New York *Times'* composing room. So, by the thousands, nude, they wandered in and out of the river.

Then there was the disorganization. The musicians, unaccountably, didn't turn up until about ten o'clock at night, though the crowd had been waiting for them since dusk. And when they did come, it was hard to hear them, so erratic were the amplifiers. Then there were the "fringe" groups who bore down using violence and the threat of violence. In place of the Hell's Angels, the promoters hired the services of a New Orleans motorcyclist group named the Galloping Gooses. These gentlemen carried shotguns and also used chains, which was not the idea of Woodstock Nation, not at all.

The most striking feature of it all was the use of hard drugs. "Everywhere you look it's uppers and downers and heroin. I've been to a number of festivals before but I've never seen anyone shooting in the open like here," one participant is quoted.

What happened to the carefree message of *Hair?* Already it is as much legend as the Pied Piper of Hamelin or the Wizard of Oz, reminding us of the premonitory line, "Now that I've dropped out / Why is life so weary weary / Answer my weary query / Timothy Leary, dearie." Timothy Leary, dearie. The first of the bards of the new class. Where is he? In North Africa, waging impenetrable vendettas with Eldridge Cleaver and others, making less and less sense, his mind manifestly atrophied by the liberating drugs he pressed on a whole generation bent on unwholesomeness. John Lennon, another of the gurus of the age, has come tumbling down, speaking endlessly and mindlessly about what it was that he went through, knowing only this, that he would not have it again. In New York City, Fillmore East has closed down. It is as if the Catholic Church had closed down Lourdes. Woodstock Nation, R.I.P.

Yesterday I approached a train conductor who stood by as the passengers disembarked, and I asked him, "Is this the 4:52?" No!!

he belched out, not bothering even to turn his head, nor to indicate which train it was, or whether the 4:52 was soon to come. I asked again: "What did you say?" No!!! he replied, boarding the train and slamming shut the door, as if to protect himself from a Hound of Hell. That man is what the trouble is with America, and whatever caused him to explode with annoyance, frustration— to rupture the bonds of affection, in the phrase of Garry Wills— is what we need to poultice. It was always clear that the narcotic frenzies of rock and tumult and drugs would not root it out, though it was not so obvious that the greening of America via Woodstock Nation would wither so soon. "The rock concert is definitely over," one observer commented. Why not?

The Young Conservatives

September 11, 1971

The surprise is that there should be so many who were surprised by the resolutions of the Young Americans for Freedom at their eleventh annual convention in Houston. The delegates at the convention voted to suspend their support of Richard Nixon, and in a straw ballot they nominated Spiro Agnew for President.

Straw ballots and mock conventions do not mean very much in the practical political order. But then it could as well be said that resolutions made at the great big conventions sponsored by the major parties do not mean very much in the practical political order.

Of course the Young Americans for Freedom are purists. Why should they not be? If the intention of the founders of the organization was to advance the fortunes of the Republican Party, they could have enrolled as Young Republicans. President Richard Nixon told us on Monday that he disapproved of price controls, and on Tuesday he invoked price controls: so Young Americans for Freedom should abandon their opposition to price controls? Better to appeal from Philip drunk to Philip sober.

The enthusiasm for Mr. Nixon grew from a series of positions

Mr. Nixon has taken over the years. Most conspicuously in the air at Houston were Mr. Nixon's a) opposition to price controls; b) commitment to the military superiority of the United States; and c) opposition to the recognition of Red China.

Now the YAFers have, indeed, produced some grist for the Condescending of this World. The New York *Times* hasn't been so mirthful since Barnum and Bailey was last in town. Commenting on the popularity of Spiro Agnew at Houston, the *Times* constructed itself a little fantasy:

"If the Vice President should nevertheless care to justify the Houston convention's confidence in him by breaking with Mr. Nixon, he has a ready-made model in the Henry A. Wallace of 1948. Running as an independent against his own former chief, Mr. Wallace got 2.3 percent of the popular vote and none of the electoral. But such is the comparative scarcity of Republican youth, let alone Republican mavericks, that Mr. Agnew could hardly expect to do as dazzlingly well as that."

It is lucky for the New York *Times* that it has such an extensive historical memory. It makes it possible to leap over more recent precedents. In the state over which the New York *Times* presides, a conservative maverick struck out on his own, on a third party ticket, as recently as a year ago, and what do you know: he was elected Senator. When things get very gloomy around these parts, it is an absolutely reliable stimulant to remind oneself that the New York *Times* is represented in the Senate by James Lane Buckley.

Youthful purists don't run countries, and (to be sure) shouldn't. But they are very important. Increasingly important, since the amendment giving the vote to the eighteen-year-olds. Mr. Theodore White, the best general practitioner in American politics in the business, quite candidly confronts the possibility of having to become a pediatrician. He reminds you that there are 27 million people who are newly licensed to vote, and that at the election in 1968 approximately 70 million people voted, and the election turned on a few hundred thousand votes.

What the young people are saying is of considerable bearing. Richard Nixon's election will probably be close, and if he wins it he will win it because he has generated two things: enthusiasm for himself, and fear for the alternative.

The youth are the principal enthusiasm-mongers. And the youthful insistence on principle, though it can be a great drag at places like the Congress of Vienna, keeps you seeing things through unjaded eyes. And that is a contribution the Young Americans for Freedom make to pro-Nixonites and anti-Nixonites alike.

IX. Politics

John Lindsay Snubs Pompidou

February 10, 1970

Back in 1958 Robert Wagner, who was Mayor of New York, refused Ibn Saud the routine reception to which visiting heads of state are traditionally entitled. The following year, Mayor Wagner presided over an enormous affair in honor of Nikita Khrushchev, who was head of the Soviet state.

There were those who remarked the anomaly. Myself, for instance. "Last year," [I wrote in *National Review*] "Mayor Wagner ostentatiously announced his refusal to greet Ibn Saud on the grounds that Ibn Saud discriminates against Jews in Saudi Arabia. Now, as everybody knows, Nikita Khrushchev not only discriminates against Jews, he kills them. On the other hand, he does much the same thing to Catholics and Protestants. Maybe that is why Mayor Wagner has consented to honor Khrushchev: Khrushchev murders people without regard to race, color, or creed . . . and therefore, whatever he is guilty of, he is not guilty of discrimination."

Whatever Mr. John Lindsay's dedication to a New Politics in 1965, it did not carry over to extending the routine courtesies to King Ibn Saud's brother and successor, King Faisal, when he came to town in 1966. The same boycott was promulgated. And now Mayor Lindsay has announced that he will boycott the President of France, who has helped the Arabs, who are at war with Israel.

At this rate, after the next election, Mr. Lindsay will refuse to receive the head of a state that helps any state that helps the Arabs to hurt the Jews— but no, that would mean he would not be able to tender the courtesies of the City to the President of the United States. We have helped France in the past and continue to do so: indeed, we share a major treaty with the French, the Atlantic Pact.

What rounds off the paradox is that a typical week does not go by without Mr. Lindsay's entertaining or being entertained by some functionary of the Soviet Union. Granted, it is not possible to bring Mayor Lindsay into dudgeon, any more than his predecessor, for what the Soviet Union does routinely to the freedom of the Czechs or Hungarians or Rumanians or Poles or whoever. But the same Soviet Union is almost single-handedly responsible for arming the Arabs, who went to war against Israel in 1967 armed by an estimated $2 billion worth of Soviet military hardware.

By contrast, the French commitment to Libya is for $100 million. But, you see, it is unfashionable to be anti-Communist in New York, and fashionable to be pro-Israel. So that the one negative fashion more or less balances the other positive fashion, and they check themselves out. On the other hand, being anti-French is not particularly unfashionable, to say nothing of being anti-Arab. So the mayor, feeding all of the political prejudices into the computer, comes out with a boycott of Pompidou. I ask you to imagine what would have been the reaction if, say, it was Mayor Yorty, boycotting the President of the Soviet Union.

A thought or two:

1) Those of us who hoped fourteen years ago that Israel would reach Cairo, who deplored the assassination of King Faisal II of Iraq, who have applauded Bourguiba's moderation, warned against the communization of Algeria done in the hot Western impatience for anti-colonialism, and cheered the Israeli victory of 1967, feel safe in observing that the boycott of Pompidou under the circumstances is just plain stupid.

In the first place it will not affect French policy. In the second place it neglects to understand what Pompidou is plainly up to. He is concerned to do two things. One is to secure France's interest in Libyan oil. There is no more reason to condemn his doing so than there is to condemn Mayor Lindsay's stake in the Federal treasury: France depends on its oil, even as Mr. Lindsay depends on taxation. Second, Pompidou is attempting to persuade the Mideast to lessen its reliance on Soviet arms, in preference for French arms, intending, that way, to reassert a Western, and presumably more benign influence on Mideast politics, from which Israel would ultimately profit. It is exactly this that the United States, greatly applauded by the liberal community, sought to do after 1948 in sending arms to Yugoslavia.

2) Jewish leaders in New York City should surely speak out against the vulgarization of diplomacy by Mr. Lindsay. "I do not think it is fitting that our great city pay homage to a foreign president who displayed such contempt for world peace," commented Congressman Podell of Brooklyn. Can anyone imagine his saying the same thing if the French had just finished sending $100 million worth of jet planes to Israel? It is humiliating for a proud people to be treated to the social and diplomatic equivalent of currying favor by eating blintzes.

The Strategy of Agnewism

March 5, 1970

Mr. Agnew's speeches are justly celebrated for their color and for the zest with which they profane the icons of Eastern Seaboard liberalism. I mean, imagine saying in a speech, "Senator Fulbright hasn't said anything new or interesting or clever in five years; his intellectual well dried up the day after Walter Lippmann stopped writing his regular column." Really, Mr. Agnew is accomplishing the liberation of the Vice Presidency. If you can say things like that, I think I'd consent to be Vice President.

What's more, Mr. Agnew is not fazed by the horrified reaction of his critics. I cherish his handling of a young editorial potentate who made it in the social-intellectual world of New York as head of a fashionable journal. He found himself, incredibly, at an affair at which the Vice President, incredibly, also found himself. So our hero approaches Mr. Agnew and says, "Mr. Vice President, in one of your speeches last fall you mentioned my magazine in such a way as implied approval of it. That has terribly damaged me. I wonder if I could persuade you to say something critical of it?" Mr. Agnew looked down, for all the world like Charles de

Gaulle, patted the editor on the shoulder, and said in clipped tones, "No favors, young man."

But reading Mr. Agnew's speeches is more than watching late-night wrestling matches. One begins to see, limned in through the flurry of half nelsons, a strategy for the Republican Party, which Mr. Agnew believes is headed for a romantic rendezvous with destiny. What has happened, says Mr. Agnew, is that the Democratic Party is coming apart at the seams. The old Roosevelt coalition, Mr. Agnew observes, rested on four pillars. Namely, the South, the working classes, the Negroes, and the intellectuals.

The South, says Mr. Agnew, is all but won. It is deserting the Democratic Party at a reassuring rate. The workingman, says Mr. Agnew, is on his way over to the Republican Party, for reasons specified and unspecified. For one thing the working class is becoming a middle class. But also there is his resentment over the collapse of law and order, and his resentment of inflation. "In the 1960's the Democratic National Party went on one of the greatest spending binges in history. Yet when the workingman looks to Capitol Hill, what does he see? The leadership of the Democratic Party bellied up at the same old bar—ordering the same old whiskey that brought us the economic hangover in the first place."

The Negro community, Mr. Agnew concedes, is still moon-struck, for the most part, by the Democrats. But the suggestion therefore that the GOP is developing as a regional party is belied by the figures of the 1968 election. "We are hardly in the business of writing off the urban industrial northeast when every large state in the region has a Republican Governor—one recently elected in New Jersey by a landslide."

And, to be sure, the GOP has not won over the class of intellectuals. At whose expense Mr. Agnew has a thoroughly good time. Before the intellectuals can become totally convincing in prescribing for America, why not ask them to show us folks how good they are at running things by asking them to put their own house in order? "Just as other institutions and organizations were challenged and questioned, so too, the academic community went through a decade of crisis. And when the crisis came, the defenses of the academic community—like the British guns at Singapore—were all pointed in the wrong direction. . . . And then the years of permissiveness and indulgence finally culminated in the days of disorder—in violence in our cities and on our campuses. And if you walked through Harlem, or Berkeley, or Columbia or Watts at the height of the disorders, you could hear—through the din of the battle between police and rioters—that unmistakable sound of chickens coming home to roost."

I think it is Mr. Agnew's point that the Republican Party will settle for less than 100 percent of the vote. "Senator Fulbright said some months ago that if the Vietnam war went on much longer the 'best of our young people' would be in Canada. Let Senator Fulbright go prospecting for his future party leaders in the deserters' dens of Canada and Sweden; we Republicans shall look elsewhere." Where most people live.

Election Hysteria

November 7, 1970

Really, we do manage to get excited. It isn't surprising when such as Mr. Pete Hamill traffic in hysteria, it being a necessary part of the paraphernalia of their social rhetoric. But the New York *Times?*—which has preached us so many sermons on the subject of the necessity to avoid panic. . . . Their comment on Senator Charles Goodell's speech announcing his determination to stay in the New York Senatorial contest reads as though it had been tossed out in a bottle from Devil's Island, in the hope that a rogue sea would waft it to shore, and to civilization. Senator Goodell's voice, said the *Times*, is that "of a public official determined to keep freedom from being assassinated by the ruthless night riders of the political right." One can only conclude from this that Richard Nixon and Spiro Agnew are bent upon assassinating freedom, and that James Buckley is their instrument.

Then there is Miss Harriet Van Horne, the syndicated columnist. "If this election goes as President Nixon would like it to go, the long trail will soon be entering a dark tunnel. The

Omnibus Crime Bill . . . will not curb crime but it will drastically curtail freedom. It wipes out in one terrible blow the major guarantees of the Bill of Rights. It gives J. Edgar Hoover and John Mitchell the kind of authority enjoyed by Gestapo chiefs and hanging judges. . . . We shall all be living [a nightmare] as the long train winds through the dark tunnel." I don't remember the rest of the column, but I think she spent it bemoaning the excesses of Spiro Agnew's rhetoric. Now I appeal to the higher intelligence of Miss Van Horne, how can night riders live in tunnels? Really, the voices of moderation ought to concert their metaphors. If you think it's easy to have one foot in the tunnel and the other foot in the stirrup of a horse, well, you are . . . unrealistic.

The *Times's* dirge raises any number of interesting questions, not the least of them how very insecure the editors of the *Times* must judge freedom to be in New York State. And, among other things, how poorly they think of their own colleagues in the journalistic profession. At this writing, three newspapers in New York have come out for the election of Charles Goodell, three for Richard Ottinger, and twenty-nine for James Buckley. Fellow assassins?

The current excitement comes back to the intrusion into this campaign of the Vice President, Mr. Agnew. It is difficult to know just why, inasmuch as Mr. Goodell keeps reminding us that he, Senator Goodell, is a national asset. Surely if he considers himself a national asset, then it is reasonable that the Vice President of the United States, who was certified by the voters two years ago as being a national asset, should be permitted to speak his views on Senator Goodell, even if they are views that contradict Mr. Goodell's?

I mean, I do not understand why Senator Goodell insists that it is right, and indeed noble, for him to exercise his independent judgment, but wrong and ignoble for Mr. Agnew to exercise *his* independent judgment. It is the judgment of Mr. Goodell that he is a blessing to the country, and it is the judgment of Mr. Agnew that he is not. All right, take your choice. Mr. Goodell seems to be saying that Mr. Agnew is depriving the voters of New York State of the opportunity of exercising their choice. His exact words are that Mr. Agnew is undermining the democratic process. I do not understand how Mr. Agnew is contriving to do that. Mr. Agnew is saying what *his* choice is, and— inasmuch as Mr. Agnew does not specialize in ambiguity—presumably what is the choice of the President. How does that deprive the voters of New York of the right to exercise their choice?

If I were a New York State registered Republican voter determined to vote for Mr. Goodell, I simply don't know what would prevent me from proceeding to do so. Is Mr. Goodell suggesting that J. Edgar Hoover will reach in and deflect my voting hand? Or if not Mr. Hoover—he is very discreet—a Greek colonel? Or Chiang Kai-shek?

And I do not understand why someone so fastidiously attached to the processes of democracy as Mr. Goodell is, should have gone along in permitting the Republican Party, at the direction of Governor Rockefeller, to refuse James Buckley the right to contest Mr. Goodell in a Republican primary last summer, on a technicality that the Democrats waived for Robert Kennedy and were prepared to waive for Morris Abram as a matter of course. Actually, that is a silly point. The answer to it is given by the polls, which show that twice as many Republican-registered voters intend to vote for Buckley as for Goodell. So that Mr. Goodell's position reduces to the following: it is extremely undemocratic for the democratically-elected Vice President of the United States to recommend democratic procedures for electing the next Senator from the State of New York to replace the non-democratically appointed incumbent, who declined to face a democratic primary. If that is too complicated for you to follow, read the New York *Times*. If the New York *Times* is too complicated for you to follow, then you and Euclid have something in common.

A few years ago, the *Times* sniffed at the candidacy of another New Yorker, who presented himself on the Conservative line. Said the *Times* (June 25, 1965), "Whether New York is ready for [the candidate] is another matter. Popular demand that he become a candidate has been thunderously absent." Last year, there were two primaries in New York City. John Marchi won the Republican primary. Mario Procaccino won the Democratic primary. Both John Marchi and Mario Procaccino have endorsed the candidacy of James Buckley. Which would appear to make him the nearest thing to a democratic imperative in recent New York history. Had enough?

Moynihan on Nixon

January 2, 1971

Really, people ought to take turns hiring Daniel Patrick Moynihan if only for the pleasure of his leave-takings. His apopemptic graces are exquisitely developed, and what he said about Nixon and his Administration was overdue to be said by someone with high standing in the academic community, particularly someone whose own preferences in politics are liberal, and who grew up in the gardens of Camelot, first as equerry for Averell Harriman, and later as servant to the king himself. The question now is whether the liberal community will listen to what he said because it was their old, accredited pal Moynihan who said it. Or whether they will simply say that Moynihan has gone daft, and go back to treating Nixon and Nixon's ideas with the discrimination of Herblock.

To the end that his words shall not be quickly forgotten, I repeat one or two of them. Remember, here is Moynihan in the East Room of the White House, speaking to several hundred members of Mr. Nixon's Administration. He comes now to his final words, or exhortations, as he calls them.

"The first is to be of good cheer and good conscience. Depressing, even frightening things are being said about the Administration. They are not true." These words, incredibly, are of revolutionary, or if you prefer counter-revolutionary, moment. Because it is quite literally true that the nation's academies are crowded with people who teach that Nixon and the men who surround him are *evil*. That they are mass murderers, who do it for fun and profit. That they care not about human suffering, or indeed about anything more wholesome than their own rancid self-interest. It may seem odd that it should be necessary to speak these words of denial. "*They are not true*" — an elegant meiotic simplicity that lends special eloquence to the sentence, which is normally rendered with verbal extravagance, of which an example might be, "People who say that kind of thing about the Administration are sowing seeds of division and hatred," etc., etc., etc.

And then Mr. Moynihan said something else which is sub-stantively arresting. "Time and again, the President has said things of startling insight, taking positions of great political courage and intellectual daring, only to be greeted with silence or incomprehension. The prime consequence of all this is that the people in the nation who take these matters seriously have never been required to take us seriously."

A brilliant perception. Now those who are wise in the ways of the world know that undoubtedly Mr. Moynihan had in mind some of the words and concepts which he, Moynihan, had sold to the President, or written in for him in some of his speeches. Poor Patrick, he did not understand. Any conservative who has ever been scratched in action understands perfectly. Most liberals, who are moralists, are taught to believe that an idea is to be appreciated or rejected depending on its provenance. If it happened that Adlai Stevenson and Everett Dirksen made the identical proposal on the same day, Stevenson's ideal would have been celebrated, Dirksen's ignored.

Good ideas have come out of conservative hatcheries by the truckload during the last ten years or so and they are simply ignored. That this should be the case even when the ideas come out of the mouth of the President of the United States, who is charged by the Constitution with proposing laws to Congress, is not merely intellectually scandalous, it is politically stultifying.

It is, finally, remarkable that Mr. Nixon succeeded in touching so deeply a man as sensitive as Moynihan, as worldly-wise and as obstinately liberal. Remember, this is the Nixon that Joe McGinniss made a fortune out of by mocking, and that Garry Wills (in his fascinating book) scarifies as a bum human being. Moynihan said: "[I] have seen him late into the night and through the night and into the morning, struggling with the most awful complexities, the most demanding and irresolvable con-flicts, doing so because he cared, trying to comprehend what is right, and trying to make others see it, above all caring, working, hoping for this country that he has made greater already and which he will make greater still."

Dr. Johnson said that epitaphs are not where to look for lapidary judgments on a man's behavior in this world. But Nixon is very much alive, and Moynihan will have to live with these words. I wish him luck.

Lindsay on the Morning Line

January 12, 1971

About twice a week, Mayor John Lindsay denies that he is seeking the Presidency; indeed one can imagine a press conference at the end of which Mr. Lindsay would accidentally say, "You forgot to ask me if I am running for President. The answer is No."

Mr. Lindsay's aides are less demure than their coy master, and the morning's news is that they are making a systematic study of the nation's primary laws, the better to concert the Presidential drive. On the lighter side, a staff member reports that the Mayor has been sent a "Lindsay for President" bumper sticker from a fan club in Los Angeles, which is about the closest you can get to New York City and escape the odor of Mr. Lindsay's spectacular maladministration. But as we know the Presidency does things to people, and vanity is wonderfully resourceful. One simply cannot doubt that Mr. Lindsay gets up in the morning, looks into the mirror, asks, "Who is the fairest mayor of them all?", and blushes boyishly.

What are his prospects? Approximately as follows. Within the Republican Party, not very good. In fact, quite awful. It is true that he enjoys a general popularity, but it is also true that that popularity comes rather from those who have appreciated him on the Johnny Carson show, than from those who have been governed by him over a period of five years. The polls are quite explicit on the subject even within New York State, where two out of three people appreciate him outside the city, and only one out of three within the city. But remember, that includes Democrats, who find the rhetoric of Mr. Lindsay comfortable, as he recites his beads— stop the war in Vietnam, give amnesty to the draft-dodgers, curb Agnew, unleash Ralph Nader: that kind of thing.

But the Republican pros do not give him a second glance. What, after all, would it take to make Lindsay the obvious man? You would have to crowd every prominent Republican in America into a boat larger than the Titanic, and sink it— no survivors— before the Republican Party would go, in receivership, to Mr. Lindsay. Remember, that with all his resources, with New

York State solidly behind him, with his incandescent liberalism of yore, Nelson Rockefeller was never willing to persevere in a single primary against Richard Nixon, and lost the critical primaries to Barry Goldwater. Nelson Rockefeller would rather vote for Bella Abzug than for Lindsay, however indistinguishable their positions.

No, it has got to be the Democratic Party. This requires the active cooperation of a few prominent Democrats, who will need to kill each other off. To this end, the script is coming along nicely. Senator Muskie, in pursuit of the interests of the voters of the great state of Maine, is in Europe, where one goes in order to emerge as a serious Presidential candidate. Senator George McGovern is about to do the same thing. It is really awfully early to start running for President thus conspicuously, but I suppose one might argue that Senators Muskie and McGovern have nothing better to do.

Now let us assume for a minute that these two will be the only candidates, if only for the sake of simplicity, and with apologies to Fred Harris, Ramsey Clark, and a few others who might enter the primaries. Let us suppose that McGovern wins the first primary, Muskie the second, McGovern the third, etc.; but that upon arriving at the convention they are deadlocked. Do they go for John Lindsay? Surely they would begin by considering Senator Kennedy, who, at that point, will (presumably) have gone two whole years without drowning anybody. Will he be forgiven? Not inconceivably. So then what does Mr. Lindsay do?

There is a lot of itch in left-Democratic circles. My own retrospective view is that it was only Robert Kennedy who prevented the formation of a significant third— or more properly fourth— party from organizing in 1968: because such a party could not hope to prosper while Robert Kennedy remained a loyalist. But now? Suppose that a conventional Democrat is nominated to run against Mr. Nixon. Under the Supreme Court's ruling in Ohio, to the advantage of George Wallace, the usual nonsense through which states have discouraged parties from appearing on the ballot is over. And no doubt Mr. Lindsay's staff is studying not only the question of how to enter primaries, but the question how to file directly for the Presidency.

State of the Union, 1971

Santiago, Chile—February 2, 1971

The text of President Nixon's message to Congress takes a little time getting down here, but the delay appears to harmonize with Congress's ho-hum reaction to it. In any event, a few observations.

1) The address was over-publicized. Such was the build-up that one-half expected that Mr. Nixon was going to propose repealing the Constitution, and adopting Robert Hutchins' in its place. Instead, they got what the President called "six great goals." They turned out to be a congeries of substantive and formalistic "goals" which do not really appear to advance the diminution of central power which Mr. Nixon throughout refers to as desirable. The most conspicuous is the "great goal" of giving money to the states. It is hard to see just how, under the present program, that is truly to diminish the power of the Federal government.

Look at it another way. If the Federal government undertakes to give money to the individual states, why isn't that yet another accretion of power in the Federal government? It isn't as if Mr. Nixon had said that the Federal government would reduce its taxes by $16 billion. No, the $16 billion will be levied. And then the dollars will be dispatched to the states, which will spend them as the states choose. What's more, it is pretty plain, at this point, that the $16 billion Mr. Nixon proposes to give to the states are going to be raised through deficit financing, which we are nowadays pleased to call a "full employment budget." So that the individual citizen will now be taxed to support additional inflation, the proceeds of which will be distributed by lesser government officials. The only way to return power to the individual states is to decrease the Federal budget and permit the states to raise their own taxes, if that is what, in the dialogue between the state legislators and the people, it is decided should be done.

2) The people. A remarkable, anaphoric insistence on the phrase "power to the people." Mr. Nixon desires to "start power and resources flowing back from Washington to the states and communities and more important, to the people." He desires us to

remember "that the truly revered leaders in world history are those who gave power to the people."

The sentiment is balm for the conservative soul, inasmuch as that is the kind of thing we have been talking about for years. Only— and this is an important distinction— we use the word "individual." "Power to the people" is everywhere the phrase that is used by the collectivists in America: the Panthers, the SDS, the Weathermen, the Socialists. By "the people," they mean the central authority, or the mob: as in, "the people's courts," or "the people's justice."

Whether Mr. Nixon is trying suddenly to co-opt the rhetoric of the hard left, one cannot know. But unless one does know that his intentions are crafty, one is left despondent. One cannot forget the address that President Eisenhower gave at Dartmouth shortly after his inauguration, wherein he said amiably that all he wanted of government was that it should be the "big brother" to its citizens. George Orwell, freshly dead, was spared the humiliation of discovering that the news about Big Brother had not yet lapped up on the banks of the Potomac. The students are said to have giggled. Senators and Congressmen don't giggle when the President is speaking, and shouldn't, but at the offices of the *Berkeley Barb*, they must have smiled and broken out a case of reefers.

3) The Presidential rhetoric was out of trim. For one thing, it is positively unguarded, in one and the same speech, to say a) that most Americans "will not— and should not— continue to tolerate the gap between promise and performance" in the government; and b) that "this"— *i.e.,* Mr. Nixon's program— "can be a revolution as profound, as far-reaching, as exciting, as that first revolution almost 200 years ago"; and c) that the 92nd Congress can emerge as "the greatest Congress in the history of this great and good nation." How? By doing Mr. Nixon's bidding.

And the language! Our beloved language. "America has long been the wealthiest nation in the world. Now it is time we became the healthiest nation in the world." One is only grateful to the speechwriter for forebearing to add, "and the wisiest nation in the world." And why do we have to have new Cabinet posts labeled, respectively, "Human Resources, Community Development, Natural Resources, and Economic Development"? *Kyrie eleison, Christe eleison.* Why not, Human Resources, Community

Resources, Natural Resources and Economic Resources? The inelegant variation. And if you think *I* quibble, watch Congress go to work, or rather fail to do so, on the President's proposals.

President-Talk

March 13, 1971

Concerning the Presidential contest, a few observations.

1. The disparagement of Mr. Nixon is concentrated, but somehow unimpassioned. It cannot compare with the quality of the disparagement of Lyndon Johnson a year before the 1968 primaries. On the other hand, Lyndon Johnson established, at least temporarily, a tradition of Presidential instability which, although the circumstances are greatly changed, endangers Mr. Nixon. Johnson was tumbled by his own party, following the New Hampshire primaries. There is no foreseen challenge to Richard Nixon from the Republican Party. Even so, the shakiness of Johnson carries implications of instability for any incumbent. In that sense Mr. Nixon is shakier than normally a President is at the completion of his first term; or so it would appear.

The formal popularity of Mr. Nixon is put at 49 percent, down 10 points over a year ago. The obvious reason for the drop is natural public restiveness. A particular reason is the internalization of American distress during the past season. A year ago the campuses were exploding, and the intellectuals were signing their manifestos of estrangement. Now we undergo what has been called the Cooling of America.

This means two things. For one, the agitators are exercising restraint, whether because they believe it to be strategically useful or because they are worn out doesn't matter: the fact is, their resentment is unshaken. For another, those who respond to defend the stability of American institutions feel a certain release. It becomes less necessary to defend the establishment if you believe that the essential stability of the republic is not being challenged. This means that many Americans will be looking to Mr. Nixon in the ensuing months demanding that he seduce their support, rather than extending it to him automatically as a gesture of resistance to the agitators.

2. Senator Muskie's strength and his weakness issue from the same attributes. He is this season's Liberal Alternative, which puts him in the mainstream, and does not rouse the anti-revolutionary enzymes. It is as safe — the typical American voter who tends to go Democratic will reason — to vote for Muskie, as it was to vote for Humphrey, and before that for, say, Truman.

On the other hand, the romantics are bound to find him wanting, and it is unlikely that a year from now the youthful legions will flock to New Hampshire to be Well-Bred-For-Ed. He has a little latitude, *i.e.*, he could permit his rhetoric to take a slightly more jacobinical and pacifist turn, but if he goes too far, he will lose his institutional Democratic support. Besides that, a position to his left will, by New Hampshire-time, have been pretty well staked out by, say, George McGovern. And, even more likely, by

3. John Lindsay. He is the Bobby Kennedy of 1972, by authority of the relationship of forces. Even his background as a Republican, which I have said he became only as a matter of baptismal affirmation, makes him sort of glamorous, even as, once the dark datum was assimilated, it became glamorous that Jack and Bobby Kennedy had once been McCarthyites. Granted, he lacks the formal dynastic designation. If only, on the same day that he changes his registration to Democrat, he would change his name to Kennedy. But when last heard from, his advisers had rejected this proposal, by a narrow vote. Then too, as I say, there is George McGovern, who is determined not to let any grass grow on his left, and before New Hampshire will probably be calling for the removal of our bases from Hawaii.

But Lindsay's strength as the natural left-candidate is hard to dissipate. For one thing, Lindsay *says* nothing. It is a minority of Americans who know that he says nothing because he has nothing to say. The kids will wring from that silence a trance-like communion between Lindsay and their common muses, which he dare not interrupt, lest his afflatus as savior of the republic be only half-received. So that they will applaud his continued silence, which others who have heard him speak will also applaud, if for other reasons. But at some point he will be heard from, and if I were Mr. Nixon, I would look forward to that day most happily.

Mr. Nixon's Critics

April 20, 1971

Richard Nixon is in for a very very rough time during the next period. He does things to people, causing even very decent folk to behave quite incomprehensibly. Joe McCarthy had the same knack. I used to point out that I never knew anything McCarthy had said that could equal in vileness some of the things that were said about him.

Take, for instance, Mr. Allard Lowenstein. He is a civilized man, of incontinent idealism, who will be remembered as the person who launched the program to retire Lyndon Johnson in 1968 by fielding an opponent in the Democratic primary in New Hampshire. Subsequently, he served a term in the House of Representatives, and now he is back on the road, organizing to beat Mr. Nixon in 1972. He stopped by recently at the John F. Kennedy Center at Harvard, where he delivered a paean on the memory of Robert F. Kennedy. Then he announced his plans, making the remark that "Nixon is making Johnson look retroactively very credible, which is an extraordinary achievement when you think about it."

Now we are all used to the hurly-burly of polemics, but when you stop to think of it, in what significant way has Nixon let the liberals down? Or, more exactly stated, in what significant way has he deceived them? He never said that he would have American troops out of Vietnam within six months or sixteen months of taking office. He said he would wind down the war, and he has done so. He said he would pull out of Cambodia by the end of June, and did; said that American foot soldiers would not fight in Laos, and they haven't. What is Lowenstein so excited about? It is mysterious. It is partly what Nixon does to Lowenstein, and partly what Lowenstein does to Lowenstein, because Al Baby is going to be looking pensive and sad about the state of the world before the New Hampshire primary of 1996, when he will announce that the world cannot survive a second term by John-John.

Then there is the columnist and author Garry Wills who, did one not know that he is capable of making distinctions only

Bertrand Russell and Alfred North Whitehead could follow, is beginning to sound like a slogan-writer for the John Birch Society.

For instance, there were those (myself included) who commented that Mr. Nixon's recent refusal to give a date when all American troops would be out of Vietnam was a sign of courage, given the clear indication that the overwhelming majority of the American people desire to be given such a date. Wills' comment? "I prefer heroes who are not 'brave' with other men's lives." At an intellectual level, that comment is the equal of "If you don't like our foreign policy, why don't you go live in Russia?"

Mr. Wills, if he would permit himself to reflect on the matter, would recognize that we are called upon, in our lifetime, to be courageous in different ways. As soldiers, we are asked to show courage on the firing line, and it is reported that, when Mr. Nixon was a soldier, he did so. Later in life, courage is needed in many different situations, in facing personal and public crises. Is Mr. Wills saying that it is improper to consider the courage of Julius Caesar, or Alexander the Great, or Napoleon Bonaparte, or Winston Churchill, because more often than not they were engaged not in exposing their own lives to the enemies' weapons, but the lives of the soldiers whom destiny put them in command of?

Wills then takes offense at Billy Graham who, commenting on the fate of Lieutenant Calley, said: "Perhaps it is a good time for each of us to re-evaluate our life. We have all had our My Lais in one way or another, perhaps not with guns, but we have hurt others with a thoughtless word, an arrogant act or a selfish deed." Observes Wills: "To equate My Lai—multiple coldblooded murder of women and children—with a thoughtless word does not so much diminish My Lai's importance as destroy any claim Graham has to speak seriously about morality."

Really, it requires the Nixonization of the spleen, so to affect a critic's reasoning powers. Graham did not *equate* My Lai with "a thoughtless word," he observed merely that many men were tempted by special circumstances to quite hideous lengths. The objective harm done differs: perhaps it is the killing of helpless children, as at My Lai. Perhaps it is the psychological castration of the human being, as in Albee's *Virginia Woolf*. Sadism, hysteria, and thoughtlessness, in different mixes, are generically responsible for My Lai—and for some of the criticisms made of public figures. Garry Wills has written imploring me please to learn to distinguish between Fathers Daniel and Philip Berrigan, and I am writing back today promising to make the effort, in return for which I ask that he learn to distinguish between Nixon and Satan.

Nixon: A Public Performance

April 22, 1971

Three years ago, just before the national political conventions, the American Society of Newspaper Editors invited Candidate Richard Nixon to appear before it, and to answer questions put to him by prominent newspaper editors. I was there, and saw Mr. Nixon in action, answering the questions put to him and—his principal mission—endeavoring to persuade this community of tough-minded men that, notwithstanding the weaknesses so greatly celebrated, he was Presidential material. I remember Mr. Nixon insisting that the podium be removed before he approached the microphone. His point was that unlike other Presidential candidates, he didn't need notes, or set paragraphs. He wanted the editors to see him there standing directly in front of a gaunt microphone. He wanted, in other words, to take the credit for his unusual capacity to extemporize neatly. Even when he delivered the so-called Checkers speech, he did not use a prepared text. It is natural to desire to exhibit one's strength.

Last Friday, it was almost exactly the same audience: the newspaper editors of America. But it was after dinner, rather than after lunch. The audience was dressed in black tie. The principal speaker was not seated at the dais during the meal. (I sometimes think it would be worth becoming President of the United States in order to dispose of that usufruct alone.) The president of the American Society of Newspaper Editors delivered short, graceful, witty remarks, compressing business and just a hint of the antic, into a brief address which was hard to hear because the amplification wasn't quite right, and the editors and their ladies were busy fussing with the dessert and coffee and exchanging stories, most of them to the effect that it was a shame everybody was talking and therefore making it difficult to listen to the words of the president of the Society.

And then at about one minute to nine, the chairman began calling the audience to attention, only to find it distractingly easy to do. Obviously he had supposed it would take a minute or so to quiet the audience. Instead he found himself confronted with total silence: and that, children, will not do. Because when the President of the United States is scheduled to come into the room at 2100 hours, that does not mean, because the room is ready for him at 2059 hours, that you can just push the button and say, come on in, Mr. President. Those who are patient in these matters will say to themselves: there is a reason for clockworkolatry, and we must not permit our natural impulses for spontaneity to get in the way of our recognition that reasons of state come first, and if it has been arranged for the President to come in at 2100 hours, you may not, must not, usher him in thirty seconds earlier, let alone a minute earlier. Suppose it was Cape Kennedy, would you expect Apollo 11 to blast off at 0731, when it was set for 0732, merely on the grounds that Walter Cronkite had run out of steam a minute before the scheduled time?

It isn't only the formalities, it is the Secret Service. The Secret Service is permanently traumatized as the result of its indifferent performance in Dallas, in 1963. I am among those who did not affix the blame for that tragedy on the Secret Service, believing, as Mr. Kennedy himself once resignedly put it, that anyone who is willing to sacrifice his own life can probably succeed in taking the life of the President. On the other hand Dallas was one of those situations where the taking of the President's life was one operation, and the surrender of one's own life was an entirely different operation, *i.e.*, it was altogether providential that the killer was caught. That, really, was the blow to the pride of the Secret Service, who had nothing whatever to do with the apprehension of Lee Harvey Oswald.

One supposes that the Dallas experience, and the subsequent tragedies at Memphis and Los Angeles (for which the S/S had no direct responsibility), are the reasons for the precautions they take. Anyway, what obtains nowadays is: The Rule. And The Rule was: an appearance at 9:00 P.M.

This was effected well, with the United States Marine Band

playing "Hail to the Chief." The United States Marine Band is not yet a target of Senator William Fulbright. He has not even suggested that it is the secret intention of Henry Kissinger and Melvin Laird to send the United States Marine Band to Laos, so it performs serenely. The President came on, with Mrs. Nixon, who was also there three years ago, and looks more and more like a Dresden doll, fine, ornamental, indestructible, alluring. Mr. Nixon, as President, didn't need notes, any more than he needed notes before he became President. On the other hand, there was the Presidential Seal. The Presidential Seal is that great circle that hangs in front of the President whenever he appears. It is the eagle, together with paraphernalia, surrounded with the legend, The Seal of the President of the United States of America. You obviously cannot hang that Seal in front of a spindly microphone — not possible. So, Mr. Nixon apparently consented to a podium, in order to accommodate the Seal.

The questioners circled him, and the questions were direct, intelligent, probing: the questions you and I would have wanted put to the President. One interrogator smoked a cigarette while he asked his question, and that didn't seem quite right — on the other hand, that was the same day that the rock group, Warm Dust, was received by the Pope, the female members allegedly dressed in hot pants. So, why can't a guy puff smoke into the face of the President, while asking him whether he intends to recognize Red China? The Secret Service is not mobilized to object. Though who knows. Perhaps, in the future, the Secret Service will instruct newspaper editors when they may smoke. After all, in Russia they instruct the President in what he can say.

Impeach Nixon?

May 8, 1971

Well, well. So young Al Lowenstein is going around the country mobilizing the troops to dump Richard Nixon in 1972. That is the sober, responsible Al. The other Al recently got himself elected president of the Americans for Democratic Action, and I for one think that, like Papa Doc, Al should be elected president of ADA for life. I fear they were meant for each other: which is too bad because Al is a nice guy, and the ADA is pretty unpleasant.

The most important act of the 24th Annual Convention of the ADA was a resolution to impeach President Richard Nixon. Impeach him for "high crimes" in Indochina. This makes Mr. Lowenstein's activities in New Hampshire and elsewhere rather formalistic. If Richard Nixon is guilty of high crimes, sufficient to impeach him, it is hardly appropriate to go about the country urging that he be defeated in a mere general election. To engage in the latter activity is to suggest that the former commitment is frivolous. Rather as if the generals engaged in the July 20 plot to assassinate Hitler paused, early in July, to launch a grass-roots movement to recall Hitler as chancellor.

Really, the liberals are something—one needs to remind oneself how very kooky they can be. The ADA, remember, is the organized intelligentsia of American liberalism. The last president of it was the Reverend Joseph Duffey, the quiet, fervent man of the people, who set out to save Connecticut from Dodd, and gave Connecticut a Republican Senator. The president before that was none other than John Kenneth Galbraith, liberalism's Disraeli: the philosopher-king. Perhaps the next most conspicuous member is Arthur Schlesinger, Jr., which brings me to the morose acknowledgment— he can no longer be ignored— that there is yet another Schlesinger to cope with, son Stephen, who alas is not suffering from any generational revolt against his father's policies, which he adopts as his very own, only more so. Then Joseph Rauh, Jr., James Wechsler: the lot of them.

What do they have in common? Above all, their early devotion to Franklin Delano Roosevelt. Out of that devotion developed an ultramontanism not known outside the Roman Curia. Anything Roosevelt did was all right, and any challenge to Roosevelt's executive prerogatives was reactionary, nihilistic, and anarchistic. Roosevelt used to make secret commitments in behalf of the United States every couple of weeks, with extras on Halloween— armies to Iceland, fleets to the Mediterranean, marines to Singapore. Never mind, what now we are taught to call the military-industrial complex, in those days we called the arsenal for democracy— you couldn't do business with Hitler— we had to shoulder the responsibilities of a great power—had to have a strong President. Impeach Roosevelt? As well impeach the Statue of Liberty.

It was the same with Harry Truman, one of the most imperious Presidents the United States ever had, who loved to flirt with rampant unconstitutionality, as for instance when he nationalized the steel industry and took us to war in Korea without even sending Congress a postcard. It was Truman who also refused, insisting on the executive prerogative, to give to duly-constituted committees of Congress information Congress demanded in order to pursue lawful inquiries. The ADA cheered: oh, how it cheered, egging on the Presidential arm of government. If John F. Kennedy had asked for a constitutional amendment to give him the right to eliminate the Republican Party and hang Everett Dirksen, it could not have failed to pass through the Americans for Democratic Action. And so it went.

Until LBJ and Vietnam. Up until that moment, it had simply never occurred to the gentlemen of the ADA that it was possible to have an American President who pursued policies substantially different from those the ADA would pursue, if the ADA were President.

Oh how they laughed ten years ago when Robert Welch announced that his solution to it all was to IMPEACH EARL WARREN. They threw up their hands in constitutional disgust in 1966, when a few uninformed conservatives in Idaho undertook to recall Senator Frank Church, in punishment for his opposition to the Vietnam war. Now they want to impeach Nixon, who has executed policies pursuant to an all but unanimous resolution of both Houses of Congress, carried forward by two Democratic Presidents; policies fully congruent with the pledges Nixon made to the people of the United States, in partial recognition of which he was elected President in 1968. Impeach Richard Nixon! ADA's latest contribution to American political understanding.

It is recorded that when Al Lowenstein called his lovely wife to advise her that he had been made president of ADA, she said to him: "I know Mrs. Roosevelt is sitting up there smiling." There can be absolutely no doubt about it. Though I expect that by now FDR has whispered to her, "No, Eleanor. It doesn't work that way."

McCloskey vs. Nixon

June 3, 1971

Congressman Paul McCloskey is the gentleman from California who proposes to Dump Nixon, which is the elegant phrase
we are encouraged to use nowadays, and of course the very use of
it contributes to the humpty-dumptiness of Mr. Nixon's image.
Imagine, by contrast, a movement called: Dump Lorenzo the
Magnificent. Somehow, the words cannot navigate their way out
of one's mouth.

Speaking of mouths, Mr. McCloskey uses his with extraordinary
looseness. The kind of things he goes about the country saying—
that Mr. Nixon and his ambassadors and representatives are liars
and enemies of the Constitution, that they are engaged in
unlawful and genocidal activity, "exactly the same thing we
hanged the German generals for,"—would have made Joe Mc-
Carthy blush for the immoderation of it all. But, of course, in
criticizing Nixon, every good liberal is expected to sound like
Herblock, and nobody is going to blow the whistle; especially not
against Pete McCloskey, an attractive war hero whose grasp of the
issues is, well, indistinct.

Mr. McCloskey, for instance, is determined to cultivate the
legend that in Laos, the United States is systematically engaged in
wiping out villages—"thousands of villages," is his phrase. Our
ambassador in Laos, Mr. George M. Godley, told him face to face
that this simply was not so, that he himself authorizes any
bombing of a village, and never when the village is occupied: that,
to be sure, our bombs have fallen on civilians as the result of
defective intelligence. So also have our bombs fallen on American
soldiers from time to time because of defective communications,
but it makes no more sense to charge that we are engaged in
genocidal warfare against Laotian citizens, than against
American citizens.

Besides, Mr. McCloskey chooses to interest himself not in the
whole of Laos, most of which is in friendly hands, but in a
relatively small area, the Plaine des Jarres, which regularly
changes hands after bitter fighting. Approximately 35,000
refugees have been driven from this area, fleeing from American

bombing in response to North Vietnam assaults. The other figure is 700,000. That is how many refugees have, in a decade, resettled as the result of North Vietnam and Pathet Lao aggression. To focus on the refugees caused by American action is on the order of an ecologist's complaining about the litter on the Normandy beach left by the Americans after D-Day.

Then Mr. McCloskey talks vaguely about impeaching President Nixon. No,— when you accost him directly about it—he never said he was *in favor* of impeachment, merely that impeachment ought to be *considered*. As a matter of fact, Mr. McCloskey is absolutely right. If Nixon is engaged in direct lies, in destroying the Constitution, in exterminating Asians for genocidal reasons, I'd vote for impeaching Nixon, and then hanging him.

Mr. McCloskey has a curious turn of mind. He greatly objects to what he insists is the illegality of the current conflict, but he is hardly a pacifist. He was in favor of declaring war against Korea if Korea didn't return the *Pueblo* and the crew of the *Pueblo*. During our last adventure in Korea, there were 3 million refugees. Mr. McCloskey seems to be saying that Mr. Nixon is too reckless in Laos, where we have lost one American killed, and not nearly reckless enough in Korea: an interesting position, which will no doubt intrigue the voters in New Hampshire when they are asked by the solemn, dedicated Mr. McCloskey to ponder it.

Or will it be someone else? Mr. McCloskey tells his audiences that he is willing to step aside in deference to any "abler Republican." I asked him who was abler than he, and he answered, well, for one, John Lindsay. I asked, did that mean that he, McCloskey, being less able than Lindsay, would have made a worse mayor of New York than Lindsay? I wish I had had time to ask him: what would you have done to damage New York more than Mr. Lindsay has done? I can't imagine what he'd have answered, except maybe declare war against New York. Mr. McCloskey is a man of utter legal rectitude.

Senator Muskie's Gaffe

September 28, 1971

Concerning Senator Muskie's observation, for which Senator McGovern has given him hell— that there would be little point in putting a black Vice President on his ticket, inasmuch as both of them would proceed to lose— a few observations.

1. President Nixon's retort that Senator Muskie had "libeled" the American people is both disingenuous and misleading. Disingenuous because we have all been told that when Henry Cabot Lodge, running for Vice President on Richard Nixon's ticket in 1960, promised somebody somewhere that if Mr. Nixon were elected he would name a Negro to the Cabinet, Candidate Nixon almost fainted. And no wonder.

Misleading because to suggest that there is no race prejudice in this country is about the same as saying there are no rivers that run, or grass that grows. But it is not *anti-Negro* to observe that *there is anti-Negro prejudice*. It is not anti-Semitic to say that there is anti-Semitic prejudice. Anybody who wants to become President tends to begin by disencumbering himself of any positions or associations which he believes are net liabilities. When, in late 1959, Mayor David Lawrence of Pittsburgh announced flatly that he was opposed to nominating John F. Kennedy because there was too much anti-Catholic prejudice in the country to make possible his election, nobody called Mr. Lawrence anti-Catholic. To be sure, he was himself a Catholic, which was a good hedge against that charge. But even if he hadn't been, he could have made that statement without disgracing himself.

2. Senator Muskie counted on getting the Negro vote to begin with, for no better reason, nor worse one, than that the Democratic Party has for quite a while now won the overwhelming majority of the Negro vote. Acknowledging that that is the way Negroes tend to vote is to acknowledge that a political prejudice will inevitably be stimulated against that particular bloc. Consider a formal construction of the syllogism: John doesn't like Democrats. Most Negroes are Democrats. Therefore John does not like most Negroes. Is that a racist conclusion? But

consider: the syllogism tells you nothing about John's prejudice being racial in origin. Racial bias takes off from an ethnic point. If approximately half of the American Negro community voted Republican, and the other half Democratic, there would be a considerable lessening of the prejudice one here discusses.

3. The most frequently cited data intended to "document" American racial bias as it touches on politics are inconclusive. Congressman Dellums— and others— cite the presence in Congress of a mere thirteen black members of the House, and one Senator. Why shouldn't there be— he asks— fifty black Congressmen, and ten Senators, reflecting the population figures? Because, a) although there are 22 million blacks, the black population does not in fact exceed the white population in any single state, or in any single city except Washington, D.C., and Newark, New Jersey, and our political system is based on the single-member district, winner-take-all principle. It is a more significant datum by far that Senator Brooke was overwhelmingly elected in Massachusetts, notwithstanding that only 2 percent of the population there is Negro. It is, however, probably true that the majority would not have voted for him for President.

And, finally, what the commotion is all about is that the Negro in America began behind— way behind. That is the meaning of a National Association for the *Advancement* of Colored People. The Negro people's disadvantages, though distinctive, are not unique. A Jew has yet to be nominated for the Presidency. And this notwithstanding that the spectacular Jewish contribution to American civilization is merely suggested by the fact that 30 percent of the undergraduate body of Harvard is Jewish (my figures are a few years old). It is not to be anti-Negro to recognize that the same politicians who until a few years ago were afraid to name a Catholic, are still afraid to name a Jew, haven't even considered naming a woman, as a Presidential candidate— should cavil at naming a Negro.

4. So that the case against Senator Muskie had better be made on more substantial grounds. And let those who fret remind themselves that progress is being made, very fast. I wrote some years ago that I hoped to see a Negro in the White House in 1980. Why 1980? Because it is a symbol for some future time. To say I'd like to see one nominated today, in the hope of being elected tomorrow, would make me, like unto thee, George McGovern, a hypocrite.

What Is the Strength of Nixon's Right?

November 11, 1971

An underground conservative social scientist sends me a document which has gone utterly unnoticed even though it is over a year old. It is the *Western Political Quarterly*, 1969, 22 (4). The study is by Edmond Constantini (Political Science, University of California at Davis), and Kenneth H. Craik (at the time, in the Department of Psychology at Berkeley). The provocative title of the article: "Competing Elites Within a Political Party: A Study of Republican Leadership." And the import of the findings goes beyond the adjudication of a hot historical argument dating back to 1964. The findings should be front-page news for Richard Nixon.

In 1964, the approved understanding among enlightened gentry of what had happened to the Republican Party in San Francisco was that a horde of primitives, whose god was Barry Goldwater, had as the result of successful conniving by some deft political operators like F. Clifton White, Stephen Shadegg and others, simply taken control of the Republican Party. Here, for instance, is how Richard Rovere, premier spokesman on political matters for the Eastern Seaboard Liberal Establishment, put it in *Encounter* magazine for October, 1964. "The language of sedition is relevant . . . to what happened to the Republican Party over the last three or four years. It has been 'infiltrated, captured,' and made (as Richard Hofstadter says) a 'front organization' by an organized faction whose loyalty to Goldwater and Goldwaterism far transcends its loyalty to Republicanism."

Indeed, Professor Hofstadter, the influential political scientist from Columbia, said it more extensively in the same issue of *Encounter*. "Goldwater's true believers promptly moved in to fill the structural and moral vacuum, while the moderate leaders rested on their oars, assuming that they would be able to move in, as they had always done, in the next campaign year. Goldwater men infiltrated the party much as the Communists in their days of strength infiltràted liberal organizations in order to use them as front groups. Working with highly disciplined cells or cadres, they rapidly took over county and town committees, developed their own local candidates, and prepared for battle at the national level."

Well, the two scholars in question went to work. They selected for interrogation a scientifically satisfactory cross-sample of the delegates pledged to Rockefeller and the delegates pledged to Goldwater and, for good measure, the delegates pledged to Lyndon Johnson.

As regards their location on the ideological spectrum, there was an extraordinary consistency between self-evaluation, and objective valuation, based on exploring the views of these delegates on fourteen separate issues. It transpired that the distance (moving right) between the Johnsonite and the Rockefellerite was approximately the same as the distance between the Rockefellerite and the Goldwaterite. And— very interesting— that the Nixonite fell almost exactly in between Rockefeller and Goldwater.

Now on the matter of who were the Republicans: The Republican people fell like ninepins. The Goldwaterites had:

— Participated in more county and state Republican organizations over the years.

— They had contributed more money to the party, from smaller incomes— even though their money went, in many cases, to liberal Republicans (*e.g.*, Nixon in 1960, Kuchel in 1962).

— They had attended more conventions (two to one in an official capacity prior to 1964).

— They had more years of active involvement in the Republican Party.

— On the record, they were more likely than the Rockefellerites to support the Republican nominee whoever he was. For instance, they had backed Eisenhower when Eisenhower beat Taft, in far greater number than the Rockefellerites backed Goldwater after Rockefeller lost.

And finally— but I would not risk a paraphrase, and so quote the authors' own version of it: "With respect to the 'why' of party involvement, the members of the Goldwater elite were more likely than the members of the Rockefeller elite to have entered politics as the result of public-serving motives (*e.g.*, out of concern for public policy issues) and less likely to have entered politics as the result of personal-serving motives (*e.g.*, to achieve certain social satisfactions or to enhance one's personal influence)."

The meaning for the historians is absolutely clear: the official version of what happened in 1964 is baloney. The current meaning for Mr. Nixon is: the backbone of the Republican Party is to his right. On the other hand, he can take comfort from the knowledge that they are slow to defect.

X. The Issues

Pollution

January 27, 1970

The President's message on the State of the Union was pleasing to Mr. James Reston, a datum which no doubt will send the Dow Jones average up ten points. Much that Mr. Nixon said was, of course, predictable: one hardly expects a message on the State of the Union at which a President expresses the hope that the years to come will usher in war, poverty, and hunger. The meaty sections of the address were a rhetorical flirtation with the notion that the government can do something substantial about the quality of our lives, and the passages concerning our obligations to nature.

It is widely accepted that Mr. Nixon has promised to do something about the quality of our lives, and it is important to examine the question whether he did so, and if so, what did he mean by it. Important because there are those of us who believe that the principal mistake made by Lyndon Johnson in enunciating his dream of a great society was precisely in suggesting that the government could utopianize the human condition: that essential human relations and spiritual needs can be looked after by government.

It is as obvious that this is not the case as it is obvious that there are people in this country with no material worries of any kind who nevertheless harbor foxes in their bosoms which drive them to drink, to a psychiatrist, or to utter, desperate boredom. Mr. Johnson's celebrated speech concerning the shape of the Great Society seemed to be saying that under Johnson such maladies, which are of the spirit, could be made to go away, presumably after elevating them to Cabinet rank. What happened, as they say, is history.

Is it to improve the "quality" of human life, to do something

274

about pollution— the concretely phrased objective of Mr. Nixon's address? Perhaps, though it is to stretch the meaning of "quality." I take it as axiomatic that no one has the right to pollute the air I breathe, or the water I drink, and that the latitudinarian habits of a society whose frontier was always bigger than any of us, have finally caught up with us, generating a common revulsion. It is overdue for government to assert its responsibility in these matters.

Whoever said that it was the responsibility of free enterprise to clean the water or purify the air? Mayor Alioto recently took a shot at Governor Reagan by alluding to the million pounds or whatever of sulphur poured into the air over Los Angeles every day by private users. To which Governor Reagan replied deploring the 70 million pounds of human offal dumped every day into San Francisco Bay by municipal sewers.

An unprofitable dispute. Adam Smith himself, by the extension of his notion that the government is uniquely responsible for public monuments, would surely have accepted the notion that it is the government's responsibility to see to it that the people do not despoil the land, depriving future generations of their birthright.

What we need now to worry about is the nature of the great bureaucracy which is inevitably going to build up around the $10-billion national anti-pollution project. As my friend Mr. William Rusher so adroitly puts it, how much, after the bureaucrats have taken their share, will actually be left over for the chipmunks? Here is where one hopes that there will be an observable difference between a Republican and a Democratic administration of a project which concededly belongs to the government.

The trick, of course, is to lay down general laws, impartially, gradually, and let the enforcement of them be done by the use of private mechanisms, and by mechanisms of the lowest feasible unit of government. Mr. Nixon has promised us an elaboration. One looks forward to it eagerly, hoping to find in it accents on local responsibility, and as little as possible of such rhetoric as suggests that natural hygiene will elevate the human condition. Natural hygiene is good because it is good, but it does not follow from it that people will become happy, any more than it follows from the condition of a hospital that its inhabitants, carried away by the quality of a local condition, will die happy.

End Conscription

It is going to require a considerable act of will to put into effect the recommendations of the Gates Commission as we gradually turn over the next year and one-half in the direction of an all-volunteer army. The Armed Services Committee of the Senate doesn't much like the idea, and went so far as informally to reject Mr. Nixon's proposed successor to General Hershey because of his undiluted enthusiasm for the idea.

On the American scene in general, the libertarians and conservatives are in favor of the all-volunteer military because we believe in the presumption of voluntariness in all things. The left-liberals oppose conscription less because of their attachment to individual freedom than because they see here an opportunity to deflate the military.

In between is a large group of people whose objections are, roughly, in two parts. On the one hand, they argue that there is great danger in a typically military class. That the opportunity might then come to the military class to dominate the civilian executive and even, as they do on Mondays, Wednesdays, and Fridays in Latin America, take over the government.

An additional argument is the notion that military training is good for any young man, and that moreover it does something to incorporate him into America— to Americanize him, if you will. In the great debate on what was then called "universal military training" in the late forties, President Truman fought to clinch the case in favor of conscription by saying proudly, "Look, I've served in the military, and look what it did for me!" That was not taken by the public as a conclusive argument in favor of UMT, but along came Korea, to make the argument academic.

Abolitionists of conscription must concede a couple of points to the opposition. It is true that a professional military class is less desirable than, say, a militia. Arguing the point in the Federalist Papers, Hamilton wrote, "There is something so far fetched and so extravagant in the idea of danger to liberty from the militia, that one is at a loss whether to treat it with gravity or with raillery: whether to consider it as a mere trial of skill, like the paradoxes of rhetoricians; as a disingenuous artifice to instill prejudices at any price; or as the serious offspring of political fanaticism."

But the virtues of the militia—which, like Switzerland's, stays and works at home except when in training, or when engaged in duty—are transferable to an army which needs, let us say, to keep three hundred thousand men in Western Europe. And the question is whether such as they should be volunteers, or conscripts.

The other objection, less often stated, is that things being as they are, inevitably the army will emerge much higher than 10 percent black. The objection is raised not because there is anything undesirable about the black fighting man. But because we will have come up with what will strike many as a mercenary army, collected from those same ghettos fostered by our system, and utilizing the victims of those ghettos who are now invited to protect with their lives their white brothers who make life intolerable for them at home.

I grant this is caricature. But so are the rantings of Herblock—precisely because the world is full of men and women who seek to hobgoblinize and, if at all possible, to dishonor the motives of America. (There is absolutely no doubt that tomorrow's economics textbook will be saying that in the post-Vietnam age, America solved its unemployment problem by recruiting a highly paid volunteer army.)

How does that add up? Surely we should end conscription, and the sooner the better. The additional cost is easily compensated for in a fairly short run by the economic productivity of those who do not enter the army, and therefore remain home and pay taxes. And, in the long run, by the lowered cost of training—the fruits of professionalization. Meanwhile, we shall have asserted once again our devotion to the principle that that which is not required of a citizen, he should not be compelled to do.

The Strike of Public Employees

March 26, 1970

At this writing the word is reassuring about the postal strike, so it is time for the postmortems. They will appear (as in this column), but just as surely they will be forgotten. It is hard to remember when last the nation mobilized itself in order to prevent the recurrence of a commonly-acknowledged outrage.

The point of the matter is that a society cannot function which extends to its civil servants the right to immobilize that society. It is as plain as that. The right of a citizen of the United States to communicate with another citizen, whether his mother, his boss or his supplier, is about as close to an absolute right as exists. The postal workers never struck before, no doubt in tacit recognition of the sacredness of their responsibility. But defiance is in season, and it can hardly be expected that they should exercise the restraint that others have not recognized. It is no more against the law for the postman to strike than for the teacher in New York City, who struck and got away with it. It is, I suppose, especially ironic that it was the teachers' union in New York that conducted the last, most spectacular strike in the country. After a couple of months of which the teachers returned to their classrooms to pursue the teaching of civic virtue.

What we need is a means of devising a decent answer to the economic question of whether we owe sympathy to a particular striker. Because in the absence of that knowledge, enough Americans will sympathize with the striker to undermine the will to enforce no-strike laws. As, for instance, in the current case involving postmen in New York City, or, to take another example, the striking motormen who paralyzed New York on January 1, 1966. It is widely acknowledged that pay for postal carriers in New York City is simply insufficient. The argument that an alternative is for the postman simply to quit, is strategically sound but not tactically sound. In the long run the postmen will quit if wages are insufficient. But in the short run, especially if they feel the lure of collective action, they will attempt a form of tactical resistance— striking. What government— and the public— needs is a reliable measure of whether the essential demands of any group of public employees are just.

Some time after the motormen's strike, Professor Yale Brozen of the University of Chicago suggested a formula. In a moderately fluid society, he observed, there is going to be job movement, that continual quitting of one job in search for a better one, the whole operation resulting in an ongoing series of adjustments and readjustments whose concatenation is called the free market.

Now it is impossible, Mr. Brozen points out, to say about any particular employee that he is overpaid, or underpaid, because the variables in his job situation are almost impossible for any person other than himself to evaluate competently. Perhaps in one situation the pay is apparently poor— but the fringe benefits high. Or perhaps the working conditions are especially pleasant. Or perhaps the prospects for advancement are good. And so on.

The only reliable guide, said Mr. Brozen, is the rate of replacement, as compared with the rate of replacement of employees in a roughly comparable situation. If, for instance, the Post Office in New York City loses 15 percent of its employees to other jobs in the course of a year, compared to say 5 percent who pull out of the Telephone Company, then moderately reliable conclusions can be drawn, and there is at least a prima facie case to suggest either that the Telephone Company is greatly over-paying, or that the Post Office is greatly underpaying. Bring in the figures for a half-dozen other service industries, so as to establish a base; and a profile emerges.

Surely an effort ought to be made by which, with reference to Brozen's formula, the public can know instantly what is the relative economic situation of any group of public employees. If they are being underpaid, they should be raised at the beginning of every year. But a national commitment having been made to guard against such inequities, then it becomes proper to resort to draconian reprisals against public employees (or certain groups of private employees) who strike. Professor van den Haag has suggested that the only convincing deterrent is the irreversible day-by-day reduction in pension coupons. But whatever it is, it has got to be made to stick. One sighs at the inconceivability that the requisite measure will become law during an election year. But the time between now and the convening of the next Congress could at least be used to study the possibilities of the Brozen formula.

"Mediocrity" and the Supreme Court

April 4, 1970

Our intelligentsia have had a wonderful time with the offhand remark of Senator Roman Hruska to the effect that if it is true that Judge Carswell is a "mediocre" legal mind, then maybe he would be especially useful to the Supreme Court. That of course is a natural for Art Buchwald, who is amusing in his treatment of such matters, and Herblock, who will be savage. It will be wonderful fodder for the next six speeches of John Kenneth Galbraith, and the next six hundred of Arthur Schlesinger.

Fair enough. But it is worthwhile to make a couple of points before it becomes settled doctrine that the Nixon Administration sees mediocrity as the apogee of the curve.

1) What Senator Hruska obviously intended to say was that the Warren Court got itself a reputation for legal virtuosity among those people who applauded its decisions: which decisions were not popular, for the most part, with the people of the United States. Therefore, if in order to redress the balance on the Court it becomes necessary to name to it someone who does not inhabit the peaks where the air is pure, why maybe we'd be better off stopping halfway up the mountain where there is a little more oxygen. The thinking is the exact equivalent of Lincoln's on hearing that General Grant drank whiskey.

2) It is true that the Warren Court became extremely popular with America's liberals. It is also true that it was popular precisely because the Court reached conclusions that were ideologically congenial to these gentlemen. As a matter of fact, the shrewdest legal minds in the land were utterly appalled by the quality of a great many of the decisions of Earl Warren and his epigoni. Alpheus Mason of Princeton, for instance, although greatly sympathetic to the decision reached in *Brown v. Board of Education*, tore his hair at the legal reasoning that led to it. Learned Hand, whose mind was anything but mediocre, went up to Harvard to say of Mr. Warren and his constitutional combo that they appeared to think of themselves as a third legislative chamber. Edward Corwin was considered probably the top

constitutional expert in the land, and his opinion of the Warren Court was that it was inexpressibly slovenly.

And it wasn't only outsiders. A professor from Notre Dame amused himself— and his readers— by publishing a pastiche of comments about the legal reasoning and conclusions of the majority of the Warren Court. It read like calls from the John Birch Society for the impeachment of Earl Warren. At the end, one discovered that one had just finished reading excerpts from the dissenting opinions of members of the Supreme Court about the work of their honorable colleagues. At one time or another Earl Warren, for instance, was accused by his colleagues of historical ignorance, self-contradiction, logical fatuity, a failure to grasp the elements of the argument, legal sciolism, and double parking.

In other words, the Warren Court is greatly appreciated by its admirers mostly because it came to the right conclusions, from their point of view. And inasmuch as people tend to believe that what they believe in is the profoundest achievement of the human mind, they simply deduced that the judges who gave them those conclusions were the most brilliant of men. Of course, it does not follow.

3) The meritocratic argument that the brighter you are the better off you are guiding the affairs of state is something the liberals ought to feel just a little uncomfortable about, when they consider their total situation. After all, they do believe— do they not?— that a man should be tried by a jury of his peers? Why not by a jury of Ph.D.'s? They were extremely enthusiastic about Harry Truman, were our friends who are laughing at the idea of putting a mediocre judge into the Supreme Court. Mr. Truman was, by most accounts, a very good President. By no one's account was he ever more than a mediocre mind.

And 4), if mediocrity means that when you read the Constitution and the Constitution says two plus two equals four, and you therefore rule that two plus two equals four, rather than rule that it depends on whether you had an underprivileged educational background then precisely what we need is a little more mediocrity.

Conservatism and Ecology

April 7, 1970

They are saying—the Right-watchers—that American Conservatives are not showing sufficient enthusiasm for the antipollution war. I believe that the accusation needs understanding.

A few months ago, when all the world, as it were on the same day, discovered Ecology, I ventured privately to predict that the enthusiasm for environment was in for some trouble. What will be the reaction—I asked—when the Hudson River Anti-Pollution Act comes into law providing a billion dollars to clean up the Hudson, and the politician, white or black, campaigning in Harlem stands up and says, "Why are we spending money to make life more comfortable for the fishes in the Hudson River, when we have right here living conditions that are intolerable for human beings? Are water rights greater than human rights?"

And indeed, we have already seen a little ideological skepticism. A Midwest SDS group has officially abandoned antipollution as one of its major demands, on the grounds that now that the Nixon Administration has embraced the goals, we have an Establishmentarian objective and that's no fun.

The politician's point, although demagogic, is not absurd. I (as an individual, and as a conservative) deeply yearn for clean air and clean rivers. But I know that I cannot have them, suddenly; and know, moreover, that the cleansing of the environment cannot reasonably take first priority in national attention. Years ago, applauding the attitudes of Secretary of the Interior Stewart Udall, I observed that he showed a commendable zeal for preserving the open spaces of society, but that sometimes he sounded as though he resented any human habitation whatsoever, on the grounds that it might get in the way of a meandering buffalo. In point of fact there is a built-in conflict of interest between social organization and natural abandon: as it is simply unrealistic to say, for instance, that because automobiles poison the air, we are going to do without automobiles.

A scholar in California has begun a careful effort to analyse the issues. Having done so, he has come up with a few useful observations—useful to those who on the one hand wish to arrest the pollution of the atmosphere, but on the other hand do not believe in a program unrelated to reality.

The scholar (who desires anonymity for the time being) believes that there is available to us a "bureaucratic" approach, and also an "institutional" approach. The former would consist primarily in issuing a complex set of instructions based on telling people what they can do, and what they cannot do. Almost always this is the less desirable way of accomplishing national objectives: because it involves coercion, because it is undiscriminating, and because it gives rise to an enormous new bureaucracy charged with the unappealing responsibility of overseeing sumptuary laws.

The institutional approach is designed to cause people, as individuals, themselves to desire and to take the necessary steps to forge what is socially desirable. An example of the latter, as distinguished from the former, would be the large bump in the road that forces the driver to slow down his car in the roadway; as an alternative to the hidden cop or radar unit that detects the miscreant.

Applied to the environment, we have in effect a situation somewhat as follows: You can pour a certain amount of waste into the Hudson River, or emit a certain amount of carbon monoxide into the air over Los Angeles, without making the water prohibitively impure, or the air fatally noxious. The problem then is to decide how to lessen— without making the effort to eliminate— the flow of pollutants into the natural system. And, as ever, the market mechanism comes in not necessarily to the rescue, but definitely to the aid of the party.

The way to reduce, for instance, the emission of dirty exhaust into the air by a factory burner is not by forbidding the factory from emitting it, but by taxing a factory according to the noxiousness of its exhaust. The factory owners then sit down to make complicated calculations guided by commercial questions. The state responds by increasing, or lessening the tax, according as it overstrains, or understrains, the system. The manufacturers of filters are given an incentive to produce filters of varying sensitivity in harmony with the likelihood that the factory will want Filter A in order to effect Saving A or Filter E to effect Saving E. Those few who desire to be wanton, may proceed to be wanton: at a cost. Thus the best way to regulate the flow of car travel into a city is to raise or lower the tolls of the arterial entrances to the city; and the best way to cut down on the use of water where water is scarce is to meter the water, so that the man who wants to waste water will have to pay for his waste.

The results are not merely the obvious ones. The residual benefits are the encouragement of an institutional acceptance of the national objective in place of an authoritarian insistence on uniform standards. That is the conservative, as distinguished from the abstractionist, approach.

The Family Assistance Plan: Nay

April 14, 1970

The moment is at hand to declare oneself for or against the Nixon-Moynihan plan to give money, no questions asked, to the indigent so as to put a federal floor on poverty. If I were in Congress, I would vote against the measure. A decision I have come to reluctantly. A few observations:

1) There is no doubting the desirability of radical reform of the existing welfare patterns. As the laws now stand, an individual seeking government help has access (at the last count) to eighty different state and federal welfare measures. It wasn't ever presumed that every single one of them would be subsumed into the $1,600 per year minimum proposed by the Nixon plan. For instance, catastrophic illnesses could never be tended to out of such a meager basic allowance. But surely other forms of federal subvention might have been. And yet as it now stands, with the exception of unemployment relief and aid to dependent children, the lobbyists for different welfare proposals stand fast, and the plan emerges as yet another federal prop, to be added to a house already jerry-built.

2) The greatly attractive provisions in the bill which suggested that recipients would be trained to work so as to remove them from the poverty rolls have not been convincingly put forward. One does not doubt that it is the intention of Mr. Nixon and of Mr. Moynihan that the measure should lead a great many indigents into vocational training schools and finally into

productive jobs. But the failure of the WIN programs, which were also designed to do the same thing; and the general acceptance of the figures constantly given us, to the effect that the overwhelming majority of those on relief cannot be expected to work because they are old or crippled or mothers or children, suggest that one should favor the measure or oppose it with little reference to this particular feature of it. In fact, there are those—one can tell it from the inflection in their comments and in their speeches—who talk about the "workfare" aspects of the bill merely as boob-bait for conservatives. They do not really believe that it will bring people to work, and they don't particularly care.

3) It is always difficult to predict the cost of new welfare proposals. Initially, I heard a cost estimate as low as $2.3 billion—*i.e.*, in excess of current welfare costs. I have not recently seen one at less than $5.5 billion.

One thinks less, at this particular moment, about the absolute sum involved, more about the expenditure of it at this particular moment in our economic history. There are those who believe that in recent weeks Mr. Nixon, frightened either by the threat of a real depression or by the prospects of political upheaval at the forthcoming election—or both—has retreated from his firm anti-inflationary stance. Certainly he has taken measures, such as the release of federal funds for various projects that had been held in abeyance, the result of which will be to goose inflation along. The effects of the postal settlement alone are said to have wiped out the modest little surplus we had programmed for fiscal 1970. Meanwhile inflation zooms along.

The notion that this is the ideal time to launch a great new welfare program, the cost of which we cannot reckon with any assurance, is at least doubtful. It will surprise a great many people to discover Mr. Moynihan is surprisingly keen on the subject of inflation. This is not something he learned at the knee of Averell Harriman or his New Deal mentors. But close association with Arthur Burns before Mr. Burns went to the Federal Reserve Board taught Mr. Moynihan a lesson, and he is one of the best learners in the business. It is that inflation is perhaps the single cruelest imposition on poor people, and that when inflation is given its head, it becomes almost impossible to make the myriad adjustments necessary to achieve justice.

So that 4), shouldn't we at least wait until the economic house is in order, cognizant precisely of the net damage that will be done if we do not control federal spending? The demagogues' easy answer that the obvious solution is to end the Vietnam war, is as satisfactory as the proposal that if we run short of concrete, we should take chunks out of the nearest dam. In this vale of tears we cannot have everything exactly when we want it. The ledger points to the desirability of voting, however reluctantly, Nay.

Women's Lib

August 15, 1970

For those of you who do not live in New York City, let it be known that it is front-page news here that McSorley's Ale House has opened its doors, and for the first time this century, to women patrons. The regular clientele are said to be disturbed by the change in the atmosphere (although it is not certain whether that change will endure). Because, on the day that the bill denying any public house the right to discriminate on account of sex became law, it was the Women's Lib types who went to McSorley's. And the Women's Lib types, whether they are women or men, would change the atmosphere. There are not enough Women's Lib types to stand guard forever at McSorley's, so that the question is who will replace them?

Perhaps just plain women, by which it should be understood that I refer to anybody from Helen of Troy to Margaret Chase Smith, who are on the one hand most indisputably women, but on the other hand, the kind of women who would move over to the opposite end of the room when Gloria Steinem comes in. McSorley's could more easily assimilate them, of course. Even so, let us face it, the atmosphere would be different. I am careful not to say that the atmosphere would be worsened — merely that it would be different. And here, I think, is the point, or one of the points, behind the inchoate opposition to the lengths that Women's Lib is nowadays going.

The ladies are busy writing books like *The Feminine Mystique*, and *Sexual Politics*, and there is much that is engrossing and brilliant in these books, but inevitably the taxonomical ambition to make men and women "equal" breaks down under the unassailable insight that, at McSorley's things *are* different when women are admitted. It is, needless to say, the same, stated the other way around: Things would be different, at New York's Colony Club, if men were admitted. Really, one oughtn't to have to go any further than that. Those who believe that all one's emotions and instincts and preferences can be nicely situated and explained away do not know the virtues of a limited curiosity. For one thing, as Wyndham Lewis pointed out, if you succeed in exactly categorizing everyone, you rob everyone of his freedoms.

From the rhetoric of equality that is being used today one has a glimpse into the future, when it will become necessary for John to give his reasons, not one of which must be even vestigially anti-social, for desiring to marry Jane. Because Jane is pretty would automatically invalidate the marriage as anti-social: surely we will not permit discrimination against non-pretty people? Because Jane is bright, ditto. Because she is Jewish, and so is John? A felony. Because she is the same age as John? Prove, scientifically, that marriages with older or younger girls do not work out. And so on, ad absurdum to be sure, but the question is whether the absurd is not already being treated seriously.

Not by everyone, granted. Charlötte Curtis of the New York *Times* is the most perceptive, and certainly the most amusing, cause-party watcher in New York. It was she who blew the whistle at Leonard Bernstein's party to protest those who stand in the way of the Black Panthers' sublime calling to kill the pigs, and later it was Charlotte Curtis who spotted the party in East Hampton of socialites raising their glasses of champagne in a toast to the boycott of California grapes.

Now Miss Curtis reports on a Women's Lib party in Long Island at which the (alas) unsinkable Mrs. Betty Friedan was going on and on about Women's Lib, including such gems as demanding that in the future it be called "*her*story, not just *hi*story," and then she called on the next speaker, Representative Patsy Mink of Hawaii, who however had mysteriously disappeared—who knows, perhaps to join the guys at McSorley's. So they introduced Gloria Steinem, at which point Jill Johnson, a writer for the *Village Voice*, jumped into the swimming pool, removed her shirt (she was, of course, bra-less), backstroked lazily up and down the pool saying how nice the water was, and altogether disrupting Miss Steinem's speech, so that not even Mrs. Friedan, seizing the mike, could reclaim the attention of the one hundred important guests who had paid $25 each to advance their cause.

It was little short of fiasco, but the very next day the House of Representatives passed a bill which, if it gets through the Senate and three-fourths of the state legislatures, would become a constitutional amendment: illegalizing any discrimination whatsoever based on sex. So far as one can see from a very quick survey of the kind of legislation the amendment would inconvenience, it would result in at least the loss of as many special privileges (*e.g.*, alimony, maternal leave, protection against rape, etc.) as the ladies would gain. The House voted without hearings, without debate, and without, if we may say so, deliberation. It is a pity that Jill Johnson wasn't there to throw herself into the House swimming pool and distract the attention of the gentlemen legislators. Perhaps she is holding out for the Senate.

October 19, 1971

The House of Representatives has passed (by a very wide margin, though by slightly less than last year's margin) the so-called Women's Rights Amendment, which forbids in all classes of activity any discrimination against women. It is not easy to project the consequences of this amendment, if it should get through the Senate and through the States, which is one reason why there is talk about a possible Senate filibuster against it.

It is mind-frazzling to imagine the kind of action that might be brought under the new amendment. In recent years we have, for instance, seen great big grown people insist that there is anti-Negro discrimination if, say, the undergraduate population is less than the percentage of the Negro population of the United States. Might it be alleged, under the new amendment, that IBM practices discrimination until the day when one-half of its senior executives are women?

And so on. But, understandably, it will be difficult to find the Senators who will step forward, because the feminists are quite prepared to say—"That man is a sexual fascist," rather than, "That man believes the proposed amendment would make bad law." No doubt, ten years hence, Senator Jones will be disqualified for a position on the Supreme Court, on the grounds that in the early seventies he showed himself sexually biased against women . . .

It does of course sound ridiculous, perhaps because the literature of Women's Liberation is so stupefyingly awful; oh dear, it is awful. I do believe that there are quite a few men, and that I am one of them, who have never even flirted with the notion that women are inferior, and perhaps that is why the glaze comes over our eyes when we come across the diatribes of some of the ladies who, having rejected the hearth, assent only to the driving of Mack trucks. Miss Gloria Steinem is the most conspicuous of them, and I read now, belatedly, the commencement address she delivered last spring at her alma mater, Smith College.

Miss Steinem reminisced about what it was like to be a student at Smith during the fifties, in an age of "racist and sexist values." She said that she was given the impression that she was "maybe even biologically and therefore immutably inferior— unlike black men whom [sic] one insisted were just as good." Her teachers should have confined themselves to pointing out that Miss Steinem was merely grammatically inferior.

She told of consulting her tutors about the advisability of going to law school, and of being told "Why study three extra years and end up in the back room of some law firm doing research and typing right away?"— a reflection, I would say, on the lady or gentleman who gave the advice, which sounds especially strange to the ear during a season when the President of the United States is considering two women for the Supreme Court, both of whom went to law school much before Miss Steinem graduated from Smith.

Miss Steinem's war against racism and sexism finds her saying things which are, curiously, well— racist, even as the demands recently for Black Studies programs have been, many of them, racist. But the lady's logic has never been her principal contribution to the scene. Having told us that she was brought up to feel biologically inferior as a woman, she then says, "We [ladies] have been discovering, in all areas of academic study and personal experience, that the so-called masculine-feminine differences are largely societal, not biological." Well, biological inferiority in the sense that Miss Steinem uses the term was never alleged; biological differentiation, as she now uses the term, is not an allegation but a fact, the elimination of which not even a constitutional amendment can accomplish. But to such lengths does she go in attempting to do so, that she finds herself talking about "so-called abnormal sexual behavior, whatever that is."

Her notion is that history shows that all our dread institutions resulted from the sudden discovery of paternity, after five thousand years of gynecocracy. It was that discovery that led, for instance, to "the idea of ownership . . . of property and of children, the origin of marriage (which was really locking women up long enough to make sure who the father was) . . . the notion that the state owns the body of a woman, a notion we still see in our abortion laws." This kind of thing is painful enough at a commencement address. That kind of thing armed with a constitutional amendment is enough to cause us all to go home to mother.

Are We Moving Right?

October 8, 1970

They are saying that the country is moving right, and lo there are those who are sore afraid. I do believe that they are a superstitious lot, and that those who examine the meaning of the term — as used, for instance, by the Attorney General, or by the public whose political inclinations the New York *Times* is nowadays polling — will find it a good deal less spooky than they have been taught to expect.

"Right" can mean a good many things. In the context of what troubles American society at this point it means, primarily:

A stricter enforcement of the law. Granted, this will get in the way of the licentious habits of some of our priests (*e.g.*, Berrigan), and poets (*e.g.*, Lowell); but also it will restrain others, who tend to express their dissent from public policies by, *e.g.*, blowing up buildings at the University of Wisconsin. Now: no one who believes in laws (and those who don't believe in them will simply have to be domesticated) should object to the laws' enforcement. If there is a law that says that individual A must not impede individual B's access to the chemistry lab, then presumably, there

is very little disagreement over the proposition that when individual A nevertheless proceeds to do just that, the police should
be summoned, B should be restored his rights, and A should be
punished according to the specifications of the law.

Now what troubles many liberals is less the prospect of
deterring A than the proposed means of identifying and ap-
prehending him. If A is clearly visible, standing guard over the
entrance to the building, shotgun in hand, that is one thing. But
suppose that A is the man who organized the blockade of the
building; or the man who intimidated B over the telephone from
even trying to get into the building; or the man who fired up the
crowd which then proceeded, under the forensic impulse of what
A said, to go to the barricades?

There you have problems, because typically the liberal resists
extraordinary ways of finding and convicting the criminal, while
the conservative, typically, believes that it is more important to
find him than to countenance the victimization of B, or to permit
his oppressors to go unpunished. The current debate over— for
instance— the No Knock law, is of this character. One of the
decisions of the Warren Court (*Massiah*) overruled the traditional arrangement by which the prosecution was permitted
to introduce into evidence such proof as it happened upon which
was incriminating in nature. It was Judge Cardozo who had held,
in an important decision in the twenties, that it is more important
to detect and to punish transgression, than to elaborate endlessly
the abstract rights of the free citizen.

Now there is no denying that there are secondary, as well as
primary, victims of almost any crime. The mugger not only
aggresses against the old lady whom he knocks down in order to
steal her purse. He also aggresses against all those other men,
women, and children who, knowing that the muggers patrol the
streets, deny themselves the freedom of those streets. A few weeks
ago, at a foreign airport, my bags were roundly examined:
because it was suspected that a bomb was being introduced into
the airplane in which I was to fly. There was certainly no
doubting the dimunition of my privacy— of my freedom, which is
an aspect of my privacy— under the circumstances. In that sense
the bomb-threatener has won a partial, and quite irrevocable,
victory. He succeeded in assaulting, however indirectly, every
passenger on that flight whose bags— and persons— were searched.

A turn to the right in American politics means, of course, many things. But mostly they are talking about the prospective dimunition of the privacy of secondary victims of current lawlessness. I join my brothers in the liberal camp in deploring the prospective losses, but I differ from them in believing that, on balance, the exchange is worth it. The important point is to grant to the state not one more ounce of power than it needs in order to return a net profit to the individual in the transaction. Government is a prehensile organism that feasts on the freedom of its citizens. But government is also, in the altogether desirable absence of vigilante justice, the single institution whose primary reason for being is to protect the individual from his aggressive brother. Clearly, as things now stand, in an age when the individual American is threatened and intimidated by a lawless communion of professional and amateur thieves and revolutionists, a turn to the right is a turn towards the maximization of human liberty in our dire circumstance.

What does turning to the right mean in the field of foreign policy? What does it mean to be "liberal" vs. "conservative" in foreign policy? At this moment, the divisions are pretty clear. The liberal is against ABM, against MIRV, against an expanded military budget, against maintaining our presence in Southeast Asia, against military aid to countries whose rulers govern other than by such authority as Americans consider to be democratically hygienic.

1. Concerning ABM (and MIRV) the arguments can be extremely elaborate, but they can also be relatively simple. The American Right (and here one can include Mr. Nixon, if not necessarily all those who work for Mr. Nixon) clings to the notion that ABM is an effective instrument of *deterrence.* Now the argument is complicated on the matter, but it is hardly arguable that the country stands to lose more than the monies spent on ABM. A turn to the right, *i.e.,* towards a more vigorous implementation of the ABM program, is a turn towards prudence in international affairs. Never let anyone wrest from you the axioms, which are that the United States does *not* intend to wage offensive war against the Soviet Union, whereas to believe that the Soviet Union would not under certain circumstances wage offensive war against the West is anti-historical.

So: a move "to the right" in military matters is a move towards, at best, the prevention of a world war; at worst, towards the unnecessary expenditure of a few billion dollars. Liberals and conservatives are opposed to the unnecessary expenditure of "federal" monies; the Right's disposition to risk the conceivable loss of a few billion dollars on defense, as opposed say to the liberal's disposition to risk the conceivable loss of a few billion dollars on the Alliance for Progress, or on the "war" on poverty, is best judged by the odds. In the latter case, if the money is misspent, why the poor are still with us, as alas they prove in substantial numbers to be; and the unstable Latin governments are still with us, as alas they are and worse, in the case of Chile and Bolivia. In the former case, "failure" is defined as something that did not succeed in deterring the aggressive impulses of the Soviet Union or Red China. Or— to be strictly fair to the liberals' argument— as the adoption of a program (ABM) which had the effect of preventing the enemy from amicable pursuits it would otherwise have pursued.

For instance, if you are disposed to come to terms with your neighbor about his disputed right to use the beach you had hitherto insisted was exclusively your own, you might be put off, on the day that you intended to make the grand gesture, if you looked up to see that your neighbor had mounted a 50-caliber machine gun on his porch. However, it requires— to believe ABM and MIRV have this potential effect on international disarmament— to believe also that the rulers of the Soviet Union are as tractable as Mary Poppins; and therein the liberals do have a problem.

2. So, turning to the right, the United States continues to give military aid to such repressive governments as that of the Greeks, or of Franco. The "turn" to the right amounts to nothing more than the continuation of broad policies originated by Franklin Delano Roosevelt (who kissed the devil's nose by giving aid to Stalin), and continued under Truman, Eisenhower, Kennedy, and Johnson. To refuse, suddenly, to give military aid to Chiang Kai-shek, or to the Colonels, because the board of directors of the Americans for Democratic Action disapproves of the governments of Formosa and Greece, is to take a turn towards that radical interventionism which has the unhappy effect of hurting real people, and damaging the prospect for real peace.

Put it this way. Could you find one (1) Israeli, who would favor an American embargo against military aid to Greece? No, and for the best of reasons. A country (like Israel) that is truly threatened, does not make foreign policy according to rules set down by Gloria Steinem for the satisfaction of Eugene McCarthy. Take one of those people and put him in a position of actual responsibility and hesto presto, you get John Kenneth Galbraith writing to President Kennedy suggesting that the United States guarantee militarily the border of Pakistan! A move to the right in foreign policy would tranquilize the world, so let's get on with it.

The Right-Anarchists

February 16, 1971

The "movement" Murray N. Rothbard announces as causing a "burgeoning split" with the conservative movement reminds me of the legendary conspiracy to overthrow the state, entered into by an assistant professor and two poets. Mr. Rothbard broke with *National Review* eleven years ago on the question of Khrushchev's visit to the United States, our position being that manifestations of displeasure with "K" were altogether appropriate, it being known that he had taken an active part in the Stalinization of the Ukraine. Rothbard took the position that there was no discernible moral difference between Nikita Khrushchev and Dwight Eisenhower, because as commander in chief of the Allied Expeditionary Force Eisenhower had killed as many people as Khrushchev had in the Ukraine. It requires that one take seriously such an analogy in order to take seriously Mr. Rothbard.

But surely—it will be said—this was mere frolic on Mr. Rothbard's part, tasteless to be sure, but hardly a reflection of the pure libertarianism whose songs he sings? One wonders. Because here now is Karl Hess, taking up the same theme. Is the United States any better than the Soviet Union? No, he says, the Soviet Union is slightly to be preferred, because they got rid of the chief of their secret police, while we have not. So even as Khrushchev is to be likened to Eisenhower, Beria is to be likened to J. Edgar Hoover. The first two both "killed" people, the second two both managed a federal police.

All right, you will say, perhaps Rothbard and Hess are moral naïfs, what does that have to do with their movement? It has this to do with their movement: they are its acknowledged leaders. It is as difficult to prescind the "movement" from such extravagances, as it finally became to prescind the body of doctrine of the John Birch Society from the distinctive lunacies of its founder.

Well, but don't they have a program? Yes they do: the cessation of all state activity. My all-time favorite is Mr. Rothbard's proposal that the lighthouses that throw out their welcome to storm-tossed ships should be privately owned, the lighthouse keeper zooming out to collect a dollar from any ship which can be proved to have treated itself to a bearing drawn from the private stock of the owner's electricity. Now you may judge that Mr. Rothbard is totally humorless. Believe me he is not. Having known him, I give you that as an instructed verdict. It is merely that he is a fundamentalist who begins with the assumption that the state is evil and marches on to the conclusion that all uses of the state are accordingly evil.

Mr. Henry Hazlitt, reviewing a recent volume by Mr. Rothbard, was forced to sigh that Mr. Rothbard suffers from "extreme apriorism," which is a nice way of putting it. Henry Hazlitt, for those members of the "movement" who may have forgotten, has done more to popularize the free market in the United States than any living man. He is as happy to make common cause against statism in *National Review* as we are to be joined with him.

If there is any danger, of course, it is that the kind of anarchy represented by Mr. Rothbard, as distinguished from the poised antistatism represented by, say, Ludwig von Mises, F. A. Hayek, Henry Hazlitt, John Chamberlain, Wilhelm Ropke *et al.*, could help to discredit the antistatist movement, whose journalistic fortress continues to be *National Review* magazine. The appeal of anarchy is not new, and the movement will have votaries long after Mr. Rothbard's has finished needlepointing his solipsisms for the benefit of those who find distinctions too heavy a burden.

The ideological licentiousness that rages through America today makes anarchy attractive to the simple-minded. Even to the ingeniously simple-minded. There are young men and young women who are attracted to Mr. Rothbard because they are attracted to extremists, or (more exactly stated) fanatical extremisms of plain truths. Oliver Wendell Holmes said it well when he commented that while common sense tells us that a man owns the air above his rooftop, the fanatic will reason that he owns a shaft of air stretching from his rooftop up into the heavens, such that no supersonic transport, or child's kite, may overfly him except with written permission. The American conservative believes that the state is as often as not an instrument of mischief as of good: it required the state, remember, to transform *Mein Kampf* into Buchenwald, and *Das Kapital* into concentration camps.

But no, children, one does not therefore argue against the existence of the state. The conservative harbors the *presumption* against any growth in state power. The question, in any given situation, whether that presumption is overridden by the evidence is for intelligent men to discuss. I am by no means assured that in every case *National Review* has concluded correctly. But I am quite, quite sure, that if, with *National Review*'s support, the United States had not supported such statist activity as has been necessary over the past generation in order to contain aggressive powers in another part of the world, Mr. Rothbard would nowadays be inhabiting a very real zoo, instead of the zoo he now voluntarily inhabits, which, thanks in no small measure to *National Review*, he is perfectly free to leave, any time, in order to join with those who strive meaningfully for an augmentation of personal liberty.

XI. The Economy

Railroad Reform

January 13, 1970

I do not know the particular situation elsewhere, but in New York the commuter railroads are a mess, and I for one do not believe that this was necessarily meant to be. This morning a friend began his telephone conversation, in reply to the routine question How are you? by muttering stoically that he had no complaint in the world except against the Penn Central Railroad.

What was it this particular morning? The "third track" wasn't working—on account of the bitter cold, the conductor had said. On the other hand, neither does the third track work regularly in the summertime, on account, presumably, of the bitter heat. Yesterday, on the line from Greenwich, Connecticut, the three count 'em three rear cars had absolutely no heat at all, so that the passengers had all to crowd in the forward cars passing an hour eyeball to eyeball, without space enough, even, to hide their tears with a copy of the New York *Daily News.*

My friend, who is a lawyer, waxed wrother and wrother, and reminded me that a year ago a passenger, protesting against some casual brutality of that morning's train, had refused to surrender his ticket. He was thereupon taken away and sentenced there and then by the judge for deprivation of service, which means that he deprived the railroad of money which belonged to the railroad in compensation for its services. What, my friend asked cogently, about the railroad's deprivation of its passengers' time? The gentleman in question is worth seventy-five dollars an hour on the open market. The figure is rough, but one can safely assume that in the course of a year, his commuter railroad costs him, in delays, oh, say, five thousand dollars.

I say it was not meant to be because I continue to believe that if no one had invented the railroad, and suddenly one were to call a press conference and divulge the idea of a track running in a straight line from city to city on which an enormous engine, an adaptation of an automobile, could pull enormous buses at speeds of a hundred miles per hour, the whole country would stop in amazement and every Congressman and Senator would rise in a chorus to appropriate money to make the dream come true. Yet, incredibly, railroads are grinding to a halt. Most of New England you cannot now reach by railroad.

I am in the mood to make a few practical proposals.

1. Is there any reason at all why the ICC shouldn't be abolished? It was set up primarily to guard against excessive abuses by the railroads of their advantages as monopolies. To guard against such abuses in this day and age is the equivalent of protecting the public against American Motors' selling its cars at too high a price.

2. It is, in my judgment, too late to turn the railroads completely over to free enterprise, but not too late for first economic principles to come to our help. The railroads' two principal economic encumbrances are a) taxes, and b) union monopolies. I propose legislation under which the government would acquire the railroad beds. The sole reason for doing so would be in order to prevent the states and the municipalities from taxing the railroads, most particularly the land over which their trackage runs.

3. The government would then proceed to lease the railroad beds for fees only just large enough to attend to the maintenance of the railroad beds, even as the highways are publicly maintained. Anyone paying the fee could use the bed and provide public services, subject to observance of safety rules, and central coordination. So that, for instance, the Greyhound Company, say, and Eastern Airlines, or even the Buckley Syndicate, could offer services to commuters, or even to longer haul passengers at a price to be arrived at by competition, and by the quality of the service and equipment they furnish. And, just as railway unions are covered under special legislation, so would they be covered under special legislation in the future: no union shop.

A sensible set of proposals, with the compliments of a former patron of the railroads, who is a prospective patron of the new railroads.

Inflation and the Unions

January 22, 1970

A high Administration official (as the saying goes) is fascinated by the number of businessmen who have lately come to the conclusion that only wage and price controls can bail the economy out. They reason (and they press their reasoning on influential ears) that there is no other way of curbing the extraordinary demands being made here and there by organized labor. The obvious way to resist outrageous demands is for the employer to decline to give in to them. But as arrangements have evolved in America, this simply does not work.

Consider General Electric. The strike is weeks old, and there is no prospect for settlement. True, General Electric does not need to settle in the sense that, say, the city of New York absolutely needed to settle with the Transport Workers Union. One cannot go more than a day or two without public transportation, whereas it is not necessary to buy another electric toaster tomorrow, and anyway there is a pretty good inventory. But every day that General Electric postpones settlement its competitors gain an advantage off which they might profit for years and years to come.

On the other han ` if General Electric were to capitulate, the cost of the new contract would mean a spectacular rise in the price of its products, which would of course be contagious, forcing up the price of Westinghouse's products when that company's contract came due and the union made similar demands. In the interim, General Electric would suffer grievously, a lesion which could gravely affect the economic health of the company. And of course, in the long run, the public would be forced to pay more money for the whole range of products manufactured by General Electric, from light bulbs to generators. Which is another way of saying that there would be more inflation. Which is what the government of the United States is pledged to resist.

So wage and price controls? No. Because although they would work for a very short period, inevitably wage and price controls freeze an economy into distortions which are strategically intolerable. England's success in reversing its economy's slide is in some quarters being attributed to wage and price controls. In fact they were of minor consequence. Most important was the devaluation of the pound, which because of the commanding role of the dollar in the world scene we are not in a position to do to it: plus heavy taxes on imports and foreign spending.

Wage and price controls work in essentially static economies, where Jones VI works for the counting house even as Jones I did a hundred years before. An economy based on kinetic capital and labor markets quickly loses its potency if Company A is told that it cannot lure Worker B from his present job to a competitive position by paying him more. Price controls almost inevitably bring a black market— and should. Even Russia tolerates a black market, so that, voyeuristically, the commissars can see what is the true value of a product.

Now there is an obvious solution, but it is taboo to mention it. The National Labor Relations Act, beloved of the New Dealers and the constellation of legislation giving to organized labor unique privileges, keeps the General Electrics of this world from doing what is in their and the public interest: the requirement of the Act that one bargain exclusively with the union— on the one hand; and, on the other, the requirement of state laws (most state laws) that one belong to said union in order to hold down a job with General Electric. Add to the whole the exemption of labor unions from the various anti-monopoly laws, and one sees, finally, the nature of the beast.

Congress and the Administration are wrestling with inflation. Why not organic reform? Why compel General Electric (or anybody else) to bargain collectively after, say, a strike goes beyond a fortnight? Surely, at that point, a company should be protected in its right to bargain with individual workers who, in turn, should be emancipated from their union: so as to diminish unemployment, to service the public, and to discourage the inflationary spiral.

June 20, 1970

Mr. Nixon has stood up very resolutely against wage and price controls in, however, an address that combined, and not so very harmoniously, the analysis and the rhetoric of the free market, with that of *dirigisme*. What Mr. Nixon said (good) was that we intend to go forward with a free economy in which the principal economic decisions will be made by the consumer through the mechanisms of the marketplace. All of which, he added (bad), will work provided people exercise a proper restraint— provided that they understand the threat of inflation, and govern themselves accordingly. What, under this analysis, ever happened to the doctrine of the Invisible Hand?

That was the doctrine of Adam Smith, who wrote the charter of economic liberty two hundred years ago by arguing that the invisible hand of the marketplace transforms into social usefulness that which was determined by the individual merely to be privately useful. For instance, the farmer who decides for altogether selfish reasons to increase his productivity by investing in, say, a tractor, ends by lowering the cost of the food, which is publicly useful; and so on.

During the Johnson years, when the war in Vietnam reached its full pitch, the idea was to keep down inflation by persuading people to limit their demands: by persuading corporations to keep down their profits, and labor to keep down its wages. The movement had its more or less world premiere when John F. Kennedy in 1962 decided publicly to castigate the head of United States Steel for announcing a price rise. Mr. Roger Blough instantly capitulated, giving rise to an editorial in *National Review* entitled, "Roger Blah, President, U. S. Putty." The editorial writer was making more than an *ad hominem* point. He was saying that if there had been good economic reason for the projected rise in the price of steel, then the steel company was being governed by necessity, not by greed: and had no business allowing the President to bully it out of that decision. If the rise in the price of steel was truly capricious, then what was needed was tougher anti-monopoly laws, but who was proposing these?

Still, the policy seemed to work there for a while during which, as John Kenneth Galbraith put it, "enforcement was hortatory." That it could not work over the long term seemed obvious, as inflationary fires were stoked by budget deficit after budget deficit. Prices had to rise, and did. Meanwhile, across the sea in England, the Socialists met their economic crisis— inflation, and a deficit in the balance of payments— with rigorous measures, including price controls, such as Mr. Galbraith and the Democrats are heartily urging for us at this moment.

A summary of the effect of price controls on inflation in

England, together with tables, was recently done by Enoch Powell. "From the end of 1964, when the government secured a 'Declaration of Intent' from the employers of the unions, to the end of 1969, when the attempt to regulate prices and wages by statute was virtually abandoned, the positive effect was exactly nil. Indeed it might more plausibly be argued that the policy was counter-productive: inflation accelerated, and was faster than during the previous period." With price controls, England's inflation rose from 108.2 in 1965 (1963 equals 100), to 127.2 in 1969. The rise here was from 103 to 119.7, or two points less.

What solved the problem in England was the devaluation of the pound, followed by the revaluation upward of the mark. What has not been solved in England is the problem of price inflation, although it is interesting that a socialist government has abandoned price controls, even as the Galbraiths in this country are advancing price controls as the truly sophisticated way of dealing with the problem of economic freedom. Their argument comes down to this: Look, certain corporations and labor unions are powerful enough to proceed towards inflationary levels by the use of their own power. So, since the prices and wages they command are arbitrarily fixed in the first instance, why not fix them arbitrarily in the public interest?

The reasoning is, in context, plausible. What they fail to suggest is what Mr. Nixon also failed to suggest, namely that true regulation is done by competition. And that the only way to regulate socially— to restore the Invisible Hand, if you will— is to apply anti-monopoly legislation. And since such legislation already exists against business, it follows that what is primarily needed is the extension of such legislation to the monopoly unions. But that is not the kind of talk we will hear from Republicans during election year, or from liberal intellectuals ever.

Subsidizing the Subways

January 10, 1970

The national attention given to the rise of the subway fares in New York City is instructive, as also the suggestion, published in the Washington *Post*, that after all, why shouldn't the subways be free, like public schools, and (adds the author) free private hospitals?

Instructive because it suggests how far away we have got from what would appear to be a rudimentary understanding of how things work. There are two reasons why the subway fares in New York City rose. The secondary reason is that the Transport Workers Union is utterly unafraid of breaking the no-strike laws of the State of New York, particularly in an election year, so that it disposes of the effective power to blackmail the city administration.

But the primary reason is that New York City subway workers weren't making enough money and needed a raise. And the reason they weren't making enough money is because the government is spending too much money. One way to put it is this, that the cost of riding the subway will rise because the American people are receiving so many things free of charge. That would appear to be paradox. It is the beginning of economic wisdom to recognize that it is not a paradox.

Inasmuch as it is predictable that before these words appear in print, Mayor John Lindsay will have blamed the rise in the fares equally on Nelson Rockefeller and the Vietnam war, it is appropriate to point out that during the Johnson Administration money spent on defense rose by 50 percent, while money spent on welfare rose by 100 percent.

As for the argument that Nelson Rockefeller is responsible, the counter-argument that comes most readily to mind is also the best argument, namely that there simply is no obvious reason why Cayuga County applepickers need to be taxed in order to subsidize the 5 million New Yorkers who regularly ride the subways. And if they were taxed (to quote myself ten years ago) a reciprocal obligation would be implicitly lodged, by the terms of which, very soon, the subway riders in New York City would be taxed in order to help the applepickers of Cayuga County, and before you know it, the sky is blackened by crisscrossing dollars, and one contemplates, yet again, the mysterious axiom of contemporary liberalism, that one should continually elongate the distance between where a dollar is collected and where a dollar is spent.

John Lindsay would be happy if Albany were to subsidize New York subway riders, happier still if Washington were to do so, and presumably elated if the United Nations were to do it.

What the raise means, to most people, is one dollar extra per week. Since getting to work is a necessary expense, that dollar will either shrink the individual's disposable income; or, in due course, he will wrest the dollar from his employer, who in turn will charge more for his product, and back we go again.

But the assumption that the way to handle the matter is to subsidize the subway is of course ludicrous, not merely because arguments at least as cogent could then be made for providing free food (in order to work you have to eat) and free shoes (in order to get from the subway to the offices you have to use shoe leather). But because after you reach a certain point it is all but impossible to effect a subsidy.

That point is easily reached by the 5 million subway riders of New York City. That bloc of people is so numerous as to belong solidly in the economic bloodstream of the country. Among them are income tax payers, property tax payers, excise tax payers, and sales tax payers: so that the idea of subsidizing them from funds into which they are not already contributing, and into which they will need to contribute more if the "subsidy" were enacted, is, well, a political shell game. It is our old friend the Economics of Hallucination without which, one might add, most of the people who are elected to office could not have got there.

A Program for Revenue Sharing

March 9, 1971

It sometimes happens— have you noticed?— that a subject gets so sliced up, one despairs of trying to pick up a piece of it that will not fragment: and, rather than start again from scratch, the temptation is to give up. It is so, for instance, with the disarmament proposals. And it is so with the revenue-sharing business. At this point so many people have been heard on the subject, often saying contradictory things, one has the feeling that the public simply turns the dial when the subject comes up, like the English and the Common Market.

Well, some recent figures are in front of me, from which, without very much coaxing, it appears to me that a story line emerges. First, one or two surprises— to stimulate the mind, and to break up the stereotypes. New York is the richest (highest per capita income) state in the Union, right? Wrong. Connecticut is. Alaska is one of the poorest, right? It is the second richest; Nevada is third, and only then, New York.

Mississippi— surely— is the poorest state in the Union? Yes, it is. And socially the most backward? How do you usually define socially progressive states? By the size of state and local taxes. Mississippi takes, in taxes, $117 for every thousand dollars of personal income. By contrast, New York State taxes $140. Inasmuch as New York is one of the very richest states, and Mississippi is the very poorest state, then the tax-strain on the Mississippians can be seen to be far greater than on New Yorkers: which collapses one old saw.

New York has the highest rate of taxation in the nation? No, the second highest. Hawaii's is the highest.

What is the spread between the poorest and the richest state? Connecticut's per capita income is $4,595. Mississippi's is $2,218, so that the richest American state has about double the per capita income of the poorest American state. What state is closest to the average? Missouri, whose per capita income is $3,458 (the average is $3,406— almost three times Japan's).

How many states are poorer than Missouri? *I.e.*, have per capita incomes less than the national average? Twenty-three. They are:

Alabama, Arizona, Arkansas, Georgia, Idaho, Kentucky, Louisiana, Maine, Mississippi, Montana, New Mexico, North Carolina, North Dakota, Oklahoma, South Carolina, South Dakota, Tennessee, Texas, Utah, Vermont, Virginia, West Virginia and Wyoming.

How does Missouri, as the average state, make out in the welfare game? Well, it pays over to the U.S. Government $500 million per year in taxes. How much does the U.S. Government pay to the state of Missouri in welfare grants? $502 million.

Is that round trip really necessary?

The Congress of the United States should resolve that henceforward no state richer than the average, *i.e.,* no state whose per capita income exceeds Missouri's, shall qualify for any federal grant.

What about the poorer states? Let Congress, which in 1969 put out $24 billion in welfare grants, scale down its brokerage function by addressing itself exclusively to the poorer American cousins. The poorest American state, Mississippi, has been getting federal aid at the rate of about $200 per capita, compared to Missouri's $125 per capita, and (inexplicably), New York's $140 per capita. The parameters are suggested. Why not begin at $100 per capita for the underprivileged states? The total population of the less-than-average states is 53 million. Times $100, you have just over $5 billion. If experience reveals that that is not enough, raise the figure. Meanwhile, the individual states are emancipated, and can look after their own welfare problems in their own way: and that is the true meaning of decentralization.

Having scaled down the brokerage function of the Federal Government by relieving it of the responsibility for taking money from the richer states in order to return money to the richer states, what can it usefully do? Two things, one of which I have described. Namely, to act as the agent through which money passes hands from the richer to the poorer states, as the philanthropic or redistributionist impulse moves the Congress.

A suggested formula might be based on the distance of any given state from the national median. Thus, for instance, Mississippi, where per capita income is $2,218, presumably needs more help than Montana, where per capita income is $3,130, close to the national median of $3,406.

The second thing the Federal Government could usefully do is

to lease its tax-gathering facilities to the individual states. I do not
see any substantial argument, based in theory or in practice,
against such cooperation. Thus, on day X in the future, the
resident of New York, having filled out his federal tax return,
would go on to consult the table for New York; which would give
him the exact sum of money he would need to add to his federal
return in order to discharge his state obligation. Exit, with the
single deed, all the state internal revenue agencies that occupy
themselves with income taxes. The Federal Government, on
receipt of the grand total, would put aside the indicated sum for
the credit of the individual state, less a service charge.

Now ideally, the Federal Government would get out of the
business of graduating the tax. As Professor Friedman has
demonstrated, it could do so with no pain at all to itself, and with
great benefit to the body politic.

A very few reforms would be needed. Those Mr. Friedman has
advocated are: 1) eliminate all deductions, 2) double dependency
allowances; and lo, you could raise as much money as the
government now raises from personal income taxes by having a
set rate of 20 percent. You could even throw in a $1,500 negative
income tax floor, by increasing the flat rate to only 23 percent.
The figures are suggestive of how relatively little is the money that
is taken from the rich. They are simply not numerous enough to
constitute a significant tax factor.

The states could then devise income taxes of their own
choosing, setting the rates according to their fancy: and, dutifully,
the tax would be collected by the single internal revenue agent,
and remitted to the states. But the taxpayer would always be
aware who it is that is taking his money. That nexus, so greatly
stressed by Wilbur Mills, is indispensable to enlightened self-
government. Under Mr. Nixon's plan, the Congress of the United
States ordains the tax, then remits a part of it to the state, whose
legislators then assemble in order to discuss merely the matter of
how the money should be spent: not whether it should have been
raised in the first instance.

To separate the one function from the other is the device of
those who wish to conceal from the taxpayer what are the
economic realities. In his book *The Affluent Society*, Professor
Galbraith, always on the prowl for means of substituting himself
for the marketplace, suggested automatic increases, pegged to
inflation and cost of living, for schools, and such, to spare the

legislators the occasional agony of having to levy more taxes, or letting the schools run down.

Better the agony, I say: and surely all taxpayers would say as much, and would hope that Congress will address this opportunity to engage in revenue-sharing, by adopting genuine, radical, reform.

Is Nixon a Keynesian?

January 19, 1971

A lot of people are snickering about the remark Mr. Nixon reportedly made to Howard K. Smith of the American Broadcasting System after the televised interview of a week or two ago. "One interesting thing Mr. Nixon said to us after the interview was, 'I am now a Keynesian in economics.' That," Mr. Smith remarked, "is a little like a Christian Crusader saying, all things considered, I think Mohammed was right."

Well, not quite. There are several levels at which to understand Keynes. Clearly Mr. Nixon was using "Keynesianism" in the most popular sense of the word, which is defined in *Webster's Third* as, "the economic theories and programs ascribed to John Maynard Keynes and his followers, specifically: the advocacy of fiscal and monetary programs by government to increase employment."

The best-known American conservative economist is Professor Milton Friedman, and he most enthusiastically backs the use of monetary policies in order to achieve economic goals. In the ideological wars, the recent battles have been between those who desire to stress fiscal policies, *i.e.*, the rate of taxation, deficit spending — that kind of thing. And those others who believe that the key to the problem lies in the money supply. Both sets of people, should they choose to do so, could call themselves Keynesians, though as professionals, they would be unlikely to do so, because they know too much about Keynes to use him as a particularly useful eponym.

A few years ago the British magazine *Encounter* conducted an almost endless symposium on the theme, "We are all Keynesians now." The editor's thought was to establish that there simply wasn't anybody around anymore who didn't accept Keynes as the spokesman for a new way of doing things in economics, whose policies are everybody's policies. He had a far less easy time of it than he expected, as individual economists weighed in insisting that, far from it, Keynesianism did not prevail.

One of them, for instance, gave it as his opinion that Keynes considered that the single most important objective of money-managers should be low interest rates. And by low interest, Keynes meant something like 2 percent. At that point, the interest rate in England was about 7 percent. How then could we say that England was "Keynesian"?

Then the subject is mystified by the rodomontade of some of Keynes' followers, who took Keynes' insights and kneaded them into an entire economic cosmology. Some of these gentlemen-fanatics were heard to say that there was nothing now that we didn't know about economics, thanks to Keynes, plus their exegesis of him. But during the late forties and the fifties the application of Keynes' formulas was shown quite simply not to work, for many reasons, some of them as yet undiagnosed. For instance, it was Keynes' breezy prescription that at times of boom, the government should skim off enough surplus money to finance its pump-priming activities in times of depression. Try it. Then, for a while, the economists would say: well, Keynes taught us how to come down from the highs, but he never taught us how to climb up from the lows. Then, for a while, they said exactly the opposite.

Today, if you say that you are a Keynesian, you are either saying a) nothing at all; or you are saying, b) that you are a reactionary. There hasn't been a Keynesian in the entire sense of the word since the feverish Harvard acolytes of the late thirties, who have gracefully disbanded.

It is often pointed out that Lord Keynes took delight in saying of himself that he was "not a Keynesian." And indeed, shortly before he died, the apostle of central economic management was writing enthusiastically about the young economist Friedrich Hayek, who had just published *The Road to Serfdom*, which predicted that the surrender of power to the government inevitably meant the surrender of liberty.

So that Mr. Nixon's remark to Mr. Smith is not quite so striking a declaration of heresy as he would have us believe. Why did he say it? I think Mr. Nixon meant to acknowledge that the mere mention of the word "Keynes" is no longer so frightening as once it was. Rather like saying, breezily, "we are all Machiavellians."

Nixon and Deficit Spending

March 25, 1971

Professor John Kenneth Galbraith, who is a great tease, has gleefully sent me the remarks of Mr. Herbert Stein, a member of the President's Council of Economic Advisers, as delivered recently before the Annual Financial Outlook Conference in New York City. Mr. Galbraith's covering note says: "Here is a thoughtful restatement of the fiscal principles of modern conservatism. I feel that similar repetition would be valuable for your own neo-Keynesian readers and should be recommended strongly to the Voice of America when next you gather to advise it."

The first sentence of Mr. Stein's speech was: "The Federal Government had a deficit in fiscal year 1970; it will have a large deficit in fiscal year 1971, the current year; it will have another deficit in fiscal 1972."

The second sentence was: a repetition of the first.

The third sentence was: still another repetition of the first.

And then Mr. Stein explained. "You may ask why I repeat these simple statements three times, and I will tell you. I am trying to demonstrate that the Administration is not ashamed of the fact that we had, have, and will have deficits and is not trying to conceal the fact. We do not talk about the full-employment budget in order to deny the existence of deficits. We do not project a Gross National Product of $1,065 billion for 1971 in order to reduce the prospective deficit.

"If we can suspend these natural but superficial and erroneous political and journalistic suspicions we can begin to discuss seriously what the Government is doing in fiscal policy. . . . Probably the most convenient way to get into this subject is to recognize that for at least the last 40 years we have had deficits when the economy was declining below full employment. The last serious attempt to bring the budget into balance in such conditions was Herbert Hoover's in 1932, although Franklin Roosevelt made a brief and halfhearted move in that direction in 1937. The Hoover experience did not invite imitation." And so on.

Now, Professor Galbraith is very well entitled to remind Mr. Nixon and his conservative backers of the rhetoric we have directed over the years at unbalanced budgets. But the learned professor is flirting with a most dangerous species of epistemology. Can he be saying that because Mr. Nixon and his conservative economists have adopted the deficit-budget, now finally we know that it is correct policy?

The traditional opposition to deficit spending, as enunciated by classical economists, has hardly been discredited by the American experience. One argument, for instance Lord Keynes', in favor of deficit spending is that it will make unemployment go away. Franklin Delano Roosevelt's colossal failure to end unemployment is excused on the grounds that his deficit spending was insufficient. Let it go. General Eisenhower, in the course of eight years as President, overspent by $27 billion (the figures are approximate). When he came into office, there were 2 million unemployed. When he left, there were almost 4 million unemployed.

John Kennedy sustained a deficit in each one of his three years, and Lyndon Johnson, as we all know, ran deficits totalling $50 billion. The unemployment figures were high in the early years of Mr. Kennedy, and were headed towards the present highs when Lyndon Johnson left office.

What Mr. Nixon and his Administration really mean to say when they plot a budget deficit is that a democracy will not support such measures as are necessary to test the theses of the classicists. Consider. It was Keynes who spoke about the advisability of budget surpluses during good years, which would be drawn upon during bad years. Now who is a Keynesian in that sense? When last did Professor Galbraith suggest that the time was right for the Government to spend less, tucking some of it away for a rainy day? Not Galbraith, not Lyndon Johnson—and not Richard Nixon. Mr. Nixon was not elected President in order to liquidate human nature. Because a member of his Council of

Economic Advisers repeats three times that there will be a deficit, it does not follow from the doxology either that a deficit is economically wise, or that it is technically virtuous.

Will Price Controls Be Next?

July 29, 1971 ⁚

While it is not clear what Mr. Nixon will accomplish by his convulsive Far Eastern policies, a distinction needs to be made between these and his domestic policies, towards which his critics, temporarily confounded, are turning their fire. Those who desire employment and can't find it would be grateful if the Nixon Administration found the means to help them find it. Those who suffer from inflation would be grateful to Mr. Nixon for a dollar whose buying power ceased to dissipate. So that it remains the question: Does Mr. Nixon know what to do about the soggy economic situation?

Concerning his problems, a few observations:

1. It becomes clear what is the Administration's attitude towards those industries in the United States whose impoverishment means a startling rise in unemployment: help them. In other times, to help the industries directly would have been neither the New Deal answer nor the answer of the classical economists. The New Deal's answer was direct intervention in behalf of the unemployed. The classicists' answer was: hands off the situation.

Mr. Maurice Stans, Secretary of Commerce, in discussing the textile situation a year or so ago was altogether blunt about it. If Japanese imports continued at the current rate, 100,000 Americans per year would be cast into unemployment. Now, he said, since it is government policy to provide welfare for those who need it, it is manifestly more efficient to protect them in their jobs, and allow foreign competition to displace them only gradually, rather than to permit them to be unemployed suddenly, greatly aggravating the problem of finding new jobs. Thus, in coming out for a flexible tariff policy, he spoke the mind of the Nixon Administration clearly: use existing organisms of employment, in order to soften the blow. The operative imperative? Social welfare.

It is exactly the same thing with Lockheed. It is preposterous to assume that Mr. Nixon's concern is with the stockholders of Lockheed. It is with Lockheed's thirty thousand unemployed. He reasons that it is more efficient to bail out Lockheed—or, to be more precise, to be instrumental in the possibility that Lockheed can bail itself out—than to plop the thirty thousand Lockheed employees into the unemployment pool: which means, in the advanced condition of state welfarism, to plop them into situations in which they derive their living from state and welfare programs.

2. The great switch of the past generation is from private to public initiative. Mr. Nixon's assumption that only 4 percent is a tolerable unemployment rate means that the stimulus to provide employment for the difference between 4 percent and the currently unemployed 6 percent has got to come from somewhere. Under the new dispensations, the initiative is the government's. In yesteryear, it would have been the private sector's. But the old mobility is gone. For one thing, the average American has been willing to trade off more and more of his salary in return for welfare measures, public and private.

The cost to American employers of fringe benefits is a staggering 30 percent of the payroll. The cost to the various governments, local, state, and federal, of all services rendered is in the vicinity of 35 percent. One gradually deduces from the relative apportionment of responsibility that necessarily the initiative devolves upon the government. There isn't enough slack in the private sector.

Assume, for one minute, that Congress were instantly to a) reduce corporate taxes by 25 percent; b) abolish unemployment benefits altogether; c) crack down on monopolies of every character. In such a situation the old, the disabled, dependent children, would still receive care. But the private sector would rush to expand, even as the unemployed rushed to seek work, never mind the union scale. How far away such free market solutions appear. The psychology of welfarism dominates.

3. The critics of Mr. Nixon are determined to hold out wage and price controls (an "incomes policy," as they nowadays call it), as the *deus ex machina*. The classicists insist it wouldn't work, that indeed it would cause great harm. I wonder, mightn't it be

worth trying? The free market analysis is not wrong, but is there a better opportunity to discredit the price control theory than the current one? Inasmuch as unemployment stays the same, the national deficit approaches spectacular reaches, inflation goes robustly forward: why not experiment? It would be no more shocking, at the domestic level, than the recognition of Red China at the foreign level. If we are so far into welfarism that we cannot seek out classical solutions, why not admit it? And force a confrontation with the results of the truly managed, totally managed economy? Even if, after we were through, we were to discover that about the only freedom we have left is to steal secret papers?

The Publishers' Problem

September 23, 1971

I too regret the death of *Look* magazine. But scanning the obituaries in search of an answer to the question: Why should a magazine that six and one-half million Americans desire to read every fortnight go out of business?, one finds only the standard lucubrations. Rising costs, diminished revenues. The latter are accepted as seasonal afflictions. The former were judged to be decisive by the directors of the corporation.

The new bogey is the Post Office. Mr. Gardner Cowles put it graphically. The rise in the postal rate, as projected by the postal corporation, would have brought the costs of mailing *Look* from $4 million a year before the rate increase set in, to $10 million by the time the scheduled rate is fully levied. That is a lot of increase, $6 million. That's practically one dollar per *Look* reader. FLASH! Why didn't *Look* try charging its readers a dollar more apiece?

The grave crisis in the magazine publishing business is, in the humble judgment of one practitioner, an aspect of the general refusal to raise the rates substantially. Take *Look*. It charged $3 a year to a subscriber, $5 for two years. In the latter case, that

meant 52 issues for $5, or about ten cents per copy. For ten cents
you get delivered to your home a great fat package full of colored
pictures and enough text to keep you busy, if you should read it
all, for three to four hours. Permit me to say, ten cents is too little
to pay for that much attention.

Time magazine has gravely raised its subscription rates— so
that if you look at the posted rate, it is up to $15 per year. But
open a typical copy of *Time* (this week's, say), and out falls a card:
thirty-three issues for $4.93, which comes to fifteen cents per copy.
On the newsstand, it's fifty cents per copy.

Fifteen cents per copy is too little to pay for what *Time*
provides— too little, I mean, in a society that charges thirty-five
cents for a hamburger, and three bucks for a movie. *Life*
magazine, which recently editorialized to the effect that the Post
Office is about to bankrupt the magazine publishing industry,
charges, in its promotion package, twelve cents for an issue of
Life. That is not enough for an issue of *Life*.

I have reminded my despairing brothers in the magazine
publishing business that the *New Republic* charged $6 per year in
1933, and thirty years later, costs having risen over 300 percent,
was charging $8 per year. Why? Because the little opinion
journals are locked into a price structure which the giants impose. The giants are subsidized by the big advertisers. The big
advertisers are manifestly unwilling to continue their subsidies in
such large measure. Thus *Collier's* went down almost fifteen years
ago, with over 3 million readers.

Then, in 1969, the great *Saturday Evening Post*, with over 5
million readers. Down and down we go— but still the major
publishers, when they manage to choke their sobbing, do so in
order to authorize a new promotional mailing: *Look* magazine,
for as many weeks as you want, at the sensational price of eleven
cents per copy! And then one day *Look* magazine dies.

One thing I do not understand. And that is: why don't people
give their readers a vote? Why not say: subscriptions beginning in
January will be at twenty-five cents per copy, no bargains, no cut
rates. If enough readers are willing to pay the price, continue to
operate. Otherwise fold.

The rumors are everywhere and have been for over a year that
Life is going down. I hope it doesn't, and hope that before it does,
it will try raising the rate, and put the burden where it should
primarily rest, on the man or woman who wants to take a couple

of hours a week away from television in order to savor the special pleasures of pictorial journalism.

February 17, 1972

I had a call the other day from an old friend, a magazine publisher in deep distress who had calculated what the planned increase in the postal rate would do to his enterprise: namely, transform it from a robust property, into something altogether marginal. And you will remember that when Gardner Cowles announced the liquidation of *Look* magazine, he placed the blame on the shoulders of the Post Office. Indeed, the projected increase in postal rates for magazine publishers, over a period of five years, is about 150 percent.

What to do? My friend was soliciting support for a measure pending in Congress which would subsidize magazines as educational matter. After all—the rationale goes—if it is the business of the Government to subsidize education, as everybody nowadays agrees that it is, what is more educational than reading matter? And anyway, at the proposed $50 million per year, aren't we talking about less than the price of one torpedo, or whatever?

My friend being a stout believer in the free enterprise system, I recalled once again La Rochefoucauld's dirge, "Sad is the lot of the woman who is at once passionately inflamed, and inflexibly virtuous." But actually, it requires something less than inflexible virtue gently to resist the temptation which is, after all, forever to shield the consumer from the true cost of what he seeks to do, whether to ride a subway, attend college, or buy *Time* magazine.

Here are some interesting figures just out from the Magazine Publishers Association, which give us an idea of what happened to magazine publishing during the five years between January 1, 1966, and December 31, 1970. In 1966 (I round the figures off), the magazines surveyed took in advertising revenue of $720 million. Five years later, that sum was down—to $714 million. Revenue from subscriptions had been $203 million, almost three times the single copy revenue of $75 million. Five years later, these revenues had risen substantially to a total of $370 million; subscription revenue was now over three times that which a publisher gets from sales at the newsstands.

During those five years, postage rose from $74 million to $96 million—a very substantial increase, but only a hint of what was—is—to come. And during that period, profits collapsed—from $99 million to $37 million.

So that, one calculates, 66 percent of magazine revenues came from advertising, 23 percent from the readers—who pay about one-third the cost of producing the magazines they fondle. The profit is down to a dangerous level—2.6 percent. Profits were down 50 percent between 1969 and 1970 alone.

What is wrong with that picture seems plain enough. It is the heavy reliance on the advertiser, and the under-reliance on the consumer. For some reason, the traditional psychology in America calls for making the product cheaper to the reader if he will permit you to wrap it up, put a stamp on it, and deliver it to your door. Thus the notices we are all forever receiving: $5.29 for 52.9 weeks of the *National Weekly,* saving you $15.28 over the newsstand price.

Now, when the Post Office decides against subsidizing publishers, the publishers protest. They have every reason to protest the impacted inefficiencies of the Post Office, which the Post Office gets away with only because it is non-competitive—if Pan American were the exclusive transatlantic carrier, it would take us 27 hours to fly London-New York, and cost a thousand dollars. But they cannot, with very good conscience, ask the taxpayer to share the cost of delivering Mrs. Jones's *Cosmopolitan* merely because she refuses to waddle over to the newsstand to buy it, or to pay the extra cost of having it delivered to her house.

The answer is surely what British publishers are increasingly relying on. Magazine subscriptions should be sold at $X—plus postage.

The Airlines' Problem

Seattle, November 16, 1971

There is an air of resigned depression here, the assumption being that Boeing will never rise again. Boeing isn't out, but it is down, and it will be a while, longer than the economy of Seattle would like, before the supply of its airplanes wears so thin that it will need to re-employ the dozens of thousands of men and women who have been let go. Wernher von Braun was here the other day, and he reassured the community by saying that the Luddite spirit of the day will soon be spent, and before long, America will turn back to technology and go confidently forward. This would mean, among other things, the resumption of the SST program, and a happier economic future for Boeing.

The chances would appear to be happier even for Boeing, than for the American-run carriers. Figures recently published by *Aviation Daily* make the point with spectacular lucidity. The magazine made a study of five major employee categories at TWA, Pan Am, Air France, Lufthansa, and Alitalia. The statisticians studied the minimum and maximum wages paid to: mechanics, ramp servicemen, ticket agents, accountants, and captains.

Pan Am pays its captains a little more, its mechanics and ramp servicemen a little less than TWA, but the differences are, for these purposes, negligible. Air France pays a little more than Lufthansa, which in turn pays a little more than BOAC, but again the differences are, for these purposes, negligible.

The lesson, then, is conveniently communicated by comparing the figures for Pan Am and those for Lufthansa. Pan Am begins its mechanics at $11,000 (I round out the figures), and pays them a maximum of $12,000. Lufthansa's comparable figures are $4,000 and $5,000. Pan Am begins its ramp servicemen at $9,000, and pays them a maximum of $10,000. Lufthansa's comparable figures are $3,000 and $4,500. Pan Am begins its ticket agents at $9,000, and pays them a maximum of $10,500. Lufthansa's comparable figures are $4,000 and $6,000.

Pan Am begins its accountants at $9,000 and pays them a maximum of $13,000. Lufthansa's comparable figures are $4,000 and $6,000. Pan Am begins its 727 pilots at $40,000, and pays them a maximum of $49,000. Lufthansa's comparable figures are $20,000 and $27,000. Pan Am begins its 747 pilots at $48,000 and pays them a maximum of $71,000. Lufthansa's comparable figures are $20,500 and $33,000.

"Added together," the survey concludes, "the five maximum salary levels for Pan Am and TWA (an average of the two carriers at each level) total $118,500, while the same figure for the four European carriers is $58,500." In other words, it costs the

American carriers almost exactly double what it costs the European carriers to operate the airlines.

The classical concept of competition between nations with widely differing pay scales is that the richer nation will make up for the disparity by a higher capitalization per job. Thus, in the textbook example, although Mary Jones is paid five times as much per hour as Juanita Garcia, in a textile plant, the difference is absorbed by Mary Jones's increased productivity, the result of the tools that capitalism places at her disposal, permitting her to produce fabric at at least five times the rate of Juanita with her hand loom.

But how does this apply to the aircraft industry? Here in Seattle they will sell anyone a 747 for the same price. And when these carriers are put into operation between Europe and New York there is the identical vessel there for the passengers to fly on. Gasoline may cost a few pennies more in Europe than in the United States, but even that difference disappears from the reckoning: European carriers can pay American prices for the return trip, and Americans have to pay the European rate for their return trip.

Manifestly, there is no way out. Unless . . .

Unless what? Well, unless the American carriers take on a lot more passengers than the European carriers. Here they have at least a temporary advantage. There are more Americans who want to go to Europe and can, than Europeans who want to come to America, and can. And when someone from Kansas City books a passage to London, he gravitates naturally towards an American carrier. But let Lufthansa offer a lower rate, and the Kansas City shopper will quickly shift—why not? That is the reason why the American carriers are so deeply disturbed by the rate war. In order to pay the much higher wages, the carriers have need of the extra business. Obviously, paying the wages they do, the foreign carriers can afford to transport passengers at lesser fares. And when the free market comes finally to the airplane companies, the American airlines are going to have to do one of three things: 1) lower their pay scales; 2) apply to the government for subsidies; or 3) go out of business, like the American oceangoing passenger lines. The likeliest of the three alternatives is the last.

The Economics of Professor Ho

December 21, 1971

There is a lot of economic ignorance in the world, and most of it is in the academy, where professors and students believe things about economics which are on the level of believing that the moon is made out of green cheese. What is surprising is when people of such limited understanding impose themselves on the general community quite obviously expecting that they will be taken seriously.

For instance, one Ping-ti Ho, who is described as a "University of Chicago professor of history and Far Eastern languages and civilizations," just back from Mainland China which he left in 1945 in order to become a Canadian citizen. Professor Ho treats Mao's China, in his articles in the Chicago *Tribune* (the Chicago *Tribune!*) like the Emerald City of Oz. To use his words, ". . . what China has achieved in the last 22 years may already be the envy of the Third World."

Herewith a little bit of analysis which should make the anthologies of economic solecism, with which Professor Ho launches his series. In China, food is very cheap. "I purposely took some of my meals in the extremely crowded backlane restaurants of Shanghai and other large cities. A northern Chinese-style breakfast or lunch which would cost me at least $2 in New York or Chicago cost me only 7 to 15 cents in China. Because restaurants are owned and operated by the state, they do not make profits. Meal prices are therefore extremely low." One wonders how the professor of history would greet a student paper which said: "Because of the Mississippi Bubble, Napoleon lost the battle of Waterloo." The latter is etiologically tighter than the former. Approximately 6 percent of the gross of the restaurant business in the United States is profit. Less than one-half of one percent of the gross in retail groceries is profit.

And anyway, how could China get to feed its people, if it charged more than 15 cents per meal? The average wage for a Chinese who works in a city is $25 per month. At 15 cents per meal for himself alone, three meals a day, he has spent over one-half his salary. If his wife is to eat also, that's $27 for the two of them, or more than he earns, never mind the children — how are *they* going to eat?

In the fairyland described by Professor Ho, it takes more than one month's salary to buy a wristwatch. As for all that food, rice is still rationed, as is meat and even cooking oil. Only vegetables and fish are not. When you go to Shanghai's Maxim's, you take your ration coupon. The country that Professor Ho lists as the marvel of the Third World lets its citizens buy 18 feet of cloth goods per year. *Per year.* A washcloth counts as one foot. Eighty-five percent of the working population is engaged in the production of food, and China has had to import food.

In the United States, where farmers do indeed insist on making a profit, 12 percent of the working population produce a gross excess of food. The Japanese, studying all available figures, calculate that the per capita income of the Mainland Chinese is $80 (other estimates put the figure at $120). The per capita income of the Taiwanese is $300. The per capita income of the Japanese is in excess of $1,200. The envy of the Third World indeed!

So it goes. American scholars *will be* brainwashed. They insist on it. And because some people find even the simplest economic axiom impenetrable, mystification is easy. The other day, at a lecture at Oakland University in Michigan, a student rose to inform me about what American capitalists had done in Argentina. First, said he, American companies in general are paying Argentine labor one-fourth as much as they pay American labor. Secondly, they are trying out experimental drugs on Argentine citizens, on the theory that killing odd Argentinians, in order to develop profit-making drugs, is perfectly okay.

Well, I said, American companies in Argentina pay what they have to pay to get labor, the lower the better. If American companies can desert Maine and go to South Carolina in order to reduce the cost of their product, and make it available cheaper to the consumer, why shouldn't American firms go to Argentina to do the same thing? As for the drug companies, I said, the chances are against the story's being true, for the simple reason that major pharmaceutical companies would get a rather bad press if it were known that they were engaged in killing innocent Argentinians.

But you can just see Professor Ho nodding his head, when somebody tells him the one about Argentina, and making a note to include that in his next series for the Chicago *Tribune*.

The Galbraith-Nixon Affair

February 22, 1972

John Kenneth Galbraith is one part economist, one part social critic, and one part tease. He has lately taken to sending me reports from the economic battlefront where General Nixon is surrendering Republican legions by the thousands, of which a typical example follows:

"Memorandum from John Kenneth Galbraith. Dear Bill, You are much on my mind. Is there anything I can do to help? Affectionately, Ken." He attaches a front-page story headlined, "U.S. PAY-PRICE/CURBS TO STAY/AT LEAST TO '73."

Professor Galbraith, who has for years now advocated permanent wage and price controls, circles with red ink the statement by a representative of President Nixon's Council on Economic Advisers, to wit, "Speculation that the Administration will abandon the controls prematurely—out of fatigue, ideological aversion, or other causes—is groundless." Professor Galbraith is having the time of his life.

And then the New York *Times*, in a much-discussed editorial, lifts the point to a level of generality, in a piece asking "Are There Any Issues?" left to divide Republicans and Democrats. The sentences that touch on the economic point are wonderfully revealing, in ways I suspect the writer did not intend. ". . . in 1960 many Republicans including General Eisenhower himself could still in good conscience cling to their traditional opposition to big government, unbalanced budgets and government 'interference' in the economy." That is quite true, though the tacit sequel of it—that no Republican can nowadays in good conscience oppose big government—is rather less than true.

"He [Mr. Nixon] has imposed wage and price controls which until very recently had been seriously advocated only by the most liberal Democrats," the editorial goes on. "He has espoused the Keynesian doctrine of government spending and has had successive budget deficits totaling nearly $100 billion. He has requested another increase of $50 billion in the national debt ceiling. He has devalued the dollar."

You will have noticed that the rhetorical cadence in that

paragraph is that of a citation leading to an honorary degree or
to the awarding of a Silver Star ... "He swore that Fort
Douamont could be taken notwithstanding that everyone
disagreed with him. He advocated the use of tactical air power at
a moment when most people thought that planes wouldn't fly. He
succeeded in losing one hundred thousand men. He has sworn to
lose another fifty thousand men per week for the next two years.
He has triumphantly attacked the population problem!"

One's ear has to be carefully cocked to catch the transition
from sense to nonsense. In economics, everybody is an expert, and
no one listens very acutely. It is one thing to say: he has had
successive budget deficits totaling nearly $100 billion— *but* he has
brought us: an end to inflation, full employment, and un-
paralleled prosperity. The non sequiturs do not bother anyone.
The triumphant irony is that last sentence: "He has devalued the
dollar."

Of course he has devalued the dollar! What conservative ever
said he shouldn't have devalued the dollar? Conservatives believe
that the value of the dollar is fixed beyond Presidential power to
affect it. It is fixed by the gnomes in Zurich and the fat Japs, and
every time the United States overspends by a billion dollars, the
people out there bid the dollar down. And if we can't shore up the
price of the dollar by giving them gold, which we can no longer
do, or persuading them to increase their dollar reserves, we clip
off a part of the dollar and, by that amount, tax the capital of the
entire dollar-owning world.

It is curious that the elated Mr. Galbraith, and the New York
Times, should now be assigning to Mr. Nixon powers which no
Republican would want to give him, namely the power to write
economic dogma. Mr. Nixon hasn't altered any theories, any
convictions. He has yielded to such pressures as Mr. Galbraith is
too easily seduced by, including the witchcraft of wage and price
controls. What Mr. Galbraith and the *Times* owe us, say two years
from now, is an assessment of the success of the new Nixonian
economics—measured in price stability, dollar stability, full
employment, and rise in per capita income. In case they forget to
make the assessment, and I'm not around, do bring it up, won't
you?

XII. The Decline of
the Catholic Church

The Sinners of Netcong

November 14, 1970

Now hear this. Netcong is a little community in New Jersey, U.S.A., land of the free. It happens that the community is composed almost entirely of Roman Catholics, many of them second-generation Italians attracted to Netcong because it is a service center for the Delaware, Lackawanna, and Western Railroad. When the Supreme Court ruled a few years ago that the saying of a common prayer as a part of the official activities of a public school is unconstitutional, the community of Netcong was disturbed, like most other communities. But unlike most other communities, the elders there decided to do something about it. What?

Why not have prayers beginning five minutes before the school officially begins, on the understanding that attendance at said prayers is voluntary? The plan was instituted, and to drive home the ecumenical spirit of it all, the organizers decided to take the prayers recited in the Senate and in the House of Representatives the previous day. In other words, to read from the *Congressional Record.* We all now know the ending. The state court has banned the Netcong Compromise. The court pronounced it an evasion, which it certainly is. What one tends to lose sight of is the main point: that it should be necessary to evade anything at all, in order to pray.

Mr. William J. Smullen is the editor of the Netcong *News Leader,* a weekly newspaper that supported the prayer movement. He is quoted in the New York *Times* on the general subject of the changes going on in the Roman Catholic Church. "The Church has been practically destroyed in the last few years. I'm a Notre Dame graduate and I wouldn't set foot on that campus now. I got one of those underground papers they put out there. . . ."

It would seem to me that Mr. Smullen's taking this opportunity to speak in general about the decline in Catholicism deftly takes hold of the central question. It is only in the light of the current apathy that a people would put up with the injunction against the Netcong Experiment. We have, to begin with, a Supreme Court decision so outrageous in its interpretation of the clause in the First Amendment that goes no further than to guarantee the separation of church and state, as to startle orderly legal minds.

Very well, the Supreme Court can certainly err; indeed during those years, that was its specialty. So, instantly, when the prayer decision was handed down, every governor in the United States save one called for a constitutional amendment which would draw a line between establishing a national religion, and permitting a common prayer in the public schools. Senator Dirksen undertook to shepherd the amendment through Congress, but although it was close, he never succeeded in coping with the opposition of Emmanuel Celler in the House. Why? Primarily because of the absence of public pressure. We fought a general election two weeks ago. How often did anyone hear the subject raised? How many Congressmen bothered to include in their programs, support for the Right to Pray Amendment?

Essentially that is what happened to Netcong. As we approach a stage of rabid secularism, it pays to remind ourselves of it. The villains are not the Justices of the Supreme Court— they are trivial figures who ratified the fanatical renderings of a small minority who cluster about the American Civil Liberties Union. Those who are really responsible are the people, and their spiritual leaders. There are many clergymen who have shown themselves disposed to go to jail for this or that cause in recent years. How odd that none has elected to do so in behalf of a cause that is integral to their calling?

It is largely forgotten that most of the saints produced in human history have been laymen, not clergymen. On the matter of obeying the law, I stand with the strict constructionists. But even they, following the long exegesis of the covenant to render to Caesar what is his, and to God what is His, have recognized that certain rights the state does not have, and one wonders that at a time when clergymen are disposed to go to jail to challenge the government's right to use DDT on the DMZ, no one is disposed to go to jail to invite a final confrontation between an aroused public opinion, and their elected officials and judges, on the issue of whether the community of Netcong, New Jersey, can proceed to read aloud before classes begin, the prayers so hypocritically entered as a part of our *Congressional Record.*

The Abortion Laws

October 20, 1970

It has greatly surprised many non-Catholics, and for that matter not a few Catholics, with what ease the abortionists have succeeded in making their permissive laws, as of this writing in five states of the Union, which permit, let's face it, abortion-on-demand. It not only *seems* only yesterday, in fact it *was* only yesterday, that the accepted idea was that the Catholic political lobby made it impossible to permit the sale of contraceptives. To have proposed abortions *ad libitum* was quite simply unthinkable for a politician.

Now, the trend is very clear. Although a few states (one thinks of Massachusetts, Rhode Island, Connecticut, and perhaps Louisiana) will resist, their resistance will be meaningless. Why would it matter to the Connecticut legislature to permit abortions, when any resident of Connecticut who wants one can take the Penn Central to New York and, assuming the child does not arrive first, proceed to get an abortion there? It is reasonable to suppose that abortions will be as widely available in the United States, notwithstanding that only five states now permit them, as they are now in England. What of the Catholics?

Among them is that strange indecision that is the condition of the Church ever since Vatican II. The formal teaching of the Church is that abortions are the taking of human life, to be sure life which is biologically distinguishable from such life as exists after birth; but life just the same. There are those among Catholics who insist that the difference between the two estates is negligible, others who believe that the difference is substantial. There are those who believe that abortion is "murder" in the quite factual sense, others (the majority, one must suppose) who believe that wrong as it is, it is something less than murder.

The Catholic Church is, as a result of Vatican II and what came after it, much much weaker than it has been at any time during the last hundred years. They speak, in New York City, about the decline in Catholic political power. The evidence of that decline abounds. There is the failure to repeal the anti-Catholic Blaine Amendment, the results of which are to deny to students of parochial schools those elementary privileges which in a free society ought to be available to anyone who patronizes a school of his choice, even if it is oriented towards a particular religion. There is the spectacular failure of the Catholic Church to attract to essential Christian doctrines the hordes who allegedly were repelled by Catholic insistence on narrow doctrinal positions. The Catholic Church threw away fish-on-Friday, liturgical Latin, tough rules for the priests and nuns; and, for their pains, got emptier and emptier churches.

When the time came to rally protests against permissive abortion laws, the troops were simply not there. It is very difficult for a Catholic fundamentalist to go on about Murder, while his Cardinal is photographed speaking amiably to the leader of the Assembly that passed the abortion bill a few months before. How would it have appeared if, let us say, Cardinal Spellman of New York had been seen shaking hands and chatting amiably with Martin Borman? The answer is that Cardinal Spellman would have avoided doing any such thing. And that Cardinal Cooke's willingness to traffic with legislators from New York who voted for the abortion bill seems to suggest that New York Catholics must regard permissive abortion policies as something less than the kind of thing that inspires mutinous relations between the subject and the state.

Any minority living under pluralistic auspices has available to it a range of responses, which go from mild dissent to tyrannicide. A Catholic in New York can, in his opposition to abortion laws, vary from advising his assemblyman that he opposes that law, to (at the other extreme) waylaying and assassinating the leader of the movement within the Assembly to pass that particular bill. What has happened in recent years is that Catholic sentiment has moved very substantially down the scale towards permissiveness. Whereas say ten years ago the furor against abortion would have imperiled the political life of almost any state legislator, now they go mostly unscathed.

Catholic voters are confused. Their bishops and their priests are complacent, or if that is not the word for it, they are un-decided about what ought to be the rights of others, in pluralistic situations, notwithstanding the dogmatic convictions of the few that in certain essential matters, the few are the guardians of the many. The majority of Germans might have conceded (one thanks God that the question was never put to them) the necessity for the genocidal extermination of the Jews. The few who after such a plebiscite nevertheless resisted, would be hailed today not as extremist dissenters, but as moral heroes.

There aren't, given the surrounding ambiguities, many Catholics in the United States disposed so to act at this moment. But the absence of them is arresting. It seems to say that the Catholic Church is nowadays acting not only out of political confusion, but out of moral uncertainty; in which case one wonders what force it will speak with ten years hence, and whether God will tolerate the total etiolation of what some have fancied all along as His Church.

The Campaign of Father Drinan, S. J.

September 22, 1970

Up Boston way is a Catholic priest who is running for Congress, who just now beat the incumbent in the Democratic primary. His name is Robert J. Drinan, he is an ordained Jesuit, the Dean of the School of Law of Boston College, and the greatest threat to or-derly thought since Eleanor Roosevelt left this vale of tears.

Father Drinan is, alas, extremely prolific. I find that sometimes that is the case when one is trafficking not so much in thought, as in the incondite matter which Fr. Drinan specializes in, and which his thoughtless sheep adore. Needless to say, the moral overlay is predictable. Fr. Drinan hates war, torture, genocide, racism, and income disparities. In his book, *Vietnam and Ar-mageddon: Peace, War and the Christian Conscience*, Fr. Drinan instructs all Catholics and all Christians in his moral code, commanding us to take it as our own, the assumption being, of course, that on moral matters Fr. Drinan's thought is greatly advanced over, say, that of the Pope.

Fr. Drinan, as a lawyer and as a trained Jesuit, is capable of being foxy, though one suspects that he is not quite lucid enough to know when he is being foxy. For instance, he writes: "If one accepts the stark fact that the United States can contribute to peace only by some courageous, unilateral method of slowing the arms race then it follows that Catholics in America are involved in a collective silence which makes the silence of German Catholics in the decade of Hitler's atrocities almost insignificant by contrast."

Now the rhetorical burden of that sentence is very clear: American Catholics are guilty of unforgivable moral sloth. In fact, the operative phrase in the sentence, which gets lost in the fuzz, is crucial. What if one were to hear a priest say: "If one accepts the stark fact that the United States can contribute to peace only by a courageous recognition of the fact that Richard Nixon is a paid agent of the Communist conspiracy, then it follows that. . . ." The point is that if the assumption is valid, so is that which deduces from it. It being my own judgment and that of approximately 99 percent of the American people that unilateral disarmament would bring instant chaos and misery to the world, then the stark fact is that anyone who favors unilateral disarmament is, by conventional standards, stark mad.

Like Fr. Drinan? Well, now, the gentleman, as I said, can be crafty. He doesn't exactly come out for instant disarmament by the United States. At least not without a suggestion for an alternative which he describes as "an entirely new international order based on justice and motivated by brotherly love." If you think that there is already more pasta than is good for the system in that sentence, pray chew on the following:

"For Christians and humanists who believe in the inviolability and sanctity of every human life, the imperious call to disarmament is a summons to subdue those fears that have made prisoners and cowards of the millions of people who are victims of the illusions and delusions of the nuclear era." The philosophical and verbal cholesterol in that sentence is enough to repeal declarative thought.

What would we do about, say, Russian nuclear missiles, tanks, armies, and submarines, under Fr. Drinan's new dispensation? Simple. We must come up with "a policy of passive resistance or militant nonviolence towards any nation which would seek to conquer America, seize our assets, and control our minds. . . . Disarmament would be accompanied by a warning to the entire world that the American people will not be governed by any foreign power. If conquered by superior military force, they will become a totally ungovernable people who will drive out the aggressor by highly sophisticated techniques of nonviolence developed, if need be, with all of the fantastic resources which America now puts in the hands of its military complex." I wish Fr. Drinan were running for office in Czechoslovakia.

Can we, then, simply assume that the poor gentleman is simply addled by idealism? That to skewer his thought is as pointless— as dastardly— as, say, to parse a sentence by Sam Goldwyn? Alas, Fr. Drinan does not leave us even with the kind of satisfaction we would have in dealing with Peter Pan. The question was raised, well, Father, do you think we should abandon the military even where Israel is involved?

Well, ho ho ho, huh huh huh, eh eh eh, Fr. Drinan replied, "the United States must stand by its moral commitment to the survival of the Jewish state." The Elmer Gantry of disarmament hath spoken.

The Bishops and the War

November 25, 1971

Garry Wills begins a long paean to the Berrigan brothers in the current *Playboy* by citing two sentences from Fidel Castro spoken in 1967. "The United States shouldn't worry about the Soviets in Latin America because they are not revolutionaries anymore. But they should worry about the Catholic revolutionaries, who are."

The words are apt, appearing in print a few weeks before the Catholic bishops, who earlier in the month opposed an amendment to the Constitution which would have permitted non-denominational prayer in the schools, denounced the continuation of the Vietnam war. It is only left for the bishops to proclaim that American soldiers have no business fighting for a country that permits prayer in its public schools.

Whatever the bishops are up to, let us not permit ourselves to think of them categorically, to think of them as if they are all alike, all united behind the effronteries of what Auberon Waugh, surveying the post-Conciliar wreckage, calls the "silly season" of the Catholic Church. But the bishops did issue a statement in their name, and they must answer for it. It is kindest to say of it that it did attempt to reason. "At this point in history," said the bishops, "it seems clear to us that whatever good we hope to achieve through continued involvement in this war is now outweighed by the destruction of human life and of moral values which it inflicts."

One bishop, from Detroit, drew from this resolution the breathtaking inference that anyone who agrees with the "Catholic position" "may not participate in this war." This startled Archbishop Philip Hannan of New Orleans who snapped that he did not "agree with that conclusion."

The resolution must be considered abstractly, and concretely. Abstractly, the bishops appear to be saying that the maintenance of our treaty obligations in South Vietnam is wrong, because it is now "clear" that our maintenance of these commitments causes more harm than good. But the good that the administrators of our Vietnam policies, both Democrat and Republican, pursue, is the maintenance of public confidence in our network of treaties, a collapse of which could bring on a world war.

The political meaning of the bishops' resolution is surely that they are dissatisfied with President Nixon's rate of withdrawal. We are losing fewer dead per week in Vietnam than we are in the streets of New York City, and the projections are that our forces in Vietnam will be less than those in Korea within one year, and that South Vietnam will survive. A precipitate withdrawal at this point would change all that; would result in thousands upon thousands— hundreds of thousands, some say, to whom the situation is at least as clear as to the bishop of Detroit— slain by a vindictive aggressor. What was the point of the bishops' resolution, if not to undermine the President's program for withdrawal?

"True religion does not look upon as sinful those wars that are waged not for motives of aggrandisement, or cruelty, but with the object of securing peace, of punishing evildoers, and of uplifting the good." Those words, of St. Augustine, are quoted by St. Thomas Aquinas in his passage on the just war. And he went on to write, "Those who wage war justly aim at peace, and so they are not opposed to peace, except to *the evil peace, which Our Lord came not to send upon earth (Matt. 10.34)*."

One wonders how long we can hold out, in America. Garry Wills, in an age when priests are tortured by two of the world's major powers, writes about the "hysterical repression" against the Fathers Berrigan in America; and the Catholic bishops, when twenty Americans per week are giving their lives to guard a frontier linked by a network of treaties to the critical frontier that separates us from a race of madmen who in a single century have slaughtered many times the number of men who gave their lives for their faith during the first two millennia of Christendom, rail against our military policies.

Such is our moral paralysis. Thus do we go whimpering for the approval of the Underground Catholics, whose transfiguration teaches them that the enemy is J. Edgar Hoover and Richard Nixon, in a world that gave us Josef Stalin and Mao Tse-tung. What overwhelms one is the historical frivolity of these confused, confusing men.

XIII. Personal

LBJ

October 21, 1971

Lyndon Johnson has released his memoirs, and we learn from them much that we expected to see confirmed, and some things—as publishers always hope—that are surprising. Mr. Johnson has (as of this writing) released only the beginning of the story he intends to tell, but it is itself fascinating. He confesses (that perhaps isn't the friendliest word for it) that President Kennedy's trip to Texas was done for purely political purposes. And he divulges the reason why he, Vice President Johnson, was getting along especially poorly with Senator Yarborough, which strained relationship resulted in the celebrated incident of Mr. Yarborough's declining to participate directly in the motorcade, on D-Day Minus One, greatly aggravating the President whose purpose in traveling to Texas was to stitch together a majority for the forthcoming election of 1964.

Why was Senator Yarborough angry with Vice President Johnson? On such trivia empires hang. Well—the memoirs confide—it was this simple. When Kennedy asked Johnson to run with him as Vice President, Johnson asked him a couple of direct questions. For one thing, Johnson wanted to know whether Kennedy was merely making a sentimental gesture, of the kind needed to glue together the entire Democratic coalition. No, Kennedy said—as we learn from Johnson—he, Kennedy, truly believed that sentiment aside, Johnson's position on the ticket would probably mean the difference between victory and loss.

At which point—one gathers from his own narrative—Johnson, rather than fall on his knees and say something on the order of, Whither thou goest, John, thither also will go thy servant Lyndon, said: Jack, one thing. If you make it to the White House, the usual rule on Federal appointments will be suspended. Normally, a President checks in with Senators from the state in which he is making Federal appointments. In this case, you are to check not merely with Senator Yarborough, but with me— Lyndon— your Vice President. Okay?

Okay, said Kennedy.

Senator Yarborough, Mr. Johnson tells us, deeply resented this extraordinary arrangement. The outrage will be shared by other sensitive political creatures, whose feelings are sensitized to the iniquities imposed by Lyndon Johnson on the Federal system.

It transpires that the very last words spoken to Johnson by Kennedy on that tragic day were, "We're going to carry two states next year if we don't carry any others: Massachusetts and Texas." Mr. Johnson explains the meaning of this remark: Jack Kennedy had no reason, in November of 1963, to take for granted his re-election. His national ratings were extraordinarily low. In Texas in a popularity poll taken a few weeks before his disastrous visit there, he had gotten a rating spectacularly low, sharply contrasting with the rating given to Governor Connally, who rode with Mr. Kennedy on the fateful ride.

Mr. Johnson tells us that Mr. Kennedy's unpopularity, at least in Texas, was the result of several things, including the Bay of Pigs (Texans do not like to lose wars), the fiscal situation (Texans tend to be conservative on money-matters), and the civil rights question (Texans were opposed to the Civil Rights Bills, which Mr. Kennedy had begun to push, although there was not, at the time of the assassination, a bill passed which bore his imprimatur). And then Johnson goes on to say that the very good mood of the President, on November 22, 1963, was the result of his feeling that the enthusiasm of the crowds gainsaid the polls. Whence the statement that he felt he could count on Texas the next time around.

All of which, elaborately, reminds us of something we have not dwelt much upon during the last eight years, even as if to do so would be profane. It is this: that President Kennedy was not all that popular. Shortly before he died, *Time* magazine was openly speculating on the question whether President Kennedy would or wouldn't succeed in beating Candidate Goldwater. *Look* magazine was not able to recall an issue which circulated post-Dallas, the lead article of which asked the question: Can Kennedy win in 1964?

In other words, it was an open question. The knowledge of that simple datum does much to illuminate the recent history of the United States, so greatly obscured by the prevalent superstition that Mr. Kennedy was as unbeatable as King Arthur at his prime. It was otherwise. Now the detractors of Mr. Kennedy spring up— not from the Right, but the Left. And the revisionist season is with us. That, of course, was inevitable. One supposes that eight years is a decent interlude. Even so, one feels just a little regret. Impeach King Arthur! One listens to the arguments, perforce; but sadly.

Lady Bird

November 6, 1970

A White House Diary. By Lady Bird·Johnson. Holt, Rinehart & Winston. $10.95.

It might have been something else. Almost anything other than what it is. It might have been history (it isn't: there is a dumb-founding indifference to history. You don't find out from these diaries, except inferentially, that Barry Goldwater was nominated at San Francisco or that Eugene McCarthy beat L.B.J. in New Hampshire). It might have been Lady Bird revealing her thoughts about people who opposed her husband (in this endless book, there are only two animadversions, one of them against Theodore White, the other against Arthur Schlesinger, and added together, they do not amount to a teaspoonful of ginger, which is not enough, not nearly enough, to flavor this vatful of dough). A book by a First Lady published so soon after her abdication is going to be either a) scandalously exciting (as one hoped would be the case, on hearing about these diaries from the publisher) or b) blah (which is, alas, what these diaries turn out to be).

Whose fault is it? Mrs. Johnson apparently kept a journal of which only one-seventh is reproduced here. One must charitably assume that the very worst one-seventh is here, the balance having been judged unsuitable for public disclosure so soon after the events it records. One discerns from reading the introduction and the acknowledgments that Mrs. Johnson had very expert help. One therefore deduces that *force majeure* caused, for instance, the fabled editor Maggie Cousins to authorize such sentences as appear in this book and to go along with the exclusion of such sentences as (we must assume) were left out of this book.

Skeptical? Here are some submissions for an Atlantic City contest in:

●Awshucksfolksism. "Later in the day Lyndon asked me to go to Austin to a couple of parties. But I'd much rather sit around the fire and watch the embers glow and talk to the folks close to me, so I begged off."

●Inspirationwiseism. "Lyndon delivered the State of the Union address. . . . So might Sir Edmund Hillary have felt when he at last reached the top of Mount Everest."

●Readerswillbelieveanythingism. "There is something [John Steinbeck] didn't know and I didn't tell him, but long, long ago Lyndon— who almost never took time off to see a movie— went with me to see *The Grapes of Wrath* and sat in his seat crying quietly for about two hours at the helpless misery of the Okies. I do not think he has ever forgotten it."

●Thingsareroughism. "After Mrs. [Charles] Lindbergh had gone, I went back to the desk to work. Later Lyndon asked me to join him in the pool. By that time it was 9 o'clock. So I went for a swim with him, for it had been a bad day. Cyprus, then Panama and a few troubles in Texas don't all mix up to make a cream puff of a life."

The writing is so very dreadful—"It began in a low-key manner"; "Rest at the ranch is a complete misnomer to me." The thinking so embarrassingly jejune—"The line I like best in Lyndon's speech was 'no one can bury us or bluff us or beat us so long as our economy remains strong.' " The social anfractuosities so, really, depressing—"Alas, the very graciousness of the hosts in asking so many guests resulted in a crowd that was overwhelming."

What is the point of it? Mrs. Johnson, the above notwithstanding, is an admirable human being, as are many people who do not, or should not, write books. This volume is only for the cult who will read anything written by anybody who slept for a while in a temple of power. I haven't read Crawfie, but I cannot imagine that her book, written about the childhood years of Elizabeth II and her sister, could be less interesting than this volume of edgy glucose, which, precisely because there is something that stirs within it giving one confidence in Lady Bird, suggests the master hand of censorship. Why? We do not reason why. "Lyndon," records Lady Bird on one occasion, "had asked me to make a tiny speech, which I did reluctantly and rather uncomfortably. . . . Sometimes it's easier to do what Lyndon asks than explain to him why you think it is inappropriate."

Millhouse

Millhouse, A White Comedy. By Emile de Antonio.

The current anti-Nixon documentary (it is called *Millhouse* for anagrammatic reasons which, like the penetration of *Oh! Calcutta!*, are not worth the archeologist's time) is of course an insult to the intelligence, but of course insults to the intelligence can be fun. Not necessarily praiseworthy fun, but who said fun had to be praiseworthy? If Dwight Macdonald could have fun seeing *MacBird!*, you can have fun seeing *Millhouse*, and your neighbor can have fun reading the Blue Book of the John Birch Society.

I gather that the director-producer Mr. Emile de Antonio is not very bright, which suggests a divine success in the distribution of talent which we mortals can only seek vainly to emulate. If Mr. de Antonio had been created Bright, he would not have blown the opportunities he had to discredit Richard Nixon, which is the intention here. He rolls along, with his anti-Nixon collage, piling anti-Nixonism on anti-Nixonism, until the audience begins to groove with him, leering with pleasurable contempt at, for instance, the (very nearly intact) Checkers speech, the McCarthyite Nixon campaigner of the early fifties, and so on. Then de Antonio brings in, of all people, Alger Hiss with the clear suggestion that Alger Hiss was framed by Nixon ("Hiss was the bad guy. His guilt was predetermined," comments Fred Cook, whose judgment on Alger Hiss is as valuable as Mussmano's on Sacco-Vanzetti). Poor Mr. de Antonio. His desire to torpedo Nixon is total, but not enough so to cause him to give a little prudent berth to the Hiss case. It is as if a Republican WASP had given us a long, eloquent, sincere, overwhelming documentary on why it would gravely injure the United States if we should nominate Abe Fortas to the Supreme Court, and ended it, "Besides Fortas is Jewish."

Everyone has his weaknesses, and as one plods through *Millhouse*, after the Hiss bit, one thinks, well, maybe Alger Hiss is de Antonio's wife's brother, a passing exoneration of whom was a nepotistic imperative. But no, before the film is over, Mr. de Antonio is giving us the motivation for the Vietnam war, and you will not guess, no— I promise you, you will not guess what it is. The motives for our involvement in Vietnam are the commercial interests of a hundred or so American concerns whose products play a role in Vietnam, everything from Firestone Rubber Company to Colgate toothpaste, it being left to the viewer to assume that anyone in Vietnam who uses rubber or brushes his teeth is doing so in order to further American imperialistic interests. By the same token, the war on poverty is the chauvinistic enterprise of United States Plywood and Bayer Aspirin, and Albert Schweitzer was a scout for the medical cartels. Odd that men who have a natural affinity for drama should be so easily tripped up by ideological ambushes. I remember the war movie by Carl Foreman in which, in order to drive home the paradoxes, he found it necessary to film the execution of an American deserter to the music, blaring forth from the PX's nickelodeon, of "Have Yourself a Merry Little Christmas." Needless to say, the execution took place on Christmas Day. De Antonio's execution of Mr. Nixon is intended to suit the convenience of the spontaneous shopper. It is only required that you leave your wits at the entrance; and, as I say, why not? Wit can be a nuisance.

Mr. de Antonio's film has some wonderful things in it, which isn't surprising. The reviewer for the *New Yorker* remarked, after the famous Edward R. Murrow film on Senator Joe McCarthy, that the kind of documentary journalism which Mr. Murrow had just consummated presented quite extraordinary opportunities to the caricaturist. On that celebrated occasion Mr. Murrow began by showing Senator McCarthy— belching. If you have available several hundreds of thousands of feet on somebody, the chances are reasonable that you can find a shot of him belching, and not altogether unreasonable that you can find a shot of him cursing, and, with a little luck, a shot of him urinating behind a tree.

So it goes in de Antonio's *Millhouse*. And of course he catches Mr. Nixon in moments unattractive, laying open the question whether they are typical; *i.e.*, does Mr. Nixon, typically, belch?

Well, Mr. Nixon most certainly guarantees, single-handed, the price of corn, no doubt about it. In the Checkers speech he spoke the words, "Because, you see, I love my country and I think my country is in danger. And I think the only man that can save America at this time is the man who is running for President on my ticket, Dwight Eisenhower." And, sixteen years later, it hadn't greatly changed. "Sixteen years ago, I stood before this Convention to accept your nomination as the running mate of one of the greatest Americans of our time or of any time, Dwight D. Eisenhower."

And there is fun in catching Mr. Nixon up on the Broken Campaign Promise. "We're going to stop the rise in prices . . . We're going to balance the federal budget . . . I will see to it that these laws will be enforced. We are going to make America free from fear again." I rather like that kind of thing, even as I like to run my fingers every now and then over the Democratic Party's Convention pledge on Vietnam ("Our most urgent task is to end the war in Vietnam by an honorable and lasting settlement. We reject as unacceptable a unilateral withdrawal of our forces which would allow aggression and subversion to succeed"). And anyway, I believe in a little secular impiety, where Presidents and princes are concerned, so much so that I like it when I see on the screen candidate Nixon saying, "Let me make one thing very clear. . . . If there's going to be unemployment next year, it's going to be the ones who got us into this mess that's going to be unemployed." Jolly good. I am a paid-up member of the Anti-Beatification League.

But is there in this film a relative assessment? Here is the most damaging of Mr. de Antonio's anti-Nixonisms. Nixon on the stump: "Hubert is a loyal American. Hubert is against the Communists. Hubert is for peace. Hubert is a good speaker.

Hubert is a very plausible man. He's a very pleasant man. He's a good campaigner. But Hubert is a sincere, dedicated radical." Sounds bad. On the other hand, in a wholly other connection, Mr. de Antonio permits us to have a glimpse of Adlai the Good, and he is saying, in his 1956 campaign against Eisenhower, "Every consideration, the President's age, his health, the fact that he can't succeed himself, make it inevitable that the dominant figure of the Republican Party under a second Eisenhower term would be Richard Nixon." Interesting that Adlai, the prophet, was wrong in that Eisenhower's health proved to be better than Mr. Stevenson's, who pre-deceased him, that Eisenhower's health was altogether serviceable during his second term, and that Nixon proved not by any means the dominant figure of the Republican Party while Eisenhower was President— so what? De Antonio was so anxious to cash an anti-Nixon chip, he didn't even notice that it was counterfeit. Adlai Stevenson went on: "*Now I say to you, do you trust this gentleman to be fair?* (CROWD YELLS NO)—[as Mr. de Antonio's script records]. *Do you want him as commander in chief to exercise power over war and peace?* (CROWD YELLS NO) *Do you want to place the hydrogen bomb in his hand?* (CROWD YELLS NO) *Do you believe that Richard Nixon has the confidence of other countries?*(CROWD YELLS NO)." Poor crowd. One wishes that Oscar Wilde hadn't ruined it by saying it so definitively: "I hope you have not been leading a double life, pretending to be wicked, and being really good all the time. That would be hypocrisy." You will understand then, why Nixon is such a wicked man, and how it must torture de Antonio not to have been reduced, long since, to nuclear ash.

James Lane Buckley

October 17, 1970

I am asked to give the reasons why you should vote for James L. Buckley as your next Senator. The crafty editor of these pages, Mr. Mike McGrady, gave *me* the assignment of urging you to vote for him because he knew that I would be outrageously partisan. I knew Mike during the wars of 1965, when I ran for mayor against John Lindsay. (For those who are not history-minded, I lost.) He is a foxy fellow; perhaps he thought that if he secured the services of somebody as patently partisan as I, he would clearly inflict damage on Jim because, after all, nobody is going to take seriously advice given by Laurel about Hardy, or by Gilbert about Sullivan.

I take the opportunity to recall that Gilbert and Sullivan couldn't stand each other; indeed (if my memory is right), they ended up refusing to have any personal dealings with one another, so that in fact their wonderful collaborations were coordinated through an agent, and they were spared, except perforce on opening nights, the pain of laying eyes on one another. Without mentioning names, I think it is fair to remind ourselves that so has it been, under the surface, with a number of figures, historical and contemporary, who had close biological or professional ties with each other, but who in fact never got on off-stage. I am being very discreet, but if pressed, I could give you a very modern and wonderfully scandalous example. There, now, that is a long introduction, the purpose of which is to attempt to neutralize the pernicious auspices of *Newsday*'s kind invitation to write about my brother Jim. Because what I want to say about him is—

He is out of this world. I mean by that that he is the only person I have ever known who has no enemies. It is extraordinary to be able to say this about Jim, because he is a very steadfast human being. He is, although always tactful, absolutely resolute about what he thinks. But there is something about him that has always persuaded everyone with whom he has contact that his fairness is, in a sense, a tribute even to those who are the immediate victims of that fairness. For instance, if Jim were a witness to an automobile accident in which his very best friend (I grant that that is hard to conceive, because he has no Very Best Friend: he likes too many people equally. If one were to conduct a contest as to who is Jim's best friend, there would be a world war), collided with an automobile driven by Eldridge Cleaver, and Jim saw that Cleaver had the green light, the testimony would be very direct on the matter, and Jim's good friend would—somehow—bear no resentment at all against Jim, even if he really and truly believed that at the moment of impact, the light had turned against

Eldridge Cleaver, which come to think of it, lights would, if the muses were nowadays at their proper stations.

He does that to people. To achieve his disfavor is something of an accomplishment. It was so even when he was very young. Since I must proceed by talking about Jim as a human being, I would be less than useful if I neglected to divulge what I know about Jim in virtue of having grown up as his younger brother. We are a large family, Jim was the fourth child, and I, born three years later, the sixth. His interests were different from mine. He cared, always, for nature, and for things natural. So that as a boy Jim could not wait to enter Millbrook School, mostly because he had heard (at age fourteen), about the fabulous zoo that the biology teacher there had founded. My father indulged him, and, if I may say so in the safety of my beloved father's demise, rather overdid it. I mean by that that Jim persuaded father to invite the biology teacher and his wife to come to our home in Sharon, Connecticut, to spend the summer, in order to teach the rest of the family Everything There Is to Know About Biology and Animal Husbandry. When my father got a sniff of life with the biology teacher morning, noon and night, he discreetly left, with my mother, to spend the summer in Europe, leaving us helpless at the hands of Jim's favorite teacher. The result was a summer at which our free time was spent either in discussing the singular virtues, ecological and moral, of leaving snakes unmolested; or in making graven images in plaster of Paris out of various leaves taken from otherwise innocent trees; or in helping to build cages for what would become, before my father came back and presided promptly over its liquidation, the next largest zoo north of the Bronx. Now the purpose of relating this story is that, notwithstanding the sheer torture of that summer inflicted by Jim on his eight brothers and sisters, somehow it didn't occur to any of us— not even to me, whose spleen, even at age ten, was hungry hungry hungry for objects of antipathy— to blame Jim for that most miserable summer: our Vietnam Summer, if I may profane that term, always hoping that you will understand how terrible it is for a ten-year-old to have to spend his time, if he is not disposed so to spend it, evacuating the racoon's evacuations, or documenting, in plaster of Paris, that a maple leaf looks like a maple leaf. Never mind that I and my brothers and sisters probably thereby spent the most useful summer of our lives. The important thing to remember is that gruesome though it was, somehow we didn't blame it on Jim, though there was never any doubt that he was PERSONALLY AND WITH MALICE AFORE-THOUGHT RESPONSIBLE.

Jim was a sophomore at Yale when the Japanese struck Pearl Harbor. He had been majoring in English literature, and, on the side, watching birds and keeping snakes. Yes, snakes, or at least one snake. I hesitate to reveal this datum, since it is not likely that *Newsday* addresses itself to many voters who incline to her-petology, *Newsday*'s political tastes notwithstanding; but it is a fact that Jim had a pet boa constrictor, left over from that summer zoo, which he used to take with him to class. Martha (as she was called) wound 'round his neck, then down his sleeve, to the shirt-cuff, where she would sleep, or listen, depending, one supposes, on the professor. The master of Jim's college in due course got wind of all of this, and ordered the expulsion of Martha forthwith. It was not in those days known that the thing to do with obnoxious deans is throw them into the river, hence Jim complied, and a big party was given for Martha, who was given her fortnightly ration of one white mouse. Ladylike, she declined to gobble him down, in the company of so many oglers. Mind you, Jim didn't then abandon Martha. Martha was his Israel. He brought Martha to South Carolina for the vacation with his family, and, greatly distressed a few minutes before train time to go back to Yale, reported that Martha had got out of her cage. Distress does not do justice to the state of mind of those of us, young and old, who were *not* leaving the house in order to go back to the safety of Yale. We had to live in that house in the constant fear that one night Martha might take one of us for Jim, snuggle up, and give us a rapturous embrace, which might well have been our last, since boa constrictors do not fool around when they embrace you. It was several months later that the local paper reported, in a tiny item, on a farmer who had shot an enormous snake, seven feet long. "If I didn't know better," the farmer was quoted as saying, "I'd have thought it was one of them bore constricters they grow in Africa." Even after *that*, we didn't hate Jimmy.

At school, he·was on the newspaper, for which he wrote a thrice-weekly column on world affairs. World affairs didn't heed his column, which is why things are rough. In the Navy he served on an LST in the Pacific, and I remember receiving a letter from him when I was in basic training, I having complained about this or that. "Don't worry," he said, "things go slowly in any bureaucracy, even in times of war. I am tempted to write an autobiography, which will be called: 'My Meteoric Career in the Navy: From Ensign to Lt. J.G. in 39 Months.' " But on the fortieth month he was back, having survived a great deal of war, and having laid eyes on Peking. He went to law school, practiced in New Haven, Connecticut, then to New York City, the home base for his travels, and many months in the Philippines, Canada, Latin America and Israel. His interest in public affairs was always marked, but somehow he adopted, as so many people do, the idea that public affairs are for *other* people to take on. From this happy state I guess I have some guilt for wrenching him, when I asked him to serve as my campaign manager in 1965. He consented to do so only because he will do anything any friend asks him to do; not because the life of politics engrossed him. Then, a few years later the 1968 election . . . And now?

Why do I go on about this kind of thing? In part because it would be artificial if I were to write a piece about the Senatorial contest in behalf of my brother, without dwelling on his personal characteristics. In part for other reasons. I had a conversation, a few years ago, with a very interesting and very well-informed Englishman. He is the editor of the *Sunday Telegraph* and he was in this country when John F. Kennedy was assassinated. He is considered, in England, the compleat Tory. During the years when he lived in Washington, he was steadfastly pro-Kennedy. A few days after the assassination, he visited with me and I remarked on the anomaly of his being at once a conservative and a great enthusiast for the liberal Democrat. He replied that increasingly he thought less and less about ideology, more and more about human beings. His judgment was that John Kennedy was an exceptional human being, and that exceptional human beings would, somehow, come forward in due course with desirable policies. I let the matter drop, in part because I do not like to wrestle with guests, in part because I wanted to think through, a bit, what Mr. Peregrine Worsthorne meant. Well, I have done so, and have come to the conclusion that there *is* a trans-ideological attraction to my brother Jim, something that brings people to him even though they associate him with political programs they tend to disapprove of; something that causes them to believe that, notwithstanding explicit differences on explicit issues— like having to build zoos in their spare time— somehow, they believe in *him*. I do not believe that that is necessarily an anti-intellectual impulse. I agree with Mr. Worsthorne that sometimes one comes by whatever road to the conclusion: *that man I trust*. I think that that quality in Jim has been his principal asset in this extraordinary contest. There are others— myself, for instance— who tend also to believe in the positions he believes in. But I do not think that any of us would have attracted, so quickly, so much general support. I think that people who listen to Jim, or who see him, somehow feel: Well, the issues are very complicated, and I know that there are very complicated reasons for saying yes or no to this or that answer to this or that question, and so I am going to vote for Jim Buckley. Because I believe that he is less tied than others to political fashion, less enslaved than others by ideological abstraction.

Jim wrote me a couple of years ago, when it had been suggested to him that he should run for the Senate, to say with his instinctive modesty, "I can't imagine why I'd be useful to the public, still less why the public should want me." I liked that then, and I like that still more now, in the light of the overwhelming evidence, given by so many of you, that you *do* want him to speak for you, on so many of the problems, so very vexing, that are coming up. We used to tease Jim, in the family, that he was never available for any family function on Saturday, because Saturdays are when people get married, and Jim was always away at marriages, usually as best man, sometimes as usher. His friends felt instinctively that they wanted him around at critical periods in their lives. I think that many voters of New York feel the same way about Jim, wanting him in the Senate in this critical period in our lives.

The Return of Edgar Smith

December 11, 1971

Last Monday, at Hackensack, New Jersey, at 6:45 P.M., Edgar Smith was released from prison as the American titleholder: longest sojourn in a death cell in the history of the United States. In order to effect his release, he played out the role assigned to him most dutifully. "Did you, on the night of March 4, 1957, pick up Victoria Zielinski?" "Yes, sir." "Did you drive to the sand pit?" "Yes, sir." "Did you kill Victoria Zielinski?" "Yes, sir." "Did you kill her by yourself?" "Yes, sir." "Was there anyone else present?" "No, sir." That was Smith's part of the deal.

The presiding judge, Morris Pashman, then performed his part of the bargain. Well, he told the crowded courtroom, now finally we have Smith's own admission that he killed the girl . . . The case against Smith is "devastating" . . . Everyone now believes him to be guilty . . . However, he has served more than 14 years in prison and his rehabilitation is impressive . . . He has written two books, learned a great deal about the law, submitted to a psychiatric examination . . . Under the circumstances . . . I sentence him to 25-30 years in prison, and I suspend the balance of the sentence, and place Edgar Smith on probation.

The State of New Jersey was well pleased with itself.

In a way, it had a right to be. Smith had been convicted at a time when it was unanimously believed that he killed the girl. But there were doubters, stubborn doubters. Judge after judge turned down Smith's appeals, based on alleged irregularities in the procedures that brought him to trial. Every state court in New Jersey denied him, and twice he came within hours of execution.

Then, finally, the Supreme Court acted, a lower court heard the case, and the conviction was reversed. The State of New Jersey was given an ultimatum: either try Smith again within 60 days, or let him go free. In the jubilation felt that day by Smith's friends and supporters, we did not know that the worst agony was now programmed.

At first, he was resolute. He wrote on June 23, "I told SFL [one of his lawyers] that my intentions at this time are to force the state to a new trial if Judge Gibbons' ruling holds up. I know of nothing that might change my mind."

When the courts denied him bail pending the new trial he egged on his lawyers. "I want to know why we quit. I can take losing the bail; I cannot tolerate giving up, not trying, quitting."

And on August 24. "I have said it before, and I restate it here. It is my desire to be retried as ordered by Judge Gibbons, and I fully expect this case to go to trial again. I do not expect to change this position except in the face of an exceedingly favorable offer from the other side, which I regard as highly unlikely. . . . The longer I contemplate standing up in court and pleading 'Guilty,' the more unlikely it becomes that I will ever do it. If I were you, I would bet against it ever happening."

For a while, admiring though he was of his exhaustively loyal and able lawyers, Smith considered appearing as counsel in his own behalf, pleading for bail. He asked my opinion and I gave it. He replied, "I was pleased to receive your letter about acting as counsel and arguing the bail myself. What costume would you suggest? My regular prison clothes? That would add a nice touch, especially the faded, blue denim work shirt with my number stencilled across the back. 'May it please my Lords and Ladies . . . ?' That's what I like about you, Bill— you're one of the few people I know who is smart enough to take me seriously."

But then the realities began to crowd in. Another trial. Before there could be a trial, there would have to be pre-trial motions. Was the indictment proper? Shouldn't they apply for a change in venue? Couldn't the state reintroduce the excluded statement— wrested from Smith, in the opinion of the federal courts, by the gray-flannel suit equivalent of the third degree— by introducing into evidence his book wherein he gave the contents of that statement? Did he really want to identify and call in as a witness his former wife, now happily remarried and living in a community where no one knows that she was once Mrs. Edgar Smith? And his daughter, months old at the time of the crime, who is unaware that her stepfather isn't actually her father? Who would raise the money for all of this? What if the jury proceeded to find the circumstantial case against him convincing, and convicted him of murder in the second degree? Was he prepared to run the risk, after all that effort, of another four years in solitary confinement?

October 31. "I do not like this deal," he wrote. "I think it is about as bad a deal as we could have made, but I do not see that I have any choice unless I want to sit in this place. . . . I have no doubt that I will always regret the decision to quit, but I also see that I have no choice. We will talk about it some day. P.S. Do me a favor. Don't plan any celebrations for me. I am not going to be in a celebrating mood after this, and I would rather get away by myself for a while."

To live is to temporize. Smith mused over a year ago that everyone who thought him guilty would continue to think him guilty irrespective of how a jury at a new trial decided. And that everyone who thought him innocent would continue to think him innocent, irrespective of how another jury ruled. Why a new trial, in that event? Pride.

A court of law is many things besides a truth-finding mechanism. It is a chamber in which subtle social and institutional conciliations are effected. The wounded pride of the State of New Jersey had to be healed, after the humiliation it suffered from the federal courts. How to do that?—except by insisting that however illegal the means by which the evidence was collected, in fact they had got the right man? Edgar Smith's claim to liberty had crystallized undeniably from his protracted struggle, at the low point of which he had left only a doting, proud mother, and a fine, unhoned mind which became, after his dark night, a file by which, working at high sweat, he finally sawed through the bars that kept him caged in an 8-by-8 cell from the time that Dwight Eisenhower began his second term of office.

Well, he may not be in a mood for celebration. But I cannot believe that his struggle will be uncelebrated in the annals of the human spirit. And it is always possible that the man who really did it will one day identify himself. Meanwhile, Smith can stop fighting. The knock on his door won't be the executioner's.

Tom Wolfe

December 24, 1970

Those of you who are not aware of Tom Wolfe should— really— do your best to acquaint yourselves with him. For one thing, he is probably the most skillful writer in America. I mean by that that he can do more things with words than anyone else: a greater variety of things. He is like the pianist, Henry Scott, who can play "Flight of the Bumblebee" while wearing mittens. That is of course stunt-stuff, but Wolfe, the virtuoso, does not depend alone on his flashy cadenzas. He can do anything. Meanwhile he is a leading figure in the New Journalism, which weds the craft of the novelist to the obligations of the journalist. And on top of that, he has written a very very controversial book, for which he has been publicly excommunicated from the company of the orthodox by the bishops who preside over the *New York Review of Books*.

Mr. Wolfe was born in Richmond, Virginia, in 1931, and took his B.A. at Washington and Lee University. His principal enthusiasm at college was baseball, in which he hoped to become a professional. He failed and, dropping out, went to Yale, taking there a doctorate degree in American Studies. He worked briefly as a copyboy for the New York *Daily News*, principally because an editor there desired the experience of having a Ph.D. bring him his Coca-Colas. Then the Washington *Post*, then the *Herald Tribune*, and now he is an editor of *New York* magazine. His articles, published there and in *Esquire*, are regularly compiled into books with crazy titles. The first was *The Kandy-Kolored Tangerine-Flake Streamline Baby*; then there was *The Pump House Gang*, and *The Electric Kool-Aid Acid Test*. And, now, *Radical Chic and Mau-Mauing the Flak Catchers*, the first part of which is about the famous party that Leonard Bernstein threw to raise money for the Black Panthers who had been indicted for conspiring to bomb a few department stores, presumably racist department stores, in New York City, during Eastertide.

Well, sir, what happened shouldn't happen to an honest hangman, let alone an artist. What Mr. Wolfe did in his book was MAKE FUN of Bernstein *et al.,* and if you have never been told, you

MUST NOT MAKE FUN of Bernstein *et al.* when what hangs in the balance is Bernstein's moral prestige plus the integrity of Black Protest; learn the lesson now. Tom Wolfe, although thoroughly apolitical, focused on the paradoxes involved in the spilling of Black Rage over the extra-porous sensibilities of an antimacassar liberal who has been trained to salivate over the plight of any Negro, even one whose cause is the absolute right of Black Panthers to commit revolution, bomb department buildings, and rage against the Jews while they are at it.

Anyway . . . Tom Wolfe is an unfortunate victim of ideological ire. His wit attracts the witless among the critics. For instance? Well, here is Wolfe, talking about how some of the black militants in San Francisco succeeded in terrorizing Poverty Program types into giving them money, namely by Frightening Them . . . "There was one genius in the art of confrontation who had mau-mauing down to what you could term a laboratory science. He had it figured out so he didn't even have to bring his boys downtown in person. He would just show up with a crocus-sack full of revolvers, ice picks, fish knives, switchblades, hatchets, blackjacks, gravity knives, straight razors, hand grenades, blow guns, bazookas, Molotov cocktails, tank rippers, unbelievable stuff, and he'd dump it all out on somebody's shiny walnut conference table. He'd say, 'These are some of the things I took off my boys last night . . .' "

This is the kind of thing that is met (by Mr. Jason Epstein of the *New York Review of Books*) with such embarrassing moral pith-and-moment phrases as that Mr. Wolfe is "cruel and shallow," that his "sin is a lack of compassion," that his is an "intellectual weakness" because he "finds himself beyond his depth, frailties that commonly accompany moments of great personal or public stress," and so on and so forth; Cotton Mather reviewing Peter Pan.

Tom Wolfe will survive the humorless of this world— that or else the world will not, should not, survive. If he feels down, after such reviews as Mr. Epstein's, he can go back and reread Karl Shapiro's that appeared in *Book World* after his previous book: "Let us . . . pay homage to Tom Wolfe right off the bat. He has given us the finest mug shots of the soi-disant revolutionaries we shall see in a long time. He has pinned their little wriggling personnae to the bulletin board for all to gape upon. He has performed necessary acts of vilification with a superb aristocratic cool. He is a master of intonation and an extrapolator who can put to shame the regnant sociologists of guilt and hedonism. . . . Tom Wolfe is more than brilliant . . . Tom Wolfe is a goddam joy."

In Memory of Drew Pearson

December 17, 1970

The news is that an annual Drew Pearson Award will be given ($5,000), to the contestant who does the best investigatory reporting of the year "in the manner of the late Drew Pearson." Herewith my entry: . . .

The Lockheed Corporation's $700-million loss, which will now be paid by the taxpayers, is being palmed off by Congress as related to the national security. Actually, this column has developed the facts.

Mrs. Lockheed was years ago friendly with Wilbur Mills, all-powerful Congressional leader whose approval of the Lockheed relief bill is a necessity. Although Mrs. Lockheed, the former Alicia Boeing, had not seen her old friend for many years, it was resolved at a secret meeting of the Board of Directors of Lockheed held last June, on the Greek island of Patmos, that the only way to assure the future of the struggling company was to press on Mrs. Lockheed the necessity of renewing her old friendship.

The board met in Greece because the colonels have been in secret negotiation with Lockheed to purchase the assets of the company for virtually nothing, in the event that Mrs. Lockheed failed in her mission with Wilbur Mills. The Greek government is being backed by Aristotle Onassis, who for many years, according to intimates, has been frustrated by not owning a large airplane manufacturing company to supplement his great shipping and air transport enterprises. The Greek interests, in other words, had a lot to gain from Lockheed's going under, so a great deal of pressure was put on Mrs. Lockheed, and it is reported that representatives of Onassis rushed to Patmos by special Olympia charter flight, recent photographs taken of Wilbur Mills attempting to emphasize his age, and overweight.

Meanwhile, members of the Boeing family, getting wind of what was going on, and desiring the end of their great competitor, Lockheed, joined forces with the Greeks. Young Smiley Boeing was selected to be the family's representative.

Smiley is Mrs. Lockheed's half-brother, by Tallulah Bankhead, whose father, the Speaker of the House, pushed through the original bill, designed to give the young Boeing Company special tax advantages, as reported by this column at that time. Smiley was always the favorite of Alicia, and they were together, holding hands, when the *Titanic* went down, but were picked up by a young seaman, who went on to become the executive vice president of Boeing, having driven a very tough bargain before scooping the young heirs up out of the water.

Historians have recently told this column that the reason the *Titanic* went down is that monopoly shipbuilders were paying back money under the table to the Duke of Salisbury, instead of putting the money into making a truly seaworthy hull. The fact that the Duke of Salisbury's first wife is the first cousin of John C. Boeing, the founder of the Boeing empire, has given rise to speculation.

Smiley reportedly arrived at Patmos just as Alicia was leaving, having resigned herself to fly to Washington to call up Mills. He persuaded her to postpone her trip for three days, during which they wandered about the ruins of Ephesus, while Smiley tried to persuade his sister that that is what California would look like if the country tried to support two, instead of just one, major aircraft producing companies. Alicia was very nearly persuaded by her attractive younger brother (he has been married nine times), when she dropped a pebble in the famous fountain of Pirsos. Legend had it that if young Roman virgins, torn between two lovers, would throw a coin into the fountain, the goddess would indicate which of the suitors was to be preferred. The ripples struck the letter *W*, and Alicia decided her destiny was to seek out Wilbur (Mills). Smiley tried to persuade her that if she moved to the other side of the pool, normally used by Roman virgins, what looked to her like a *W*, would actually appear to have been an *S*— for Smiley. He traced out his point on the ground with a stick, but Alicia, although patient with her brother, was adamant that *W* was what the gods intended, and flew back on the next plane to Washington.

It's an open secret that she has been seen with Wilbur Mills at least on one occasion since last June— at the summer White House Party for Congress, and there is actually a photograph of Mrs. Lockheed going through the receiving line of Congressional leaders, and shaking hands with Congressman Mills as if he were a perfect stranger, which did not fool this column.

Jerry Rubin

April 11, 1970

I do not care about the depravities of Jerry Rubin, who is one of the lost souls sentenced at the Chicago conspiracy trial, except that he is a fellow human being, bent on destroying himself, preferably in cinemascope. But I do care very much that Jerry Rubin should have found a panderer this side of the underground.

Mr. Rubin's book is called *Do It!* Do what? Well, whatever you like, provided it involves enormous amounts of drugs, sex, protests, obstructionism, obscenity, and the killing of non-members of the sect, hereinafter called pigs. Mr. Rubin went all the way to Algeria to get an introduction for his book from Eldridge Cleaver. He could not have gone to a more appropriate person to open the gates to Mr. Rubin's lower intestine for the long long passage ahead.

Mr. Cleaver, the spiritual leader of the Black Panthers, urges that "the people" "rise up and kill pigs and destroy their power." From his asylum in Algeria (he is wanted by the courts in California to resume his sentence for rape), he recalls as the sweetest moment of his politically active life, the shoot-out at Oakland when "the shadow of death was created by the blaze leaping from the barrel of a gun. A pig white lay dead, deep fried in the fat of his own b--------." The hyphens are mine.

Rubin's book has only the single virtue that it confirms the hypocrisy of many of the activists. He reveals quite unabashedly that their campaigns are often based on consciously invented lies. "Our tactic was exaggeration. Everything was 'the biggest,' 'the most massive.' " His use of obscenity is so witless as really to all but drive it out of fashion. One thinks of Norman Mailer's *Why Are We in Vietnam?*, and is tempted to advocate legislation that will forbid printed obscenity by those who, if one may say so, debase it. The book is filled with drawings and photographs of porcine nudes who could not have qualified to pose for *Sunshine & Health*. They all look like Jerry Rubin, and one begins to suspect that in those circles the love is free because they couldn't possibly sell it.

So much for Rubin. What about the distinguished firm of Simon & Schuster? Listen to what is printed on the back jacket — by the publishers. "This book will become a Molotov cocktail in your very hands." (Who wants a Molotov cocktail in his very hands?) "Jerry Rubin has written the Communist Manifesto of our era." (If that's the case, *Hair!* is the *Paradise Lost* of our era, and our era may as well give up.) "This book is the most important political statement made by a white revolutionary in America today. *Do It!* is to be danced to. Read aloud. Studied. Memorized. Debated. Burned. Swallowed. Eaten. But most important, after living through the experience of this book, take its final advice: Do it!" The promotion editor who wrote that, you see, tries to swing by using the words, "swallowed, eaten."

A limp performance, which does not dispose of the problem of having counseled the readers to Do It — above all to do it, doing it being: the destruction of oneself, of other human beings, of free institutions, of any sense of order and goodness and restraint.

It is not to come out for censorship to wonder at the sponsorship of this book. Though arguments — very sound arguments — could certainly be mustered for suppressing a book which incites to sedition, and arson, and killing, and which is guilty of criminally libelous charges against named individuals, my own disposition would have been against suppressing these pages of human and political ordure. But I want my dirty pictures sold to me by dirty little men and hidden in Russian Easter eggs. Not passed out ceremoniously by men and women who pride themselves on their contributions to thought and literature and who regularly publish great tracts of prose devoted to the maintenance of humane standards.

So, Simon & Schuster will make themselves a hundred grand or so from the publication of this book, forever reminding us of Lenin's wry dictum that when the last of the bourgeois is hanged, a capitalist will sell the rope. I shall think of Simon & Schuster when I think of Jerry Rubin, as no doubt will the estates of Bertrand Russell and Winston Churchill, and Charles de Gaulle and Malcolm Muggeridge and Joseph Alsop, who no doubt will wonder at the company they keep.

John Lennon

March 16, 1971

A letter from a spirited and incisive correspondent on the West Coast has cost me the better part of a day. . . . "I send you, untouched by human hands, Issues 74 & 75 of *Rolling Stone* that carry the complete interview with John Lennon, running to some 30,000 words.

"These sheep-witted Beatles, fawned on and reverently looked up to by most of the young across the earth, although their dispositions are as mean as their intelligence and their morals are as base as their lineage, I make so bold as to suggest to you, started it all, and have dealt Western Society such heavy blows that it will be a century in recovering, if, in fact, it ever does.

"These men are not innocents— they are sophisticated scoundrels capable of the most swinish behavior and their influence poisoned the headwaters of the Sixties and we now see that trickling stream of history as it gathers and deepens and broadens and rolls its mighty tides of drugs and antinomian attitudes, now already engulfing what remains of civilization in a few walled towns. I am led to believe that what I am sending you is an historic document."

Because my friend believes, after all is said and done, in the virtue of moderation, he adds the P.S., "There are northwest winds today, and the horses are restless— also my 51st birthday— tomorrow will be better." Well, I have read all 30,000 words, and I also hope that tomorrow will be better, having no alternative:

despair is a mortal sin. Despair is very nearly what the reading of this gargantuan interview brings to you.

What was Lennon's point in granting the interview? He had a minor and major point to make, respectively to promote an upcoming album, and to talk about himself. Several times, with his complete approval, he refers to himself as an egomaniac, a frailty a great many people have: but not all of those who have it, have the complementary failing of supposing that that part of the world (always a majority) that fails to interrupt all other activity in order to give itself over to the veneration of you is a) philistine, b) ungrateful, c) wasting its time.

Lennon manages to convey these conclusions, which could have been done much more economically if he had eliminated as redundant, say, every other use of his favorite obscenity, which makes him sound like a musician who cannot graduate beyond the use of the two-four beat.

It is remarkable to achieve in combination what Mr. Lennon manages to do here, namely a) to demonstrate how he laid waste his life during the 1960's, and b) to proclaim so apodictically on how others should govern their lives: (recipe: adore Lennon, and [favorite verb] your neighbor).

By his own admission Lennon was never happy with the Beatles. 1) He greatly distrusted Paul, whom he always suspected of attempting to satellize the other Beatles; 2) to have joined the Beatles was in any case an artistic cop-out; 3) he was victimized by a succession of commercial predators who have managed to get everything snarled up; 4) the music the Beatles ended up playing was arid and formalistic and an imposture on good creative music; 5) he was stoned for the better part of two years on acid, which he took "literally" thousands of times; 6) the sex orgies in which he engaged, particularly when on tour, cloyed, and gave him no satisfaction; 7) on flying out to India in search of spiritual solace, he discovered that the fakir in whom he reposed confidence was a commercial old lecher; 8) oh yes, he discarded a wife; 9) everybody is jealous of him; and 10), it is only by chance that he met his Yoko, whose least song is better than "Sergeant Pepper," widely hailed as the Beatles' best; wherein Mr. Lennon achieves credibility at last. The balance of the magazine is devoted to endless copy about other rock groups, classified advertising for abortion seekers, and home-growing advice for marijuana users, plus a great deal that is inscrutable except to high-honor students in the sub-culture which strains through 30,000 words of John Lennon in search—

Of what? Lennon is greatly talented as a musician. As a philosopher he is as interesting as Jelly Roll Morton: less so, as a matter of fact. He is interesting only to an anthologist of pieces on How I Wrecked My Own Life, and Can Help Wreck Yours.

Little Lord Haw Haw

February 20, 1970

But let him introduce himself. "My name is David Ifshin, and I'm president of the National Students Association of the United States, and I was student body president at Syracuse University last year. I just graduated. I came to North Vietnam after being denied admission to South Vietnam, where you are right now. We had hoped to go to South Vietnam to meet with the students there and to discuss, find out the situation regarding the Thieu-Ky regime and their oppression of the Vietnamese people. . . ."

Having been denied entry into South Vietnam where he was determined to "find out the situation," young Ifshin apparently realized that what the hell, he knew the situation anyway, so he went on to Hanoi and explained the situation, over the radio, beamed to United States troops in South Vietnam. South Vietnam's ability to see through this preposterous little phony speaks well for it. One cannot easily imagine General MacArthur granting an interview to Tokyo Rose.

There are various available levels of indignation. 1) By siding thus directly with the enemy, he becomes an enemy of the United States. It is one thing to argue against the Vietnam war in the United States. It is another to attempt to demoralize American troops on the field. Psychological warfare is a recognized branch of—warfare. There is no philosophical difference between what Ifshin did during that broadcast from Hanoi, and the firing of bullets at American soldiers.

Then, 2), there is the effrontery of the thing. He might have begun his broadcast by saying, "I am David Ifshin, and although I'm president of the National Students Association, I am a member of a tiny minority of American students who believe the Communist Party line on all matters that relate to North Vietnam." G.I.'s listening in might at least have recognized the auspices of the speaker. Or if he had said, "Although I am president of the National Students Association, I must confess that Wall Street imperialists so greatly dominate American colleges and universities that the overwhelming body of the students are blinded to the truths."

But no: he simply presents himself as president of the National Students Association; which is as representative of American students as Charles Manson is of American Boy Scouts. But that is for the National Students Association to fret about, and one doesn't particularly care what they do about it, because, long since, no one has particularly cared what the National Students Association does or says about anything.

3) But in a sense the worst is to come. Young Ifshin has been so active politically in his young career, one can only assume he has not had time to study. Presumably, as a freshman, he set out for Syracuse University to "find out the situation." The authorities at Syracuse were at once (a) misguided in letting him matriculate, because clearly he did not want to "find out the situation" in the world of learning; and (b) misguided in letting him graduate, in view of the fact that clearly he had not learned anything.

Listen: "The Thieu-Ky regime is one of the most oppressive regimes in history." Could Ifshin have studied *any* history, ancient, medieval, or modern? Any political science? Economics? "I realize especially after this trip, that the U.S. Government does not go to South Vietnam to fight for democracy, or to defend the rights of the people, but they go there and send us to murder the people of Vietnam in order to make South Vietnam into one large U.S. military base, not to defend the United States but to aggressively threaten other countries. The fear is that if the people of Vietnam are allowed to have their own country, are allowed to determine for themselves their own interests, they will not support the investments of private capital."

As though American capital, bleeding from the expenses of the war, needs *support* from "the people" of South Vietnam! Probably the young man's teachers thought better of trying to teach him anything, and sent him off instead to serve as president of the National Students Association, for which his ignorance qualifies him.

April 15, 1971

A few weeks ago I wrote about the president of the National Students Association, young David Ifshin, and his activities in behalf of the enemy in Hanoi. Little Lord Haw Haw has now objected to what I said, and you will not believe the sanction he threatens against me! He proposes to lead a movement to persuade the Senate of the University of Syracuse to withdraw the honorary degree conferred upon me two years ago. Here is the reasoning of young Ifshin. I charged in my column that he is ignorant. But in fact, he says, he got very high grades at Syracuse. Therefore I have defamed Syracuse. And if I defame Syracuse, Syracuse has no business honoring me.

"If Buckley is so disgruntled with the academic quality of Syracuse University," the student newspaper writes, "he ought to resign his honorary degree from this institution. Of course, he probably won't, and so that leaves the resolution of the dilemma up to the university community. It is incumbent upon us to safeguard the good name of Syracuse University by affirming that a real degree from SU is more substantial than an honorary degree. The best way to affirm that is to divest the ungrateful Mr. Buckley of his SU diploma, and a number of students intend to propose doing just that in the University Senate."

I have not been advised by the Senate of Syracuse University of the disposition of the motion that pends against me, and will meanwhile make my way under the Damoclean burden of the suspense. On the other hand, having learned that Mr. Ifshin got high grades at Syracuse, it might be worth the Senate's attention to ponder the relation between high grades and what one used to call *recta ratio*, or right thought, it being the purpose of universities not merely to turn out graduates of intellectual dexterity, but also men who are other than barbarians. It would have been better, I think we might all agree, if, say, Hitler and Stalin had received no education, rather than such education as they did receive.

I repeat two statements uttered by Mr. Ifshin, the president of the National Students Association, over Radio Hanoi, beamed to American fighting men in South Vietnam.

1) "The Thieu-Ky regime is one of the most oppressive regimes in history."

Now, at this point one deduces that young Ifshin majored in astronomy, or structural linguistics, or perhaps home economics. No such luck for Syracuse. I have been informed that he majored in English, over which he has, manifestly, an uneasy grasp; and in religion, which is pretty brinky, if you ask me: Further, My God, From Thee is a much safer place from which to go around acting chummy with Communist atrocity-nabobs; and in political science. Yes, *political science*. How is it possible to have read a single book on political science— any book: whether by John Stuart Mill or Karl Marx, or Herbert Marcuse— and emerge believing that the Thieu regime is "one of the most oppressive regimes in history"?

And then, 2) Ifshin told the troops: "The [U.S.] fear is that if the people of Vietnam are allowed to have their own country, are allowed to determine for themselves their own interests, they will not support the investments of private capital."

That is the kind of reasoning that would cause sophisticated Communists to titter, in the privacy of their quarters. It is adolescent Marxist Tarzan-talk, and by God as an honorary doctor of laws from Syracuse University, I demand that the Senate do something about it: either call back Little Lord Haw Haw and explain a few things to him, or else beg him not to bring up, while exhibiting his ignorance, the matter of his having been graduated from Syracuse University. It's too embarrassing to us Syracuse degree-holders.

Clare Boothe Luce

April 11, 1971

Clare Boothe Luce, A Biography. By Stephen Shadegg. Illustrated, Simon & Schuster. $7.95.

You are a young, beautiful woman, Pearl Harbor was only yesterday, you have spent several months poking about disconsolate Allied fronts in Asia and the Mideast, you have written a long analysis, cruelly objective, infinitely embarrassing to the Allies, and correspondingly useful to the Axis powers, and then, on the last leg of your journey, a British customs officer at Trinidad insists on examining your papers. He discovers the dynamite, calls in British security, which packs you off under house arrest. What do you do?

Well, if you are Clare Boothe Luce, you get in touch with the American consulate, and the American consulate gets a message through to your husband, Henry Luce. Harry calls Colonel Bill Donovan, head of American Intelligence, and Colonel Donovan arranges to appoint you *retroactively* as an intelligence official of the United States Government. The British thereupon agree to let you fly to New York, and there they give your report to the British Ambassador. He is so impressed by it that he instantly apprises Churchill of its contents. Churchill pauses from the war effort to cable back his regards to "Clare," who is thereupon asked by the Joint Chiefs of Staff to brief them on her analyses, which, suitably bowdlerized, appear in successive issues of *Life* magazine, and are a journalistic hit. That's Clare Baby, and let's face it, they don't come down the road that way very often, and when they do, they are worth reading about.

If only, for instance, to pick up such an episode as this one, and the dozens of others chronicled by Stephen Shadegg in his biography. It is a favorable biography, though not gushy. It obviously required a degree of cooperation from Mrs. Luce, for instance access to her press clippings. Yet the book's stylelessness suggests that Mrs. Luce's relationship to it was perfunctory; that she flatly declined (assuming that she was asked; Mr. Shadegg is a professional himself) to shape the book, and so she must not be held accountable for distortions in it, and, of course, she cannot be held responsible for the principal failure of the book, which is that somehow it does not sufficiently communicate the flavor of her, and that has nothing whatever to do with the silly question whether you do or don't approve of her political views.

I remember a few years ago reading a biography of Westbrook Pegler whose principal failure was its short ration of Pegler's art. As much must be said of Shadegg's Mrs. Luce. When he does vouchsafe her to us directly, whole chapters light up. As when, in his account of Mrs. Luce's exchanges with Fulton Sheen that led to her conversion to the Catholic faith, Shadegg tells us that

Father Sheen told her he did not want to hear her confession himself, and would she like to designate a priest to execute that duty? "Bring me someone who has seen the rise and fall of empires," said Mrs. Luce.

Thus the book tantalizes, and also by giving us unpursued (and unpursuable) leads, such as that Clare somehow "transferred her resentment" over the tragedy of her daughter's accidental death onto her husband's shoulders, because he (Luce) "had never suffered a defeat." He touches upon frequently, but never explores, a professional and maybe even personal hostility between the Emperor's wife and the court, over at the Time-Life Building. We do not really know how such critics of Congresswoman Luce as Clifton Fadiman can have got away with derogating her intelligence ("no woman of our time has gone further with less mental equipment"). On the other hand, the account of her Ambassadorship in Italy is satisfying. Indeed, there is a sense in which the whole of the book is that, because it deals with a woman who is quite simply fascinating, and gives us information about her and the famous people she knows and knew which isn't otherwise available.

Is it a key to the essential Luce? Once again, there are clues there. She is an active member of the social community, easily engrossed by ideas, particularly ideas of altruistic potential. A young economist, Amintore Fantani, writes a book extolling the economic "reforms" of Mussolini, Charles Poletti gives Clare a copy, she calls it to Hugh Johnson's attention, he gives it to Ray Moley, who sells it to F.D.R., and what comes of it is the National Recovery Act.

She played a role in the midwifery of other monsters ($1,000 to the Abraham Lincoln Brigade), but also to building some great bridges (the Marshall Plan, the Trieste treaty), and she could also give some very trenchant negative advice. "When Willkie asked her opinion [about what to do in the spring of 1944], she bluntly advised him to 'stop drinking, lose 40 pounds, and adopt a more realistic understanding of the Communists' announced plan to conquer the world.' "

And her penetrating mind gladly shattered myths from which she profited, *e.g.*, that the characters around whom she wrote *The Women* were somehow admirable. "The women who inspired this play deserved to be smacked across the head with a meat axe and that, I flatter myself, is exactly what I smacked them with. They are vulgar and dirty-minded and alien to grace, and I would not, if I could, which I hasten to say I cannot, cross their obscenities with a wit which is foreign to them and gild their futilities with the glamour which by birth and breeding and performance they do not possess." So much for the beautiful people, and how greatly such a passage as this accents the need for an autobiography. Until then, Mr. Shadegg's book is the one to read.

William F. Rickenbacker

June 5, 1970

William F. Rickenbacker suffers whatever it is you call it being the son of a very famous man. We know about such people that their way is very hard; and indeed I recall (the words may be wrong, but the sense is right I think), that somewhere in Homer it is fatefully remarked about Telemachus that he could never be the equal of his father Ulysses, any more than anyone's son can ever be the equal of his father, *pace* Darwin.

It is the response most usual in sons of famous fathers that they fade away; or, here and there, they Revolt, not merely against their fathers' personal authority, but against their fathers' praiseworthiness (*e.g.*, here and there the Krupp, or the Lamont). But Bill Rickenbacker wholeheartedly approves of his father Captain Eddie. Add to the problem a name so distinctive, such that when you run into it the tendency has been rather to speculate on the relation between William and Captain Eddie, than to meditate on the reasons why you heard of William to begin with. I have found it amusing, but can understand it that Wm. does not. And the careful good manners of the gentlefolk who, in my field of vision, have confronted him, feigning either ignorance or indifference as regards his progeny, have never really let him off. I think as an analogy of the hostess who was informed a year or so after the Battle of the Bulge that her guest of honor General McAuliffe reacted almost violently to any reminder that at the moment of supreme stress when the Nazis demanded that he surrender he had replied "Nuts." The hostess accordingly mentioned Bastogne not at all during the whole of the evening, but when she bade the guest of honor goodnight, she gushed, in the manner of Billie Burke, "Goodnight, General McNuts."

All of which is to suggest that William F. Rickenbacker ought to be more widely recognized, at this point, than merely as a most successful son of Eddie Rickenbacker. I came to know his background only very gradually as I became his friend and colleague and, month after month, year after year, tripped across yet another accomplishment of a young man who had attracted me, at the beginning, very simply because his hold of the English language was so captivatingly secure: that and because there was a streak of madcap irony in his person and in his work that I have found very nearly indispensable in those with whom one cohabits in the house of ideology. Mr. Rickenbacker and his colleagues are dissenters from the American zeitgeist, but to pretend that we are persecuted in the sense that, say, Pasternak and Solzhenitsyn and Daniel are persecuted, is to profane heroism. What we are made to suffer is, by contrast, bearable: so that we can not only indulge a wryness of outlook, but even require it. Rickenbacker's smile, although he is very good at suppressing it, is a part of his temperamental and philosophical equipment.

But on with his curriculum vitae. He was born in California in 1928, went to preparatory school in Asheville, North Carolina, and after that to Harvard. Now brace yourself.

1) As a boy he became interested in music, and in piano playing, and he won first place in the juvenile division of the National Steinway Contest in New York in 1935. He gave his first solo piano recital in 1945. He is even now engaged in recording piano classics, and has released, I think, his fifth record at this writing. Needless to say, he writes and publishes music criticism. Holden Caulfield? Hardly. 2) At Harvard he took a varsity letter in swimming, and also in golf, having served as captain of the golf team, and as medalist in the New England Intercollegiate Golf Championship. All of which suggests that he neglected his studies? 3) He graduated cum laude. His fascination with English absorbed his verbal energies? 4) He is fluent in French, German and Spanish. He is expert in Russian, Italian, Portuguese, Latin, and Greek. He reads Dutch, Anglo-Saxon and Hebrew. 5) His hobbies include aviation. He has a commercial pilot's license and

three thousand hours of pilot time (an interesting contrast with his famous father, whose total is three hundred hours).

In the late 1950's, Bill Rickenbacker was making his living as a stock market analyst (the Renaissance man goes to work, dreaming of Michelangelo). He began to do a little free-lancing, the target of which was, mostly, omnipotent government; which is to say the most nubile target of this or for that matter any age, in this or for that matter any society. And then, in 1960, he sent to the editors of *National Review* a piece which would become historical. He called it "The Fourth House," and proclaimed therein his refusal to complete the famous Blue Form issued by the census-takers, which form asked among other impertinencies how many toilets did Mr. Rickenbacker have in his house, stopping short (and out of no apparent recognition of any other bounds than a lapsed curiosity) only of questioning how often was each toilet flushed.

Now Bill Rickenbacker can be very provocative, and the Justice Department elected to pounce. There was an indictment, and a trial, and Rickenbacker, with the aid of a brilliant and resourceful attorney, argued valiantly against the constitutionality of this invasion of privacy, but lost. He was fined one hundred dollars and given a suspended sentence. His satisfaction came ten years later with the census of 1970, when it was revealed by the chief census-taker, dubbed "Snoopchief" in Rickenbacker's famous article, that any citizen receiving the 1970 version of the Blue Form who had conscientious objections to filling it out, would go unmolested. The beneficiary of Rickenbacker's favors.

Bill Rickenbacker has collected a number of essays and short pieces written during the ten years in which he published two best-sellers on money: *Wooden Nickels*, and *Death of the Dollar*. During most of that time he served nobly and eloquently as a senior editor of *National Review*. A year or two ago he resigned in order to bring out a weekly market letter, the *Rickenbacker Report*. *National Review* is not the same without him, and I wish that his new book could have, somehow, communicated a little bit more of the harum-scarum that adds, I think, rather than subtracts, from the gravitas that gives force to such opinions as Bill Rickenbacker so gravely holds. Some of it, to be sure, is inside stuff, dangerous to give out, lest it cause (dangerous) perplexity, or even (fatal), a yawn. For instance, at our shop we have a publisher most learned in political machination who flatly predicted, on the basis of super-inside knowledge, that Ronald Reagan would be nominated for President by the Republican National Convention at Miami in 1968. The elaboration of his analysis the editors listened to patiently, as a rule, and sometimes a little bit impatiently. A month or so before the Convention, Bill Rickenbacker elected to circulate a memorandum in which he commented on no less than five of the publisher's preceding memoranda. Rickenbacker's read as follows:

> I owe it to you to make my position irrefragably clear. If Rockefeller fails on the first ballot, Romney tosses his kerchief to Nixon, Reagan squares with Percy, and O'Doherty and Rusher remain above the conflict, then McKinley is a shoo-in. If, however, Stassen and Dewey announce for Nixon *before* the third ballot, Clif White swears off martinis, Mahoney and Alessandroni arrive at an understanding with Nixon, and Rockefeller undercuts Reagan's early strength by divorcing Happy and remarrying the former Elizabeth Todhunter Clark, then it seems entirely possible that Claude Kirk of Florida and Charles Percy of Illinois will be the immediate (though by no means final) beneficiaries. There remains the possibility of a premature combination between Rockefeller, Reagan, Nixon, Stassen, Romney, Scranton, Lindsay, Javits, and Spinoza to thwart the rapidly expanding Presidential ambitions of Buz Lukens. In this event, I would look for a brokered convention.

One never knew, at *National Review*, what news event would catch his fancy. Sure, economics; sure, politics. Of course, anybody's solecism. Music, certainly, and aeronautical engineering. I asked him in the spring of 1963 to submit a short editorial on the subject of the Soviet's launching of the first female cosmonaut. To this day I pat myself on the back for having had the guts *not* to print it. But the days have passed, and I herewith divulge Rickenbacker's unpublished editorial, of June, 1963, entitled, "Song of the Wild Goose."

> The orbitch clumb the termagantry
> Go, no go, girl, go.
> Yon sputwich cum within her pantry
> Apogee-string, go.

Into the nosecrone clumb astrollop
Gynecosmonaut,
Set her capsulass for wallop
Why? Because . . . monaut.

Yon zoombie astrobabe doth say
All systems go, virago—
Then padlaunched from the cuntdown, year,
She'll hump Yuri Garago.

Oh hark, galacrobat, perhaps you'll
Take my counsel free-ah:
And don't import into your clapsule
Go, no gonorrhea.

Ah, I can hear you beginning to say. He is not serious . . .

> 23 October 1965

Dear Bill [he wrote me at the height of my mayoralty campaign against John V. Lindsay]:

I remember that when we all had supper with Milton Friedman last spring, we wondered how to pronounce the name of the wine we were enjoying— whether, specifically, the t should be sounded in Montrachet. I had always intended to find out. Today I finally looked. The n-t-r combination in French is lawless, I find:

T sounded	*T silent*
Montrésor	Montrachet
Montret	Montréal
Montreuil	Montredon-Labessonnié
Montreuil-sur-Mer	Montréjeau
Montreuil-Bellay	Montrevel
Montreux	Montrose
Montrevault	Montrouge
Montrichard	

It would have been a shame to come to the end of the mayoral campaign with items like this untended to.

> Yours ever,
> wfr

About politics he can write very gravely. But for all that he desires that we should understand politics and economics, because an understanding of them is absolutely necessary to the securing of our liberties, somehow I have never found him unflinchingly serious except when he is talking about music. "For all of Schubert's supposed simplicity," he wrote me once sternly, "there are things in his slightest work which reward the student. I have noted in red [in an accompanying manuscript] a few of the prominent details. 1) The extremely rare interval of the diminished octave, here in cross-relation: C sharp, C natural. 2) Diminished fifth as harmonic interval. 3) Parallel fifths. 4) The G is a stroke of genius. Without the G the measure is banal. 5) The great flowing power of the melody is supported by asymmetric phrase-writing: a four-measure statement, followed by a four-measure reply, followed by a secondary statement of six measures, and then the repeat begins. It is that six-measure phrase that gives us the feeling of floating off somewhere into the blue, liberated for the moment from the tyranny of the $2 + 2$ world. Here for a moment we know how it feels when $2 + 2 = 6$, how it feels when a miracle happens . . ."

I remember writing him from Switzerland that I had begun to dabble with oils. "How interesting, and good, that you're taking a crack at painting. Your nicest perceptions are, I think, visual (mine are not). . . . I tire of the sea and the surf because they assail my ear after a short while with a mindless roar. I could never understand Whitman's infatuation with the surf, though I am dumb with wonder at the words he found to describe that primeval rote— 'Out of the cradle, endlessly rocking'— say that to yourself very slowly and very deliberately, and the accompaniment of waves *a capella* leaps to your ear. We just stumbled through an oxymoron. Sorry about that. In any case, have a good long partnership with paint. I think it's your substitute for words, as music is mine— or to be terribly forthright, I might say that words are my substitute for music."

I do not doubt that the reader of his book will concur in that judgment, after he savors the quality of the prose, and the harmony of the thought. I do not know that he will get the flavor of the individual, or that that flavor can be communicated, except as one shares an office, over a period of time, with the author of this book. I would not want to make the point heavily that only physical proximity serves to cause understanding between people: it was never stressed during the ten years he shared offices with his colleagues. He wrote me once, "One of the most pleasant aspects of the relation between you and me is, at least for me, the feeling that it is not necessary to touch bases too often. I know that you are covering your immense territory with your accustomed vigilance; you assume that I'll keep the dust from collecting too deep in my corner of the barrack; we assume we agree on the important matters, and I do believe we do. The occasions in life when I have offered my trust only to find it returned in handsome amplification can be counted on the thumbs of one hand. Naturally I have three hands. . . . When two lifetimes of reading go into a conversational interchange on Keynes or Chaucer shall we savor the interchange— or the lifetimes? Or Chaucer? No one knows . . . At the end . . . one remembers a style of mind, a tempo of interplay, a seriousness or flippancy of mood, a yes or no person. One is grounded again in the reality of one's confreres, and therefore readied for another assault upon the mice in the attic."

I am glad that the pressures of the mind and the style and the insights of my old friend and colleague are being made generally available. The public and the author deserve each other. Ladies and gentlemen, Bill Rickenbacker.

John Dos Passos

October 6, 1970

I have come back from the funeral of John Dos Passos. It was in a way typical of him to die a few minutes after Nasser, who of course swamped the obituary headlines, so much so that Dos Passos's own young stepson, away at law school, who reads the papers lackadaisically and listens not at all to the radio or TV, was not aware of the death until a few hours before the funeral, to which he hastened, registering the grief felt universally by everyone who had known Dos Passos, let alone been brought up by him. There was no way to keep his death off the front page (geniuses have a pre-emptive right to die on the front page), but the reader felt that the editorial handling was somehow harassed. Nasser had died, the chancelleries of the world were in turmoil, and the death of mere literary giants doesn't substantially occupy the front page (nor should it: front pages are correctly devoted to news of immediate and transitory significance. Never mind that few people can now remember who reigned over England and Spain during the week that Shakespeare and Cervantes died).

On the other hand it is worth noting that Dos Passos did not suffer the pains that torture those artists who cry over the neglect of them by their contemporaries. The only reason why he did not treat the literary press with the total aloofness of, say, an Edmund Wilson, or a Charles Lindbergh, is that he was too good-natured. He could not bring himself to say No to the tenacious literary reporter who wanted to interview him and write a profile of him.

Mr. Dan Wakefield, a most conscientious journalist and novelist, wrote a considerable profile of Dos Passos a few years ago, and I remember asking him what his opinion of it was, to which he replied with a shyness which neither he— nor David Garrick— could have feigned, that in fact he hadn't read it. "I find," he said, with a self-effacing giggle that his friends knew as his conversational signature, "that when I start reading those things"— by which he meant profiles of himself, or reviews of his books— "my eyes just dribble off the page, so I just don't look at them."

Did this mean that he had no self-esteem? No, that would be inaccurate. It means that he was a genuine artist, who did the very best he could every time he sat down to write a novel, or a book of history; but that since he had absolutely nothing to contribute to the improvement of a book after it was published, what was the point in reading reviews of his books? Or— for heaven's sakes— reviews of himself, as author of said books? "If I had to describe him in a single sentence," his next-door neighbor told me after the funeral, "I would say that he was a modest man; the most modest man I ever met."

We are talking about someone who stupefied the literary generation of the twenties. Critics as disparate as Jean-Paul Sartre and Whittaker Chambers were to remark matter-of-factly that he was the greatest novelist in America. The formal tributes did not, all of them, come in. It was an open secret that he was scorned by the Nobel Prize committee because of his political sympathies. He began his career as an ardent sympathizer of left-wing political movements. After the Spanish Civil War, he identified the Communists as the great evildoers of his time, an insight that caused him to do that which pained him most, namely to break a friendship: in this case, with Ernest Hemingway. But he pursued his conviction that man was best off untrammeled by political authority, and of course when he died, the obituarists merely repeated what had been said about him so often before, namely that his literary work was at the service of political reactionaries.

Translation: JDP was a political conservative, and the rules of the game being that no one can simultaneously be a literary genius and a political conservative, you must draw your own conclusions about Dos Passos. In the event that you are slow at doing that kind of thing, here is the key: JDP was a genius during his left-wing period. After that, he was pedestrian, a time-server. Never mind the two dozen books he wrote, the extraordinary histories of Jefferson, of Brazil, of Portugal; the novel *Mid-Century*. Forget them. If you can.

The answer is that no one can forget Dos Passos, and the working press, somehow, sensed it. The reporters and the television people were at his funeral. I was accosted by one, who asked me to assess the literary work of JDP. I was at that moment in the company of John Chamberlain, whom William Lyon Phelps once called the principal literary critic of his generation, and to open my voice on Dos Passos in Chamberlain's presence would have been doubly to profane the situation inasmuch as what I wanted to say was simply that I would have been present, here at the Episcopal Church of Towson, Maryland, as sorrowfully if JDP had never written a word, because I knew him primarily as a friend; but if literary taxonomy was what the press wanted, why didn't they ask Chamberlain? The widow, firm, tall, beautiful, moved serenely through the vague confusion, the result of an uneasy apprehension that the death of this modest man who came closest to explaining America to the world, might just turn out to be a historical event the neglect of which would above all proclaim the philistinism of the country he loved so very much more than his literary detractors love it.

It was all so very hard to sort out, because the historical meaning of the occasion was clearly secondary to all who were there except the press. I traveled to Baltimore with an extraordinarily self-disciplined attorney (it was his seventieth birthday) who had known JDP for *fifty* years, and on three occasions, my traveling companion had to turn away from a conversation, overcome by tears at the awful prospect of facing life without the friendship of John Dos Passos. If C. D. Batchelor were active, he'd have done a drawing of the Statue of Liberty weeping over her loss; this irreparable loss.

XIV. Manners, Mannerists, Vexations

You Are the More Cupcakeable for Being a Cosmopolitan Girl

September 22, 1970

I knew nothing about Helen Gurley Brown until undertaking to write about her *Cosmopolitan*. But as often happens in such situations, the moment I embarked on the project—suddenly all the world became a gathering system and for a week or so it seemed that there was never a conversation anywhere in which her name didn't figure. And then I was given to read a trunkload of articles from a year of *Cosmopolitan,* articles which were Distinctively Helen Gurley Brown. Halfway through reading them, I found myself rejecting the common suspicion that HGB (as she often signs herself) is putting us on. I was absolutely certain that she was not, until I came on one paragraph from *Cosmo*'s monthly Editor's Column, which is pure HGB, wherein the editor introduces the reader to that particular issue, and chats. *Great God,* I found myself wondering. Could it *possibly* be? (as she would put it). Read it carefully . . .

"In her article, 'How Sexually Generous Should a Girl Be?' (p. 138), Gael [Greene] tells some of the right and wrong reasons, in her opinion, for going to bed with a man. Do read it! Gael and her husband, Don Forst, New York Times *culture editor, have renovated a church for a weekend house (they're photographed there)."*

But of course! The whole of *Cosmopolitan* has become a renovated church. Who needs a *church*? Not the Cosmopolitan Girl. She needs Helen Gurley Brown. Who will tell her *everything*. Listen . . .

Are you, sir, a breast fetishist? I mean, *madam,* is your *lover* a breast fetishist? Don't despair. Don't go away. Hear what *Jill* did. *Cosmo* reveals that on her wedding night she *"came to bed with a big dollop of Hershey's milk-chocolate syrup tipping each breast. Honest! Stan is still a fetishist. But his fetish is his wife. And they keep a can of Hershey's by the bed. Does that hurt anyone?"*

And you can get *Cosmo* at the newsstand for only seventy-five cents, the same newsstands where they sell Hershey's.

Mind you, the new *Cosmo*— the other great publishing success of the decade along with *Playboy* (the greatest coincidence since *Love* begot *Screw*)— is not without a sense of morality, provided you lean hard on the metaphorical uses of the word. For one thing, there is the high-up management that keeps an eye on it. It is a Hearst Magazine. One time, Helen Gurley Brown asked the girls at the office to recount in unsigned memos whether their men had any extraordinary uses for their (sorry to go back to them again, but although Raquel Welch has discovered that the Mind is an erogenous zone, HGB has not)— breasts. One girl (HGB called her a "bitch," which is the opposite of a Cosmopolitan Girl) sent a copy of the memo anonymously to *Women's Wear Daily*, which printed it, and right away there was a commotion upstairs, because you see not all the Hearst Management are Cosmopolitan Girls. "I tread a very careful path with Hearst Management and I don't want to get them exercised about anything. If I just very quietly develop these articles and show them the finished product, it's *much better*. Furthermore, we have trouble with supermarkets in the South and I didn't want them stirred up ahead of time." Ahead of time means before the article itself is printed. Because the articles, well, they say things in a way which, if you then object to them, you are against Candor and Love. And you are, simply, *against* cupcakeability. Understand that that is the purpose of the New *Cosmopolitan*— to instruct its girl readers in a single Commandment in which the previous Ten are subsumed. As HGB put it, *"You've got to make yourself more cupcakeable all the time so that you're a better cupcake to be gobbled up,"* and not all Southern supermarkets are ready, because they are Behind the Times.

Mrs. Brown is quite aware that some people believe there are things people *should* do and things people *shouldn't* do. She just wants to *help* you if it happens that you *want* to do the things you *shouldn't* do. Mrs. Brown is always helping people out, for instance her friend Joyce, who was looking for a title for her new book on adultery. "The trouble with your friend," said Joyce

about one of Helen's friends, "is she's acting like a *child.*" Helen
shot back: "And, of course, adultery is for *adults.* The book was
born!" writes HGB. *Adultery Is for Adults.*

Mrs. Brown took that as a lesson for the day, and went on, "I
personally think a lot of people would like adultery for *themselves*
(feel they could handle it with maturity, eclat, elan, and so on),
but it's their *mate* they don't want messing around. Well," she
says— and you know, I think there's a trace of a wink there, don't
you?— "Well, nobody around here is *for* adultery, but you ought
to know how to cope in case it hits one near and dear, yes?" Indeed. *"See page 178."*

There are those who believe that what it all adds up to is
promiscuity. They will be surprised. The author of "How Sexually
Generous Should a Girl Be?" can sound like Cotton Mather. She
calls for a *frein vital.* As the author says, "While you're wondering
things, do you ever wonder whether you've worked out the right
sexual code for yourself? We [*vide* Aristophanes] have the 'vote,'
so to speak . . . but now we often say yes, yes, yes— not because
we're 'free,' but for reasons that have little to do with sexual
enjoyment. It's a dreary slavery of habit. It's not giving, but a
colossal waste of a girl's resources. Better *one* good satisfying
orgasm and all that."

You do understand? It's your duty, madam, not to go to bed
with anybody, unless you *want* to. Who says the Cosmopolitan
Girl is without a sense of restraint?

Of course, things *can* go wrong. For instance, there was the girl
who was raped. She, naturally, wrote an article, called, "I Was
Raped." The reader's sympathy quickens as she recounts the
experience and the skepticism with which her story was treated by
the police and later at the clinic. But then the sun begins to shine,
as you realize that the Cosmopolitan Girl is never really taken
altogether by surprise. In the midst of her despair, she recalls,
"Thank God, I was taking birth-control pills!"

It has been observed that the Cosmopolitan Girl has many
problems, while the Playboy has absolutely none. Well, that may
be, but it is certainly on account of the pains the Cosmopolitan
Girl is instructed to take in order to please. Simple things. "How
Not to Get Dumped on His Way Up" tells the wife how not to get
dumped on his way up, for instance Point Six, "Love may be
blind, but it's not deaf. Have you ever listened to yourself screech

lately? Borrow a tape recorder and *hear* how you sound. Voices can be changed. . . ." ("How Do You Sound?" *Cosmo*, April.)

And not-so-usual things. "What Turns Men On— Humming . . . What Turns Men Off— and Running. Thirty-Eight Men Tell Their Secret Pleasures." One man's secret pleasure came on discovering "the word 'love' [tattooed]on her behind, surrounded by flowers. She wouldn't tell me how she got it and I didn't care." (The *questions* some people ask!) Now whatever a Cosmopolitan Girl puts on her *behind*, she must *never* fail to keep her false eyelashes on her *eyes* ("Why I Wear My False Eyelashes to Bed"). Granted, there are problems. The Shower. But for every problem there is a solution. "Toy with the shower dial so that it is fixed at its weakest pressure and only a pathetic drizzle results. When it's turned on, tilt your head so that the spray catches you only from the neck down. If all else fails and your shower companion is scrubbing you with his pumice stone" (pumice stone? This shower companion apparently *didn't* like it on her behind) "hurl soapsuds in his eyes. This way, if your makeup has worn off, he won't be able to see how you look!"

So, life can be very complicated, to be sure, but though there are silver linings, silver linings themselves beget complications. For instance, the Q and A on The Pill. "Do drugs or alcohol interfere with the working of the Pill?" Think think think, what if the answer should turn out to be *Yes!* . . . But *of course* not . . . "*No* drugs have been found to have this effect." Sigh of relief— but then ZAP!— "although an obvious risk from taking a lot of alcohol is that it might prevent you from remembering to take the tablets." *Remember to take your pill with your orange juice.*

And so it goes, issue after issue. "What's in *Cosmo this* month?" HGB can hardly wait to tell you. "Oh, you know . . . making it . . . making good . . . making love . . . loving men . . . loving yourself . . . a great mystery novel, short stories . . . the usual birthday package. I hope you like *all* of it." If you like to learn, you'll certainly never stop learning from *Cosmo*. For instance, about the group-therapy-through-nudity prophet just sixty miles from Los Angeles. Twenty-four patients including the author assemble at this particular twenty-four-hour session, half girls, half men, no sexual highjinks, that was made quite clear at the outset, but then they all went right to work, and by midnight were all stripped down and cozy. By the next day they were *wonderfully* familiar with each other. "Childhood traumas were explored, some of them acted out. Barbara expressed long-buried hatred of her father by beating on a sofa cushion until, exhausted and drained, she said calmly, 'I think it's finally, completely, gone.' " That doesn't mean that if you have a hang-up you should automatically stop wearing clothes, an idea that would hardly appeal to *Cosmo*'s advertisers. The author, who cherishes her experience, nevertheless explains, "I'm still more comfortable with the window dressing in place, but no longer apprehensive should it happen to slip a bit. My makeup is more subtle, softer, and I smile more easily, even at strangers— and they smile back."

Nudity can be so *wonderful*. So can the life of ("I Was a Nude Model") a nude model. The author was writing a novel, and of course had to work to support herself, and chose modeling. The only trouble came when her mother heard about it, because her mother's "friends" were *always* sending Mother pictures of her nude daughter snipped out of magazines. "I got another imperative note from Mother: 'You must stop that filthy nude modeling.' The Puritan ice may be melting in most Americans' veins, but not in Mother's. I could understand, but I couldn't do what she wanted." Mother apparently thought that Alice would lead an abnormal life under the circumstances. *Imagine!* "How did the modeling affect my love life? It didn't. During that period I went with a philosophy professor, a press aide to a governor, a mathematician, a psychologist, a Mexican architect, a Spanish doctor, and a young English banker. *They* weren't put off by my profession." They gobbled her up, just like they'll gobble *you* up, if you will just remember to do what Helen Gurley Brown tells you.

Antarctic Summer

McMurdo Station, Antarctica—January 22, 1972

I am not very good at science, and will not pretend to know what I am talking about. But that should not prevent me from calling to your attention the Antarctic, where fascinating things are happening under the aegis of a little-known treaty among a dozen nations which, incredibly, was also signed by the Soviet Union. I say incredibly, because the treaty calls on signatory powers not only to adjourn without prejudice any territorial claims in Antarctica, but to publish all scientific information developed in Antarctica, and to permit representatives of other nations to visit each other's scientific installations and to probe into the work being done.

This means, if you can imagine it, that an American scientist can actually take residence in a Soviet installation, and rummage about, looking through Soviet telescopes, or whatever it is scientists do, taking notes, feeding computers, and exchanging scientific shoptalk.

What kind of talk? The lineaments of the situation are as follows. Antarctica is about the size of the United States and Mexico. Its coastline is 18,000 miles long. During the winter, the ice doubles the size of the continent. The ice at the South Pole is about two miles thick. If the continent were to melt, it would raise the water level of the world by 200 feet, which means that the first twenty-eight stories of the Empire State Building would be, well, useless. The ice in Antarctica is a deposit of 90 percent of the fresh water supply of the earth.

Now hear this. Ocean water absorbs 90 percent of the sun's heat. Snow and ice reflect 85 percent. One can see— even I can see— that Antarctica is the principal generator, potentially, of the kind of energy that governs the metabolism of the earth. Its effect even as things are— on weather, currents, and temperature— is critical. Its potential uses, if we come to know how to domesticate Antarctica, is something very like the uses of a key to the universe. There is everything there, potentially. The control of the weather. The answer to the fresh water problem. A vat of energy greater than the known supply of the world's oil.

That is why we are spending $30 million a year in Antarctica, a modest sum of money, niggardly, in fact; but enough to secure a foothold in the developing scientific melodrama. The Russians, needless to say, are all over the place. Our own venture there is the business of the National Science Foundation. If you have an idea you want to flex in the Antarctic, you write to the National Science Foundation. If they think it has merit, they put up the money to get you out there, equip you with the instruments you need, and give you the help you need. You may be interested in meteorology, in biology, in paleontology, in astronomy, in oceanography, you name it.

I discovered that there are people in Antarctica who are engaged in magneto hydrodynamics. I begged an eloquent scientist to please explain to me what is magneto hydrodynamics, and he talked nonstop for ten minutes, but he might as well have been speaking in Russian. Even so, from the rapture he felt, I can report confidently that there is a magneto hydrodynamic in your future.

It comes down to 210 scientists, engaged in 65 projects, sponsored by 35 American colleges and institutions. All this is made possible by the United States Navy and Coast Guard charged by Congress and the President with making possible the scientific enterprises envisioned by the treaty, and launched formally during the International Geophysical Year in 1957. The Navy and Coast Guard break the ice, bring in the ships, supply the bases, fly in the scientists, drop the provisions, furnish the power, deliver the mail, oil the wheels of the entire enterprise. Because Antarctica is so remote, it requires ten dollars of logistics to sustain a dollar of research.

During the short summer, from November to February, the Navy has 1,300 men engaged in what they call Operation Deep Freeze. During that period there is no night in Antarctica. But then the dark comes, the terrible, endless night, and 300 Americans endure it, in total isolation— no ships, no airplanes, no intercourse with the outside world. We have a half-dozen stations, one of them squatting right on the South Pole, where the average temperature is 57 below, and two dozen men are there, funneling information taken from the ionosphere above, and from the ocean floor below, into the great memory bank of mankind. The idea is to outwit a universe which is essentially unfriendly, given to afflicting us with heat, cold, flood, and drought. Antarctica is America's great current scientific frontier.

As the crow flies, we are ten thousand miles from New York, 2,300 miles south of Christchurch, New Zealand. We are, as they say in these parts, "on the ice," and because it is summertime and the ice on the landing field is suspiciously soft, we came not by jet, but on "the Herc," as we call the C-130 Lockheed turbo-prop, which is the Navy's workhorse in this part of the world.

McMurdo is Antarctica's New York. It has a church, a nuclear energy plant, and lots of storage tanks, one of which holds 2 million gallons of fuel. The summer population is about 1,000, nine-tenths naval personnel, the balance scientists. It is from this area that the great exploratory expeditions to the South Pole were launched in the early years of the century. Shackleton, an Englishman, seeking to traverse the continent, turned back, found his ship beset by ice, struggled through blizzards and scurvy to a point which proved to be deserted, set out in an open boat in the fiercest seas in the world on an 800-mile voyage to a whaling center, landed on the wrong side of an island, scaled a mountain to get across to safety, and sailed happily home. There'll always be an England.

Scott made one exploration and went back for more, finally reaching the Pole— only to find there a taunting note of welcome from the Norwegian Amundsen, who, having arrived thirty-six days earlier and made history by being the first man to reach the Pole, left a cocky note for Scott, who read it despondently, trekked back the 800 miles toward McMurdo, but perished from cold and fatigue 11 miles short of safety.

Now you can get to the South Pole not in the fifty-six days it took Roald Amundsen to get there, but in three hours, by naval airplane, landing on skis. Not that the trip is without peril. I was wounded there. And I intend to consult Lloyd's of London about a policy to guard against a recurrence of what happened.

There I was, smack at the South Pole, and two gentlemen of the Navy suggested that if I stood on my head, they would snap a photograph of me which, turned upside down, would represent me, atlas-like, bearing the weight of the world on my shoulders. That being what I habitually do anyway, I readily consented, and the Navy, which is after all officially in charge of logistics, pulled up my ankles skyward, while I braced the earth.

At that precise moment, the junior Senator from New York, standing 20 yards off, decided to set off a firecracker designed to propel skyward an American flag which would then billow down to earth by parachute: a most patriotic sentiment, when at the South Pole— typical of the junior Senator from New York. However, for some reason— perhaps because the temperature was 35 below zero— instead of the flag shooting up, the cork shot out from the bottom of the firecracker. And instead of shooting down towards the earth, for some reason— perhaps because at that point, everywhere you go is south— the cork hit me smack on the nose, causing me suddenly to collapse my burden, gravely upsetting the Richter scale the world over.

In Antarctica you can't sue anybody, because of the anomalous civil situation: there is no civil authority, no laws. Indeed, it is the ideal place for a civilian to murder another civilian, which I suspect was the purpose of the junior Senator, the American flag and parachute being nothing but window dressing.

We were assigned custody of the geographic South Pole, under the dispensations of the International Geophysical Year, and the Russians got the geomagnetic pole, over which they preside at Vostok, two and a half air hours inland from McMurdo. I could not imagine what interest the Russians had in the Antarctic, supposing that they went there in order to study ways to make Siberia colder. But they too are interested in pure scientific research, and the twenty-three Russians who greeted us in their ice ghetto did so with great warmth, crabmeat, caviar, and vodka.

A young American scientist had been interned with them for thirteen months, and such tensions as arose were the result not of ideological, racial, or cultural differences, but of the utter isolation of igloo life. The cliché is to be treated with suspicion, but it remains true that there is a natural community of scientific interest, and that the last thing it occurs to a Russian scientist to dwell upon, in the relative security of the Antarctic, is the inspirational leadership of Marx, Engels, and Lenin.

At the American polar station, the public rooms are an endless collage of quite naked ladies. In the Russian station, the ladies share the walls with color pictures of— American sports cars. That, one takes it, is what they dream about in the Arctic wastes. Beautiful women, and beautiful cars.

The Secretary of the Navy presented the commander of the Soviet station with a dart board, on which to dissipate any latent hostilities. And a Soviet technician embraced me, tiptoed me away to the laboratory, and gave me an ice core, ten pounds heavy, taken from 1,800 feet below the surface: ice formed from water 25,000 years ago. I was told to disguise my gift, and so I hugged it to my bosom under my Arctic jacket, and, back at McMurdo, I have melted it, and poured the contents into twenty little bottles, feeling, for all the world, like Louis Pasteur.

I wish I might have returned the favor of my Soviet friend. But the only disposable thing in my possession that day was a novel by

Alexander Solzhenitsyn, and I would not have wanted to break the peace of the Antarctic by giving it to him.

Cancel My Subscription

December 2, 1971

I have a letter from an irate lady informing me that she declined ostentatiously on a recent occasion to purchase a copy of one of my books "because I don't want to have a hand in making you rich." It isn't so often that one receives letters announcing the writers' intentions not to buy one's book in order, if only prospectively, to impose economic punishment. But of course all publishers are used to receiving notices of cancellation, whether of magazines or of newspapers, and the superstition afflicts almost every able-bodied American that these cancellations are economically critical. It is for that reason that the subscriber addresses his/her cancellation, typically, to "Mr. Henry Luce, PERSONAL, Time-Life Building . . ." Or to Mr. Arthur Sulzberger, New York *Times*. Even as one writes directly to the President of the United States instructing him in his peccadilloes, copy of said letter usually going to friends, and relatives.

On the whole, I approve of the gesture. It is, really, the only way of expressing oneself in vexed situations. Sometimes it imposes considerable burdens on the vexee. I have in mind one gentleman who regularly cancels his subscription to the magazine I edit, but who cannot apparently live without it, so that he is driven to re-subscribing under an assumed name, causing innumerable complications for the circulation department.

While approving the gesture, I think it odd how little knowledge there is of the economics of the publishing business, and thought today to tell the little I know, so that readers may gauge more accurately what is their economic leverage.

Consider the book writer. It is commonly thought that authors of books make a great deal of money. The answer is: some writers of books make a great deal of money. Most do not.

If you are an experienced book writer, you can wrest from your publisher a royalty of 15 percent of the retail sale price of your book. That means that for every book that sells at, say, $6, the author earns 90 cents. A typical sale is 10,000 copies. From which the (experienced) author would earn $9,000.

The particular book my correspondent informed me she did not intend to buy happens to be out on the newsstands in paperback. It sells for 95 cents (call it a dollar). Now the paperback book is licensed to a paperback house by the publisher of the hard-cover edition. That ravenous gentleman gets to keep one-half of the royalty paid by the paperback house, remitting the other half, grudgingly, to the author. The typical royalty for the paperback is 8 percent. Thus it is readily seen that for every paperback sale of the book in question, the author makes four cents. He needs to sell 100,000 copies in order to make $4,000. Very few paperbacks sell 100,000 copies.

Since the publishers want to keep the royalty schedule as low as possible, they have devised a very neat trick for bidding for the high-selling authors, like the sex-book writers, and here and there a very popular historian like William Shirer, or the fascinating chronicler of a Mafia family, Mr. Gay Talese. What they do is to offer a guarantee wildly in excess of anything the author could hope to realize from actual sales. In the case of Mr. Shirer's book about Nazi Germany, the guarantee was reputedly $450,000, and so is it, in that neighborhood, for Mr. Talese. That means, assuming a dollar book, that an author would have to sell 10 million copies before he earned back his guarantee.

Not even *Love Story* sells 10 million copies. But the paperback houses are in effect saying: Our own profit rises so steeply when we can sell several million copies of a book, we are willing to share those profits with the author, but we must couch the deal in such a way as not to undermine the normal contract between publisher and author. It is sad to think that the lady who wrote to deprive me of four cents, had to pay twice that to send me the letter.

In the magazine business, the penalty for a lost subscription is much higher. If the magazine sells for $10, it is reasonable to assume that, say, $5 is profit— on a renewal. (Usually, on subscriptions that come in from circulation promotions, there isn't any profit at all.) Five dollars is a lot more than four cents, but, alas, the imposition of a $5 fine is generally not enough to attract the personal attention of the publisher, and it is reputed that the computer has no feelings. Still, it is a robust habit, like refusing a candidate your vote, and I am all for it.

Hair (Kids')

June 30, 1970

Some months ago a conservative journal published a plea by a young man to those of his elders, which is to say the great majority of them, who engage in hostilities against everyone who wears long hair. His point is he was in the Youth for Goldwater movement in 1964, and will gladly join the Senior Citizens for Goldwater, Jr., movement in 1984: but meanwhile, wouldn't we please allow him to wear his hair long, without visually frisking him every time he comes into a restaurant on the assumption that he is concealing a Molotov cocktail?

And then I have a letter from the formidable critic Hugh Kenner, who raises the point apropos a discussion of the serious students who have survived the general dislocations. Listen as he describes a "College of Creative Studies" at the University of California in Santa Barbara . . .

"Its gimmick is simply to select extra-bright freshmen, the sort who win nationwide essay contests at 16, or work their way through calculus text books on the side, while enrolled in high school algebra, and give them individual tailormade programs, free of requirements. They can take graduate courses while freshmen if they want to. One boy, a junior, took a graduate course of mine last year and wrote a publishable paper which is a genuine contribution to knowledge. Now. These young folk tend to blue jeans and long hair. They tend to freewheel. I could designate four or five the sight of whom would bring down every portcullis in Pasadena, or bring R. R. leaping from the executive chair, forefinger quivering. And throughout all disturbances, the CCS students go about their business, which they find more interesting than revolutionizing can hope to be."

And third, I have just finished reading a long article called "Why Hair Has Become a Four-Letter Word." It is a very scholarly piece, by one Warner Brown, which is, however, sexed-up for the benefit of the magazine in which it is published, and it comes to absolutist sexual conclusions of the kind that delight Freudian fundamentalists.

The essay is rich in historical interest, pointing out that the long hair-short hair argument is not centuries old as we have supposed, but millennia-old. It is here that, incredibly, I first came across St. Paul on the subject, who wrote: "Does not nature itself teach you that if a man have long hair it is a shame unto him? But if a woman have long hair it is a glory to her?" And, also, a quotation from 1881 by a Mrs. Jane G. Austin, published in the *Popular Monthly*: "Among the minor mysteries of human nature may be ranked the feeling, deeper than custom or fashion, in favor of long hair upon a woman's head, short upon that of a man. True, caprice occasionally dictates the reverse, but these caprices generally indicate an unnatural and unhealthy state of mind in people or individuals who exhibit them."

It was generally thought by the authorities over the years that men with beards are men to be feared, and it is interesting that Fidel Castro, who did more than anybody in the modern age to identify long hair and radicalism, came quietly to, really, the same conclusion when in 1968 he banned long hair at Havana University. After all, revolution in Cuba is now, by definition, anti-Castroist. *None of that.* In other words, Castro joins the American skinheads, as we are derogatorily referred to, in accepting long hair as the symbol of iconoclasm.

My own tendency in these matters is permissive. I have always been attracted, at least in the abstract, to Chesterton's notion that we should each of us be free to be our own "potty little selves." And yet, and yet: I wonder why it is that a spirit of something halfway between disgust and anger wells up within me at true excessiveness, particularly among teenagers. I think I know the reason, and it has nothing to do with sex or revolution. It has to do with exhibitionism.

Murray Kempton once remarked that he could not understand, nor sympathize with, young people who get their kicks by uttering obscenities within earshot of old ladies. Long hair is not intrinsically evil— neither, incidentally, is an obscenity. Both, however, are shocking, to be sure one less so than the other. And cause dismay, disappointment, hurt. How account for it?

St. Thomas says that: "There is in man a certain inclination to the good, corresponding to his rational nature; and this inclination is proper to man alone. So, man has a natural inclination to know the truth about God, and to live in society. In this respect, there come under the natural law all actions connected with such inclinations: namely, that a man should avoid ignorance, that he must not give offence to others with whom he must associate, and all actions of a like nature." As usual, St. Thomas has something like the answer.

Beethoven's 200th

November 3, 1970

This being Election Day, it occurs to me that it is the 200th anniversary of the birth of Ludwig van Beethoven. And that I have not paid my tribute, which is all right because the line is very long, and anyway my flowers are pretty inconspicuous alongside those of the stellar figures of the musical world.

But I am provoked by my old friend William F. Rickenbacker (yes, son of Eddie), writer, sportsman, stock analyst, linguist, musician: and, first and foremost, provocateur. Mr. Rickenbacker has written in *National Review* to acknowledge that much of Beethoven's later music is "impossible to overrate," but that most of the early stuff is merely "manipulative bangbang." The appreciation of any particular piece of music is of course a subjective matter, as everyone knows, especially Mr. Rickenbacker, though he attempts what sounds like an objective demonstration. Beethoven, he says, is easy to imitate. "Mrs. Brown, the English mystic who claims to receive music dictated directly from dead masters, has 'introduced' some music she says Liszt gave her, but it doesn't sound like Liszt; the things she says Schubert gave her don't sound like Schubert; her Beethoven sounds exactly like Beethoven in his early, *i.e.*, awful, period." Now all that that story suggests to me is that Beethoven is cooperating with Mrs. Brown while Liszt and Schubert are not.

So what does Mr. Rickenbacker propose? A "Beethoven Suppression Society whose purpose will be to stamp out all the master's works up through Opus 52." ("And all the goddamn operas.") (He means *Fidelio*.) Mr. Rickenbacker, wise beyond his years in extra-musical matters, ends his article, "I will not answer any letters from anyone on this subject, unless it be the editor's letter accompanying the check." Well, I have sent the check. This is my letter.

By the time Beethoven came around to Opus 52 (eight songs), he was thirty-two years old. He had composed two of his symphonies, three of his piano concertos— indeed, over one-third of his entire production. Never mind the symphonies, or concertos, but concentrate for a minute on what Mr. Rickenbacker would have us exclude from among the piano sonatas.

There are 32 of them, and he would ban the first 20, right up to the Waldstein. Interestingly enough, he does not ban the "Appassionata," while passing along about it (and exaggerating) the recent slurs of Glenn Gould. Consider the carnage. Name one or two of the better known sonatas. Take the most famous of them all, the "Moonlight Sonata."

Now what is the matter with the "Moonlight Sonata" is that people play it who shouldn't play it, because the first movement is technically easy. I had a teacher who solved in one stroke The Problem of the "Moonlight Sonata": she would not permit any of her students to take on the first movement who had not developed the skill to perform the third movement. That kept all but the top 5 percent from playing that sonata and by the time you get so you can play the last movement, you probably have enough sophistication to play the first without ruining it.

Now, you cannot keep music students from permanently ruining the reputation of, say, the "Minuet in G": though when played by, say, Myra Hess, one is reminded of the simple beauty of it, like one of the pastoral couplets of Wordsworth. The third movement of the "Moonlight" is a little junky, so what: it is perfectly agreeable, and in any case it is a foundation for some of the exploits so perfectly consummated in the later sonatas.

The very first sonata, in F minor, is wonderfully pleasant: really, what a bore it is to say that having tasted the great vintages, you can never enjoy table wine. Can Mr. Rickenbacker seriously maintain that the adagio movement of the C major (#3) sonata is less than sublime? The "Pathétique Sonata" is grand and exciting, though to be sure one can skip the last movement, even though music boxes are also worth listening to every now and then.

I tell you what. Here is my propitiation to Beethoven. There is a splendid artist whose name is Alfred Brendel, a Viennese who teaches in Mexico and performs everywhere. He has recorded all of Beethoven's piano music, stereo, for Vox. And a wonderfully enterprising company, The Dollar Record Plan, Inc. of P.O. Box 86, Pearl River, N.Y. 10965, has brought out these records at the astonishing price of one dollar ($1) apiece. You can buy *all* the sonatas for $12. If you have caught the Rickenbacker virus, you can buy all the later sonatas (volumes 2 and 3) for $6.

Now, my offer is this: Buy the lot. If you don't like the first half, send them to me and I'll reimburse your $6, and transship the records to a hospital, as the anonymous gift of someone who turned deaf. And when next I ask Bill Rickenbacker to write for *National Review*, I shall ask him please to refrain from using the early letters of the alphabet.

The Oxford English Dictionary

December 19, 1971

The Compact Edition of the Oxford English Dictionary. Complete Text Reproduced Micrographically. 4,116 pp. New York: Oxford University Press. Two Vols., boxed. $75.

The *Oxford English Dictionary* was the moon-landing project of the English people, and if Sidney Webb, who was born the year the project was conceived and reached seventy the year it was completed, did not denounce it as a dreadful extravagance in an age when poverty was abundant in the groaning industrial areas of England, it can only have been because he forgot to do so. The

enterprise resulted—to use the words of its publishers in connection with the new edition—in "the most prestigious book ever
published," even as the moon-landing is almost indisputably the
most prestigious scientific enterprise ever consummated. Of
course, scientific achievement, like an athletic one, is obsolescent
in a sense quite different from a cultural achievement. The man
who ran the four-minute mile knew that he was not being given
tenure as a world-record-holder. The men who contributed to the
O.E.D. achieved a more certain satisfaction. Not exactly like the
individual artist, who defies "improvement" in any measurable
sense. But halfway there; far enough to raise the question, on
which I shall touch in due course: Why isn't the *O.E.D.* a *continuing* masterpiece?

It could only have been a sense of historical excitement that
kept successive lexicographers working over a period of seventy
years to achieve this dictionary, that kept at least one compositor
busy during the whole of his working life setting type for this
dictionary which was printed in sections that sold for 12 shillings
and sixpence each, beginning twenty-five years after the project
was conceived, on into 1928. Each of the 12 volumes required
anywhere from three to ten years to complete, depending on such
variables as whether an editor (at the peak there were three
working simultaneously) died, or whether England was fighting a
particularly engrossing war, or whatever.

There were moments of doubt and even of panic, as when the
whole of it was offered to Cambridge University, which sniffed it
away, even as Yale disdained Mr. Harkness's colleges only to
discover that Harvard instantly and greedily accepted them. But
eventually the thing was done, and a set of the volumes was
presented one each to the chiefs of state of the great English-
speaking powers, King George V and President Calvin Coolidge,
that they should know better their common philological
patrimony.

Incidentally, there were American scholars involved in the
project, and generous acknowledgment is made of their contributions. Indeed, the principal editor, Dr. James Murray, ad-
journed the meiotic tradition of his countrymen to say, as early as
1880, that he had discovered in Americans "an ideal love for the
English language as a glorious heritage and a pride in being
intimate with its grand memories, such as . . . is rare indeed in
Englishmen toward their own tongue; and from this I draw the

most certain inferences as to the lead which Americans must at no distant date take in English scholarship." Dr. Murray was, of course, correct: The study of linguistics is all but a protected American industry.

And it was the idea of an American, Mr. Albert Boni, head of the Readex Microprint Corporation, to take the entire *O.E.D.* and bring it out in two volumes. This involved shrinking 13 volumes, not 12. The editors brought out the supplemental volume in 1928 to deal with words that had come into being too late to be included in the previous volumes— it was too expensive to collate the new words typographically. And, as lagniappe, they threw in a list of "spurious words" the scholars had come upon in dictionaries dead and extant, which imposters had got into them as the result of typographical or other errors (sample: "*Depectible, a.* Error in Johnson's Dict. and some later Dicts. for *Depertible*") and finally, the Supplement gives the long list of books cited in the great dictionary.

The principal motive for bringing out the new edition is of course to reduce the cost of the dictionary to the reader. The original costs $300, so that the current edition of two volumes is if not quite two-thirteenths of the price of the entire set, a large step (at $75) in that direction. Most human eyes will need a little help, and that is tactfully furnished— a magnifying glass mounted on a wooden rectangle a few inches by a few inches, along the base of which lies a groove whose purpose is nowhere explained. If it is intended somehow to permit the reader to manipulate the glass, as a periscope, by remote control, I must report that the motor, or drive shaft, or whatever, was missing from my set. No matter, there are other and better magnifying glasses on the market, and very strong eyeglasses will do.

The economy apart, there is the advantage of space saved, and the general feeling of accessibility that comes from dealing with two instead of 13 volumes. I am surprised that the publishers neglected to provide a lettered thumb index, but I installed my own without much trouble. The books are well bound and the pages fall open easily, without crowding— four of the original appearing in each page of the miniaturized volumes, which total 4,116 pages. I cannot imagine that anyone who has the money will put off the purchase of a set; or that anyone who hasn't the money will put off borrowing to buy the set. That is the way I feel about it, and if you are a doubter, stay with me for just a moment.

The dictionary is best described by its own editors. They explain, for instance, that they did not include words that had become obsolete by 1150 A.D., giving the reasons why. Beyond that, ". . . it is the aim of the Dictionary to deal with all the common words of speech and literature, and with all words which approach these in character; the limits being extended farther in the domain of science and philosophy, which naturally passes into that of literature than in that of slang or cant, which touches the colloquial. In scientific and technical terminology, the aim has been to include *all words English in form* . . . except those of which an explanation would be unintelligible to any but the specialist; and such words, not English in form, as either are in general use, like *Hippopotamus, Geranium, Aluminium, Focus, Stratum, Bronchitis*, or belong to the more familiar language of science, as *Mammalia, Lepidoptera, Invertebrata.*"

The thought given to the arrangement of the words bore exotic fruit, beyond anything for which mere catalogues are useful. The richness of the work is suggested in the passage that gives the thinking of the editors on how to deal with *Combinations:*

"Under this term are included all collocations of simple words in which the separate spelling of each word is retained, whether they are formally connected by the hyphen, or virtually by the unity of their signification. The formal union and the actual by no means coincide; not only is the use of the hyphen a matter of indifference in an immense number of cases, but in many where it is habitually used, the combination implies no unity of signification; while others, in which there is a distinct unity or specialization of meaning, are not hyphened. The primary use of the hyphen is *grammatical:* it implies either that the syntactic relation between two words is closer than if they stood side by side without it, or that the relation is a *less usual* one than that which would at first sight suggest itself to us, if we saw the two words standing unconnected. Thus, in the three sentences, '*After consideration* had been given to the proposal, it was duly accepted,' '*After consideration* the proposal was accepted,' '*After-consideration* had shown him his mistake,' we have *first* no immediate syntactic relation between *after* (conjunctive adverb) and *consideration; secondly,* the relation of preposition and object; *thirdly,* the relation of attribute and substantive, closer than the first, less usual than the second, (since *after* is more commonly a preposition than an adjective). But *after-consideration* is not really a single word, any more than *subsequent consideration, fuller consideration;* the hyphen being merely a convenient help to the sense, which would be clearly expressed in speech by the different phrase-accentuation of *a'fter considera"tion* and *a"fter considera'tion.* And as this 'help to the sense' is not always equally necessary, nor its need equally appreciated in the same place, it is impossible that its use should be uniform. Nevertheless *after-consideration,* as used above, is on the way to become a single word, which *reconsideration* (chiefly because *re-* is not a separate word, but also because we have *reconsider*) is reckoned to be; and indeed *close grammatical relation* constantly accompanies close union of sense, so that in many combinations the hyphen becomes an expression of this unification of sense. When this unification and specialization has [?]* proceeded so far that we no longer analyze the combination into its elements, but take it in as a whole, as in *blackberry, postman, newspaper,* pronouncing it in speech with a single accent, the hyphen is usually omitted, and the fully developed compound is written as a single word."

Is that not beautiful? One can read it again and again, once for the analysis, again as philosophy, twice more for the music; and there isn't an entry in the dictionary that does not present itself as manifestly the object of the lovingcare (note, no hyphen) these grave, and lively, and penetrating craftsmen gave us; and, no doubt, when the volumes were received by the critics, and for years after, workmen sat as nervously as Mission Control in Houston, lest error be found, or the tiniest miscalibration, such as might propel a future statesman towards war instead of peace. As far as I know, their principal humiliation lay in having omitted the word APPENDIX, which had to wait to debut in the Supplementary Volume. It is rumored that, buried deep in the dictionary, is a SPURIOUS WORD of the editors' super-secret devising, so that their grandchildren might know the contemporary estate of plagiarism. If it is true, the identity of the word is a well-kept secret.

The limitations of the *O.E.D.* are I should think unavoidable. There are a great many words one needs to know about which simply aren't there, so that one always has to have another dictionary—a more contemporary dictionary—at hand. And then, here and there one comes across anti-metaphorical rigidity.

**Or, as Dwight Macdonald would say,* [?!]

For instance, ENTROPY is not permitted, in the *O.E.D.*, to stray out of its thermodynamic cage, so that one gets no hint of Webster's 4th meaning, "The ultimate state reached in the degradation of the matter and energy of the universe. . . ."

The Compact Edition, now that it is done, strikes one as so obviously a useful idea, one cannot imagine why it wasn't done before. So, now, a proposal for the next edition. Probably two stout volumes of supplementary words could now be listed, if the successors to the editors who laid down their burden in 1928 were to address themselves to the word explosion of the succeeding four decades. No doubt the enterprise hasn't been revived because the economic cost of typographical collation is discouraging. But—but—now we have the computer print-out! Why not an edition of the *O.E.D.*, made current say every ten years, in which the new words are fed alphabetically into place on the mastertape. The user would buy the tape, which would come in a unit that would look like a portable typewriter, a small screen perched on top of the carriage. Whereupon—you guessed it—you would need merely to type out the word you wished to explore, and there you'd have it, illuminated on the screen. The *O.E.D.* as a continuing masterpiece. The *O.E.D.* needs updating even as the Census does, and the *Encyclopaedia Britannica*, and the ingenuity of the publishers in bringing out the current *Compact Edition* ought not to be terminal (lest we reach ENTROPY). But even now, there is no literary excitement quite like the ownership of these volumes, the experiencing of which is like having been out there in the early morning at Cape Kennedy, and seeing the missile stagger up, knowing that it will travel all the way to the moon.

Swiss Sojourn

Rougemont, Switzerland—March 24, 1970

I have always thought that Switzerland is the way station to Paradise. I have been coming here for almost forty years. The first few winters, at age five or six, I would amuse myself by asking any old Swiss, any old time, "Excuse me, but could you please tell me the name of the President of Switzerland?" The record, thus far, is 100 percent: nobody has known the name of the President of Switzerland. Inevitably there is a nervous silence, and then a whisper to the neighboring partner, which whisper goes down the length of the room, the last man tiptoeing out to the telephone, or to an almanac, and eventually the name of the President is triumphantly divulged.

The reason nobody knows the name of the President of Switzerland is because it doesn't much matter who is the President of Switzerland. Switzerland is so well governed, the responsibilities are so diffused, the national sense of purpose is so explicit, that there simply isn't very much left over for the President to do, except to get very angry when a terrorist blows up one of his airplanes.

The other day, by mistake, a clerk in a little post office dropped a carton that contained emergency military summonses to duty for the male population of that town, everyone between the ages of twenty and fifty. The next morning the postman routinely stuck the summonses in the boxes, and by that afternoon all the men of the town had simply gone off— reporting for duty at the cantonal capital. All except two or three, who not having had news of any national emergency, thought to telephone to the capital to verify their summons. They were of course told that there was no summons, that it must have been a clerical mistake. Now the interesting thing is that all the newspapers criticized not the gullible majority who had gone automatically off to duty, but the inquisitive minority. Switzerland expects that every man will do his duty unquestioningly, even if it is a clerical mistake.

That is true efficiency. Speaking of which, the Swiss Post Office is easily the most efficient in the world, the mail traveling faster between any part of Switzerland and the United States, than between Chicago and New York— even in non-strike conditions. To be sure, it needs to be efficient, if only to understand its own postage rates. If you desire to airmail a letter abroad, you must know, just to begin with, whether you are in category One or in category Ten, Twenty, Twenty-Five, Thirty, Forty, Fifty, or Seventy. Now reflect on the progression of those numbers. Crazy, isn't it? Why shouldn't the Twenty-Five be eliminated, and a Sixty inserted?

The United States is in category Twenty-Five, and it costs .75

centimes to airmail a letter that weighs up to 5 grams. Up to 10 grams, one franc. Up to 15 grams, 1.25 francs. Up to 20 grams, 1.50 francs. Got it? Oh no you don't: in Switzerland, that's hubris. Up to 25 grams isn't the expected 1.75 francs, but— for reasons as obscure as the identity of the President of Switzerland— 2.05 francs. You climb that scale at 25 centimes per 5 grams for four times, and then you skip again, to another interval of 60 centimes. It takes a first-class mathematical education to send a letter in Switzerland, which is a good way of cutting down on the post office load. And oh yes, if you want to airmail a postcard to America, the postage is— a flat 55 centimes. But of course you can't buy a 55 centime stamp— they just don't make them. You buy a 50 and a 5. It all gets very expensive. I figured the other day that it would cost me about five times as much to wrap myself up and send myself airmail to the United States as it would to travel first-class on the *Queen Elizabeth.*

There is a price— and a penalty— for everything in Switzerland. Going up on a ski gondola a while ago it was very hot and I noticed that the window could be removed by prying it out of its rubber frame. This I did, and on reaching the top received a most royal and lengthy dressing down from the attending mechanic in a most flustered French, ending with a simple declarative, "That will be seven francs fifty centimes." It was known exactly how much to charge even for so rogue an infraction.

I know, I know, that if, having established his identity, anyone were so foolish or so evil as to shoot the President of Switzerland, he would be most severely tried and tongue-lashed, and then told that the penalty for shooting presidents of Switzerland is 78,450 francs. It is a most glorious country and, after my own, I love it best, and do herewith, in the presence of witnesses, plight to it my troth.

The Great Cadonau War

Gstaad, Switzerland— March 14, 1972

Gstaad is a sleepy little town that bustles two or three months per year, when people descend on it in great numbers, most of them to ski or to look at the skiers, or to drink with them. Everyone runs into everyone at Cadonau's, which is where one picks up the daily edition of the Paris *Herald Tribune*, paint supplies, scotch tape, stationery— and, occasionally, a book.

Madame Cadonau's window is a showcase for a few recently published books which are there in three languages, available for the occasional tourist in Gstaad who knows how to read. The saga of the past few months has to do with my looking into the showcase to find prominently displayed David Niven's best-seller, *The Moon's a Balloon*. Mr. Niven is a local resident who is very highly regarded. It came as something of a blow to the professional writers in residence when Mr. Niven managed to dash off a superbly written best-seller. The comment of the playwright George Axelrod was dead on: "How dare he write so well? Do I go about playing British colonels?" Fortunately, Mr. Niven is not a professionally qualified skier— otherwise he would be intolerable.

I felt no resentment at all against the display of his book. But just next to it was another book by a famous local resident. *Economics Peace and Laughter*, by John Kenneth Galbraith. Bad enough, I thought, to pollute this unspoiled Alpine retreat by displaying a book by Mr. Galbraith, but altogether intolerable in the light of the fact that a chapter in it is devoted to the disparagement of a classic on municipal government written by a third distinguished writer-in-residence of the area, to wit, me.

Added to this slight was the mysterious non-appearance of my own recently published book, a lacuna which Madame Cadonau embarrassedly explained on the grounds that the book, though ordered months ago, had not arrived presumably because of the New York dock strike. I replied that New York's longshoremen are distinctly my kind of people, and I could not imagine their consenting to load the innocent bottoms of Liberian transports with books by Galbraith, and declining to ease their conscience by supplying them with my own. I called New York and had air-expressed six copies to Madame Cadonau, and then went to China.

I returned to find, in the window, all the old entries, plus a paperback of Mr. Galbraith's *Ambassador's Journal*. I thereupon collected from an old trunk a copy of my anthology of conservative writing, and handed it, wordlessly, to Madame Cadonau, who dutifully shoe-horned it into her feverish window. The next day, I saw there a copy of *The New Industrial State*— in German, which is the kind of thing that happens when Galbraith decides to pull rank. I wired New York and got hold of the single extant copy, in German, of a book I had a hand in writing eighteen years ago on Senator McCarthy, which desiring not to lose it (there were only eighty-seven copies printed), I priced at a level beyond the reach even of the ski-set of Gstaad.

At this point it had become necessary to retire from the window *Everything You Always Wanted to Know About Sex*, by Dr. Reuben, and everything you didn't want to know about sex by Harold Robbins. Everyone has been moved out except of course David Niven, and now the showcase has in it the original doctoral dissertation of Professor Galbraith, written in 1936, and entitled, "Economic Reasons Why the Government of South Vietnam Cannot Last Another Fortnight." That one was hard to beat, but I have written to Buckingham Palace for the original of a letter I dispatched to King George when Mr. Galbraith was a sophomore at college.

Late last night, a tall, lean man was spotted going into the back door of Madame Cadonau's with a lock of graying hair, so I have today written to Dr. Kissinger to ask him please to make a secret visit to Madame Cadonau, who has for days now refused to move from her upstairs apartment, and to promise mutual de-escalation, and the repatriation of all American incunabula, as tensions diminish. I believe in taking the initiative, where peace is concerned.

Path to Rome

Rome, March 27, 1971

Having business in Rome, I thought to go there by sleeping-car from Montreux, my wife having endorsed the conveyance as exemplary after using it a few years ago. I booked a double stateroom, inasmuch as my wife and I together with paraphernalia tend to overflow; and as we set out by car for Montreux, I thought our gesture particularly appropriate on the very day that the House of Representatives in Washington would decide the fate of supersonic travel.

We waited on the platform as a turbulent sky blackened over the still and misty lake that stretches 80 miles from Geneva to Montreux. The train pulled in dead on schedule at 19:05, as they call 7:05 P.M. in these parts, and we boarded. In the bustle of bags and porters and ticket-showing, the darkness of the sleeping car was unremarkable, but as the train slid out I lightheartedly asked the steward, who was wrestling with the bags while holding a mini-flashlight in his mouth, when ho ho would the lights go on? He mumbled, like a patient trying to communicate to his dentist, something that sounded awfully like "when we get to Rome." He led us then to a minuscule cabin, the upper and lower bunks already made up, and heaved the bags onto the overhead rack until there was no more room, so that the last two were dumped on the floor, leaving the lower bunk to sit on provided you crouched forward at a 45-degree angle, else you bumped into space pre-empted by the upper bunk.

The steward explained that because of a recent strike in Rome the electrical system had not been repaired, and because of an administrative oversight we had not got the second cabin, and the car was full. I asked him in choked accents which way was the restaurant car, and he said there is no restaurant car on this train, hasn't been for three years, but that when we crossed the border into Italy three hours from now we could run out and buy a picnic basket. I overcame paralysis sufficiently to ask formally for a second flashlight, and he replied that there was only one available per cabin. My French was simply inadequate to the depths of my indignation. I mean, *"maintenant j'ai tout vu"* somehow doesn't accomplish what "now I've seen everything!" does.

Now I like to think that my wife and I, if summoned to rampart-watching by dawn's early light, could manage quite stoically along with everybody else. But we were not here forwarding any grand patriotic purpose. The little light was insufficient for reading anything except the larger headlines in the afternoon paper. I thought of reciting poetry, only to recognize that in my misspent youth I had managed to memorize a total of one poem by Ogden Nash, one couplet by Wordsworth, one sonnet by Sor Juana Inés de la Cruz, and one exhortation from *Paradise Lost*.

We thereupon resolved to take leave of the Geneva-Rome express, only to learn from the steward that the very next stop, forty-five minutes down the line, would leave us stranded in a remote and taxi-less part of Switzerland. So we decided instead to laugh about it; but to pass along these lapidary lines for the benefit of future romantics who think, when headed from Switzerland to the Eternal City, to disdain jet travel.

That day in the life of William Buckleyvitch seems remote, twenty-four hours later. This morning there was high Mass at St. Peter's, a brilliant organist, absorbed in the beauty of his music and the purpose it served, transmuting the noisy tourists into soft-shoed pilgrims. And then, sipping coffee and reading the *Sunday Times* on the Square, we await the Pope, who will appear sharp at noon at his window in the Vatican apartment to deliver the weekly homily.

Five minutes before noon, the shutters open and the Papal banner, 20 feet long, is lowered. The wind, gusty and irreverent, hurls it back up, and over, and twists it here and there, and one wonders that after 2,000 years the Vatican has not learned how to deal with unruly winds— and then a fantasy: might it happen— just possibly!— that when the Pope appeared, suddenly the wind would quiet down, even as the seas of Galilee once did?

Quite the contrary. The Vicar of Christ appeared, to address the crowd of 50,000, his voice somewhat tired and uncertain, like the Church whose voice he is, and the banner revolted right into his face, smothering the microphone. I do not know what he said, not knowing Italian, but I must suppose that he acknowledged the sacrifices that some of those, pressed into the square, had made in coming there; and I recalled that Hilaire Belloc walked all the way to Rome from Paris before I was born, and that not so many lifetimes ago, a journey to Rome consumed a major part of the lifetime of many pilgrims; and now, the journey, in modern times, takes longer and longer, as the impediments multiply, and the flesh weakens.

Happy Talk

July 10, 1971

I pause to admit a ray of light—of sunshine, if you like— having come across a speech recently delivered by the American Ambassador to Italy, Mr. Graham Martin. Mr. Martin, by anyone's reckoning, is among the two or three top U.S. diplomats. Add to this that he represents us in a country about which the very gloomiest things are being said, such as that Italy will soon go Communist, will repudiate NATO, will be satellized by the Soviet Union, that sort of thing. I do not know whether these rumors are merely the playthings of the under-spirited: or whether they are the sibylline warnings of those who trace political movements with astronomical certitude. But I do believe that human beings alter human situations, and that the internal optimism of the astringent Mr. Martin, which a casual dowser would never locate, is a great fountain of creative diplomatic energy.

The Ambassador was off to a fine start by telling his audience at the American Club of Rome that he found it difficult entirely to understand the total enthusiasm for life of his one-year-old granddaughter who was then visiting him, until suddenly "a wild thought flitted across my mind. Perhaps her radiant, contagious happiness arose from the fact that she could not read the Paris *Herald Tribune* and Mr. Anthony Lewis."

That is an inside joke, outside Europe; but in Europe, it is jocular tender as negotiable as a yarn based on Jack Benny's stinginess or on Teddy Kennedy's decisiveness. The joke is that the Paris *Herald Tribune*, read by most Americans abroad, and edited— if you can imagine a more despondent triumvirate— by the owners of the officially moribund New York *Herald Tribune*, and the New York *Times* and Washington *Post*, who hang on to life in the twentieth century only because they fear that someone, somewhere, may survive them, without a morning paper to make him sad. The talented Mr. Lewis is one of the *Tribune*'s most lugubrious undertakers.

Anyway, on this bright morning Ambassador Martin elected to quote a passage he had recently read. "It was— bad form to praise the world and life openly. It was fashionable to see only its suffering and misery, to discover everywhere signs of decadence and the near end— in short to condemn the times and despise them." As you will suspect, the passage isn't about our own age, or even about the age of McCarthy the Terrible. The passage is from a book about *The Waning of the Middle Ages*, and Mr. Martin quotes a recent historian who, commenting on the gloom in which the fifteenth century enshrouded itself, said that in the light of history we see the period quite 'differently. "We see the period that provided Columbus, Copernicus and Erasmus, as already pregnant with the spirit of exploration and intellectual inquiry, of broadening political horizons, of quickening economic activity, of deepening respect for humanity and individuality."

So it goes in our own time, says Mr. Martin. "A steady diet of only the dramatic emphasizes the chaos inevitably involved in rapid change, and thereby obscures the progress that is evolving slowly in less dramatic form."

He quoted then from a recently published father-son exchange between C. P. Snow and his eighteen-year-old son: "It is, I think, true and symptomatic," said Lord Snow, "that no great country at the peak of its power has ever through its literature, with such masochistic enthusiasm, painted so forbidding a picture. . . . [America] can't be entirely devoted to drug taking and delinquency. But that is what a foreign reader, learning the country only through books, is presented with."

Then Lord Snow, who is at once a scientist and a novelist, said this about the achievements of America: "At a rough estimate, since 1945, American universities have carried out about 80 percent of all the science and scholarship in the Western world, and a very high proportion of the science and scholarship in the whole planet. That is the effort of a single generation. It is something about which Americans might, without false modesty, pat themselves on the back."

And then Lord Snow invited his son to consider the plight we are so greatly concerned with these days. "The American problem [of pollution and environmentalism] is enormous, but it is absolutely tailored to the American genius. To solve it needs energy, resource, invention, and a certain ruthlessness. I shall have been a very bad observer"—writes sixty-five-year-old Lord Snow—"and a worse prophet, if America is not out of comparison less polluted in ten years' time" than now.

How refreshing, to use just the right word; and refreshing that Mr. Martin concluded his speech by publicizing a poll released in *Communita Europa* divulging that the countries in which European youth have the most confidence are Switzerland, 78 percent; America, 69 percent, and Great Britain, 61 percent. Oh say can you see, by the dawn's early light . . .

Index